Fodor's

NEW
ORLEANS

3

WELCOME TO NEW ORLEANS

New Orleans is a vibrant, bursting-at-the-seams melting pot of a city that famously inspires indulgence. This is the place to eat, drink, listen to jazz or R&B, take part in a parade, and immerse yourself in the atmosphere. Whether you come for Mardi Gras or the New Orleans Jazz and Heritage Festival or any other reason, a visit to this unique destination is never the same trip twice, but always memorable. Sugar-dusted beignets are a must, cocktail hour is anytime you want it, and the street musicians will have you dancing on the sidewalk.

TOP REASONS TO GO

★ **Food:** Seafood, cutting-edge cuisine, and Creole and Cajun specialties.

★ **Music:** You'll hear brass bands and funk rhythms in the street and in the clubs.

★ **History:** Frenchmen, Spaniards, Africans, and others forged the city's culture.

★ **French Quarter:** Elegant streets have everything from antiques to Bourbon Street raunch.

★ **Garden District:** A stroll here takes in centuries-old oaks and historic mansions.

★ **The Vibe:** More northern Caribbean than Southern U.S., NOLA lives like no other city.

15 ULTIMATE EXPERIENCES

New Orleans offers terrific experiences that should be on every traveler's list. Here are Fodor's top picks for a memorable trip.

1 Go Shopping on Magazine Street

Spend an afternoon on a leisurely walk down this busy Garden District street, featuring the city's best collection of vintage, art, clothing, and furniture stores. Don't miss NOLA Boards, Tchoup Industries, The White Roach, and Defend New Orleans. *(Ch. 5, 11)*

2 Get Active in City Park

This 1,300 acre park boasts the most live oaks in the world, natural bayous, manmade lakes, gorgeous greenways, and walking paths. *(Ch. 7)*

3 Indulge in Beignets

Many begin a trip to New Orleans with a plate of these square donuts, best enjoyed piping hot, covered in powdered sugar, and alongside a café au lait. *(Ch. 8, 11)*

4 Eat and Drink on St. Claude Avenue

Dubbed the St. Claude Arts District, this stretch between the Marigny & Bywater has some of the best cafes and nightlife in the city. *(Ch. 3, 8, 10)*

5 Walk Through a Creepy Cemetery

The tombs are home to famed old city dwellers and provide a spooky setting for an afternoon stroll. *(Ch. 3, 5, 7)*

6 Have a 5-Star Meal at a 100-year-old Restaurant

Indulge in brunch at Commander's Palace, one of the city's pricey but famed old restaurants. *(Ch. 8)*

7 Snack on Char Grilled Oysters

In this iconic New Orleans dish, gulf oysters are cooked over a flame grill, creating oysters that are uniquely juicy, smoky, and steamed. *(Ch. 8)*

8 See Bands on Frenchmen Street

Nowhere else in the city can you capture such a concentrated amount of local music and nightlife revelry as within these four blocks in the Marigny. *(Ch. 3, 10)*

9 Ride the St. Charles Streetcar

The oldest, most picturesque streetcar in town glides from the river bend past Audubon Park and through Uptown and the Garden District. *(Ch. 6)*

10 Take a Ghost Tour

You don't have to be a believer in ghost stories to have fun walking through the French Quarter with a guide. *(Ch. 2)*

11 Visit the Pharmacy Museum

Tucked behind a storefront on Chartres Street, this former apothecary tells the story of early medicinal practices. *(Ch. 2)*

12 Stroll Along the Sculpture Garden

This free outdoor art museum comprising of 64 scultpures inside City Park is a pleasant oasis within the city. *(Ch. 7)*

13 Eat Po-Boys in the Irish Channel

This little neighborhood includes colorful houses, busy pubs, and some of the greatest po-boy spots in the city. *(Ch. 8)*

14 Fall in Love at Bacchanal

What started as a little wine shop and backyard music show on a dead-end street in the Bywater is now a wine garden, five-star kitchen, and music venue. *(Ch. 10)*

15 Go on a Swamp Tour

The wild wetlands of Louisiana are a piece of nature unique to this part of the world, with enchanting plants and wildlife. *(Ch. 12)*

Fodor's NEW ORLEANS

TRAVEL
917.6335
Fodor

Editorial: Douglas Stallings, *Editorial Director*; Margaret Kelly, Jacinta O'Halloran, *Senior Editors*; Kayla Becker, Alexis Kelly, Amanda Sadlowski, *Editors*; Teddy Minford, *Content Editor*; Rachael Roth, *Content Manager*

Design: Tina Malaney, *Design and Production Director*; Jessica Gonzalez, *Production Designer*

Photography: Jennifer Arnow, *Senior Photo Editor*

Maps: Rebecca Baer, *Senior Map Editor*; Mark Stroud (Moon Street Cartography), David Lindroth, *Cartographers*

Production: Jennifer DePrima, *Editorial Production Manager*; Carrie Parker, *Senior Production Editor*; Elyse Rozelle, *Production Editor*

Business & Operations: Chuck Hoover, *Chief Marketing Officer*; Joy Lai, *Vice President and General Manager*; Stephen Horowitz, *Director of Business Development and Revenue Operations*; Tara McCrillis, *Director of Publishing Operations*; Eliza D. Aceves, *Content Operations Manager and Strategist*

Public Relations and Marketing: Joe Ewaskiw, *Manager*; Esther Su, *Marketing Manager*

Writers: Karen Taylor-Gist, Cameron Quincy Todd

Editor: Teddy Minford

Production Editor: Elyse Rozelle

28th Edition

ISBN 978–1–64097–036–6

ISSN 0743–9385

All details in this book are based on information supplied to us at press time. Always confirm information when it matters, especially if you're making a detour to visit a specific place. Fodor's expressly disclaims any liability, loss, or risk, personal or otherwise, that is incurred as a consequence of the use of any of the contents of this book.

SPECIAL SALES

This book is available at special discounts for bulk purchases for sales promotions or premiums. For more information, e-mail SpecialMarkets@fodors.com.

PRINTED IN THE UNITED STATES OF AMERICA

10 9 8 7 6 5 4 3 2 1

CONTENTS

1 EXPERIENCE NEW ORLEANS . . 15
New Orleans Today 16
What's Where 18
New Orleans Planner 20
Under-the-Radar New Orleans 22
New Orleans Sports:
Saints and Pelicans 24
Inspiration: Books and Movies 25
Local for a Day 26
New Orleans with Kids 27
Great Itineraries 28
A Good Garden District Walk 30
A Good Gallery Walk in
the Warehouse District 32
Best Fests and Parades 34
Free and Cheap 36
Cocktail Events and Exhibits 37
Getting Out of Town 38

2 THE FRENCH QUARTER 39

**3 FAUBOURG MARIGNY,
BYWATER, AND TREMÉ 65**
Faubourg Marigny 68
Bywater 70
Tremé 73

**4 CBD AND
WAREHOUSE DISTRICT 77**
Central Business District 80
Warehouse District 83

5 THE GARDEN DISTRICT 87

**6 UPTOWN AND
CARROLLTON-RIVERBEND 97**
Riding the Streetcar 100
Uptown 103
Carrollton-Riverbend 105

Fodor's Features

It's Mardi Gras Time in New Orleans! . . 52
The Cuisine of New Orleans 132
New Orleans Noise 178

**7 MID-CITY AND
BAYOU ST. JOHN 107**
Mid-City 111
Bayou St. John 114

8 WHERE TO EAT 117
New Orleans Dining Planner 118
Restaurant Reviews 119

9 WHERE TO STAY 147
New Orleans Lodging Planner 149
Hotel Reviews 150

**10 NIGHTLIFE AND
PERFORMING ARTS 167**
Cocktail Culture 168
Planning 170
Nightlife 171
Performing Arts 196

11 SHOPS AND SPAS 199
Shopping Planner 201
French Quarter 202

CONTENTS

Faubourg Marigny and Bywater... 214

CBD and Warehouse District...... 215

The Garden District and
Magazine Street 218

Uptown and Magazine Street,
with Carrollton-Riverbend 223

Mid-City........................... 227

12 SIDE TRIPS FROM
NEW ORLEANS.............. 229

Welcome To
Side Trips from New Orleans 230

Planning.......................... 233

Abita Springs 234

Plantation Country................ 236

Cajun Country 244

TRAVEL SMART
NEW ORLEANS.............. 261

INDEX 271

ABOUT OUR WRITERS....... 288

MAPS

A Good Garden District Walk...... 31

A Good Gallery Walk in
the Warehouse District 33

The French Quarter............... 40

Faubourg Marigny,
Bywater, and Tremé............... 66

CBD and Warehouse District....... 78

Garden District 88

Uptown and
Carrollton-Riverbend.............. 98

Mid-City and Bayou St. John...... 108

Where to Eat in the French Quarter
and Faubourg Marigny........... 127

Where to Eat in CBD and
the Warehouse District 131

Where to Eat Outside
the Downtown Area 141

Where to Stay in
Downtown New Orleans..... 152–153

Where to Stay Outside
the Downtown Area 164

Plantation Country............... 235

Cajun Country 245

Lafayette......................... 246

ABOUT
THIS GUIDE

Fodor's Recommendations

Everything in this guide is worth doing—we don't cover what isn't—but exceptional sights, hotels, and restaurants are recognized with additional accolades. **Fodor's Choice★** indicates our top recommendations. Care to nominate a new place? Visit Fodors.com/contact-us.

Trip Costs

We list prices wherever possible to help you budget well. Hotel and restaurant price categories from **$** to **$$$$** are noted alongside each recommendation. For hotels, we include the lowest cost of a standard double room in high season. For restaurants, we cite the average price of a main course at dinner or, if dinner isn't served, at lunch. For attractions, we always list adult admission fees; discounts are usually available for children, students, and senior citizens.

Hotels

Our local writers vet every hotel to recommend the best overnights in each price category, from budget to expensive. Unless otherwise specified, you can expect private bath, phone, and TV in your room. Hotel reviews have been shortened. For full information, visit Fodors.com.

Top Picks	Hotels &
★ **Fodor's**Choice	**Restaurants**
	⊞ Hotel
Listings	⤹ Number of
✉ Address	rooms
✉ Branch address	⍟ Meal plans
☎ Telephone	✗ Restaurant
🖷 Fax	⌑ Reservations
⊕ Website	⍓ Dress code
✎ E-mail	⊟ No credit cards
🎟 Admission fee	⑤ Price
⊗ Open/closed	
times	**Other**
Ⓜ Subway	⇨ See also
✛ Directions or	☞ Take note
Map coordinates	⅄ Golf facilities

Restaurants

Unless we state otherwise, restaurants are open for lunch and dinner daily. We mention dress code only when there's a specific requirement and reservations only when they're essential or not accepted. Restaurant reviews have been shortened. For full information, visit Fodors.com.

Credit Cards

The hotels and restaurants in this guide typically accept credit cards. If not, we'll say so.

EUGENE FODOR

Hungarian-born Eugene Fodor (1905–91) began his travel career as an interpreter on a French cruise ship. The experience inspired him to write *On the Continent* (1936), the first guidebook to receive annual updates and discuss a country's way of life as well as its sights. Fodor later joined the U.S. Army and worked for the OSS in World War II. After the war, he kept up his intelligence work while expanding his guidebook series. During the Cold War, many guides were written by fellow agents who understood the value of insider information. Today's guides continue Fodor's legacy by providing travelers with timely coverage, insider tips, and cultural context.

EXPERIENCE
NEW ORLEANS

NEW ORLEANS TODAY

New Orleans is the ultimate urban illustration of the Japanese concept *wabi-sabi* (literally "perfect-imperfect"). Like a sidewalk buckling under oak roots or bricks showing through a crumbling plaster wall, sometimes things are even more special when they are just a little bit broken. New Orleans is perfect in its sheer persistence; this comeback city's longevity, incredible heritage and history, and unwavering determination to live on and let the good times roll are what make it so endearing—and so easy to return to again and again.

A Highly Unique American City. It sounds like a tourist-brochure cliché, but it's true: New Orleans feels out of step with the rest of the country. It may be due in large part to geography. This port city has seen an influx of many, many cultures over the course of its history. It welcomes diversity and tolerates lifestyles that deviate from the norm—a big reason artists and other creative types have long put down roots here. And the fact that the city lies mostly below sea level lends it a certain fatalism, which may unconsciously inspire the classic New Orleans "live for today" attitude.

Chock Full of Tradition and Ritual. Red beans and rice on Monday, St. Joseph's altars, jazz funerals, a Christmas visit to Mr. Bingle in City Park—New Orleans is a destination steeped in tradition, its unique customs carefully guarded for more than a century. Take Mardi Gras, for example: some of the parading organizations, known as "krewes," have been around for more than 150 years, building elaborate floats annually and parading through the streets in masks. The Mardi Gras Indian tradition is shrouded in secrecy and ritual, with "tribes" of mostly African American revelers spending months constructing fanciful, Native American–influenced costumes in tribute to actual tribes that once helped escaped slaves find freedom.

A Cinematic Affair. New Orleans has a creative pull and fictional appeal that has been inspiring filmmakers for centuries. Movies and shows filmed here recently include *NCIS: New Orleans*, HBO's *Treme*, and *True Detective*, Quentin Tarantino's *Django Unchained*, FX's *American Horror Story*, and Bravo's *Top Chef: New Orleans*.

WHAT WE'RE TALKING ABOUT

New Orleanians buy local to keep artists, craftsmen, and entrepreneurs thinking their creative thoughts. These days, they're also "sipping local," popping tops to support a spate of new breweries and distilleries. The grandaddy of local distilleries, **Old New Orleans Rum** (✉ 2815 Frenchmen St. ☎ 504/945–9400), offers tours and tastings weekdays at 10, 2, and 4. **Atelier Vie** (✉ 1001 S. Broad St. ☎ 504/534–8590), maker of absinthe as well as rice whiskey, vodka, and gin, opens its doors on weekends from 10 to 2. An hour away in Thibodaux, **Donner-Peltier Distillers** (✉ 1635 St. Patrick Hwy. ☎ 985/446–0002) gives tours Monday through Saturday at 4 pm, and a tasting room serves samples of their only-in-Louisiana praline rum, along

Navigating the Road to Recovery. Over ten years after Katrina hit the city, the areas where tourists tend to wander—downtown, the riverfront, the French Quarter, Faubourg Marigny, the Warehouse District, and the Garden District/Uptown—all show little outward sign of floodwater devastation. But predominantly residential areas like parts of east New Orleans and the Lower Ninth Ward are still recovering. As of July 2016, Census Bureau estimates indicated that the city's population was still 81% of what it had been before the storm.

Grounded in Community. In the fall of 2017, New Orleans ushered in a new mayor in the wake of Mitch Landrieu's two-term reign. New leadership faces responsibilities to expand a successful school system, remedy a housing crisis, keep crime low, and best prepare the city for future storms. But New Orleans's strength has always been in the people that live it and love it, and local nonprofits and grassroots organizations like HandsOn New Orleans, The Gulf Restoration Network, and New Orleans's Musicians Relief Fund are just a few of the bright leaders in locally based change for the future. In the last few years, an influx of millennials have joined the community working for nonprofits, teaching, and starting innovative businesses.

Hopeful for the Future. New Orleans has survived an insane number of fires, floods, epidemics, and scandals since its founding in 1718. There are many encouraging signs—new buildings, streetcar lines, restorations, festivals—that even Hurricane Katrina couldn't keep this amazing city down. But questions remain: the repaired levees held fast against 2012's Hurricane Isaac, but will they withstand an even larger storm? Will New Orleans move past its political scandals, crime, and the ills of urban poverty? Despite the many fortune-tellers plying their trade on Jackson Square, no one knows for sure what the future holds for the Crescent City.

---

with vodka, gin, and whiskey weekdays from 9 to 6.

It's said that history reveals itself in New Orleans through both elegance and decay. And along those lines, the city's most famous museum is using sophisticated technology to knock the dust off its retelling of the Second World War. An ambitious $370 million expansion is currently underway at the National WWII Museum (⊕ www.nationalww2museum.org), with plans to eventually quadruple the museum's size, including an on-site hotel and parking garage alongside the new exhibits and pavilions. Two expansive new exhibits as part of this project are now open to the public: An exploration on cultural differences and battle strategies in Asia and the Pacific, and an exhibit focusing on the Homefront's critical role in winning the war.

WHAT'S WHERE

1 The French Quarter. The geographic and cultural heart of the city since the early 1700s, the Quarter is a vibrant commercial and residential hodgepodge of wrought-iron balconies, inviting courtyards, antiques shops—and, of course, rowdy Bourbon Street bars. Elsewhere in the Quarter, you'll find fine dining and fabulous local music.

2 Faubourg Marigny, Bywater, and Tremé. The Faubourg Marigny is home to restored Creole cottages and famous Frenchmen Street, lined with music clubs, restaurants, and bars. Bywater has gentrified somewhat, but retains its working-class credentials, with a burgeoning arts scene and an influx of hipster professionals. Tremé, the cradle of jazz and second-line parades, remains a historical hub of African American and Creole traditions in the city.

3 CBD and Warehouse District. The city's trendy urban area is undergoing a building boom; most of the newer hotels are clustered here, near Canal Street or the sprawling Ernest N. Morial Convention Center. There also are museums, art galleries, fine restaurants, and a casino.

Lake Pontchartrain

Lakesho

Robert E Lee Blvd

W. Esplanade Ave.

Metairie

Lake View

Pontchartrain Blvd

Orleans Ave.

City Park

Veterans Memorial Blvd

10

610

Metairie Rd

Besthoff Sculpture Garden

City Park Ave.

Pitot House

6

Airline Dr

N. Carrollton Ave.

Mid-City

61

10

Earhart Expy

Jefferson

Earhart Blvd

Palmetto St.

Tulane Ave.

Fontainebleau Dr.

S Claiborne Ave.

Dakin St.

S. Broad St.

S Carrollton Ave.

Tulane University

Carrollton

S. Claiborne Ave.

Maple St.

Loyola University

Calhoun St.

Washingto

Bridge City

Saint Charles Ave.

Riverside

Uppeline St.

Freret

Napoleon Ave.

Louisiana Ave.

Audubon Park

Exposition Blvd

5

Uptown

Saint Charles Ave.

4

Magazine St.

Tchoupitoulas St

Westwego

Miss

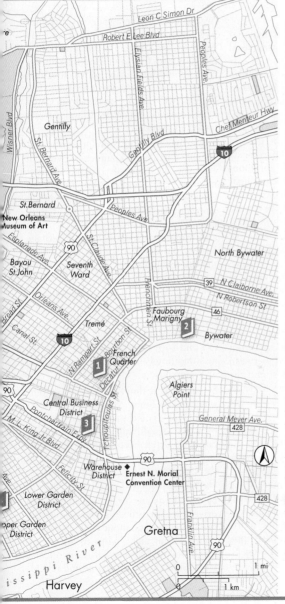

4 The Garden District. Stunning early-19th-century mansions make this a great neighborhood for walking, followed by an afternoon browsing the shops and cafés along ever-evolving Magazine Street. Take the streetcar for a gander at massive and stately St. Charles Avenue homes.

5 Uptown and Carrollton-Riverbend. Audubon Park and the campuses of Tulane and Loyola universities anchor oak-shaded Uptown; hop on the St. Charles Avenue streetcar to survey it in period style. You'll find boutiques, eateries, and pubs at the Uptown end of Magazine Street, on Maple Street between Broadway and Carrollton, and in the Riverbend.

6 Mid-City and Bayou St. John. City Park is Mid-City's playground and encompasses the New Orleans Museum of Art and the adjacent Besthoff Sculpture Garden. A stroll along Bayou St. John and a visit to Pitot House on its banks are good ways to see this residential neighborhood.

7 Side Trips. If you have time, head to Plantation Country to visit the gorgeous antebellum homes, or explore Cajun Country.

NEW ORLEANS PLANNER

Getting Here

By air: Most major and a few regional airlines serve **Louis Armstrong International Airport** (☎ *504/464–0831*), 15 miles east of downtown New Orleans. A taxi from the airport to the French Quarter costs a flat rate of $36 for two people; for more than two passengers, it's $15 per person. Uber and Lyft charge comparable rates and pick up passengers on the ground transportation lower level. Shared-ride shuttles to hotels are available for about $20 per person. If you're traveling light and have extra time, take Jefferson Transit's airport bus, which runs between the main terminal entrance and the Central Business District (CBD). Fare is $2.

By car: Interstate 10 is the major thoroughfare into and out of New Orleans, and can be used to reach downtown from the airport. Lanes can get backed up during morning and evening rush hours; plan accordingly.

By train: Three Amtrak lines serve New Orleans: the *City of New Orleans* from Chicago; the *Sunset Limited* between New Orleans and Los Angeles; and the *Crescent*, which connects New Orleans and New York by way of Atlanta. For tickets and schedules, call ☎ *800/872–7245* or visit ⊕ *www.amtrak.com*.

Getting Around

By streetcar: The St. Charles line runs from Canal Street to the intersection of Claiborne and Carrollton avenues; along the way, it passes the Garden District, Audubon Park, and Tulane and Loyola universities. The Riverfront line skirts the French Quarter along the Mississippi, from Esplanade Avenue to the Ernest N. Morial Convention Center. Some Canal line streetcars make a straight shot from the Quarter to the cemeteries at City Park Avenue; others take a spur at Carrollton Avenue that goes to City Park and the New Orleans Museum of Art. The Loyola line runs from the Union Passenger Terminal (rail and bus station) down to Canal Street, where it meets the other lines. The Rampart–St. Claude line runs from Canal Street down Rampart/St. Claude streets into the Bywater.

By Bus: Bus travel in New Orleans is reasonably reliable and comfortable; you can even get the status of your bus via text message. The Magazine bus runs from Canal and Camp streets to the Audubon Zoo entrance at the far edge of Audubon Park. The Esplanade bus serves City Park and drops New Orleans Jazz and Heritage Festival passengers off a few blocks from the Fair Grounds.

Fares for streetcars and buses are $1.25 ($1.50 for express lines); unlimited-ride Jazzy Pass cards are available for one day ($3, available on buses and streetcars); unlimited 3-day and 31-day passes ($9 and $55, respectively) are available at some hotels and grocery stores and at Walgreens.

By car: If you don't plan to drive outside the city limits, you probably won't need a car—you'll save money traveling by streetcar, cab, and on foot. If you do decide to drive, keep in mind that some streets are in rough shape, and parking in the Quarter is tight (and regulations are vigorously enforced).

By taxi: Taxis are often convenient, and drivers are used to short trips, so grab a cab if you're leery about walking back to your hotel at night. Most locals recommend Yellow Checker and United Cabs. Uber and Lyft are affordable and reliable services throughout town.

Safety

The French Quarter is generally safe, but pay attention to your surroundings and your possessions (especially expensive cameras and dangling shoulder bags). Use special caution in the areas near Rampart Street and below St. Philip Street at night, and be alert on all quiet Quarter side streets.

The CBD and Warehouse District are safe, but take a cab at night if there aren't many other pedestrians around.

Be alert and exercise caution walking around in the Bywater or the lower part of Faubourg Marigny at night, and take a cab when traveling between spread-out destinations.

All that said, the New Orleans Police Department take pains to keep violent crime out of tourist zones, with many uniformed and plainclothes officers stationed throughout the Quarter and at special events.

Helpful Websites

⊕ *www.fodors.com*: Log on to the Travel Talk Forums to get advice from New Orleanians and travelers who have recently visited the Crescent City.

⊕ *www.neworleanscvb.com*: Head here for up-to-date information from the New Orleans Convention and Visitors Bureau.

⊕ *www.nola.com*: Find out what's happening from the city's newspaper, *The Times-Picayune*.

⊕ *www.neworleans.com*: This site has often-updated special events and entertainment info.

⊕ *www.offbeat.com*: The website for the monthly *Offbeat* magazine has extensive club and live-music listings, along with features on the local music scene.

When to Go

May through September is hot and humid— "double 100" days (100°F and nearly 100% humidity) aren't uncommon. Just mustering the energy to raise a mint julep to your lips can cause exhaustion. These long, hot summers may explain why things are less hurried down here. June through November may bring occasional heavy rains or even a hurricane. But if you visit during sticky July and August, you'll find lower hotel prices and plenty of tables at top restaurants.

Tourism picks up in October, when temperatures drop and festivals (and football season) begin. Although winters are mild compared with those in northern climes, the humidity can put a chill in the air December through February. Nevertheless, the holiday season is a great time to visit, with few conventions in town, a beautifully bedecked French Quarter, and "Papa Noel" discounted rates at many hotels.

Perhaps the best time to visit the city is early spring. Days are pleasant, except for seasonal cloudbursts, and nights are cool. The azaleas are in full bloom, the apricot scent of sweet olive trees wafts through the evening air, and the city bustles from one outdoor festival to the next.

UNDER-THE-RADAR NEW ORLEANS

Bowling

Rock 'N' Bowl isn't just for bowling enthusiasts: the venue features two bars, delicious burgers, a Ping-Pong table, and dance floor. The decor and general charm is reminiscent of an old dance hall or large barn, and the music shows likewise feel more like a friendly hoedown than a concert. The stage hosts a variety of theme nights, most popular among them zydeco, southern Louisiana's unique Creole rock, famous for its lively accordion and washboard sounds.

Cemeteries

The old cemeteries in and around New Orleans, where tombs have to be built above the boggy ground to keep the remains of loved ones from drifting away, are fascinating places to visit. Those near the French Quarter (**St. Louis No. 2** and **St. Roch,** for example) are best visited on a tour or with a group. **Lake Lawn Metairie Cemetery** (✉ *5100 Pontchartrain Blvd.* ☎ *504/486–6331*), on the other hand, is safe to visit on your own: the office even has audio guides to help motorists find their way around the stately cemetery, the final resting place of luminaries like Al Hirt, Louis Prima, and Civil War general P.G.T. Beauregard. Because it's a busy cemetery, officials prefer that people visit between 8:30 and 10:30 am or after 3:30 pm, when there's less chance of disrupting a funeral.

Drag Shows

It makes sense that a city known for flair, costumes, and performance would have no shortage of drag shows. During **Southern Decadence**—New Orleans's own Pride festival held over Labor Day weekend—you'll find a packed schedule of lively shows at gay bars throughout the French Quarter and Faubourg Marigny.

Any time of year, check the weekly schedule at **3 Keys,** an intimate venue inside **The Ace Hotel,** for performances by local favorite Neon Burgundy. Neighborhood gay bars like **Tulane Avenue Bar** in Mid-City and **GrandPre** in Faubourg Marigny host showcases on Friday or Saturday nights.

Breweries

Besides serving high-quality craft beer, the few breweries that have popped up around town in recent years often host food trucks, lawn games, and live music. On Saturday afternoons, Mid-City residents mingle at **Second Line Brewery** to listen to music, sip IPAs, and eat hot dogs or tacos from the rotating local food trucks. The Tap Room at **NOLA Brewing** in the lower Garden District is a longtime favorite, and still the biggest: two stories, with a large selection of beers, a game room, and a kitchen serving McClure's barbecue. **Urban South Brewery** on Tchoupitoulas Street, the latest newcomer, hosts a free crawfish boil and beer tasting on Thursdays in the spring.

Indie Theater

Most big-screen multiplexes are far out of city limits, and the in-town movie scene is boutique and indie. Small theaters are often architectural wonders, each with their own quirky culture, careful pick of flicks, and libations and treats. The **Broad Theater** is housed in a Spanish Mission–style building that last housed a boxing gym. The opulent concessions room has a full bar, and the theater's four screens usually play three indie films and one blockbuster. The growing arts and entertainment district on Oretha Castle Haley Boulevard hosts the **Zeitgeist Multidisciplinary Arts Center,** a small one-screen theater playing foreign and indie films, often with a socially conscious theme. The cutest theater in the city might be **Prytania Theater**, tucked on a quiet uptown street. Check Prytania's website for fun events and festivals, like the Late Night Series, when the theater puts on cult classics on Fridays at midnight.

Weird Museums

Home to a small but interesting collection of art and artifacts related to voodoo history and practice in the city, the **New Orleans Historic Voodoo Museum** (⊠ *724 Dumaine St.* ☎ *504/680–0128*) offers insight into a spiritual tradition that persists to this day. If you're not squeamish about toying with the black arts, there are handcrafted voodoo dolls and *gris-gris* (magic talisman) bags sold in the small shop. (⇨ *See the French Quarter listings.*)

Louis Dufilho, America's first licensed pharmacist, operated an apothecary, La Pharmacie Francaise, in an 1823 townhouse. Today it holds the **New Orleans Pharmacy Museum** (⊠ *514 Chartres St.* ☎ *504/565–8027*), a collection of ancient medicine bottles, a huge leech jar, eyeglasses, and some truly unsettling surgical instruments. (⇨ *See the French Quarter listings.*)

In a former funeral home, the small, quirky **Backstreet Cultural Museum** (⊠ *1116 St. Claude St.* ☎ *504/577–6001*) has everything you want to know about second line and Mardi Gras Indian traditions, with fascinating displays of Mardi Gras Indian suits, the fans and umbrellas of social aid and pleasure clubs, and the vestments of lesser-known traditions, such as the Baby Dolls and Skull and Bone Gangs. (⇨ *See the Tremé listings.*)

Tiny Abita Springs, north of Lake Pontchartrain, is notable for three things: artesian spring water, Abita beer, and an oddball institution known as the **Abita Mystery House** (⊠ *22275 Hwy. 36, at Grover St., Abita Springs* ☎ *985/892–2624* ⊕ *www.abitamysteryhouse.com*). Artist John Preble's obsessive collection of found objects includes combs, old musical instruments, paint-by-number art, and taxidermy experiments gone awry. (⇨ *See the Side Trips from New Orleans listings.*)

Picnics

With gorgeous waterways and green spaces throughout the city (and a law that lets you enjoy beer and wine outside), New Orleans is a perfect city for a picnic. When the weather is nice (which it usually is), you'll see many locals out enjoying the parks, while playing music, boating, or boiling crawfish. If you're in Mid-City or the Esplanade Avenue area, shop for wine and cheese at **Pearl Wine Co.** and head to **City Park** or **Bayou St. John**. If you're in the Faubourg Marigny or Bywater, go to **Faubourg Wine** on St. Claude Avenue for your libations and gourmet snacks, then walk down to **Crescent Park** to watch the barges glide down the Mississippi.

Sno-balls

In the days before air-conditioning, New Orleanians developed the sno-ball as a way to cope with stifling summers: it's a ball of shaved ice served in a cup or Chinese take-out container, topped with flavored simple syrups and add-ons like condensed milk. A New Orleans inventor designed the patented SnoWizard machine to produce the finest shaved ice imaginable, so a sno-ball in New Orleans is different from those elsewhere. **Hansen's Sno-Blitz Sweet Shop** (⊠ *4801 Tchoupitoulas St., Uptown* ☎ *504/891–9788 May–Oct.*) has been dishing them out since 1939; another local favorite is **Plum Street Snoball** (⊠ *1300 Burdette St., Carrollton-Riverbend* ☎ *504/866–7996 Mar.–Oct.*).

NEW ORLEANS SPORTS: SAINTS AND PELICANS

For a city that loves to play so much, New Orleans once wasn't considered much of a professional sports town. Season after season of disappointment had even earned their football team the local nickname "the Aints." Things changed over the last several years, after two of the city's pro teams saw unprecedented success. The victories represented a comeback—not just for the teams, but for the entire city.

New Orleans Saints

The Saints went marching in to victory in Miami in 2010 when they became Super Bowl champions for the first time. Throughout that season—which opened with 13 wins in a row—New Orleans was abuzz, united in Saints spirit like never before. The Super Bowl XLIV victory parade fell just a week before Mardi Gras and drew 800,000 people. It was the largest parade crowd some locals say they've ever seen, which is truly impressive for America's party city.

Today, despite a so-so last few seasons, Saints fever continues unabated. Fans are as enthusiastic as ever and celebrate in Champions Square, just outside the Mercedes-Benz Superdome, a hot spot for pre- and postgame partying. Whether you're at the Dome or watching the Saints on TV, keep an eye out for some of the Saints' most famous fans: Halo Saint, who wears a gold Transformer-esque getup; Da Pope, dressed as the pontiff himself; Whistle Monsta, in black-and-gold face paint and Saints uniform, with a giant gold whistle atop his helmet; and Voodoo Man, sporting a tux jacket, top hat, and ghostly face paint.

Where they play: Mercedes-Benz Superdome (⊠ *Sugar Bowl Dr., CBD*)

Season: August–January

How to buy tickets: Individual tickets are technically not for sale (the Dome has been sold out on season tickets alone since 2006), but resale tickets aren't hard to come by. Your best bet is the NFL Ticket Exchange (⊕ *www.nfl.com*).

Famous players, past and present: Drew Brees, Rickey Jackson, Archie Manning

Past highlights: Won Super Bowl XLIV in 2010; made playoffs in 2011, 2012, and 2013.

New Orleans Pelicans

The Pelicans, who from 2002 through 2012 kept the "Hornets" moniker they arrived with from Charlotte, have seen mixed results over the years. Hurricane Katrina sent the team to Oklahoma City from 2005 to 2007, but they returned to New Orleans for the 2007–08 season and made the playoffs two years in a row. The Pelicans haven't been back to the playoffs since 2014, but a team of rising stars led by Anthony Davis, and their fans, are still hopeful.

Where they play: Smoothie King Arena (⊠ *1501 Dave Dixon Dr., CBD*)

Season: October–April

How to buy tickets: Contact the ticket office by phone or online (☎ *504/525–HOOP* ⊕ *www.nba.com/hornets*).

Past highlights: Making the NBA playoffs in 2008, 2009, 2011, and 2014

INSPIRATION: BOOKS AND MOVIES

New Orleans is a strange, wonderful, and evocative place, and it has inspired some incredible books, movies, and television shows.

Movies

To prepare for your trip to New Orleans, rent *A Streetcar Named Desire,* starring Marlon Brando and Vivien Leigh. Seedy, steamy, and emotionally charged, this is the quintessential New Orleans film. Also check out Elvis in *King Creole,* a music-filled noir tale set in the French Quarter. Other New Orleans classics include *Jezebel, The Buccaneer,* and *Easy Rider.* For more contemporary movies, check out the film adaptation of Anne Rice's *Interview with the Vampire,* John Grisham's *The Pelican Brief* starring Julia Roberts and Denzel Washington, *Double Jeopardy* with Ashley Judd, *Runaway Jury* starring John Cusack, *Déja Vu* with Denzel Washington, and *The Curious Case of Benjamin Button,* set in the Garden District.

Television Shows

The HBO series *Treme* highlights post-Katrina New Orleans music and culture. CBS's *NCIS: New Orleans* returns to the Crescent City for a fourth season. The third season of the anthology series *American Horror Story* is set in New Orleans, as was the 11th season of *Top Chef.*

Books: fiction

Essential reading for any visitor, John Kennedy Toole's *A Confederacy of Dunces* is a New Orleans classic. Ignatius J. Reilly, the book's bumbling protagonist, is as quirky as the city itself. Tim Gautreaux's *The Missing* is a literary mystery set in the 1920s. Or pick up anything by George Washington Cable and immerse yourself in the New Orleans of the late 1800s.

For more contemporary fare, look for Tom Piazza's *City of Refuge,* which looks at two fictional families—one black, one white—in the aftermath of Hurricane Katrina. (His nonfiction *Why New Orleans Matters,* written right after the hurricane, is a short but moving book about what makes the city unique and why it was so important to rebuild.) James Lee Burke's well-known series starring detective Dave Robicheaux is set in and around New Orleans (and several of the books have been made into movies).

Books: nonfiction

Several excellent nonfiction books have been written about New Orleans and Hurricane Katrina, including Dan Baum's excellent *Nine Lives,* which traces the story of 40 years of New Orleans through the lives of nine very different people. *Zeitoun* by Dave Eggers, is a penetrating look at the life of Abdulrahman Zeitoun, a resident of New Orleans who remained in his home during the storm. Zeitoun came to the aid of many people in need before he was arrested by the National Guard. Rebecca Solnit's *Unfathomable City: A New Orleans Atlas* maps the city both literally and through the essays of expert local historians, geographers, musicians, activists, and more. For a somewhat lighter look at the city, try NPR commentator Andrei Codrescu's *New Orleans, Mon Amour,* a touching and humorous collection of short essays about living in his adopted home.

While you're in New Orleans, visit any locally owned bookstore and talk to the staff for a ground-level perspective on the city's literary scene.

LOCAL FOR A DAY

Tired of time-share hawkers and tap dancers? Want to spend some time enjoying New Orleans the way locals do? Step one: get out of the Quarter.

Get Some Exercise

Go for a jog along the **St. Charles Avenue streetcar tracks.** You'll have plenty of company anywhere between Jackson Avenue and the university area—just follow the well-worn trails along the median (what locals refer to as the "neutral ground"). Keep an eye out for streetcars as well as vehicles crossing the tracks. If that sounds too risky, hit the trails in **City Park,** or rent a bicycle and head for **Audubon Park,** where you can get on a paved jogging and cycling path that runs along the Mississippi River levee well into Jefferson Parish.

Find a Market

The **Crescent City Farmers Market** sets up at the corner of Girod and Magazine streets in the CBD on Saturday morning; on Tuesday from 9 am to 1 pm, you can find it Uptown at Tulane Square, on Leake Avenue at Broadway; and on Wednesday from 2 pm to 6 pm, it's in the French Quarter. While you may not want to lug a bag of broccoli back to your hotel, you'll find good prepared foods for sale, local chefs foraging for ingredients, and an entertaining bunch of vendors. If you're in town the first Saturday of the month (except July and August), head to the **Freret Market Uptown,** a food, art, and flea market where the merchandise quality is always high and the crowd never less than colorful. The **Frenchmen Art Market,** at 619 Frenchmen Street, takes place Thursday through Saturday from 7 pm to 1 am, and on Sunday from 6 pm to midnight.

Queue Up for Breakfast

After a long Saturday of cavorting, locals need a Sunday morning recovery meal just as much as visitors. Every New Orleanian has a favorite brunch spot, where you'll find lines of hungry customers. Hit **Dante's Kitchen** (⌧ *736 Dante St., Uptown* ☎ *504/861–3121*; brunch Sun.) for buttermilk biscuits, shrimp and grits, and bread-pudding French toast. For a more elegant option, head to **Patois** (⌧ *6078 Laurel St., Uptown* ☎ *504/895–9441*; brunch Sun.) and try their bacon or hash browns paired with fried rabbit or almond-crusted Gulf fish. **Elizabeth's** (⌧ *601 Gallier St., Bywater* ☎ *504/944–9272*; breakfast daily) sees its share of tourists, but the brunch crowd still mostly consists of neighborhood denizens.

Hang Out by the River

Locals love Riverview Drive—better known as **The Fly**—the riverside stretch of Audubon Park behind the zoo, even if they have no idea how it got its nickname (probably from a butterfly-shape building that used to stand here). There is a Little League baseball complex, where spectators can sip Abita beer from the snack bar, and a football/soccer field, but most people are content to simply spread out on a blanket, have a picnic or barbecue, and watch the ships go by on the Mississippi.

Shop Local

Whether it's at the incredibly diverse array of boutiques on the "six miles of style" that make up **Magazine Street** or at the stately antiques dealerships in the **French Quarter,** locals prefer to spend their money at businesses owned and staffed by New Orleanians. Look for the lime-green-and-blue "Stay Local!" stickers on store windows.

NEW ORLEANS WITH KIDS

New Orleans is a grown-up town in a lot of ways, but there are lots of activities to keep the kids interested, too. ⇨ *See the full listings in the neighborhood exploring chapters for contact info.*

Get Out and Play

Audubon Park. This beautiful Uptown park is the perfect place to let the kids run free for a couple of hours. At the lagoon complex, they'll find ducks and an impressive assortment of (sometimes squawky) migratory birds nesting on Bird Island. Several play structures throughout the park—the biggest is at the downtown lakeside corner of the park near St. Charles Avenue—provide places for kids to swing, slide, and climb. And a walk around the 1.8-mile paved jogging path is an ever-popular family pastime. (*Uptown*) **City Park.** There's plenty to do here for the younger set, including two free playgrounds—one with swings near the Peristyle, and another for older kids, just off Marconi Drive, with more challenging things to clamber on. Storyland, a fairy-tale theme park, is open year-round, and features a number of sculptures created by Blaine Kern Studios, the maker of Mardi Gras floats. The adjacent Carousel Gardens Amusement Park has low-impact rides, a miniature train that tours the park, and a beautiful 100-year-old carousel centerpiece. City Putt offers 36 holes of mini golf. (*Mid-City*)

Animals Everywhere!

Aquarium of the Americas. Loads of exotic sea creatures, a penguin exhibit, and an interactive area where kids can get their hands wet make the aquarium a favorite family destination. There's a fun museum shop and an IMAX theater next door. (*The French Quarter: Riverfront*) **Audubon Insectarium.** This amazing attraction features insects for everyone—from a beautiful exhibit on butterflies to gross-out fun with the "bug chef." (*The French Quarter: Riverfront*) **Audubon Zoo.** A well-designed showcase with animals from all over the world, the zoo also has a hands-on area for kids, where young volunteers show off zoo residents, and a petting area with friendly goats and other beasties. (*Uptown*)

Kiddie Culture

Louisiana Children's Museum. This Warehouse District museum tries to sneak in a little education while giving kids a place to romp, role-play, and dabble in the arts. (*Warehouse District*)

For Kids of All Ages

Blaine Kern's Mardi Gras World at Kern Studios. The city's most famous float-building family offer tours of their company's vast studio, where kids can try on costumes and watch the artists at work. (*Warehouse District*) **Streetcars.** You can't leave New Orleans without taking the kids for a ride on a streetcar, which you can also use to get to several of the sites listed here, including City Park (on the Canal Street line) and Audubon Park (St. Charles Avenue). (⇨ *See the "Riding the Streetcar" feature in the Uptown and Carrollton-Riverbend chapter.*)

GREAT ITINERARIES

NEW ORLEANS HIGHLIGHTS

Including a trip to Plantation Country.

Day 1: The French Quarter

Start by getting to know the city's most famous neighborhood. The café au lait and beignets at **Café du Monde** are a good place to begin, followed by a stroll around **Jackson Square** and **St. Louis Cathedral.** Cross the seawall and take in the views of the Mississippi River from **Woldenberg Riverfront Park.** Wander along North Peters Street to the shops and market stalls in the **French Market,** followed by a walk in the mostly residential **Lower Quarter** and **Faubourg Marigny.** After lunch, explore the antiques stores and art galleries on **Royal and Chartres streets,** winding it all up with a cocktail in a shady courtyard—try **Napoleon House,** an atmospheric bar and café that makes a mean Pimm's Cup, or French Quarter mainstay **Pat O'Brien's.** Save **Bourbon Street** for after dinner at one of the Quarter's esteemed restaurants; like anything that's lived hard and been around long, it's much more attractive in low light.

Day 2: The Garden District and Uptown

The **St. Charles Avenue streetcar** rumbles past some of the South's most prized real estate; relax in one of the antique wooden seats and admire the scenery on the way to leafy **Audubon Park.** In the park you can follow the paved footpath to the **Audubon Zoo,** keeping an eye out for the zoo's white tiger and rare white alligators. Board an inbound **Magazine Street** bus near the zoo entrance and take it a couple of blocks past Louisiana Avenue, where a number of restaurants, some with sidewalk tables, are clustered. Continue along Magazine to Washington Avenue and head left through the **Garden District.** Prytania Street, just past **Lafayette Cemetery No. 1** (Anne Rice fans, take note), is a good axis from which to explore the neighborhood's elegant side streets. Catch a downtown-bound streetcar on St. Charles, or wrap up the afternoon shopping and dining on Magazine Street.

Day 3: Art, History, and Culture

Dedicate one day to a deeper exploration of the city's cultural attractions. Art lovers shouldn't miss the **Warehouse District,** where a pair of fine museums—the **Ogden Museum of Southern Art** and the **Contemporary Arts Center**—anchor a vibrant strip of contemporary art galleries, most of which feature local artists. History buffs will want to check out the **National World War II Museum,** also in the Warehouse District, and the **Historic New Orleans Collection** in the French Quarter, which hosts changing exhibits in a beautifully restored town home.

Day 4: Remembering Katrina

It may strike some as macabre, but touring neighborhoods devastated by Katrina's floodwater has become a ritual for many visitors, much the same as pilgrimages to Lower Manhattan's Ground Zero. You can opt for a guided bus tour, which takes you to **Lakeview** and the infamous **17th Street Canal levee breach;** some companies also travel to the **Lower Ninth Ward** and **Chalmette.** After a somber tour of Hurricane Katrina's destruction, take heart by looking to the many signs of renewal and rebirth. **City Park,** which sustained extensive wind and flood damage, reopened its stately botanical gardens; nearby stands the venerable **New Orleans Museum of Art** and the adjacent **Sydney and Walda Besthoff Sculpture Garden.** Wind down from the day with dinner and live music downtown at one of the clubs on **Frenchmen Street,** in the Faubourg Marigny neighborhood, where the city's inexhaustible spirit parties on.

Day 5: Head Out of Town

Consider a day trip out of town to visit one of the region's **plantation homes,** explore **Cajun Country,** or take a guided **swamp tour.** Some tour companies offer a combination, with stops for lunch. Many of the antebellum mansions between New Orleans and Baton Rouge have been painstakingly restored and filled with period furniture; nature lovers will want to set aside time to explore their grounds and lush flower gardens. Although swamp tours may sound hokey, they're actually a good way to see south Louisiana's cypress-studded wetlands (and get up close and personal with the alligators and other critters that live there). Continue the nautical theme in the evening with a ride to **Algiers Point** aboard the Canal Street Ferry for lovely sunset views of the New Orleans skyline.

TIPS

If you're venturing out in your own vehicle, be aware of massive repaving projects; with a little patience, you'll get through some gnarly construction-zone traffic patterns.

Summer in New Orleans arrives early and sticks around longer than most people would like. If visiting in the hot months, stay hydrated, limit your midday outdoor activities, and be prepared for sudden, sometimes torrential downpours.

Bring a sweater or light jacket with you: air-conditioning in restaurants and other destinations can be excessive.

New Orleanians are friendly, but odd offers from people on the street to tell you where you got your shoes—"You got them on your feet," followed by a demand that you pay for this information—or other overtures from chatty, dubious-looking types should be ignored (feel free to pretend you don't speak English). Trust your intuition.

Before you book your trip, visit ⊕ www. neworleansonline.com, click "Travel Tools" at the bottom, and download coupons for lodging, dining, attractions, tours, and shopping discounts. This site is owned by the New Orleans Tourism Marketing Corporation and is a great source for event information. The site ⊕ www. neworleanscvb.com also has a selection of downloadable coupons.

A GOOD GARDEN DISTRICT WALK

As New Orleans expanded upriver from Canal Street in the 19th century, wealthy newcomers built their majestic homes in the Garden District. Today the area is home to politicians, fifth-generation New Orleanians, and celebrities. A walk through the Garden District, just a 20-minute streetcar ride from the French Quarter, provides a unique look at life in New Orleans, past and present.

Start at **the Rink,** a small shopping complex at the Washington Avenue and Prytania Street intersection, a block from the streetcar stop. Walk east on Prytania (the main artery of the district) to the corner of Fourth Street to see **Colonel Short's Villa** (⊠ *1448 Fourth St.*), known for its ornate cornstalk fence and supposedly built for his wife, who was homesick for Kentucky. Toward Third Street, the **Briggs-Staub House** (⊠ *2605 Prytania St.*) is one of the few Gothic Revival houses in the city. No expense was spared in building the **Lonsdale House** (⊠ *2521 Prytania St.*) across the street, which was a Catholic chapel for more than 70 years. The **Maddox House** (⊠ *2507 Prytania St.*) next door is an example of the five-bay Greek Revival expansion. Across Prytania at the corner of Second is the **Women's Guild of the New Orleans Opera Association House** (⊠ *2504 Prytania St.*), with its distinctive octagonal turret; it's now a catering hall for weddings and social events. At First and Prytania streets are the regal **Bradish-Johnson House** (⊠ *2343 Prytania St.*), now a private girls' school, and the relatively modest raised **Toby-Westfeldt House** (⊠ *2340 Prytania St.*), an example of a Creole colonial home.

Turn right and walk down First Street. Built in 1869, **Morris House** (⊠ *1331 First St.*), on the corner of Coliseum, and **Carroll House** (⊠ *1315 First St.*) next door

(where *Toys in the Attic* was filmed), are decorated with "iron lace," exemplifying the era's romantic Italianate style. Across Chestnut Street, **Brevard House** (⊠ *1239 First St.*), also known as Rosegate for the ornate cast-iron gate that extends the length of the block, used to be the home of author Anne Rice. A block farther on the right is the **Payne House** (⊠ *1134 First St.*), where Confederate president Jefferson Davis died.

Walk back up First Street toward Coliseum, which takes you past some of the most beautiful and historic homes in the South. The **Italianate Mansion** at 2425 Coliseum Street is the home of actor John Goodman. Across the street from each other at Coliseum and Third streets are the white-columned **Robinson House** (⊠ *1413 Third St.*), thought to be the first house in New Orleans with indoor plumbing, and the intricate iron-balconied **Musson House** (⊠ *1415 Third St.*) built by Edgar Degas's uncle. The white-columned **Nolan House,** at 2707 Coliseum, is where Benjamin Button was raised in the film *The Curious Case of Benjamin Button.* Next door, one of New Orleans's most famous restaurants, **Commander's Palace** (⊠ *1403 Washington Ave.*), is a great stop for lunch. Across Washington Avenue is the white-walled **Lafayette Cemetery No. 1,** arguably the most beautiful cemetery in the city.

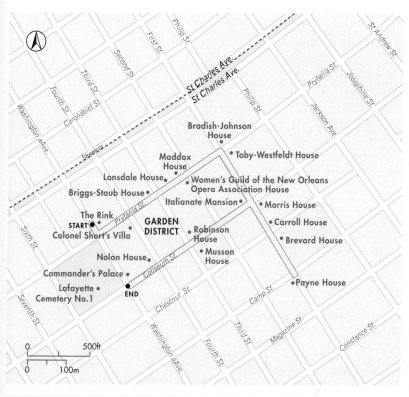

Where to Start:	The Rink on Prytania Street and Washington Avenue
Distance:	1 mile
Timing:	45 minutes (without stops inside)
Where to Stop:	Women's Guild of the New Orleans Opera Association House for interior tours on Monday (closed Memorial Day to Labor Day); Lafayette Cemetery No. 1, open to visitors daily until 3 pm
Best Time to Go:	Mornings, especially in spring and fall; Monday for the Women's Guild tours
Worst Time to Go:	Midday, especially in summer; major holidays when the cemetery is closed
Good in the Hood:	Stein's Deli, Tracey's Irish Channel Bar, Coquette bistro and wine bar, Commander's Palace

A GOOD GALLERY WALK IN THE WAREHOUSE DISTRICT

Julia Street in the Warehouse District is the epicenter of New Orleans's contemporary arts scene, and for art enthusiasts a day on (and just off) Julia is a requirement. The street is lined with galleries, specialty shops, and modern apartment buildings, and the greatest concentration of them stretches from South Peters Street to Camp Street.

Start your walk on Camp and St. Joseph streets. Whet your appetite inside the airy, contemporary, stone-and-glass-walled **Ogden Museum of Southern Art** (✉ 925 Camp St. ☎ 504/539–9600), which houses the largest collection of Southern art anywhere. Across the street, the multidisciplinary **Contemporary Arts Center** (✉ 900 Camp St. ☎ 504/528–3805) hosts performances, concerts, and lectures, and runs stimulating and eclectic exhibitions by local and foreign artists. Pop in if there's an exhibition, and then continue on your way down Camp to Julia Street. Turn left on Julia to see five gallery and studio spaces in the single block between this corner and St. Charles Avenue.

At Camp and Julia streets you'll find **Gallery 600 Julia** (✉ 600 Julia St. ☎ 504/895–7375), in the first of the Thirteen Sisters addresses that make up the historic Julia Street Row. Gallery 600 shows a mix of contemporary and historical paintings depicting Louisiana scenery and life, from wetlands wildlife to New Orleans cityscapes.

A longtime champion of the visual arts scene in New Orleans, **Arthur Roger** maintains a world-class gallery (✉ 432–434 Julia St. ☎ 504/522–1999) that occupies two adjacent Julia Street addresses behind gleaming glass-walled facades. The gallery is a leader in representing prominent local artists and works from around the globe, and is an influential presence in the national art scene.

In the next block you'll find contemporary work with a political edge and a public conscience at **Jonathan Ferrara Gallery** (✉ 400a Julia St. ☎ 504/522–5471).

Next door, the lofty whitewashed brick-and-glass space inside **Søren Christensen** (✉ 400 Julia St. ☎ 504/569–9501) provides a gorgeous backdrop for always-excellent exhibitions, largely featuring contemporary painting but sometimes photography and sculpture.

Keep heading toward the river to **Le Mieux Galleries** (✉ 332 Julia St. ☎ 504/522–5988), where contemporary Southern artists are the stars; drawings, paintings, photography, and sculpture from throughout the region are showcased here.

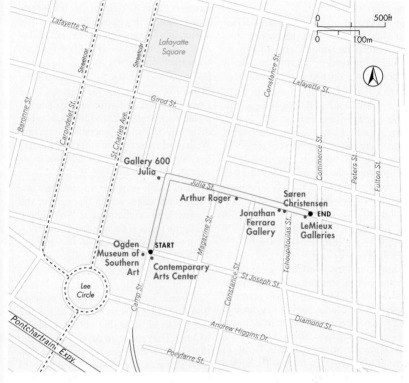

Where to Start:	Camp Street at the Ogden Museum of Southern Art
Distance:	About a half mile
Timing:	Several hours to all day, depending on how much time you have and how much you want to see
Where to Stop:	Julia and Commerce streets
Best Time to Go:	First Saturday of every month, when Art Walks are hosted by Warehouse District galleries from 6 to 9 pm. Two Saturdays not to be missed if you happen to be in town are Jammin' on Julia in April and Whitney White Linen Night in August—both wildly popular, all-out art-themed block parties enjoyed by enthusiastic crowds.
Worst Time to Go:	Sunday, when nearly all galleries are closed
Good in the Hood:	Charcuterie and Southern cuisine are showcased at Cochon (⊠ 930 Tchoupitoulas St. ☎ 504/588–2123). Next door, Cochon Butcher (⊠ 930 Tchoupitoulas St. ☎ 504/588–7675) is more casual, with sandwiches and small plates. Wood Pizza Bistro and Taphouse (⊠ 404 Andrew Higgins ☎ 504/281–4893) serves its creative pizzas in a pleasant street-facing courtyard.

BEST FESTS AND PARADES

New Year's Eve

Join the crowd on the Mississippi River near Jax Brewery for fireworks, live music, and the annual countdown to midnight (marked by a giant fleur-de-lis dropping from the top of the brewery).

Mardi Gras, February or March

The biggest event in the city's busy calendar has been around for well over a century, and for a celebration of frivolity, people here take Carnival very seriously. There are almost daily parades—even one for dogs (the Krewe of Barkus)—in the two weeks leading up to Fat Tuesday, when pretty much the entire city takes the day off, gets in costume, and hits the streets (⇨ *See our Mardi Gras feature in Chapter 2*). ⊕ *www.mardigrasneworleans.com*.

St. Patrick's Day, March

A couple of big parades roll on the weekend closest to March 17: one starts at Molly's at the Market and winds through the French Quarter; the other, in Uptown, goes down Magazine Street. On St. Paddy's Day the streets around Parasol's Restaurant & Bar, in the Irish Channel neighborhood, turn into one big, green block party. Two days later (March 19) the town celebrates St. Joseph's Day with home-cooked food and goodie bags filled with cookies and lucky fava beans. Check the *Times-Picayune* classifieds or ⊕ *www.nola.com* for announcements of altars that you can visit, and be prepared to make a small contribution to cover costs ($5 a person or so).

Tennessee Williams/New Orleans Literary Festival, March

This annual tribute to the *A Streetcar Named Desire* playwright, who spent much of his career in New Orleans, draws well-known and aspiring writers, lecturers, and a handful of Williams's acquaintances. It closes with contestants re-enacting Stanley Kowalski's big "Stella-a-a!" moment. ☎ *504/581–1144* ⊕ *www.tennesseewilliams.net*.

Easter, March or April

Three fun parades hit the streets of the French Quarter on Easter Sunday: one led by local entertainer Chris Owens, another dedicated to the late socialite Germaine Wells, and a gay parade that takes the festive bonnet tradition to a whole new level.

French Quarter Festival, April

A lot of locals consider this the best festival. With stages set up throughout the Quarter and on the river at Woldenberg Park, the focus is on free local entertainment—and, of course, food. ☎ *504/522–5730* ⊕ *www.fqfi.org*.

New Orleans Jazz & Heritage Festival, April–May

Top-notch local, national, and international talent takes to several stages the last weekend of April and first weekend of May. The repertoire covers much more than jazz, with big-name rock and pop stars in the mix, and there are dozens of lectures, quality arts and crafts, and awesome food to boot. Next to Mardi Gras, Jazz Fest is the city's biggest draw; book your hotel as far in advance as possible (⇨ *see the New Orleans Noise feature in Chapter 10*). ☎ *504/410–4100* ⊕ *www.nojazzfest.com*.

New Orleans Wine & Food Experience, May

Winemakers and oenophiles from all over the world converge for five days of seminars, tastings, and fine food. The Royal Street Stroll, when shops and galleries host pourings and chefs set up tables on the street, is especially lively. ☎ *504/934–1474* ⊕ *www.nowfe.com*.

Essence Music Festival, July

Held around Independence Day, this three-day festival draws top names in R&B, pop, and hip-hop to the Mercedes-Benz Superdome. The event also includes talks by prominent African American figures and empowerment seminars. ⊕ *www. essence.com/festival.*

Tales of the Cocktail, late July

Every summer, heralded mixologists, distillers, writers, chefs, and cocktail connoisseurs converge in the city that gave birth to the Sazerac and the Ramos gin fizz—among other libations—for several days of cocktail competitions, seminars, tastings, pairing dinners, and many more spirited events. ⊕ *www.talesofthecocktail.com.*

Satchmo SummerFest, August

This weekend-long tribute to the late, great Louis Armstrong honors Satchmo with jazz performances staged throughout the French Quarter, seminars and discussions with Louis Armstrong scholars, a Satchmo Club Strut down Frenchmen Street, and the Louis Armstrong Birthday Party. ⊕ *www.fqfi.org/satchmosummerfest.*

Southern Decadence, early September

On Labor Day weekend, hundreds of drag-queens-for-a-day parade through the Quarter. What began as a small party among friends has evolved into one of the South's biggest gay celebrations. The parade rolls—and as the day wears on, staggers—along on Sunday, but Decadence parties and events start Thursday evening. ⊕ *www.southerndecadence.net.*

Art for Art's Sake, early October

Art lovers and people-watchers pack the Warehouse District and Magazine Street galleries for this annual Saturday-evening kickoff to the arts season. What's on the walls usually plays second fiddle to the party scene, which spills out into the streets.

Voodoo Experience, October

Part music festival, part giant interactive art exhibition, Voodoo Experience is an evolving festival held every Halloween weekend; it attracts eclectic young masses with its mix of edgy national acts, local bands, and art installations in various media. ⊕ *www.worshipthemusic.com.*

Celebration in the Oaks, late November–early January

City Park's majestic oaks, Botanical Gardens, Carousel Garden, and Storyland amusement park are awash in holiday lights and decorations during this popular weeks-long event. You'll find food and rides, a miniature train decked out for Christmas, and entertainment by local school groups. ☏ *504/482–4888* ⊕ *www. neworleanscitypark.com.*

A New Orleans Christmas, December

The lighting of Canal Street kicks off this monthlong celebration. Royal Street shops and historic homes don holiday decorations, restaurants feature special *reveillon* menus, and thousands of carolers gather in Jackson Square for a sing-along by candlelight. Around Christmas, bonfires are lit on the levee at various points along the Mississippi, from below New Orleans up into Cajun Country. Legend says the bonfires were lighted by the early settlers to help Papa Noel (the Cajun Santa Claus) find his way up the river. Steamboat tour companies offer special cruises for the occasion.

FREE AND CHEAP

Free Museums and Galleries

Buy a **Power Pass** (three days, $144.50 per adult ⊕ *www.visiticket.com*) to save a significant amount on admissions to the city's leading museums and attractions. It costs nothing, however, to browse the **Warehouse District galleries** on and around Julia Street, where you'll find works by established and up-and-coming artists.

The Sydney and Walda Besthoff Sculpture Garden in City Park, next to the New Orleans Museum of Art, is free and exhibits major works by important 20th-century artists, including Henry Moore, Jacques Lipchitz, Barbara Hepworth, and Seymour Lipton, dramatically set among lagoons and moss-laden oak trees.

Uptown, on the Tulane University campus, the **Newcomb Art Gallery** hosts shows featuring work by internationally known artists—photographer Diane Arbus and master silversmith William Spratling are two examples—as well as themed exhibitions and work by Newcomb's art school alumni.

Free Music

Outdoor festivals like the **Satchmo Summer Fest** and **French Quarter Festival** are great places to hear live music for free. Street bands also serenade visitors daily in the French Quarter—but if you linger, you'll likely be asked to toss a few bucks into the hat.

The **New Orleans Jazz National Historical Park** (⊠ *916 N. Peters St.* ☎ *504/589–4806*) sponsors free live performances and lectures Tuesday through Saturday at its French Market office and at its smart new performance space in the Old U.S. Mint. The musicians are invariably good and run the full gamut, from traditional brass band music to modern jazz.

If you're in town on a Wednesday from March to late June, check out the free **Wednesday at the Square** concert series at Lafayette Square in the CBD, across from Gallier Hall. At about 5 pm, a horde of downtown workers and fest-loving residents converge on the square to dance, socialize, and hear great local bands. There's plenty of food and drink available for purchase.

On Thursday in either spring or fall, head right outside the French Quarter to Armstrong Park for its free **Jazz in the Park** series. You'll hear well-known musicians like the Rebirth Brass Band and Jon Cleary in addition to lesser-knowns, starting at 4 pm. The series runs mid-April through May and mid-September through October, and there's always plenty of food and crafts vendors nearby.

Cheap and Scenic Ride

The **Canal–Algiers Ferry** ($2) offers some of the best views of the city. It's a fun thing to do with kids, and a great way to get a sense of the Mississippi River's magnitude. The pedestrian entrance is on the plaza at the foot of Canal Street, across from Harrah's Casino; it docks on the West Bank at Algiers Point, a quaint historic neighborhood that makes for a good daytime stroll.

COCKTAIL EVENTS AND EXHIBITS

Drink & Learn: The Cocktail Tour. Culinary historian and Louisiana native Elizabeth Pearce leads a deeply informative two-hour walking tour dedicated to the city's cocktail culture. The $50 ticket includes four drinks. ⊠ *French Quarter* ☎ *504/207–4532* ⊕ *www.drinkandlearn.com.*

New Orleans Original Cocktail Tour. This Gray Line walking tour leads you through the saloons and wine cellars of the French Quarter. Frequent stops for libations along the route guarantee that you'll get firsthand experience of the city's best drinks. The 2½-hour tours cost $29 and depart daily at 4 pm from the Lighthouse ticket office at Toulouse Street and the Mississippi River. ⊠ *Warehouse District* ☎ *504/569–1401* ⊕ *www.graylineneworleans.com/cocktail-tour.html.*

New Orleans Wine and Food Experience. Serious wine drinkers skip the beach for this four-day celebration of Bacchus over Memorial Day weekend. Popular events include a series of vintner dinners at local restaurants, a wine-fueled stroll through the shops of Royal Street, and the two-day Grand Tasting, where nearly 75 restaurants serve food and 1,000 different wines are poured. ⊠ *New Orleans* ☎ *504/934–1474* ⊕ *www.nowfe.com.*

NOLA Brewing Tour. Every Friday and Saturday, beer lovers show up at New Orleans's only craft brewery (the name stands for "New Orleans Lager and Ale") to learn how beer gets made. The 90-minute free tour starts at 2 pm, but the rowdy tap room is open 11 am to 11 pm. ⊠ *3001 Tchoupitoulas St., Garden District* ☎ *407/222–0449 (marketing and sales)* ⊕ *www.nolabrewing.com.*

Old New Orleans Rum Distillery. Founded in 1995, this craft distillery is the oldest maker of rum in the continental United States. Tours ($15) start with a cocktail and end with a tasting of four different rums. Complimentary transportation from the French Quarter is available during the week—make reservations for it in advance. ⊠ *2815 Frenchmen St., Gentilly* ☎ *504/945–9400* ⊕ *www.oldneworleansrum.com.*

Tales of the Cocktail. Each July, the annual Tales of the Cocktail, billed as "the most spirited event of the summer," brings thousands of experts and enthusiasts together for an internationally acclaimed, five-day celebration dedicated to the artistry and science of making drinks. In addition to enjoying some of "the best cocktails ever made," attendees participate in dinners, demonstrations, tastings, competitions, seminars, book signings, tours, and parties. ⊠ *New Orleans* ☎ *504/948–0511* ⊕ *www.talesofthecocktail.com.*

GETTING OUT OF TOWN

Cajun Country

The land that gave the world one of its great cuisines—and a refuge for French-Canadian exiles in the 18th century—is worth at least one overnight. **Lafayette,** with its attractive downtown area and plentiful accommodations, makes a good hub for exploring the region. The Cajun kitsch can be a bit much at times, but there are some outstanding restaurants and museums, including the **Paul and Lulu Hilliard University Art Museum** and **Acadian Village,** a re-creation of an early-19th-century Acadian settlement. Venture south to picturesque **Abbeville,** where restaurants serve up some mean oysters on the half shell, or to **New Iberia** and nearby **Avery Island,** home of the famous Tabasco hot sauce and a gorgeous 250-acre botanical garden. **Breaux Bridge,** site of the annual Crawfish Festival, has antiques shops and some excellent Cajun restaurants, including **Café des Amis,** known for its dance parties. **St. Martinville,** south of Breaux Bridge, is an attractive small town and home of the **Evangeline Oak,** immortalized in Longfellow's classic poem "Evangeline."

To the north lies **Grand Coteau,** a quaint, historic village set on a natural bluff. A little farther up, you'll find **Opelousas,** a hotbed of zydeco music and home to the annual **Southwest Louisiana Zydeco Music festival** each Labor Day weekend. The normally quiet town of **Mamou** goes bonkers on Fat Tuesday, when the traditional **Courir de Mardi Gras** takes to the streets; on Saturday mornings little **Fred's Lounge** gets packed to the gills with locals and more than a few tourists two-stepping and waltzing to live Cajun music.

Plantation Country

The stretch of the Mississippi north of New Orleans offers the ultimate Southern antebellum experience. Tour buses ply the highway on both sides of the river, but with a car and a map, it's easy to explore on your own. Fortunes were made here in the 18th and 19th centuries—on the backs of the slaves that worked these plantations—and vestiges of the Old South's wealthy heyday remain in the region's lavish homes, many lovingly restored and open to the public. Highlights include **Oak Alley,** with its procession of ancient oak trees that flank the entrance; **Houmas House,** notable for its architecture, gardens, and fine Latil's Landing restaurant; and **Nottoway,** the largest extant plantation house. Several homes offer accommodations and dining. **Whitney Plantation** is the first of these homes (and only in the country) dedicated to the lives of slaves, and a trip to this moving and enlightening museum is an essential stop on your tour of plantation era history.

Many of the small towns that dot Plantation Country are fun to explore, but **St. Francisville,** about 25 miles north of Baton Rouge, deserves special mention. The historic town center is a well-preserved collection of antebellum homes and buildings, and the river landing there is one of the few places in south Louisiana where the Mississippi isn't hemmed in by levees. A cluster of fine plantation homes are nearby, including **Rosedown Plantation and Gardens.**

THE FRENCH QUARTER

Getting Oriented

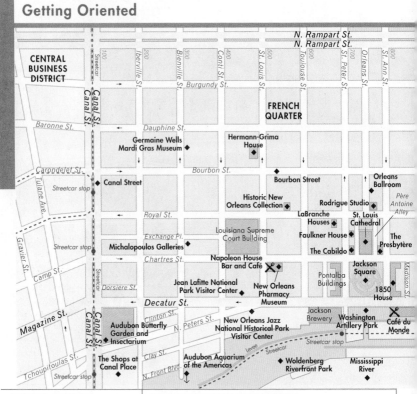

CENTRAL BUSINESS DISTRICT

FRENCH QUARTER

N. Rampart St.
N. Rampart St.

Streetcar
Canal St.
Canal St.

Iberville St.
Bienville St.
Conti St.
St. Louis St.
Toulouse St.
St. Peter St.
Orleans St.
St. Ann St.

Burgundy St.

Baronne St.
Dauphine St.

Germaine Wells
Mardi Gras Museum ◆

Hermann-Grima House ◆

Carondelet St.
Bourbon St.

Tulane Ave.
Streetcar stop
◆ Canal Street

Bourbon Street
Orleans Ballroom

Historic New Orleans Collection ◆

Rodrigue Studio ◆

Père Antoine Alley

Royal St.

LaBranche Houses ◆
St. Louis Cathedral

Gravier St.
Streetcar stop ◆
Michalopoulos Galleries ◆

Exchange Pl.

Louisiana Supreme Court Building

Faulkner House ◆

The Presbytère

Camp St.
Chartres St.

The Cabildo ◆

Dorsiere St.
Streetcar
Napoleon House Bar and Café ✗◆

Jackson Square ◆

Madison St.

Jean Lafitte National Park Visitor Center ◆

New Orleans Pharmacy Museum

Pontalba Buildings

1850 House

Decatur St.

Magazine St.
Canal St.
Canal St.

Clinton St.
N. Peters St.

Audubon Butterfly Garden and Insectarium ◆

New Orleans Jazz National Historical Park Visitor Center

Jackson Brewery

Washington Artillery Park

Café du Monde ✗

Streetcar stop

Tchoupitoulas St.
The Shops at Canal Place ◆

Clay St.
N. Front Blvd.

Audubon Aquarium of the Americas ◆

Levee
Streetcar

Woldenberg Riverfront Park ◆

Mississippi River ◆

Streetcar stop

GETTING AROUND	MAKING THE MOST OF YOUR TIME
French Quarter streets are laid out in a **grid pattern.** Locals describe locations based on the proximity to the river or the lake and to uptown or downtown. Thus, "it's on the downtown, lakeside corner" indicates that a destination in the Quarter is on the northeast corner. Locals also refer to the **number block** that a site is on (as in "the 500 block of Royal Street"). Numbers across the top of the map are applicable to all streets parallel to North Rampart Street. Streets perpendicular to North Rampart start at 500 at Decatur Street and progress north in increments of 100.	Many visitors never leave the French Quarter, which is the center of New Orleans. Daytime offers history buffs, antiques lovers, shoppers, and foodies a feast of delights; street performers around **Jackson Square** are always entertaining; and the Quarter lights up with fine and casual dining, live music, and the infamous **Bourbon Street** debauchery at night. This is a destination you can enjoy 24 hours a day.

SAFETY

Exercise the same caution here that you would in any major city. Closer to the river, the French Quarter is busy day and night, and there is safety in numbers. Farther from the river and closer to Rampart Street or the more residential area, crowds thin, and opportunities for theft grow slightly higher. It's advisable to use extra caution at these outer edges of the French Quarter.

2

The French Quarter

QUICK BITES

Café du Monde. Open around the clock for late-night treats Café du Monde has been serving up café au lait and beignets for more than a century. If the open-air café is crowded, go around back to the take-out window and enjoy your treats on the Mississippi riverfront. ⊠ *800 Decatur St., French Quarter* ☎ *504/525–4544* ⊕ *www.cafedumonde.com* ▬ *No credit cards.*

Napoleon House Bar and Café. The house specialty Pimm's Cup can be enjoyed in the lush courtyard or in the cool interior, along with bites like pulled-duck po'boys. The residence was built in 1797 and was purportedly chosen as Napoléon's New World residence in an escape plan hatched for the exiled emperor. ⊠ *500 Chartres St., French Quarter* ☎ *504/524–9752* ⊕ *www.napoleonhouse.com* ⊗ *Closed Sun.*

TOP REASONS TO GO

Queue up for beignets. Anytime is the right time for powdered-sugar-topped beignets and café au lait from Café du Monde.

Take in Jackson Square. Mule-drawn carriage tours, artists selling their wares, and quirky street performers and musicians converge on Jackson Square, with the historic St. Louis Cathedral as a backdrop.

Go treasure hunting. The French Market and the random stores and warehouses that surround it are great for finding inexpensive souvenirs.

Drink up. From rowdy Bourbon Street to fancy hotel bars, you'll never go thirsty. Savor your cocktail in a beautiful courtyard, or ask for a "go cup."

Gallery hop on Royal Street. Fine antiques, upscale boutiques, and artwork abound on this classy thoroughfare.

Groove to live music. The French Quarter has some great music venues, including Preservation Hall, the Palm Court Jazz Cafe, Fritzel's European Jazz Pub, and One-Eyed Jack's.

Sightseeing
★★★★★
Dining
★★★★★
Lodging
★★★★★
Shopping
★★★★★
Nightlife
★★★★★

Even locals love to get lost in the history and romance of the French Quarter, the city's oldest neighborhood. As you stroll through narrow side streets flanked by historic architecture, you'll marvel at the neighborhood's ability to endure. Keep walking, slowly, and take time to look up at fabled wrought-iron balcony railings or peer down cobblestone corridors for a glimpse of secret courtyard gardens.

Updated by
Cameron
Quincy Todd

The French Quarter will not run out of ways to entertain you. The Vieux Carré, French for "Old Square," is technically the entire French Quarter, but you'll notice a divide at Decatur Street, as things start to feel more modern towards the river, and chain stores and restaurants pop up. The historic part of the French Quarter is where you can slip down a quiet street, gaze up at a row of balconies, and forget for a moment that you are living in the 21st century. During the day, the French Quarter offers several different faces to its visitors. The streets running parallel to the river all bear distinct personas: Decatur Street is a strip of tourist shops, hotels, restaurants, and bars uptown from Jackson Square; downtown from the square, it becomes a hangout for hipsters and leather-clad regulars drawn to shadowy bars, vintage clothing boutiques, funky antiques emporiums, and novelty stores. Modern development along the river side of Decatur Street can make this strip feel like a suburban corridor, but some of the best of old New Orleans is still here: the massive Mississippi River, Café du Monde, and the French Market.

Chartres Street remains a relatively calm stretch of inviting shops and eateries. Royal Street is, perhaps aptly, the address of sophisticated antiques shops, glittering jewelry stores, and many of the Quarter's finest residences. Bourbon Street claims the strip bars, sex shops, extravagant cocktails, and flashy music clubs filmmakers love to feature. Dauphine and Burgundy streets are more residential, with just a few restaurants and bars offering retreats for locals.

After dark you'll find fine dining and easygoing eateries aplenty, and music pouring from the doorways of bars as freely as the drinks flowing inside (and outside—plastic "go cups" for your cocktails are standard at the exit of every bar and club, and consuming alcohol on public streets is legal in New Orleans). On any ordinary evening a stroll through the French Quarter is a moving concert. Strains of traditional jazz, blues, classic rock 'n' roll, and electronic dance beats all flow from the various bars and nightclubs, while street musicians add their unique sounds to the mix.

> ## GET A GO CUP
>
> Open containers of alcohol are allowed on the streets of New Orleans, as long as they're not in glass. So when you're ready to leave, ask your bartender for a "go cup," pour your drink into the plastic cup, and head out, beverage in hand.

For all its evening-time adult entertainment, the French Quarter by day is quite kid-friendly. Children adore eating beignets; watching ships ply the Mississippi; walking through the tunnel-shape Caribbean fish tank at the Aquarium of the Americas; munching crunchy treats made out of bugs at the Audubon Insectarium; and savoring the same delicious po'boy sandwiches and fried seafood that their parents enjoy.

TOP ATTRACTIONS

FAMILY
Fodor's Choice
★

Audubon Aquarium of the Americas. This giant aquatic showplace perched on the Mississippi riverfront has four major exhibit areas: the Amazon Rain Forest, the Mississippi River, the Gulf of Mexico, and the new Great Maya Reef gallery, all of which have fish and animals native to their respective environments. The aquarium's spectacular design allows you to feel like you're part of these watery worlds by providing close-up encounters with the inhabitants. One special treat is Parakeet Pointe, where you can spend time amid hundreds of parakeets and feed them by hand. A gift shop and café are on the premises. Woldenberg Riverfront Park, which surrounds the aquarium, is a tranquil spot with a view of the Mississippi. You can combine tickets for the aquarium and the **Entergy IMAX Theater** ($29.95), but the best deal is the "Audubon Experience": aquarium, IMAX, **Audubon Insectarium**, and **Audubon Zoo** for $44.95 (tickets are good for 30 days). ⊠ *1 Canal St., French Quarter* ☎ *504/861–2537, 800/774–7394* ⊕ *www.auduboninstitute. org* ⌨ *$29.95* ☉ *Closed Mon.*

FAMILY
Audubon Butterfly Garden and Insectarium. Shrink down to ant size and experience "Life Underground," explore the world's insect myth and lore, venture into a Louisiana swamp, and marvel at the hundreds of delicate denizens of the Japanese butterfly garden. Then tour the termite galleries and other sections devoted to the havoc insects wreak, so you can sample Cajun-fried crickets and other insect cuisine without a twinge of guilt. ⊠ *423 Canal St., French Quarter* ☎ *800/774–7394* ⊕ *www.auduboninstitute.org* ⌨ *$22.95* ☉ *Closed Mon.*

Bourbon Street. Ignore your better judgment and take a stroll down Bourbon Street past the bars, restaurants, music clubs, adult stores,

WHEN TO GO

Save Bourbon Street for after dinner at one of the Quarter's esteemed restaurants; like anything that's lived hard and been around a long time, Bourbon Street is much more attractive in low light.

and novelty shops that have given this strip its reputation as the play-ground of the South. The bars of Bourbon Street were among the first businesses of the city to reopen after Katrina; catering to off-duty relief workers, they provided their own form of relief. Today, the spirit of unbridled revelry here is as alive as ever. The noise, raucous crowds, and bawdy sights are not family fare, however; if you go with children, do so before sundown. St. Ann Street marks the beginning of a short strip of gay bars, some of which figure in the long history of gay culture in New Orleans. Although Bourbon Street is usually well patrolled, it is wise to stay alert to your surroundings. The street is blocked to make a pedestrian mall at night; crowds often get shoulder-to-shoulder, especially during major sports events, on New Year's Eve, and during Mardi Gras. ⊠ *French Quarter.*

The Cabildo. Dating from 1799, this Spanish colonial building is named for the Spanish council—or *cabildo*—that met here. The transfer of Louisiana to the United States was finalized in 1803 in the front room on the second floor overlooking the square. This historic transaction was reenacted in the same room for the 200th anniversary of the purchase in 2003. The Cabildo later served as city hall and then state supreme court.

Three floors of multicultural exhibits recount Louisiana history—from the colonial period through Reconstruction—with countless artifacts, including the death mask of Napoléon Bonaparte. In 1988 the building suffered terrible damage from a four-alarm fire. Most of the historic pieces inside were saved, but the top floor (which had been added in the 1840s), the roof, and the cupola had to be replaced. The Cabildo is almost a twin to the **Presbytère** on the other side of the cathedral. ■TIP➜ **Both sites—as well as the Old U.S. Mint and the 1850 House— are part of the Louisiana State Museum system. Buy tickets to two or more state museums and receive a 20% discount.** ⊠ *Jackson Sq., 701 Chartres St., French Quarter* ☎ *504/568–8968* ⊕ *www.louisianastate-museum.org* 🖅 *$6* ⊙ *Closed Mon.*

French Market. The sounds, colors, and smells here are alluring: ships' horns on the river, street performers, pralines, muffulettas, sugarcane, and Creole tomatoes. Originally a Native American trading post and later a bustling open-air market under the French and Spanish, the French Market historically began at the present-day Café du Monde and stretched along Decatur and North Peters streets all the way to the downtown edge of the Quarter. Today, the market's graceful arcades have been mostly enclosed and filled with shops, trinket stands, and eateries, and the farmers' market has been pushed several blocks down-river, under sheds built in the 1930s as part of a Works Progress Admin-istration project. **Latrobe Park,** a small recreational area at the uptown end of the French Market, honors Benjamin Latrobe, designer of the city's first waterworks. An evocative modern fountain marks the spot where Latrobe's steam-powered pumps once stood. Sunken seating, fountains, and greenery make this a lovely place to relax with a drink from one of the nearby kiosks. ⊠ *Decatur St., French Quarter* ⊕ *www. frenchmarket.org.*

A statue of General Andrew Jackson presides over his namesake park, Jackson Square.

Hermann-Grima House. Noted architect William Brand built this Georgian-style house in 1831, and it's one of the largest and best-preserved examples of American architecture in the Vieux Carré. Cooking demonstrations on the open hearth of the Creole kitchen are held most Thursdays from November through April. You'll want to check out the gift shop, which has many local crafts and books. ⊠ *820 St. Louis St., French Quarter* ☎ *504/274–0750* ⊕ *www.hgghh.org* ✉ *$15* ⊘ *Closed Wed. and Sun.*

Historic New Orleans Collection. This private archive and exhibit complex, with thousands of historic photos, documents, portraits, and books, is one of the finest research centers in the South. It occupies the 19th-century town house of General Kemper Williams and the 1792 Merieult House. Changing exhibits focus on various aspects of local history. Architecture, history, and house tours are offered several times daily, and a museum shop sells books, prints, and gifts. The Williams Research Center addition, at 410 Chartres Street, hosts additional free exhibits. ⊠ *533 Royal St., French Quarter* ☎ *504/523–4662* ⊕ *www. hnoc.org* ✉ *Free, tours $5.*

FAMILY
Fodor's Choice
★
Jackson Square. Surrounded by historic buildings and atmospheric street life, this beautifully landscaped park is the heart of the French Quarter. **St. Louis Cathedral** sits at the top of the square, while the **Cabildo** and **Presbytère**, two Spanish colonial buildings, flank the church. The handsome brick apartments on each side of the square are the **Pontalba Buildings**. During the day, dozens of artists hang their paintings on the park fence and set up outdoor studios where they work on canvases or offer to draw portraits of passersby. Musicians, mimes, tarot-card

readers, and magicians perform on the flagstone pedestrian mall, many of them day and night.

A **statue of Andrew Jackson,** victorious leader in the Battle of New Orleans in the War of 1812, commands the center of the square; the park was renamed for him in the 1850s. The words carved in the base on the cathedral side of the statue ("The Union must and shall be preserved") are a lasting reminder of the Federal troops who occupied New Orleans during the Civil War and who inscribed them. ⊠ *French Quarter* ⊕ *www.experienceneworleans.com.*

LaBranche Houses. This complex of lovely town houses, built in the 1830s by sugar planter Jean Baptiste LaBranche, fills the half block between Pirate's Alley and Royal and St. Peter streets behind the Cabildo. The house on the corner of Royal and St. Peter streets, with its elaborate, rounded cast-iron balconies, is among the most frequently photographed residences in the French Quarter. ⊠ *700 Royal St., French Quarter.*

Mississippi River. When facing the river with the French Quarter at your back, you will see, to your right, the **Crescent City Connection,** a twin-span bridge between downtown New Orleans and the West Bank, and a ferry that crosses the river every 30 minutes. The river flows to the left downstream for another 100 miles until it merges with the Gulf of Mexico. **Woldenberg Riverfront Park** and **Spanish Plaza** are prime territory for watching everyday life along the Mississippi: steamboats carrying tour groups, tugboats pushing enormous barges, and oceangoing ships. Directly across the river from the Quarter are the ferry landing and a dry dock for ship repair. ⊠ *French Quarter.*

Fodor'sChoice
★
The Presbytère. One of the twin Spanish colonial buildings flanking the St. Louis Cathedral, this one, on the right, was built on the site of the priests' residence, or *presbytère*. It served as a courthouse under the Spanish and later under the Americans. It is now a museum showcasing a spectacular collection of Mardi Gras memorabilia. Displays highlight both the little-known and popular traditions associated with New Orleans's most famous festival. "Living with Hurricanes: Katrina and Beyond" is a $7.5-million exhibition exploring the history, science, and powerful human drama of one of nature's most destructive forces. The building's cupola, destroyed by a hurricane in 1915, was restored to match the one atop its twin, the Cabildo. Allow at least an hour to see the exhibits. ⊠ *751 Chartres St., on Jackson Sq., French Quarter* ☎ *504/568–6964* ⊕ *www.louisianastatemuseum.org* ⊠ *$6* ⊗ *Closed Mon.*

CHESS CHAMPIONS

Frances Parkinson Keyes's historical novel *The Chess Players* is based on the life of Paul Morphy, a New Orleanian considered to be one of the greatest modern chess masters. The Beauregard-Keyes House was originally built for Morphy's grandfather. If you're interested in challenging a living chess master, stop by Jude Acers's sidewalk table outside the Gazebo Cafe on Decatur Street. A two-time world-record holder for simultaneous games, Acers is at his table most days and takes on any challenger for a small fee.

St. Louis Cathedral. The oldest active Catholic cathedral in the United States, this beautiful church and basilica at the heart of the Old City is named for the 13th-century French king who led two crusades. The current building, which replaced two structures destroyed by fire, dates from 1794 (although it was remodeled and enlarged in 1851). The austere interior is brightened by murals covering the ceiling and stained-glass windows along the first floor. Pope John Paul II held a prayer service for clergy here during his New Orleans visit in 1987; to honor the occasion, the pedestrian mall in front of the cathedral was renamed Place Jean Paul Deux. Of special interest is his portrait in a Jackson Square setting, which hangs on the cathedral's inner side wall. Docents often give free tours. You can also pick up a brochure ($1) for a self-guided tour. Books about the cathedral are available in the gift shop.

■ TIP→ Nearly every evening in December brings a free concert at the cathedral, in addition to the free concert series throughout the year.

The statue of the Sacred Heart of Jesus dominates St. Anthony's Garden, which extends behind the cathedral-basilica to Royal Street. The garden is also the site of a monument to 30 crew members of a French ship, who died in a yellow-fever epidemic in 1857. The garden has been redesigned by famed French landscape architect Louis Benech, who also redesigned the Tuileries gardens in Paris. ✉ *615 Père Antoine Alley, French Quarter* ☎ *504/525–9585* ⊕ *www.stlouiscathedral.org* ✉ *Free* ☞ *Mass daily at 7:30 am.*

Woldenberg Riverfront Park. This 16-acre stretch of green from Canal Street to Esplanade Avenue overlooks the Mississippi River as it curves around New Orleans, inspiring the "Crescent City" moniker. The wooden promenade section in front of Jackson Square is called the **Moon Walk,** named for Mayor Moon Landrieu (father of current mayor Mitch Landrieu), under whose administration in the 1970s the riverfront beyond the flood wall was reopened to public view. Today, the French Quarter Festival's main stages are erected here every April. It's a great place for a rest (or a muffuletta sandwich or café au lait and beignet picnic) after touring the Quarter, and you'll often be serenaded by musicians and amused by street performers. The park also is home to art pieces including the modest **Holocaust Memorial,** with its spiral walkway clad in Jerusalem stone. At the center of the spiral are nine sculptural panels by Jewish artist Yaacov Agam. A statue of local businessman Malcolm Woldenberg, the park's benefactor, is located near *Ocean Song,* local artist John T. Scott's large kinetic sculpture whose wind-powered movements are intended to evoke the patterns of New Orleans music. ✉ *French Quarter* ⊕ *www.auduboninstitute.org/ aquarium/exhibits-and-attractions/woldenberg-park.*

WORTH NOTING

Beauregard-Keyes House. The Confederate general and Louisiana native P.G.T. Beauregard briefly made his home at this stately 19th-century mansion. A more long-term resident, however, was the novelist Frances Parkinson Keyes, who found the place in a sad state when she arrived in the 1940s. Keyes restored the home—today filled with period

CLOSE UP

Micaela Pontalba

Every life has its little dramas, but how many of us can claim a life dramatic enough to inspire an opera? The Baroness Micaela Almonester de Pontalba numbers among that rarefied group, albeit posthumously. In 2003, on the 200th anniversary of the Louisiana Purchase, the New Orleans Opera Association commissioned an opera based on Pontalba, whose legacy you can easily see in the Pontalba Buildings, the elegant brick apartments lining Jackson Square.

Micaela Almonester was of Spanish stock, the daughter of the wealthy entrepreneur and developer Don Andres Almonester, who was instrumental in the creation of the Cabildo and Presbytère on Jackson Square. Don Almonester died while Micaela was still young, but not before passing on to his daughter a passion for building and urban design. The rest of her life would become a tale of international scope.

At the time of the Louisiana Purchase, in 1803, New Orleans was in a state of cultural upheaval. Following a period under Spanish rule during the late 18th century, the French had reacquired the colony—and merrily sold it to the Americans. The already complex blend of French and Spanish societies was further complicated by the anticipated imposition of American laws and mores, so foreign to the population of New Orleans. Micaela Almonester was right in the middle of the confusion: daughter of Spanish gentry, she fell in love and married a Frenchman, who took her to Paris with his family to avoid coming under American rule in New Orleans.

The Pontalbas' marriage was particularly unhappy, and Micaela's relationship to her in-laws was poisoned by mistrust over family property. Control of her New Orleans inheritance became part of an increasingly bitter feud that resulted in separation from her husband and, at its dramatic pinnacle, her attempted murder by her father-in-law. After the old baron inflicted four gunshot wounds on his daughter-in-law, he committed suicide, believing he had protected his son and his property. But Micaela, now Baroness de Pontalba following the old baron's death, survived her wounds. Within two years she had recovered enough to conceive the plan for the buildings that bear her name, but a long series of delays, including a bitter divorce, halted the project. Micaela finally returned to New Orleans in the 1840s in order to direct construction of the elegant apartments that would complete the square her father had been instrumental in developing. The Pontalba Buildings, designed by James Gallier in the French style favored by Micaela, were dedicated in 1851 to great fanfare. Each building contained 16 grand and lavishly detailed apartments.

Following the dedication of the buildings, Pontalba returned to France. She had been living in Paris for nearly 50 years and it had become her home. Yet the pilgrimage she made to New Orleans in order to complete a dream in the name of her father's memory hints that her heart never left her childhood home.

2

furnishings—and her studio at the back of the large courtyard remains intact, complete with family photos, original manuscripts, and her doll, fan, and teapot collections. Keyes wrote 40 novels there, all in long-hand, among them local favorite *Dinner at Antoine's*. Even if you don't have time for a tour, take a peek at the beautiful walled garden through the gates at the corner of Chartres and Ursulines streets. Landscaped in the same sun pattern as Jackson Square, it blooms year-round. ⊠ *1113 Chartres St., French Quarter* ☎ *504/523–7257* ⊕ *www.bkhouse.org* 🖃 *$10* ☉ *Closed Sun.*

Canal Street. At 170 feet wide, Canal Street is often called the widest street (as opposed to avenue or boulevard) in the United States, and it's certainly one of the liveliest—particularly during Carnival parades. It was once slated for conversion into a canal linking the Mississippi River to Lake Pontchartrain; plans changed, but the name remains. In the early 1800s, after the Louisiana Purchase, the French Creoles residing in the French Quarter segregated themselves from the Americans who settled upriver. What is now Canal Street—specifically the central median running down Canal Street—was neutral ground between them. Today, animosities between these two groups are history, but the term "neutral ground" has survived as the name for all medians throughout the city.

Some of the grand buildings that once lined Canal Street remain, many of them former department stores that now serve as hotels, restaurants, or souvenir shops. The Werlein Building (No. 605), once a multilevel music store, is now the **Palace Café** restaurant. The former home of Maison Blanche (No. 921), once the most elegant of downtown department stores, is now a **Ritz-Carlton hotel**. One building still serving its original purpose is **Adler's** (No. 722), the city's most elite jewelry and gift store. For the most part, these buildings have been faithfully restored, so you can still appreciate the grandeur that once reigned on this fabled strip. ⊠ *French Quarter* ⊕ *www.neworleanscvb.com/visit/ neighborhoods/canal-street.*

1850 House. This well-preserved town house and courtyard provide rare public access beyond the storefronts to the interior of the exclusive **Pontalba Buildings.** The rooms are furnished in the style of the mid-19th century, when the buildings were designed as upscale residences and retail spaces. Notice the ornate ironwork on the balconies of the apartments: the original owner, Baroness Micaela Pontalba, popularized cast (or molded) iron with these buildings, and it eventually replaced much of the old handwrought ironwork in the French Quarter. The initials for her families, *A* and *P* (Almonester and Pontalba), are worked into the design. A gift shop and bookstore run by the Friends of the Cabildo is downstairs. The Friends also offer informative two-hour walking tours of the French Quarter ($15) from this location Tuesday through Sunday at 10 and 1:30 that include admission to the house. ⊠ *523 St. Ann St., on Jackson Sq., French Quarter* ☎ *504/523–3939* ⊕ *www. louisianastatemuseum.org/museums/1850-house* 🖃 *$3* ☉ *Closed Mon.*

Faulkner House. The young novelist William Faulkner lived and wrote his first book, *Soldiers' Pay,* here in the 1920s. He later returned to his native Oxford, Mississippi, where his explorations of Southern consciousness earned him the Nobel Prize for literature. The house is not open for tours, but the ground-floor apartment Faulkner inhabited is now a bookstore, **Faulkner House Books**, which specializes in local and Southern writers. The house is also home to the **Pirate's Alley Faulkner Society** literary group, which sponsors the annual Words & Music literary festival. ✉ *624 Pirate's Alley, French Quarter* ☎ *504/524–2940* ⊕ *www.wordsandmusic.org.*

Gallier House. Irish-born James Gallier Jr. was one of the city's most famous 19th-century architects; he died in 1866, when a hurricane sank the paddle-steamer on which he was a passenger. This house, where he lived with his family, was built in 1857 and contains an excellent collection of early Victorian furnishings. During the holiday season, the entire house is filled with Christmas decorations. ✉ *1132 Royal St., French Quarter* ☎ *504/525–5661* ⊕ *www.hgghh.org* 💲 *$15, combination ticket with Hermann-Grima House $25* ⊘ *Closed Wed. and Sun.*

Gauche House. The cherubs featured in the effusive ironwork on this distinctive house stops people in the street. Built in 1856, this mansion and its service buildings were once the estate of businessman John Gauche, who lived there until 1882. Although the privately owned house is not open to the public, its exterior still merits a visit to snap a few photos. ✉ *704 Esplanade Ave., French Quarter.*

Germaine Wells Mardi Gras Museum. During a 31-year period (1937–68), Germaine Cazenave Wells, daughter of Arnaud's restaurant founder Arnaud Cazenave, was queen of Carnival balls a record 22 times for 17 different krewes (organizations). Many of her ball gowns—in addition to costumes worn by other family members, photographs, krewe invitations, and jewelry—are on display in this dim, quirky museum above Arnaud's restaurant. ✉ *Arnaud's restaurant, 813 Bienville St., 2nd fl. (enter through restaurant), French Quarter* ☎ *504/523–5433* ⊕ *www.arnaudsrestaurant.com/mardi-gras-museum* 💲 *Free.*

Jean Lafitte National Park Visitor Center. Visitors who want to explore the areas around New Orleans should stop here first. The office supervises and provides information on the Jean Lafitte National Park Barataria Preserve, a beautiful wetland area across the river from New Orleans, and the Chalmette Battlefield, where the Battle of New Orleans was fought in the War of 1812. Each year in January, near the anniversary of the battle, a reenactment is staged at the Chalmette site. This visitor center has free visual and audio exhibits on the customs of various communities throughout the state, as well as information-rich riverfront tours called "history strolls," offered Tuesday through Saturday. The hour-long tour leaves at 9:30 am; tickets are handed out individually (you must be present to get a ticket) beginning at 9 am, for that day's tour only. Arrive at least 15 minutes before tour time to be sure of a spot. You'll need a car to visit the preserve or the battlefield. ✉ *419 Decatur St., French Quarter* ☎ *504/589–2636* ⊕ *www.nps.gov/jela* ⊘ *Closed Sun. and Mon.*

LaLaurie Mansion. Locals (or at least local tour guides) say this is the most haunted house in a generally haunted neighborhood. Most blame

Continued on page 61

DID YOU KNOW?

Years ago, yelling "Hey, mister! Throw me somethin', mister!" probably would have gotten you beads made of Czechoslovakian glass in traditional purple, green, and yellow. Although beads come in more colors these days, they're generally plastic and made in China.

IT'S MARDI GRAS TIME IN NEW ORLEANS!

by Todd Price

Odds are, most of what you know about Mardi Gras is wrong. The bare breasts of Bourbon Street have nothing to do with the real experience—a party steeped in tradition that New Orleanians throw (and pay for) themselves. They generously invite the rest of the world to join in the fun, so hold on to your fairy wings, your tutus, and your beads; things are about to get crazy!

Mardi Gras (French for "Fat Tuesday") is actually the final day of Carnival, a Christian holiday season that begins on the Twelfth Night of Christmas (January 6) and comes crashing to a halt on Ash Wednesday, the first day of Lent. The elite celebrate with private balls, while the rest of the city takes to the streets for weeks of parades and mischief. Don't be shy—after a few moments of astonished gaping, and maybe some Hurricane cocktails, you too will be bebopping to the marching bands, yelling for throws, and draped in garlands of beads.

On Mardi Gras day, New Orleanians don costumes and masks, drink Bloody Marys for breakfast and roam the streets until dark. It's an official city holiday, with just about everyone but the police and bartenders taking the day off. Two of Carnival's most important parades, Zulu and Rex, roll that day before noon, smaller walking crews meander through the side streets, tribes of Mardi Gras Indians emerge in Tremé, and silent bands of skeletons mysteriously appear. For one day, an entire city becomes a surreal, flamboyant party.

(top) Masked revelers get in the Mardi Gras spirit

DID YOU KNOW?

Mardi Gras attendance often edges toward a million people, and sometimes it feels like they're all on Bourbon Street at once. To enjoy the fray in style, look into packages offered by Bourbon Street hotels or companies representing private balconies.

MARDI GRAS HISTORY

"The Carnival at New Orleans," a wood engraving drawn by John Durkin and published in *Harper's Weekly*, March 1885.

On February 24, 1857, a group of men dressed like demons paraded through the streets of New Orleans in a torch-lighted cavalcade. They called themselves the **Mistick Krewe of Comus,** after the Greek god of revelry. It was the start of modern Mardi Gras.

Based on European traditions, these men formed a secret society and sent 3,000 invitations to a ball held at New Orleans's Gaiety Theater. Many years later, when a 1991 City Council ordinance—later ruled unconstitutional—required all krewes to reveal their members to obtain a parade permit, Comus stopped parading. Its annual ball, however, remains one of the city's most exclusive.

Through the years, other groups of men organized Carnival krewes, each with its own character. In 1872, 40 businessmen founded the School of Design, whose ruler would be dubbed **Rex**. The krewe still parades on Mardi Gras morning and holds its lavish ball Mardi Gras night. Rex and his queen are considered the monarchs of the entire Carnival celebration, and their identities are kept secret until Lundi Gras morning.

For many decades, these "old-line" crews were strictly segregated, so other parts of society started their own clubs. The **Zulu Social Aid and Pleasure Club** was organized in 1909 by working-class black men, and they started parading in 1915. Zulu was one of the first krewes to integrate, and today members spanning the racial and economic spectrums parade down St. Charles Avenue on Mardi Gras day, preceding Rex.

Parade standards changed in 1969, when a group of businessmen founded the **Krewe of Bacchus,** named after the god of wine. The sassy group stunned the city with a stupendous show featuring lavish floats that dwarfed the old-line parades. The king was Danny Kaye, not a homegrown humanitarian, as was custom, but a famous entertainer. And you didn't have to be socially prominent—or white—to join the after-party, which they called a rendezvous, not a ball.

The arrival of Bacchus ushered in an era of new krewes with open memberships, including satiric krewes such as **Tucks** and **Muses**, that put on many of today's most popular parades.

PEOPLE STILL TALK ABOUT...

1972: Major parades rolled one last time through the French Quarter's narrow streets.

2000: The 19th century Krewe of Proteus returned after a seven-year hiatus.

2006: Despite the 2005 devastation of Katrina, New Orleanians insisted on holding a smaller (but no less enthusiastic) Mardi Gras.

2010: Saints quarterback Drew Brees reigned as king of Bacchus, tossing Nerf footballs to the crowds a week after winning the Super Bowl.

EXPERIENCE MARDI GRAS

Don't forget your costume! Mardi Gras spectators are often the wackiest.

Carnival parades begin in earnest two weekends before Mardi Gras day, with krewes rolling day and night on the final weekend. Almost all krewes each year select a different theme, ranging from the whimsical to hard-edged satire. Off-color jokes and political incorrectness are part and parcel of the subversiveness that characterizes Carnival. Throws will sometimes reflect a parade's theme, which is one reason why locals dive for the cups, doubloons, and other plastic trinkets. The floats and high school marching bands make up the bulk of the parades, with the odd walking club, dance troupe, or convertible car tossed into the mix.

Night parades also have the flambeaux, torch-bearing dancers who historically lighted the way for the parades. These days they provide little more than nostalgia and some fancy stepping to the bands, but they still earn tips for their efforts.

There are no day parades Monday, but Lundi Gras, literally "Fat Monday," has become a major event downtown by the riverfront. Rex and the Zulu King each arrive by boat to greet their subjects and each other. Zulu also hosts free concerts throughout the day. On Mardi Gras day, nearly every corner of New Orleans sees something marvelous, including walking clubs that follow unannounced routes and Mardi Gras Indians who wage mock battles to prove who's the prettiest. Mardi Gras and the Carnival season end with the arrival of Ash Wednesday.

FOR EARLY BIRDS

While most revelers arrive in New Orleans the Friday before Mardi Gras, many major parades actually start earlier in the week. They follow the traditional route down St. Charles Avenue to Canal Street. Note: times might change

Wednesday: Krew of Druids, 6:30 pm; Krewe of Nyx, 7 pm

Thursday: Knights of Babylon, 5:45 pm; Knights of Chaos, 6:30 pm; Krew of Muses, 6:30 pm

MARDI GRAS PARADE SCHEDULE: NOTEABLE KREWES

KREWES (EST.)	Rolls	Participants	Claim to fame	Watch for	Prize throws
Hermes (1937)	Friday 6 pm	Local businessmen	Oldest continuous night parade	Large line-up of marching bands	Lighted medallion beads
Le Krewe d'Etat (1996)	Friday 6:30 pm	Sardonic lawyers and well-heeled elites	Led by a dictator instead of a king	The Dictator's "Banana Wagon" pulled by mules	"D'Etat Gazette" with drawings of every float
Morpheus (2000)	Friday 7 pm	Lovers of traditional parades	Youngest parading krewe in New Orleans	Old-school floats and generous throws	Plush moons
Iris (1917)	Saturday 11 am	Upper crust ladies	Oldest all-female krewe	Flirtatious ladies throwing silk flowers	Ceramic beads
Tucks (1969)	Saturday 12 pm	Exuberant and irreverent young men and women	Took name from defunct Friar Tucks bar	Tongue-in-cheek themes	Plastic plungers and stuffed Friar Tucks dolls
Endymion (1966)	Saturday 4:15 pm	Partiers from around the country	Largest Mardi Gras parade; follows a unique route through Mid-City	Massive, spectacular floats and celebrity riders	Plush Endymion mascots
Okeanos (1949)	Sunday 11 am	Civic-minded business leaders	Queen selected by lottery	Trailer carrying a traditional jazz band	Frisbees
Mid-City (1934)	Sunday 11:45 am	Men from Mid-City	First krewe to have "animated" floats	Floats decorated in colored tinfoil	Bags of potato chips
Thoth (1947)	Sunday 12 pm	Guys with a charitable bent	Unique route passes retirement homes and Children's Hospital	Lavishing throws on children	Thoth baseballs
Bacchus (1968)	Sunday 5:15 pm	Devotees of the god of wine	First "superkrewe"	The Bacchagator and King Kong floats	Wine colored "king" doubloons
Proteus (1882)	Monday 5:15 pm	Members of the city's oldest families	Second-oldest krewe	Beautiful floats built on 19th century wagons	Plush seahorses
Orpheus (1993)	Monday 6 pm	Musicians and music lovers of any gender	Founded by singer Harry Connick Jr.	Latest parade technology, including confetti blowers	Stuffed Leviathan with flashing eyes
Zulu (1916)	Tuesday 8 am	Predominantly African American	Oldest African American Mardi Gras parade	Riders in blackface	Hand-painted coconuts
Rex (1872)	Tuesday 10 am	The most elite men in New Orleans society	King of Carnival	Crossing St. Charles to toast Rex mansion	Traditional Rex beads

WHERE TO WATCH THE PARADES

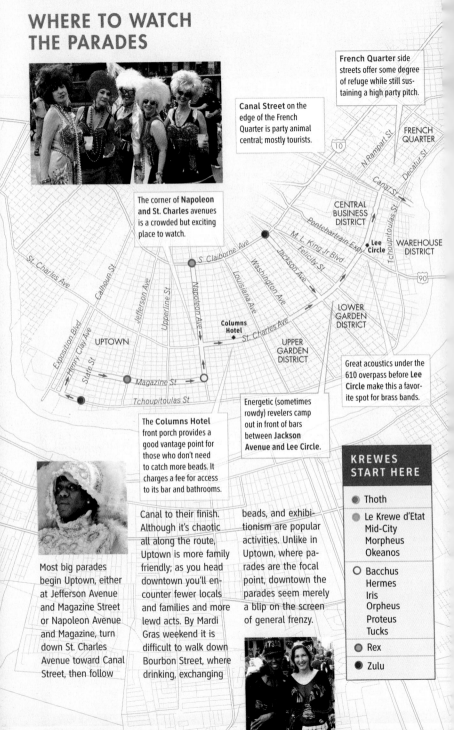

French Quarter side streets offer some degree of refuge while still sustaining a high party pitch.

Canal Street on the edge of the French Quarter is party animal central; mostly tourists.

The corner of **Napoleon** and **St. Charles** avenues is a crowded but exciting place to watch.

Great acoustics under the 610 overpass before **Lee Circle** make this a favorite spot for brass bands.

The **Columns Hotel** front porch provides a good vantage point for those who don't need to catch more beads. It charges a fee for access to its bar and bathrooms.

Energetic (sometimes rowdy) revelers camp out in front of bars between **Jackson Avenue** and **Lee Circle**.

KREWES START HERE

- Thoth
- Le Krewe d'Etat
  Mid-City
  Morpheus
  Okeanos
- Bacchus
  Hermes
  Iris
  Orpheus
  Proteus
  Tucks
- Rex
- Zulu

Most big parades begin Uptown, either at Jefferson Avenue and Magazine Street or Napoleon Avenue and Magazine, turn down St. Charles Avenue toward Canal Street, then follow Canal to their finish. Although it's chaotic all along the route, Uptown is more family friendly; as you head downtown you'll encounter fewer locals and families and more lewd acts. By Mardi Gras weekend it is difficult to walk down Bourbon Street, where drinking, exchanging beads, and exhibitionism are popular activities. Unlike in Uptown, where parades are the focal point, downtown the parades seem merely a blip on the screen of general frenzy.

MARDI GRAS TRADITIONS

Royalty

Indian   Dancer

New Orleans's many Carnival traditions often collide on Mardi Gras. Here are some of the characters you're bound to meet.

Mardi Gras Royalty. Each krewe selects monarchs to preside over its parade and ball. In old-line krewes, members choose the king, who is often a prominent local philanthropist and businessman. Super krewes like Bacchus and Endymion pick celebrity kings or grand marshals. Some krewes elect a queen; others have a more elaborate process. To become the reigning woman of the Twelfth Night Revelers, a debutante must find a golden bean in a faux king cake.

Mardi Gras Indians. The African American Mardi Gras Indians began their rituals in the late 19th century in response to being excluded from white Mardi Gras festivities. On Fat Tuesday morning—dressed in intricately beaded and feathered "suits" that often take all year to create—the tribes chant songs and square off in mock battles to decide whose Big Chief is the prettiest. You'll find the Uptown tribes across St. Charles Avenue from the Garden District between Jackson and Washington avenues. Downtown tribes generally meander through Tremé on Ursulines Street.

Dancers. First it was troupes of suburban middle-school girls—dressed a tad too provocatively for their age—that entertained between parade floats. Later, grown women thought this looked fun and created groups like the Pussyfooters and Camel Toe Lady Steppers. Despite the risqué names, many members are lawyers, professors, and other professionals; all members practice choreographed routines for months. In 2010, the 610 Stompers, the first all-male troupe, took to the streets in tight blue gym shorts and red satin jackets. Their motto was "Ordinary Men, Extraordinary Moves."

MARDI GRAS SAFETY

■ Use common sense; don't bring excess cash, valuables, or tempting jewelry.

■ Establish a meeting spot where your family or group will convene at preset times throughout the day.

■ Do not throw anything at the floats or bands, a ticketable and truly hazardous act.

■ You will probably get away with flashing in the French Quarter, but elsewhere you might get ticketed.

■ Be aware that cell phone photos and videos shot on Bourbon Street can wind up on the Internet; think twice before you flash for beads.

■ Each year accidents occur when children (or adults) venture too near the wheels of floats. If you have kids with you, pick a spot some way back from the parade.

MARDI GRAS YEAR-ROUND

A sculptor working on a float at Blaine Kern's Mardi Gras World.

BACKSTREET CULTURAL MUSEUM
This small museum in Tremé chronicles New Orleans's street culture, including the Mardi Gras Indians. Elaborate costumes are on display.

BLAINE KERN'S MARDI GRAS WORLD
Tour the workshop of one of the most prominent Carnival float builders. Floats from previous parades are on display in the warehouse.

GERMAINE WELLS MARDI GRAS MUSEUM
This free Mardi Gras museum is full of photos, masks, and more than two dozen mid-20th-century ball gowns, most worn by Germaine Wells, daughter of the restaurant's founder and queen of more than twenty-two Mardi Gras balls.

THE PRESBYTERE
Part of the Louisiana State Museum, this historic building on Jackson Square hosts a permanent Mardi Gras exhibit on the second floor.

MARDI GRAS RESOURCES

- **Arthur Hardy's Mardi Gras Guide** (⊕ www.mardigrasguide.com).
- **MardiGras.com** (⊕ www.mardigras.com).

- **New Orleans Convention and Visitors Bureau** (⊕ www.neworleanscvb.com).

MARDI GRAS LINGO

King cake: An oval cake decorated with purple, green, and gold sugar and glaze, eaten from January 6—"Twelfth Night"—until Mardi Gras. A plastic baby is hidden inside, and by tradition whoever gets it must buy the next cake.

Krewe: A term used by Carnival organizations to describe themselves, as in Krewe of Iris.

Lundi Gras: French for "Fat Monday," the day before Mardi Gras.

Mardi Gras: "Fat Tuesday" in French; the day before Ash Wednesday and the culmination of the festivities surrounding Carnival season.

Purple, green, and gold: The traditional colors of Mardi Gras (purple represents justice, green faith, and gold power), chosen by the first Rex in 1872.

Throw: Anything tossed off a float, such as beads, plastic cups, doubloons (fake metal coins), or stuffed animals.

"Throw me somethin', mister": Phrase shouted at float riders to get their attention so they will throw you beads.

the spooks on Madame LaLaurie, a wealthy but ill-fated 19th-century socialite who fell out with society when, during a fire, neighbors who rushed into the house found mutilated slaves in one of the apartments. Madame LaLaurie fled town that night, but there have been stories of hauntings ever since. The home is a private residence, not open to the public. Actor Nicolas Cage bought the property in 2007; two years later, the house sold at a foreclosure auction. ⊠ *1140 Royal St., French Quarter.*

Latrobe House. Architect Benjamin Henry Latrobe, who designed the U.S. Capitol, built this modest house with Arsene Latour in 1814. Its smooth lines and porticoes started a passion for Greek Revival architecture in Louisiana, as later evinced in many plantation houses upriver as well as in a significant number of buildings in New Orleans. Latrobe would die in New Orleans six years later from yellow fever. This house, believed to be the earliest example of Greek Revival in the city, is not open to the public. ⊠ *721 Governor Nicholls St., French Quarter.*

Madame John's Legacy. Now a state museum, this is the only example of West Indies architecture and early Creole-colonial home design in the French Quarter. The large, dark rooms of the main living space occupy the second story, and a porch (called a gallery) runs along the front and back of the house, providing ventilation during the steamy summers and shelter from both sun and rain. The house has a colorful past. Its first owner, Jean Pascal, a French sea captain, was killed by Natchez Indians. The current building was constructed in 1789, following the 1788 fire that destroyed much of the Quarter. The name "Madame John's Legacy," was adopted in the late 1800s after a short story by New Orleans writer George Washington Cable. The popular tale was about Madame John, a "free woman of color" who, like many mulatto women at that time, became the mistress of a Frenchman. Having never married, the Frenchman, John (Jean), bequeathed his house and estate to her on his deathbed. ⊠ *632 Dumaine St., French Quarter* ☎ *504/568–6968* ⊕ *www.louisianastatemuseum.org* ☜ *Free* ☉ *Closed Mon.*

Michalopoulos Galleries. One of New Orleans's most beloved artists, James Michalopoulos exhibits his expressionistic visions of New Orleans architecture in this small gallery. Michalopoulos's palette-knife technique of applying thick waves of paint invariably evokes van Gogh—but his vision of New Orleans, where no line is truly straight and every building appears to have a soul, is uniquely his own. His work has become a prized adornment of many a New Orleanian's walls. Michalopoulos was commissioned to create the official poster of the New Orleans Jazz and Heritage Festival in 1998, 2001, '03, '06, '09,

TALK OF THE TOWN

Although it's just two blocks away from Bourbon Street in the French Quarter, Burgundy Street is not pronounced like the wine (New Orleanians say "bur-GUN-dee" instead). And if you trot out your high-school French to ask for directions to Chartres Street, a bemused local will probably ask if you mean "CHAW-tuhs." Farther uptown, the streets named for the muses offer more challenges: Calliope ("CAL-ee-ope") and Melpomene ("MELL-pa-meen").

and '13, bringing a new perspective to some of New Orleans's greatest musicians: Mahalia Jackson, Louis Armstrong, Dr. John, Fats Domino, and Aaron Neville. ⊠ *617 Bienville St., French Quarter* ☎ *504/558–0505* ⊕ *www.michalopoulos.com.*

New Orleans Historic Voodoo Museum. This homegrown museum may turn skeptics into believers. Voodoo isn't just something marketed to visitors; it lingers on in the lives of many New Orleanians, who still light candles for good luck or rely on a potion to find love. The large collection of artifacts on display here include portraits by and of voodoo legends, African artifacts believed to have influenced the development of the religion, and lots of gris-gris. The gift shop sells customized gris-gris, potions, and handcrafted voodoo dolls. A psychic reader is on duty to divine your future. ⊠ *724 Dumaine St., French Quarter* ☎ *504/680–0128* ⊕ *www.voodoomuseum.com* ⊠ *$7; waived when combined with various haunted and cemetery tours around town.*

FAMILY **New Orleans Jazz National Historical Park.** In 1987 the U.S. Congress declared jazz a "national American treasure," and shortly thereafter the New Orleans Jazz National Historical Park was created to educate people about the art form and to preserve its history. The park hosts free performances and educational events in two locations around the French Quarter: the Visitor Center and the **Old U.S. Mint,** which also houses the state's jazz collection. Some of the park's rangers are also working musicians; don't miss the chance to catch their lively and informative demonstrations exploring the full range of Louisiana's musical heritage. ⊠ *Visitor Center, 916 N. Peters St., French Quarter* ☎ *504/589–4841* ⊕ *www.nps.gov/jazz* ⊠ *Free* ☉ *No performances Sun. or Mon.*

Fodor'sChoice **New Orleans Pharmacy Museum.** To tour this musty shop is to step back
★ into 19th-century medicine—the window display alone, with its enormous leech jar and other antiquated paraphernalia, is fascinating. This building was the apothecary shop and residence of Louis J. Dufilho Jr., America's first licensed pharmacist, in the 1820s. His botanical and herbal gardens are still cultivated in the pretty back courtyard (complete with a postcard-worthy fountain). Watch for free 19th-century seasonal health tips posted in the front window. ⊠ *514 Chartres St., French Quarter* ☎ *504/565–8027* ⊕ *www.pharmacymuseum.org* ⊠ *$5* ☉ *Closed Sun. and Mon.*

Old Ursuline Convent. The Ursulines were the first of many orders of religious women who came to New Orleans and founded schools, orphanages, and asylums, and ministered to the needs of the poor. The original tract of land for a convent, school, and gardens covered several French Quarter blocks. The current structure, which replaced the original convent, was completed in 1752 and is now the oldest French-colonial building in the Mississippi Valley, having survived the disastrous 18th-century fires that destroyed the rest of the Quarter. **St. Mary's Church,** adjoining the convent, was added in 1845. Now an archive for the archdiocese, the convent was used by the Ursulines for 90 years. The Ursuline Academy, a girls' school founded in 1727, is now Uptown on State Street, where a newer convent and chapel were built. The academy is the oldest girls' school in the country. The Old Ursuline Convent is open to the public for self-guided tours Monday through Saturday. ✉ *1110 Chartres St., French Quarter* ☎ *504/525–9585* ⊕ *www.oldursulineconventmuseum.com* 🎫 *$8* ⊘ *Closed Sun.*

Old U.S. Mint. Minting began in 1838 in this ambitious Ionic structure, a project of President Andrew Jackson's. The New Orleans mint was to provide currency for the South and the West, which it did until Louisiana seceded from the

DON'T BET ON IT!

At some point during your visit to the French Quarter, you are bound to come across someone on the street who will offer you the following wager: "I bet you [insert dollar amount] I know where you got them shoes." It's a con, of course, and an old one at that. The answer is: "You got them on your feet in New Orleans, Louisiana."

Union in 1861. Both the short-lived Republic of Louisiana and the Confederacy minted coins here. When Confederate supplies ran out, the building served as a barracks—and then a prison—for Confederate soldiers. The production of U.S. coins recommenced only in 1879; it stopped again, for good, in 1909. After years of neglect, the federal government handed the Old Mint over to Louisiana in 1966. The state now uses the building for exhibitions of the Louisiana State Museum collection, and the New Orleans Jazz National Historical Park has events here. After repairs from damage by Hurricane Katrina, the museum reopened to the public in 2007.

The first-floor exhibit recounts the history of the mint. The principal draw, however, is the second floor, dedicated to items from the **New Orleans Jazz Collection**. At the end of the exhibit, displayed in its own room like the Crown Jewels, you'll find Louis Armstrong's first cornet.

The **Louisiana Historical Center,** which holds the French and Spanish Louisiana archives, is open to researchers by appointment. At the foot of Esplanade Avenue, notice the memorial to the French rebels against early Spanish rule. The rebel leaders were executed on this spot and gave nearby Frenchmen Street its name. ✉ *400 Esplanade Ave., French Quarter* ☎ *504/568–6993* ⊕ *louisianastatemuseum.org* 🎫 *Free.*

Orleans Ballroom. In the early 1800s, the wooden-rail balcony extending over Orleans Street was linked to a ballroom where free women of color met their French suitors—as Madame John of "Madame John's Legacy" is said to have done. The quadroons (technically, people whose racial makeup was one-quarter African) who met here were young, unmarried women of legendary beauty. A gentleman would select a favorite and, with her mother's approval, buy her a house and support her as his mistress. The sons of these unions, which were generally maintained in addition to legal marriages with French women, were often sent to France to be educated. This practice, known as *plaçage*, was unique to New Orleans at the time. The ballroom later became part of a convent and school for the Sisters of the Holy Family, a religious order founded in New Orleans in 1842 by the daughter of a quadroon to educate and care for African American women. The ballroom itself is not open to visitors, but a view of the balcony from across the street is enough to set the historical stage. ✉ *Bourbon Orleans Hotel, 717 Orleans St., 2nd fl., French Quarter.*

Rodrigue Studio. Cajun artist George Rodrigue began his career as a painter with moody yet stirring portraits of rural Cajun life, but he gained popular renown in 1984 when he started painting blue dogs, inspired by the spirit of his deceased pet, Tiffany. Since then, the blue dog can be found in thousands of manifestations in various settings in the cult artist's paintings. Though Rodrigue died in late 2013, his

principal gallery, a space rather eerily lined almost entirely with paintings of the blue dog, remains open. ✉ *730 Royal St., French Quarter* ☎ *504/581–4244* ⊕ *www.georgerodrigue.com.*

The Shops at Canal Place. At the foot of Canal Street, this mall offers high-end shopping and the **Theatres at Canal Place,** an upscale moviegoing experience with reserved seating and waiters to deliver snacks, drinks, or even a full meal in the middle of a screening. The **Westin New Orleans at Canal Place** tops the complex; its dining rooms and lobby have fantastic river views. ✉ *333 Canal St., French Quarter* ☎ *504/522–9200* ⊕ *www.theshopsatcanalplace.com.*

Washington Artillery Park. This raised concrete area on the river side of Decatur Street, directly across from Jackson Square, is a great spot to photograph the square or the barges and paddle wheelers on the Mississippi. The cannon mounted in the center and pointing toward the river is a model 1861 Parrot Rifle used in the Civil War. This monument honors the local 141st Field Artillery of the Louisiana National Guard that saw action from the Civil War through World War II. Marble tablets at the base give the history of the group, represented today by the Washington Artillery Association. ✉ *Decatur St., between St. Peter and St. Ann Sts., French Quarter* ⊕ *www.washingtonartillery.com.*

FAUBOURG MARIGNY, BYWATER, AND TREMÉ

Getting Oriented

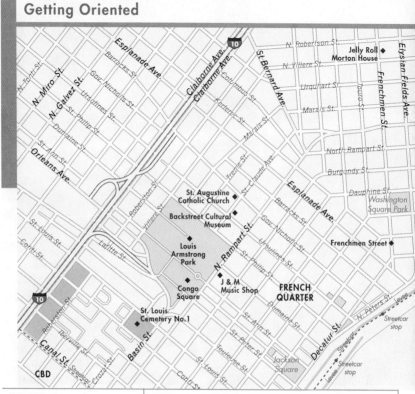

SAFETY

Use common sense when exploring these neighborhoods, especially at night. The Marigny is the easiest of the three to explore during daylight hours, and Frenchmen Street is a safe, crowded, nightlife hot spot. St. Claude Avenue and the areas of the Bywater where you'll spend most of your time are relatively safe, but adjacent neighborhoods are rough; it's advisable to travel by car, especially if you're going into the Lower Ninth Ward.

GETTING HERE AND AROUND

The Marigny and Tremé border the French Quarter to the east and north, and are within easy walking distance. The **bus** and **streetcar** will also land you in or around these neighborhoods. Biking is a great way to get around the French Quarter and the Marigny (⇨ *See Travel Smart for bike rental companies*).

Bywater is a little farther out, past the Marigny to the east. The **No. 5 Marigny/Bywater bus** runs along the south edge (river side) of the French Quarter, out to the far edge of Bywater. The **No. 88 St. Claude/Jackson Barracks bus** runs along the north edge (lake side) of the French Quarter all the way into the Lower Ninth Ward. The ride from the French Quarter takes about 15 minutes. A new Rampart–St. Claude Streetcar line runs from the French Quarter (at Canal Street) down St. Claude Avenue into the Bywater.

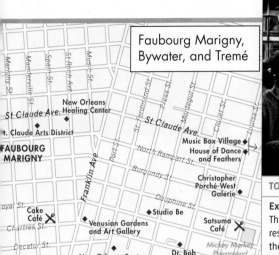

Faubourg Marigny, Bywater, and Tremé

TOP REASONS TO GO

Explore Frenchmen Street. This bustling strip of bars, clubs, restaurants, cafés, and shops is the heart of the Marigny. At night this is *the* place to hear live music and watch eccentric street artists.

Experience the birthplace of jazz. Tremé is a crucible of New Orleans musical tradition. Visit the site of Congo Square, where jazz was born (now in Louis Armstrong Park), or drop by the Backstreet Cultural Museum.

Discover the Bywater arts scene. This rapidly gentrifying neighborhood is an enclave of artists, musicians, and creative outliers, and you'll see it in everything from the decorated cars and funky boutiques to the intricate street art on warehouses and buildings.

Enjoy the Marigny architecture. In 1974 the entire Marigny neighborhood was added to the National Register of Historic Places; 35 years later it was awarded the distinguished "Great Places in America" designation by the American Planning Association.

MAKING THE MOST OF YOUR TIME

The Marigny and Tremé are within reach of the Quarter. At night, Frenchmen Street is *the* place for live music. In Bywater, spend some time exploring galleries, parks, cafés, and vintage stores. Off-the-beaten-path bars, restaurants, and music clubs light up at night.

QUICK BITES

Cake Café. A beloved local favorite, this corner bakery and café serves breakfast, lunch, pastries, and baked goods indoors and on the sidewalk patio daily until 3 pm. ⊠ *2440 Chartres St., Faubourg Marigny* ☎ *504/943–0010* ⊕ *www. nolacakes.com* ⊟ *No credit cards.*

Satsuma Café. Drop into this lively bohemian hangout for a healthy breakfast, a midday repast, or a restorative glass of juiced fruits and vegetables. ⊠ *3218 Dauphine St., Bywater* ☎ *504/304–5962* ⊕ *www.satsumacafe.com.*

Sightseeing
★★
Dining
★★
Lodging
★
Shopping
★★
Nightlife
★★★★

From Tremé's musical history to the alternative-arts scene in Bywater to their bohemian convergence in the Marigny, these three neighborhoods only look like sleepy rows of houses. In fact, they're engines at the core of New Orleans's most innovative and creative activity, where newly arrived artists and entrepreneurs add to the area's historic legacy.

FAUBOURG MARIGNY

Updated by
Cameron
Quincy Todd

The Faubourg Marigny (pronounced "FOE-berg MAR-ah-nee," though mainly referred to as simply "the Marigny") is made up of two distinct sections. The Marigny Triangle is the trendy area, with the Frenchmen Street commercial district on the border of the French Quarter. Its mazelike streets are lined with beautiful cottages, Creole plantation homes, and charming guesthouses. You'll have no problem finding great restaurants, bars, music clubs, and hip shops. The Marigny Rectangle begins on the other side of Elysian Fields Avenue.

The Marigny is one of the earliest neighborhoods in the city. It was formed in 1805 when the young Bernard Xavier Philippe de Marigny de Mandeville embarked on what is now practically an American pastime: creating subdivisions. With architectural styles ranging from classic Creole cottages to Victorian mansions, the streets are mainly peaceful and the residents often bohemian—similar to the French Quarter 30 years ago.

TOP ATTRACTIONS

Fodor's Choice
★

Frenchmen Street. The three-block stretch closest to the French Quarter is where it's at—complete with cafés, bars, and music clubs. The true magic happens come nightfall, when live music spills from the doorways of clubs and crowds gather for street performers, but it's still a great daytime destination, too. ⊠ *Frenchmen St. between Decatur and Dauphine Sts., Faubourg Marigny.*

An artist works on a Mardi Gras mural that feels right at home in the colorful Marigny neighborhood.

New Orleans Healing Center. This is a great place to get in touch with the spiritual side of New Orleans. It's the product of an innovative collaboration of more than a dozen of New Orleans's most progressive (and intriguing) organizations. Visitors can check out everything from the Wild Lotus Yoga Studio to the New Orleans Food Co-Op, from the Café Istanbul Performance Hall to the Island of Salvation Botanica, the famous voodoo shop run by the internationally renowned priestess Sallie Ann Glassman. Spotted Cat Food and Spirits, a family-friendly version of the beloved Frenchmen Street music club, serves breakfast all day here. ⊠ *2372 St. Claude Ave., Faubourg Marigny* ☎ *504/940–1130* ⊕ *www.neworleanshealingcenter.org.*

WORTH NOTING

House of Dance and Feathers. One of the most fascinating and heart-warming locations in the Lower Ninth Ward has to be the House of Dance and Feathers, a tiny backyard museum, which is a labor of love for community character Ronald Lewis, a retired streetcar conductor. Formed almost by accident—after his wife threw his extensive collection of Mardi Gras Indian and second-line paraphernalia out of the house and into the yard—this small glass-paneled building contains a trove of Mardi Gras Indian lore and local legend. Intricately beaded panels from Indian costumes, huge fans and plumes of feathers dangling from the rafters, and photographs cover almost every available inch of wall space. Lewis, who among many other things can list "president of the Big Nine Social and Pleasure Club" and "former Council Chief of the Choctaw Hunters" on his résumé, is a qualified and dedicated historian whose vision and work have become a rallying point for a hardscrabble neighborhood. ⊠ *1317 Tupelo St., Faubourg Marigny* ☎ *504/957–2678* ⊕ *www.houseofdanceandfeathers.org* ⊠ *Free.*

OFF THE
BEATEN
PATH

Jelly Roll Morton House. Jazz enthusiasts would do well to follow Frenchmen Street beyond the borders of the Marigny to pay homage to Jelly Roll Morton at the pianist and composer's modest former home, now a private residence with nary a plaque to suggest its import. The current residents, however, have put a photo of the musician in the window. Morton was a "Creole of color" (free African American of mixed race), a clear distinction from darker blacks in those days—Morton himself always described his roots as "French." The neighborhood has declined some since Morton's days, so plan to take a car or taxi at night. ⊠ *1443 Frenchmen St., Seventh Ward.*

New Orleans Center for Creative Arts (NOCCA). Many of New Orleans's most talented musicians, artists, actors, and writers have passed through this high school arts program on their way to fame, including Harry Connick Jr., Trombone Shorty, the Marsalis brothers, Donald Harrison, Terence Blanchard, Anthony Mackie, and Wendell Pierce. More than just a beautiful campus built along the Marigny's industrial riverfront area, NOCCA hosts a year-round schedule of celebrated performances, exhibitions, and other public events. ⊠ *2800 Chartres St., Faubourg Marigny* ☎ *504/940–2787* ⊕ *www.nocca.com.*

Venusian Gardens and Art Gallery. This 19th-century building, a former church, now serves as Eric Ehlenberger's otherworldly art studio, gallery, and event space, displaying his luminous sculptures and dioramas. Take a stroll beneath a sea of glowing jellyfish or bask in a neon-lit landscape. ⊠ *2601 Chartres St., Faubourg Marigny* ☎ *504/943–7446* ⊕ *www.venusiangardens.com.*

BYWATER

Bywater, a once crumbling but beautiful old neighborhood east of the train tracks at Press Street, has become a magnet for wealthy newcomers seeking to make "authentic" New Orleans their home. The Mississippi River runs the length of its boundary, and the bars and coffee shops scattered around the neighborhood's gritty and shiny parts alike combine elements of its working-class roots with the more recent hipster influx to make for a lively and distinctly local experience. It doesn't have the head-turning array of sights you'll find in the French Quarter, but a visit to Bywater gives you a feel for New Orleans as it lives day to day, in a colorful, overgrown, slightly sleepy cityscape reminiscent of island communities and tinged with a sense of perpetual decay.

TOP ATTRACTIONS

St. Claude Arts District. The Bywater neighborhood is home to dozens of alternative art spaces, many of which have banded together under the loose umbrella of the St. Claude Arts District (SCAD). From old candle factories to people's living rooms, this burgeoning scene—centered around St. Claude Avenue and nearby streets—produces some

CLOSE UP

The Lower Ninth Ward

The Lower Ninth Ward has long been a cultural touchstone for New Orleans, generating some of the most venerable artists and colorful traditions in the city. In the wake of post-Katrina flooding, the neighborhood became a touchstone for the whole nation—indeed, the world—a symbol of tragedy. No neighborhood endured as much destruction or suffering as this low-lying residential stretch, victim to the failed levees.

Nowadays the neighborhood is a changed place. Signs of the deluge persist—empty lots where houses were literally swept off their foundations, boarded-up buildings with overgrown weeds and an eerie quiet—but signs of life and renewed vigor show, too. A slow but steady reconstruction effort by hard-hit locals joined by aid organizations and volunteers is reclaiming the landscape one lot at a time. Traditional New Orleans shotgun-style homes are now joined by sleek, raised, modern houses, compliments of Brad Pitt's Make It Right foundation. In addition, groups like Habitat for Humanity and Global Green have embarked on innovative and environmentally sustainable rebuilding projects in and around this neighborhood, such as the New Orleans Musicians Village and the Holy Cross Project.

Visit the **Lower Ninth Ward Living Museum** (✉ *1235 Deslonde St.* ⊕ *www.l9livingmuseum.org*) to get a better sense of the Lower Ninth Ward's extensive history, with particular focus on the before and after of Hurricane Katrina. This small, community-run museum celebrates the neighborhood's past, present, and future through oral histories and various exhibits, and is free to the public.

of the most intriguing and innovative work in the city, with several major artists and arts organizations. In addition to galleries, several independent theater spaces have sprung up as well, offering venues for live performances, magic and burlesque shows, fringe theater, and more. The second Saturday of each month is opening night, when galleries and venues host new shows and parties. ✉ *Bywater.*

WORTH NOTING

Christopher Porché-West Galerie. Legendary independent photographer Christopher Porché-West operates out of this working studio and exhibit space. The atmosphere depends on the current focus and vigor of Porché-West's activities: sometimes it is more work-oriented, sometimes more formally organized around exhibits of his work or that of other artists. The gallery occupies an old pharmacy storefront at the hub of a hip block boasting restaurants, boutiques, and a yoga studio. Whenever the artist happens to be in, the gallery is open. You can also make an appointment by calling (he's almost always nearby). ✉ *3201 Burgundy St., Bywater* ☎ *504/947–3880* ⊕ *www.porche-west.com.*

Crescent Park. The newest park in New Orleans stretches along the Mississippi riverfront and provides for spectacular views of the New

A unique Creole cottage in Tremé, across the street from the Backstreet Cultural Museum

Orleans skyline, Algiers, and the mighty Mississippi herself. The best place to enter the park is at Mazant Street in the Bywater, where you can explore the park's promenades, green spaces, and repurposed wharfs, and walk the 1.4-mile path along the water. Plans are in the works to extend the park through the Marigny and beyond. ✉ *Mazant St. at Chartres St., Bywater* ⊕ *www.nola.gov/city/crescent-park.*

Dr. Bob. A small compound of artists' and furniture-makers' studios includes the headquarters of this beloved local folk artist, whose easily recognizable work can be found hanging across New Orleans. "Be Nice or Leave," "Be Gay and Stay," "Shalom, Ya'll," and "Shut Up and Fish" are just a few of his popular themes. Dr. Bob's shop is chock-full of original furniture, colorful signs, and unidentifiable objects of artistic fancy. Prices start as low as $30 for a small "Be Nice," and most pieces are in the $200–$500 range. The sign outside advertises the open hours as "9 am–'til"—best to call ahead. ✉ *3027 Chartres St., Bywater* ☎ *504/945–2225* ⊕ *www.drbobart.net.*

Music Box Village. A whimsical creation of repurposed urban wasteland, this artist-built sculpture garden features an interactive landscape of music-making structures and houses. The space hosts musical acts, performances, and workshops, and is open for public visits on weekends. ✉ *4557 N. Rampart St., Bywater* ⊕ *www.musicboxvillage.com* ✉ *Suggested $12 donation.*

Studio Be. Artist Brandan "BMike" Odums' larger-than-life graffitti murals and installations fill this 35,000-square-foot warehouse in an industrial nook of the Bywater, easy to spot from its bright front exterior and giant mural of a young African American girl shrugging her arms up towards the sky. Work here excites and awakens viewers, with its themes on social justice, African American history, racial violence, and other contemporary issues in New Orleans and beyond. Check Brandan's website for more projects around town. ⊠ *2941 Royal St., Bywater* ☎ *504/330–6231* ⊕ *www.brandanodums.com* ☜ *$10* ☾ *Closed Sun.–Tues.*

TREMÉ

Just across Rampart Street from the French Quarter, is Tremé (pronounced "truh-MAY"), one of the oldest neighborhoods in the city, perhaps in the country. The rows of cottages, churches, and corner stores belie the raucous historical and musical legacy of this area, originally built and populated largely by free people of color. This is the birthplace of jazz after all, not to mention the site of the old Congo Square gathering place for African and Caribbean slaves, and the location of the fabled Storyville red-light district. Through its many incarnations it has remained true to its heritage as one of the oldest African American neighborhoods in the nation. Tremé continues to be one of the great driving forces behind the musical culture of New Orleans.

TOP ATTRACTIONS

Backstreet Cultural Museum. Local photographer and self-made historian Sylvester Francis is an enthusiastic guide through this rich collection of Mardi Gras Indian costumes and other musical artifacts tied to the street traditions of New Orleans, and the museum hosts traveling and featured exhibits in addition to its permanent collection. Sylvester is also an excellent source for current musical goings-on in Tremé and throughout town. ⊠ *1116 Henriette Delille St., Tremé* ☎ *504/522–4806* ⊕ *www.backstreetmuseum.org* ☜ *$10.*

St. Louis Cemetery No. 1. The oldest and most famous of New Orleans's cities of the dead, founded in the late 1700s, is just one block from the French Quarter. Stately rows of crypts are home to many of the city's most legendary figures, including Homer Plessy of the *Plessy v. Ferguson* 1896 U.S. Supreme Court decision establishing the "Jim Crow" laws ("separate but equal"), and voodoo queen Marie Laveau, whose grave is still a popular pilgrimage among the spiritual, the superstitious, and the curious. Visitors are required to be part of a tour group in order to enter the cemetery, so join one of the many groups that come through each day. The nonprofit group **Save Our Cemeteries** (☎ *504/525–3377*) gives guided tours daily leaving from the Basin Street Station Visitors Center at 501 Basin Street. ⊠ *499 Basin St., bounded by Basin, Conti, Tremé, and St. Louis Sts., Tremé* ☜ *Save Our Cemeteries tours $20.*

Louis Armstrong Park is home to iconic Congo Square.

WORTH NOTING

J&M Music Shop. Although the patrons of the laundromat that now occupies this space probably don't pay the historical provenance much heed, this is one of the most significant musical landmarks in New Orleans. A plaque on this 1835 building marks it as the former site of the recording studio that launched the rock 'n' roll careers of such greats as Fats Domino, Jerry Lee Lewis, Little Richard, and Ray Charles. Owned by Cosimo Matassa, the studio operated from 1945 to 1955. ✉ *840 N. Rampart St., Tremé.*

Louis Armstrong Park. There's a certain sad irony to this park. On the one hand, it's a joy to behold, with its huge, lighted gateway and its paths meandering through 32 acres of grassy knolls, lagoons, and historic landmarks. Elizabeth Catlett's famous statue of Louis Armstrong is joined by other artistic landmarks, such as the bust of Sidney Bechet, and the park now houses the New Orleans Jazz National Historical Park. On the other hand, it's often nearly deserted, and bordered by some rough stretches of neighborhood—not a place to visit after dark.

Inside the park and to the left is **Congo Square**, marked by an inlaid-stone space, where slaves in the 18th and early 19th centuries gathered on Sunday, the only time they were permitted to play their music openly. The weekly meetings held here have been immortalized in the travelogues of visitors, leaving invaluable insight into the earliest stages of free musical practices by Africans in America and African Americans. Neighborhood musicians still congregate here at times for percussion jams, and it is difficult not to think of the musical spirit of ancestors hovering over them. Marie Laveau, the greatly feared

CLOSE UP

HBO's Treme

The Tremé neighborhood has always held a special place in the hearts of musicians and musical historians for its role in the development of jazz and other African American musical traditions, but it wasn't until more recently that the neighborhood captured the imagination of a much wider audience, thanks to the HBO series *Treme*. In the wake of Hurricane Katrina, the award-winning team of David Simon and Eric Overmyer (*The Wire*) decided to turn their lens on the Crescent City. They found the ornate and deeply rooted traditions of working-class Tremé to be the perfect focal point for the larger story of recovery and perseverance in New Orleans. *Treme,* the fourth and final season of which was completed in 2013, is widely regarded as one of the best and most accurate representations of New Orleans ever captured on film—no small feat for anyone trying to render the intricacies of the social, cultural, musical, and political dynamics of this city.

"The aesthetic has an anthropological quality," says Henry Griffin, a New Orleans writer, filmmaker, and professor, who plays a character in the series based loosely on himself. "They're trying to re-create an exact period of history: the years right after the storm."

To that end, the producers employed a small army of local writers, factcheckers, and historians to help ensure that the script and scene work were as accurate and realistic as possible. The casting team used locals whenever possible, and the location scouts and set producers went to remarkable lengths to ensure the authenticity of sets, props, and costumes. "What really sets it apart," Griffin says, "is that other shows or films about New Orleans are always made for a bigger audience first, and then later the directors might consider what locals think of it. *Treme,* on the other hand, is made for New Orleans first, and then developed for the wider audience."

The show cast a spotlight on many of New Orleans's underground spots. Suddenly, crowds of music lovers showed up to catch Kermit Ruffins performing at Bullets Sports Bar (✉ *2441 AP Tureaud* ☎ *504/948–4003*), a bar that has long been a staple of Tremé nightlife. Local institutions like Bywater nightclub Vaughan's (✉ *4229 Dauphine St.* ☎ *504/947–5562*), the Mid-City café Angelo Brocato's (✉ *214 N. Carrollton Ave.* ☎ *504/486–1465*), and the French Quarter restaurant Bayona (✉ *430 Dauphine St.* ☎ *504/525–4455*) were also featured.

Treme proved to be a galvanizing creative force in the city of New Orleans, bringing people together to celebrate their own world and traditions. More than that, it's a recognition, a rendering, and a celebration of the perseverance and unique temperament of this city and its denizens in the face of an unprecedented national tragedy—and that has a healing quality all its own.

3

and respected voodoo queen of antebellum New Orleans, had her home a block away on St. Ann Street and is reported to have held rituals here regularly.

Behind Congo Square is a large gray building, the **Morris F.X. Jeff Municipal Auditorium;** to the right, behind the auditorium, is the beautifully renovated **Mahalia Jackson Center for the Performing Arts,** which is home to the New Orleans Opera and the New Orleans Ballet and hosts an excellent year-round calendar of events—everything from readings to rock concerts. The St. Philip Street side of the park houses the **Jazz National Historical Park,** anchored by **Perseverance Hall,** the oldest Masonic temple in the state. Louis Armstrong Park is patrolled by a security detail, but be very careful when wandering, and do not visit after dark. ⊠ *N. Rampart St. between St. Philip and St. Peter Sts., Tremé.*

JAZZ FUNERALS AND SECOND LINES

If you're lucky, you'll get swept up in a jazz street parade while you're in New Orleans. The parades themselves are often referred to as "second lines," a term that originated in the city's jazz funerals. Traditionally, a brass band accompanies a New Orleans funeral procession to the grave site, playing dirges along the way. On the return from the grave, however, the music becomes upbeat, celebrating the departed's passage to heaven. Behind the family, friends, and recognized mourners, a second group often gathers, taking part in the free entertainment and dancing—hence, the "second line."

St. Augustine Catholic Church. Ursuline nuns donated the land for this church in 1841. Upon its completion in 1842, St. Augustine's became an integrated place of worship; slaves were relegated to the side pews, but free blacks claimed just as much right to enter pews as whites did. The architect, J.N.B. de Pouilly, attended the École des Beaux-Arts in Paris and was known for his idiosyncratic style, which borrowed freely from a variety of traditions and resisted classification. Some of the ornamentation in his original drawings was eliminated when money ran out, but effusive pink-and-gold paint inside brightens the austere structure. The church grounds now also house the Tomb of the Unknown Slave, a monument dedicated in 2004 to the slaves buried in unmarked graves in the church grounds and surrounding areas. Following Hurricane Katrina, the Archdiocese of New Orleans planned to close seven churches in the city, including St. Augustine. Public outcry, the church's historical significance, and parishioners' dedication saved the parish, and its 10 am Sunday gospel-jazz services continue. Tours are available by appointment. ⊠ *1210 Governor Nicholls St., Tremé* ☎ *504/525–5934* ⊕ *www.staugustinecatholicchurch-neworleans.org.*

CBD AND
WAREHOUSE
DISTRICT

Getting Oriented

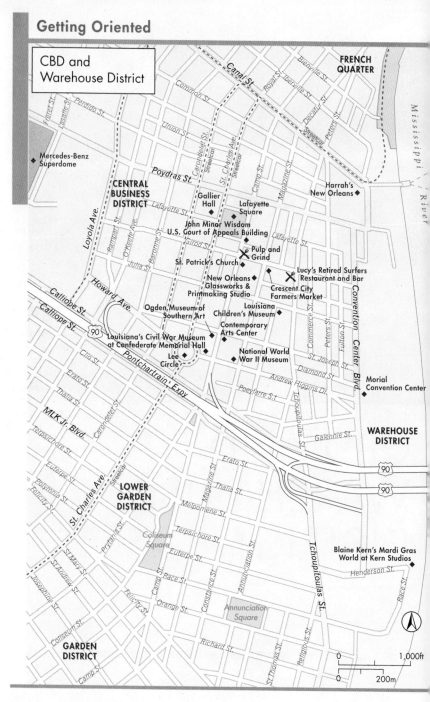

CBD and
Warehouse District

FRENCH
QUARTER

Canal St.

Bienville St.
Royal St.
Iberville St.
St.
Decatur
St.
Peters St.

Common St.

Union St.

Carondelet St.
St. Charles Ave.
Streetcar
Camp St.
Magazine St.

Fulton St.
Perdido St.
Lasalle St.
Freret St.

Streetcar

Mississippi River

Mercedes-Benz
Superdome

Poydras St.

CENTRAL
BUSINESS
DISTRICT

Loyola Ave.

Rampart St.
O'Keefe Ave.
Baronne St.

Lafayette St.
Girod St.
Julia St.

Gallier
Hall
Lafayette
Square

Harrah's
New Orleans

John Minor Wisdom
U.S. Court of Appeals Building

Lafayette St.

Pulp and
Grind

St. Patrick's Church

New Orleans
Glassworks &
Printmaking Studio

Lucy's Retired Surfers
Restaurant and Bar

Crescent City
Farmers Market

Convention Center Blvd.

Howard Ave.

Calliope St.

Calliope St.

90

Ogden Museum of
Southern Art

Louisiana
Children's Museum

Contemporary
Arts Center

Commerce St.
Peters St.
Fulton St.

Louisiana's Civil War Museum
at Confederate Memorial Hall

Lee
Circle

National World
War II Museum

St. Joseph St.
Diamond St.

Morial
Convention Center

Clio St.

Pontchartrain Expy.

Andrew Higgins Dr.

Poeyfarre St.

Tchoupitoulas St.

Erato St.

Thalia St.

MLK Jr. Blvd.

Terpsichore St.

Euterpe St.

Polymnia St.

Felicity St.

Carondelet St.
St. Charles Ave.
Streetcar

LOWER
GARDEN
DISTRICT

Erato St.

Magazine St.

Thalia St.

WAREHOUSE
DISTRICT

Gaienhie St.

90

90

Melpomene St.

St. Andrew St.
St. Mary St.
Josephine St.

Prytania St.

Coliseum
Square

Terpsichore St.

Euterpe St.

Camp St.
Race St.
Constance St.
Annunciation St.

Blaine Kern's Mardi Gras
World at Kern Studios

Henderson St.

Race St.

Coliseum St.

GARDEN
DISTRICT

St. Charles Ave.
Streetcar

Felicity St.

Orange St.

Annunciation
Square

Camp St.

Richard St.

St. Thomas St.
Religious St.
Tchoupitoulas St.

0   1,000ft

0   200m

GETTING HERE AND AROUND

The CBD and Warehouse District together make up a fairly small area and can be readily explored on foot; the close proximity of the Warehouse District's museums and galleries makes sightseeing especially easy. The CBD is adjacent to the French Quarter, just across Canal Street. To travel to or from Uptown or the Garden District, you can take a cab, drive, or take the **St. Charles Avenue streetcar**—any stop from Canal Street to Lee Circle will do. (If you have an extra 20 minutes, walking is also feasible.)

MAKING THE MOST OF YOUR TIME

Arts- and culture-loving travelers can easily spend a few days visiting the **museums**, auction houses, **and galleries** here. The area also is a great **nightlife destination**, with some of the city's most acclaimed restaurants, music clubs, and Harrah's New Orleans.

QUICK BITES

Lucy's Retired Surfers Restaurant and Bar. This bar, courtyard, and dining room are a nice spot for a margarita, fresh seafood, or a Southwestern-style snack. The menu pays homage to surfing pioneers with bios and specialty dishes. ✉ *701 Tchoupitoulas St., Warehouse District* ☎ *504/523–8995* ⊕ *www.lucysretiredsurfers.com* ⊟ *No credit cards.*

Pulp and Grind. This chic little café provides quality coffee and espresso drinks, fresh juices, and pastries. ✉ *644 Camp St., Warehouse District* ☎ *504/510–4037* ⊕ *www.pulpandgrind.com.*

TOP REASONS TO GO

Gallery crawl through the Warehouse District. Browse the many art galleries that line Julia Street and its surroundings.

Feast on cutting-edge dining. Sample some of the finest in Louisiana contemporary cuisine from chefs who are quickly becoming household names.

Get cultured. Revisit a defining chapter of our nation's history at the National World War II Museum, or discover a new favorite artist in the airy, urban oasis of the Ogden Museum of Southern Art.

Experience Carnival season year-round. At Blaine Kern's Mardi Gras World at Kern Studios, see floats from years past, watch video footage, observe artists working on next year's creations, and stock up on souvenirs.

SAFETY

Parts of the CBD are more deserted at night than other highly trafficked tourist areas. Staying close to the river while downtown and near the pulse of Warehouse District nightlife is the safest bet after the sun sets. By day, these areas are bustling with workers, shoppers, and tourists.

Sightseeing
★★★★
Dining
★★★★
Lodging
★★★★
Shopping
★★
Nightlife
★★

With a particularly welcoming atmosphere for art, design, and entertainment, the CBD (Central Business District) and Warehouse District (also known as the Arts District) are a vibrant, vital sector of downtown New Orleans that's become increasingly residential, with high-end apartments, condos, and shops taking root in once dilapidated historic buildings.

Updated by
Cameron
Quincy Todd

The CBD covers the ground between Canal and Poydras streets, with some spillover into the Warehouse District's official territory. By day the CBD hums with commerce and productivity. You'll find the National World War II Museum, the Ogden Museum of Southern Art, the Contemporary Arts Center, the Louisiana Children's Museum, and Louisiana's Civil War Museum at Confederate Memorial Hall—all within a three-square-block radius. The neighborhood also includes the Mercedes-Benz Superdome, the convention center, and Harrah's Casino. Around central Lafayette Square you'll also find historic architecture, government buildings, and office complexes. Canal Street is the CBD's main artery and the official dividing line between the business district and the French Quarter; street names change from American to French as they cross Canal into the Quarter. Served by the streetcar, the palm tree–lined Canal Street has regained some of its former elegance, particularly as it nears the river.

CENTRAL BUSINESS DISTRICT

TOP ATTRACTIONS

Harrah's New Orleans. Some 115,000 square feet of gaming space is divided into five areas, each with a New Orleans theme: Jazz Court, Court of Good Fortune, Smugglers Court, Mardi Gras Court, and Court of the Mansion. There are also table games, a covered gaming courtyard for smokers, 2,100-plus slots, and live entertainment at Masquerade,

A ride on the streetcar is a great way to tour New Orleans in period style.

which includes a lounge, video tower, and dancing show. Check the website for seasonal productions, including music, theater, and comedy. Restaurants here include the extensive Harrah's buffet, the Cafés on Canal food court, Gordon Biersch, Grand Isle, Manning's, and Ruth's Chris Steak House. The last four are part of Harrah's Fulton Street Mall, a pedestrian promenade that attracts casual strollers, clubgoers, and diners. ✉ *8 Canal St., Central Business District* ☎ *504/533–6000, 800/427–7247* ⊕ *www.harrahs.com.*

Mercedes-Benz Superdome. Home to the NFL's New Orleans Saints, the Mercedes-Benz Superdome has been the site of many Sugar Bowls, several NCAA Final Four basketball tournaments, the BCS championship game, a record seven Super Bowls (including 2013), and the 1988 Republican National Convention, as well as many concerts.

The Superdome was badly damaged during Hurricane Katrina and its aftermath, when it served as a shelter of last resort for evacuees. The stadium underwent extensive renovations in the years that followed and reopened for football in September 2006, when the Saints beat the Atlanta Falcons, at the time setting a record for the largest TV audience in ESPN history.

Built in 1975, the Superdome seats 71,000 people, and has a 166,000-square-foot main arena and a roof that covers almost 10 acres at a height of 27 stories. Since the Saints' Super Bowl victory in 2010, the Superdome has been covered in gold-hue anodized aluminum siding. It was also given a brand-new outdoor festival space, Champions Square, which is a favorite spot for game-day tailgating and the occasional festival. Exterior LED lighting added in 2011 gives the stadium an eye-catching, ever-changing facade.

The Mercedes-Benz Superdome is home to the NFL's New Orleans Saints.

The bronze statue on the Poydras Street side of the Superdome is the Vietnam Veterans Memorial. Across from it is a large abstract sculpture called *Krewe of Poydras*. The sculptor, Ida Kohlmeyer, meant to evoke the frivolity and zany spirit of Mardi Gras. A couple of blocks down Poydras Street from the Superdome is the Bloch Cancer Survivors Monument, a block-long walkway of whimsical columns, figures, and a triumphal arch in the median of Loyola Avenue. The Smoothie King Center (formerly called the New Orleans Arena) behind the Superdome is home to the NBA's New Orleans Pelicans.

■ TIP→ The Superdome does not offer public tours, but visitors can walk along the exterior plaza and Champions Square to get a better view. The plaza by Champions Square offers the best photo opportunity. ⊠ *1 Sugar Bowl Dr., Central Business District* ☎ *504/587–3663* ⊕ *www.superdome.com.*

WORTH NOTING

Gallier Hall. This Greek Revival building, modeled on the Erechtheion of Athens, was built in 1845 by the architect James Gallier Sr. It served as City Hall in the mid-20th century and today hosts special events. It's the mayor's official perch during Carnival parades, where kings and queens of many krewes stop to be toasted by city officials and dignitaries. The grand rooms inside the hall are adorned with portraits and decorative details ordered by Gallier from Paris. ⊠ *545 St. Charles Ave., Central Business District* ☎ *504/658–4000* ⊕ *www.nola.gov/gallier-hall.*

John Minor Wisdom United States Court of Appeals Building. New York architect James Gamble Rogers designed this three-story granite structure as a post office and court building in 1909. It opened in 1915, but by the 1960s, the post office had moved to larger digs, leaving it open for McDonough No. 35 High School to find refuge after Hurricane Betsy in 1965. Today, the Italian Renaissance Revival building houses the Fifth Circuit Court of Appeals in an elaborately paneled and ornamented series of three courtrooms, one of which, the En Banc courtroom, boasts a bronze glazed ceiling. The Great Hall's plaster ceiling has been restored to its original appearance and color, a light gray. As you enter the building and pass security, turn left and continue around the corner to find the library, where you can pick up information on the courthouse. Outside, a repeating sculpture of four women stands atop each corner of the building's penthouse level: the four ladies represent History, Agriculture, Industry, and the Arts. The building is named for Judge John Minor Wisdom, the New Orleans native who was instrumental in dismantling the segregation laws of the South. Judge Wisdom received the Presidential Medal of Freedom in 1993. ⊠ *600 Camp St., Central Business District* ☎ *504/310–7700* ⊕ *www.uscourts.gov* ☉ *Closed weekends.*

> **FREE FUN**
>
> From mid-March to June, the Young Leadership Council, the Downtown Development District, and several corporate sponsors present Wednesday at the Square, a weekly event that features food, beer and soft drinks, local arts and crafts vendors, and a free evening concert in Lafayette Square. Bring a blanket and enjoy the music from 5 to 8.

Lafayette Square. Planned in 1788 as a public place for Faubourg St. Marie, this 2.5-acre park occupies one city block in between the Federal Complex and Gallier Hall. The leafy square, covered by oaks, magnolias, and maple trees, and landscaped with hydrangeas and azaleas, offers a shady spot to sit. Statues include Benjamin Franklin, Henry Clay, and the New Orleans philanthropist John McDonogh. Recently, the Square has been experiencing a renaissance brought about in large part by the Young Leadership Council's Wednesday at the Square concert series, held in the spring and early summer. ⊠ *Between Camp St., St. Charles Ave., and N. Maestri and S. Maestri Sts., Central Business District* ⊕ *www.nola.gov/parks-and-parkways.*

WAREHOUSE DISTRICT

Bordered by the river, St. Charles Avenue, Poydras Street, and the Pontchartrain Expressway, and filled with former factories and cotton warehouses, the Warehouse District began its renaissance when the city hosted the World's Fair here in 1984. Structures that housed the international pavilions during the fair now make up the New Orleans Morial Convention Center and a number of hotels, restaurants, bars, and music venues.

Today the Warehouse District is one of the trendiest residential and arts-and-nightlife areas of the city, dotted with modern renovations of historic buildings and upscale lofts. Galleries, auction houses, and artist studios line Julia Street, a main thoroughfare, and you can try your hand at glassmaking and printmaking in some of the workshops. By night you'll find excellent restaurants, bustling live-music venues old and new, and numerous neighborhood and hotel bars ranging from casual to the very chic. Inside, scores of young professionals mix with tourists and longtime residents.

TOP ATTRACTIONS

FAMILY
Fodor'sChoice
★

Blaine Kern's Mardi Gras World at Kern Studios. If you're not in town for the real thing, here's a fun (and family-friendly) backstage look at the history and artistry of Carnival. The massive 400,000-square-foot complex, just upriver from the New Orleans Morial Convention Center, features an enhanced guided tour through a maze of video presentations, decorative sculptures, and favorite megafloats from Mardi Gras parades such as Bacchus, Rex, and Endymion. A gift shop sells masks, beads, and Mardi Gras posters, as well as tickets for the tour, during which participants can sample king cake and coffee, pose for pictures in front of parade floats, and see artists at work, sculpting with papier-mâché and fiberglass. For special events, visitors enter through a plantation alley that is part Cajun swamp-shack village, part antebellum Disneyworld (Kern was a friend of, and inspired by, Walt Disney). ✉ *1380 Port of New Orleans Pl., Warehouse District* ☎ *504/361–7821* ⊕ *www. mardigrasworld.com* ✏ *$19.95.*

Fodor'sChoice
★

Contemporary Arts Center. Take in cutting-edge exhibits, featuring both local artists and the work of national and international talent, at this cornerstone of the vibrant Warehouse District. Two theaters present jazz, film, dance, plays, lectures, and experimental and conventional concerts, including a New Orleans music series. Check the website for details. ✉ *900 Camp St., Warehouse District* ☎ *504/528–3805, 504/528–3800 tickets* ⊕ *www.cacno.org* ✏ *$10* ☞ *Free to children and students through grade 12.*

FAMILY

Louisiana Children's Museum. This top-notch children's museum is 30,000 square feet of hands-on educational fun. Favorites include a mini grocery store, a role-play café, a bayou-theme literacy center, and an exhibit on New Orleans architecture featuring a miniature French Quarter courtyard. If your kids still have steam, they can burn it off at the fitness center, with a child-size stationary bicycle and rock-climbing wall. A welcoming environment is provided for children with disabilities—most exhibits are accessible. Art teachers lead classes daily, and there's also daily theatrical storytelling. An indoor playground is reserved for toddlers ages three and under; Toddler Time activities are held at 10 am on Tuesday and Thursday. ✉ *420 Julia St., Warehouse District* ☎ *504/523–1357* ⊕ *www.lcm.org* ✏ *$8.50* ☉ *Closed Mon. in winter.*

Fodor'sChoice
★

National World War II Museum. This vast and still-expanding museum is a moving and well-executed examination of World War II events and its aftermath. Seminal moments are re-created through vintage propaganda from the period, including posters, radio, and film clips; more than 7,500 oral histories of the military personnel involved; a number of short documentary films; and collections of weapons, personal items, and other artifacts from the war. Highlights of the museum include "Final Mission: The USS *Tang* Experience," which re-creates the experience of being in a submarine, and the 4-D theater experience (across the street from the main exhibits) called "Beyond All Boundaries," produced and narrated by Tom Hanks. Other popular exhibits are the replicas of the Higgins boat troop landing craft, which was invented and manufactured in New Orleans by Andrew Jackson Higgins during WWII, and the U.S. Freedom Pavilion: The Boeing Center, which honors all service branches and includes a restored Boeing B-17. Galleries dedicated to the European and Pacific theaters, as well as the Homefront's role in the war, are the latest additions in a wide expansion due to complete in 2018. The Stage Door Canteen features WWII-era entertainment, and an adjoining restaurant serving a "Victory Garden-to-table" menu. Check the website for updates on the expansion and current offerings. ✉ *945 Magazine St., main entrance on Andrew Higgins Dr., Warehouse District* ☎ *504/528–1944* ⊕ *www. nationalww2museum.org* ✆ *$27; Beyond All Boundaries and Final Mission presentations $5 each.*

FAMILY
Fodor's Choice
★

Ogden Museum of Southern Art. Art by Southern artists, made in the South, about the South, and exploring Southern themes fills this elegant five-story building. The basis of the museum's permanent collection are 1,200 works collected by local developer Roger Ogden since the 1960s. It has now grown to more than 4,000 pieces, including paintings, ceramics, drawings, sculptures, photographs, and designs. These pieces, along with special exhibitions, showcase artists from Washington, D.C., and 15 Southern states spanning the 18th through 21st century. A central stair atrium filters natural light through the series of galleries, and a rooftop patio serves as a sculpture garden with lovely views of the surrounding area. The gift shop sells crafts and jewelry by Southern artists, and books and movies celebrating the South. Thursday night (6–8) comes alive with Ogden After Hours, featuring live music, artist interviews, refreshments, children's activities, and special gallery exhibitions. ✉ *925 Camp St., Warehouse District* ☎ *504/539–9650* ⊕ *www. ogdenmuseum.org* ✆ *$13.50.*

WORTH NOTING

Crescent City Farmers Market. This year-round Saturday market offers an array of locally grown produce, baked goods, cut flowers, non-farmed Louisiana seafood, fresh dairy, locally farm-raised meat, and prepared foods from regional vendors. Special events and holidays mean cooking demonstrations and appearances by local musicians. Meet and greet the local farmers, chefs, and fishers who make this city's amazing food culture possible. The market also makes an appearance Uptown on Tuesday morning, in the French Quarter on Wednesday afternoon, and in Mid-City on Thursday evening. ✉ *700 Magazine St., Warehouse District* ☎ *504/861–4488* ⊕ *www.crescentcityfarmersmarket.org.*

Lee Circle. In a traffic circle at the northern edge of the Warehouse District, an 1884 bronze statue of Civil War General Robert E. Lee, by sculptor Alexander Doyle, stood high above the city on a white marble column—until spring 2017, that is, when Mayor Landrieu responded to local protests and nationwide attention to remove glorified Confederate monuments. Plans are underway to redevelop (and rename) the circle as a public space that unites the city, rather than divides it. ⊠ *Warehouse District.*

Louisiana's Civil War Museum at Confederate Memorial Hall. Established in 1891, this ponderous stone building is the oldest museum in Louisiana and features heavy trusses, gleaming cypress paneling, and elaborate Richardsonian Romanesque architecture. It houses a collection of artifacts from the Civil War, including uniforms, flags, soldiers' personal effects, and a rudimentary hand grenade. ⊠ *929 Camp St., Warehouse District* ☎ *504/523–4522* ⊕ *www.confederatemuseum.com* ▣ *$10* ⊙ *Closed Sun. and Mon.*

FAMILY **New Orleans Glassworks & Printmaking Studio.** See free demonstrations of printmaking, glassmaking and design, and silver alchemy in this restored, 1800s-era brick warehouse (with a whopping 25,000-square-foot interior). The studio offers group and individual classes. Call in advance to make reservations for hands-on instruction. A shop and gallery display and sell the finished products. ⊠ *727 Magazine St., Warehouse District* ☎ *504/529–7279* ⊕ *www.neworleansglassworks. com* ⊙ *Closed Sun.*

St. Patrick's Church. A stark exterior gives way to a far more ornate interior in the first church built in the American sector of New Orleans, intended to provide the city's Irish Catholics with a place of worship as distinguished as the French St. Louis Cathedral. The vaulted interior was completed in 1840 by local architect James Gallier, who moved here from Ireland in 1834. High stained-glass windows and huge murals, painted in 1841, enrich the interior. ⊠ *724 Camp St., Warehouse District* ☎ *504/525–4413* ⊕ *www.oldstpatricks.org.*

THE GARDEN DISTRICT

Getting Oriented

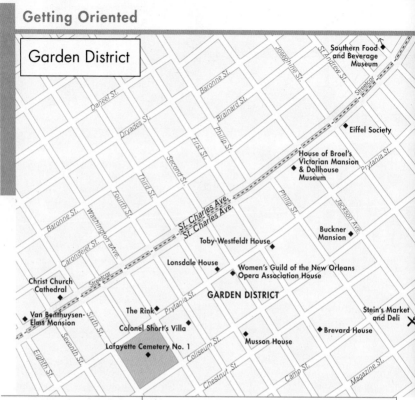

Garden District

Southern Food and Beverage Museum

Eiffel Society

House of Broel's Victorian Mansion & Dollhouse Museum

St. Charles Ave.

Buckner Mansion

Toby-Westfeldt House

Lonsdale House

Women's Guild of the New Orleans Opera Association House

GARDEN DISTRICT

Christ Church Cathedral

The Rink

Stein's Market and Deli

Van Benthuysen-Elms Mansion

Colonel Short's Villa

Brevard House

Lafayette Cemetery No. 1

Musson House

QUICK BITES

French Truck Roastery and Espresso Bar. You'll find some of the best locally roasted coffee and espresso drinks in this bright, pint-sized space. ✉ *1200 Magazine St., Lower Garden District* ☎ *504/298–1115* ⊕ *www.frenchtruckcoffee.com.*

Stein's Market and Deli. This Jewish and Italian deli serves the "Muphuletta," a Philly take on a New Orleans muffuletta with sopressata, ham, provolone, and olive salad on ciabatta. ✉ *2207 Magazine St., Garden District* ☎ *504/527–0771* ⊕ *www.stein-sdeli.com* ▭ *No credit cards.*

GETTING HERE AND AROUND

The Garden District is easily accessible by car, streetcar, and city bus, or on foot from the CBD or Uptown. It's easy and free to park your car on any side street, but you have to pay to park along the busier stretches of Magazine Street and Prytania Street.

The **streetcar** runs about every 30 minutes (more frequently during rush hour), 24 hours a day, and makes several stops along St. Charles Avenue. Because the tracks are undergoing maintenance, segments of the line are periodically out of commission, and in those instances a shuttle service is available. You may have to wait longer than 30 minutes for the streetcar to arrive at night, but it's generally a safe, if leisurely, mode of transportation. It takes about 20 minutes on the streetcar to get to Jackson Avenue in the lower Garden District from Canal Street. The **No. 11 bus** runs up Magazine Street, making stops at all major intersections every 20 minutes. The ride from Canal Street to Jackson Avenue takes about 10 minutes depending on traffic.

TOP REASONS TO GO

5

Architecture. View antebellum homes built during New Orleans's most prosperous era by renowned architects, including Henry Howard, Lewis E. Reynolds, William Freret, and Samuel Jamison.

Feast on Magazine Street. Rubbing shoulders with vintage boutiques and dive bars, the eateries along this stretch serve a mélange of cuisines—you'll find everything from po'boys to French crêpes to crawfish-stuffed sushi rolls.

Check out local art. Peruse both fine and funky jewelry, paintings, pottery, and other locally made artwork at the galleries on Magazine Street. Or visit the community art centers on OC Haley Boulevard.

Take in some history. View the aboveground tombs at Lafayette Cemetery No. 1, in continual use since 1833 and one of the most beautiful burial grounds in the city.

MAKING THE MOST OF YOUR TIME

Plan at least a day to see the Garden District's gorgeous mansions, to shop Magazine Street, and to visit **Lafayette Cemetery No. 1**, the oldest municipal cemetery in the city. Historic New Orleans Tours runs quality tours of the Garden District that includes the former house of Anne Rice and the cemetery (⇨ *see Travel Smart for more information*).

SAFETY

Safety isn't a major concern in the Garden District, as the neighborhood hires its own security service in addition to what protection the New Orleans police offer. Still, at night the neighborhood is quiet and the streets are not well lighted, so it's always wise to walk with someone, especially in the lower Garden District and Central City on the opposite side of St. Charles Avenue.

Sightseeing
★★★
Dining
★★
Lodging
★★
Shopping
★★★★
Nightlife
★

Boasting some of the most stunning homes in the city, the Garden District has acquired fame for its antebellum mansions and manicured gardens. Residents take great pride in their gorgeous properties, and the neighborhood is in bloom year-round. Although most homes are closed to the public (except for tours on special occasions), the views from outside the intricate cast-iron fences are still impressive. A stroll through the neighborhood is a peaceful break from more touristy areas of New Orleans.

Updated by
Cameron
Quincy Todd

Originally part of the Livaudais plantation, the Garden District was laid out in the late 1820s and remained part of the city of Lafayette until incorporated into New Orleans in 1852. The neighborhood attracted "new-moneyed" Americans who, snubbed by the Creole residents of the French Quarter, constructed grand houses with large English-style gardens featuring lush azaleas, magnolias, and camellias. Three architectural styles were favored: the three-bay Greek Revival, center-hall Greek Revival, and raised cottage. Renovations and expansions to these designs through the years allowed owners to host bigger and more ostentatious parties, particularly during the social season between Christmas and Carnival. Today many of the proud residents represent fourth- or fifth-generation New Orleanians.

The lower Garden District (along Magazine Street east of Jackson Avenue) boasts offbeat boutiques selling original art, antiques, vintage clothing, and jewelry, catering to the young professional and student crowds in particular. A "green light district" of eco-friendly shops has taken root in its 2000–2100 blocks. Coliseum Square, in the center of the neighborhood, features a fountain and walking trails that wind around looming oak trees, and the mansions flanking the park display a distinctly faded beauty. The neighborhood quiets down considerably in the evening, though there are a few nighttime hangouts and restaurants, especially near the triangular intersection at St. Mary Street and Sophie Wright Place.

A morning walk in the upper Garden District (west of Jackson Avenue) provides a peaceful break from the more touristy areas of New Orleans. Besides beautiful mansions with wrought-iron fences that wrap around vibrant, manicured gardens, this part of the neighborhood is where you'll find Lafayette Cemetery No. 1, one of the city's oldest and most beautiful cemeteries. Return to the present day by visiting the stretch of Magazine Street that runs alongside the upper Garden District, which boasts an eclectic mix of restaurants and chichi boutiques.

SPEAK BIG EASY

The "muse streets" that transverse the lower Garden District are not pronounced like the Greek goddess names you may recall. New Orleanians have their own way of speaking: Calliope isn't "kal-eye-oh-pee"—it's "kal-ee-ope," Melpomene is pronounced "mel-puh-meen," and Terpsichore is "terp-sih-core."

5

TOP ATTRACTIONS

Brevard House. Though Anne Rice moved out of her elegant Garden District home in 2004, the famous novelist's fans still flock to see the house that inspired the Mayfair Manor in her series *Lives of the Mayfair Witches*. The house is a three-bay Greek Revival, extended over a luxurious, lemon tree–lined side yard and surrounded by a fence of cast-iron rosettes that earned the estate its historical name, Rosegate. ⊠ *1239 First St., Garden District.*

Coliseum Square Park. Established in the mid-19th century, this lush green space is the centerpiece of the lower Garden District. With cycling and walking trails as well as a beautiful fountain, the wedge-shape park is a great spot to stop and relax after a walk through the neighborhood. Although the area bordered by Race and Melpomene streets can be bustling with activity during the day, it's best not to wander around alone at night. ⊠ *1700 Coliseum St., Garden District.*

Goodrich-Stanley House. This restored Creole cottage was a modest prototype for much of the far more elaborate architecture of the surrounding Garden District. The scale, derived from the climate-conscious design prevalent in the West Indies, made this style easily adaptable to the higher pretensions of the Greek Revival look, as well as the slightly more reserved Colonial Revival. Built in 1837, the house has had one famous occupant: Henry Morton Stanley, renowned explorer of Africa and founder of the Congo Free States who most famously uttered the phrase "Dr. Livingstone, I presume" upon encountering the long-lost Scottish missionary. ⊠ *1729 Coliseum St., Garden District.*

House of Broel's Victorian Mansion and Dollhouse Museum. This restored antebellum home was built in two periods: its present-day second floor was actually constructed first, in 1850, and in 1884 the house was elevated and a new first floor added. The extensive dollhouse collection includes 60 historically accurate, scale-model miniatures of Victorian, Tudor, and plantation-style houses and covers more than 3,000 square feet on the mansion's second floor. All were created by owner Bonnie Broel over a 15-year period. Tours are available for both walk-ins and groups, and the mansion offers a romantic setting for weddings, receptions, and parties. Visitors can only view the property on tours, which can fill up, so it's best to call ahead. ⊠ *2220 St. Charles Ave., Garden District* ☎ *504/522–2220, 504/494–2220 tour info and reservations* ⊕ *www.houseofbroel.com* ✉ *Tour $15.*

Fodor's Choice
★

Lafayette Cemetery No. 1. New Orleans found itself amid a large influx of Italian, German, Irish, and American immigrants from the North when this magnolia-shaded cemetery opened in 1833. Many who fought or played a role in the Civil War have plots here, indicated by plaques and headstones that detail the site of their death. Several tombs also reflect the toll taken by the yellow fever epidemic, which affected mostly children and newcomers to New Orleans; 2,000 yellow fever victims were buried here in 1852. Movies such as *Interview with the Vampire* and *Double Jeopardy* have used this walled cemetery for its eerie beauty. Save Our Cemeteries, a nonprofit, offers hour-long, volunteer-led tours daily at 10:30 am. All proceeds benefit the organization's cemetery restoration and advocacy efforts. ⊠ *1400 block of Washington Ave., Garden District* ⊕ *www.saveourcemeteries.org.*

Lonsdale House. As a 16-year-old immigrant working in the New Orleans shipyards, Henry Lonsdale noticed how many damaged goods were arriving from upriver. Spotting a need for more-protective shipping materials, he developed the burlap sack and made a fortune, only to lose it all in the 1837 depression. Lonsdale turned to coffee importing, and in order to stretch his supply, he thought to cut the coffee grounds with chicory, a bitter root—and New Orleanians have been drinking the blend ever since. This house includes intricate cast-iron work and a carved marble entrance hall. The statue of Our Mother of Perpetual Help in the front yard is a remnant of the house's more than 70 years as an active Catholic chapel. ⊠ *2521–2523 Prytania St., Garden District.*

Southern Food and Beverage Museum. This 30,000-square-foot museum, which opened in 2014 on the up-and-coming O.C. Haley Boulevard, was designed to educate visitors on the vast amount of knowledge and art that has accrued around two near-obsessions in the South: eating and drinking. Exhibits feature information on fishermen, farmers, and chefs as well as the many cultures that contribute to this region's tradition of cocktails and cuisine. There's a food gift shop and a tasting room with chef demonstrations; call ahead for updates, current exhibitions, and programs. ⊠ *1504 O.C. Haley Blvd., Garden District* ☎ *504/569–0405* ⊕ *www.southernfood.org* ✉ *$10.50* ☉ *Closed Tues.*

Van Benthuysen-Elms Mansion. Built in 1869, this stately Italianate mansion saw the Confederate president Jefferson Davis as a frequent guest. In the early 20th century, it served as the German consulate until the start of World War II. The house has been meticulously maintained and furnished with period pieces, and is mainly a venue for private receptions and special events. Highlights include a carved-oak staircase and mantelpiece and 24-karat gilt moldings and sconces. ⊠ *3029 St. Charles Ave., Garden District* ☎ *504/895–9200* ⊕ *www.elmsmansion.com.*

Women's Guild of the New Orleans Opera Association House. This Greek Revival house, built in 1865, has an octagonal turret, added in the late 19th century. The last private owner, Nettie Seebold, willed the estate to the Guild in 1965. Furnished with 18th- and 19th-century European and American pieces, the house underwent extensive renovations in 2008. ⊠ *2504 Prytania St., Garden District* ☎ *504/267–9539* ⊕ *neworleansopera.org/womens-guild* ⊠ *$15* ☞ *No public tours Memorial Day–Labor Day.*

WORTH NOTING

Buckner Mansion. This 1856 home was built by cotton king Henry S. Buckner in overt competition with the famous Stanton Hall in Natchez, built by Buckner's former partner. Among the luxurious details are its 48 fluted cypress columns and a rare honeysuckle-design cast-iron fence. Now privately owned, the house served as the campus of Soulé College from 1923 to 1975 and appeared in *American Horror Story*. ⊠ *1410 Jackson Ave., Garden District.*

Christ Church Cathedral. The present-day English Gothic church, completed in 1887, has pitched gables, an architectural detail that prefigured the New Orleans Victorian style. Its congregation was actually established in 1805, however, making it the first non–Roman Catholic church in the Louisiana Purchase territory. Jefferson Davis was among its parishioners, and the altar from his home is at the church, as is the grave of Confederate general Leonidas Polk. ⊠ *2919 St. Charles Ave., Garden District* ⊕ *www.cccnola.org.*

Colonel Short's Villa. Built in 1859, this house's stylistic influence was due to the two-story galleries of its dining room wing, which had railings made of cast iron. Architect Henry Howard is known for designing Nottaway, the largest plantation home in America. The fence features a pattern of morning glories and cornstalks and is the most famous work of cast iron in the Garden District. Colonel Short purchased the fence for his wife, who was homesick for her native Iowa. The house was occupied by Union governor Michael Hahn and by governor Nathaniel Banks during the Civil War. ⊠ *1448 Fourth St., Garden District.*

Eiffel Society. Thirty years ago, engineers in Paris discovered hairline fractures in the Eiffel Tower supports. To lighten the load, they removed the restaurant on the second platform. New Orleans auto dealer McDonald Stephens bought that restaurant, which was disassembled into 11,062 pieces for shipping. Stephens hired New Orleans architect Steven Bingler to build a "jewel box" out of the pieces for his four beloved daughters. Bingler's vision, assembled on St. Charles Avenue in 1986, incorporated scattered pieces from the original restaurant into a structure meant to resemble the Eiffel Tower. The building has gone through many incarnations; today it is a club and event space. ⊠ *2040 St. Charles Ave., Garden District* ☎ *504/525–2951* ⊕ *www.eiffelsociety.com.*

Musson House. This Italianate house was built by impressionist Edgar Degas's maternal uncle, Michel Musson—a rare Creole inhabitant of the predominantly American Garden District. Musson had moved to his Esplanade Street residence before Degas visited New Orleans, so it's

The Greek Revival design by
architect William A. Freret
was built for Edward A. Davis in 1859.
Dr. and Mrs. Herman de Bachelle Seebold
purchased the home in 1944 and
donated the mansion, furnishings and art
in 1965 to the
Women's Guild
of the
New Orleans Opera Association.

unlikely the artist ever stayed at this address. A subsequent owner added the famous "lace" iron galleries. ⊠ *1331 Third St., Garden District.*

The Rink. This collection of shops was once the location of the South's first roller-skating rink. Locals browse the **Garden District Book Shop,** which stocks regional and antiquarian books, along with an assortment of autographed first editions by regional writers; **Judy's at the Rink,** an upscale gifts and housewares boutique; and **Loomed NOLA,** which imports handwoven textiles from Turkey. ⊠ *2727 Prytania St., Garden District.*

Toby-Westfeldt House. Dating to the 1830s, this Greek Revival cottage sits amid a plantationlike garden, surrounded by a copy of the original white-picket fence. Businessman Thomas Toby moved to New Orleans and had the house raised aboveground to protect it from flooding. ⊠ *2340 Prytania St., Garden District.*

UPTOWN AND CARROLLTON-RIVERBEND

Getting Oriented

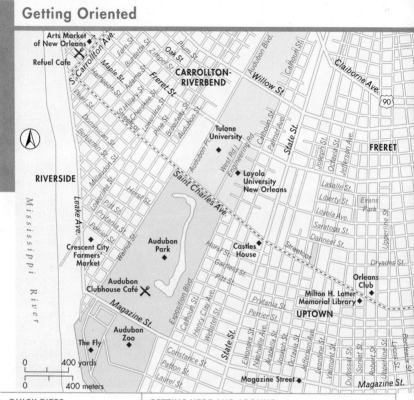

QUICK BITES

Audubon Clubhouse Café. Eat in an airy dining room overlooking Audubon Park golf course, or relax with a drink on the veranda. ✉ *6500 Magazine St., Uptown* ✛ *Turn onto Golf Club Dr.* ☎ *504/212–5285, 800/774–7394* ⊕ *www.audoboninstitute. org* ⊟ *No credit cards.*

Refuel Cafe. This modern café serves fresh salads and sandwiches. At brunch, try the hand-whisked grits. ✉ *8124 Hampson St., Carrollton-Riverbend* ☎ *504/872–0187* ⊕ *www. refuelcafe.com* ⊟ *No credit cards* ☾ *No lunch Mon.*

GETTING HERE AND AROUND

Uptown and Carrollton-Riverbend are easily walkable neighborhoods. The **St. Charles Avenue streetcar** is a reliable and picturesque mode of transportation. It runs approximately every 10 minutes, 24 hours a day (less frequently nights and weekends), from Canal Street at the edge of the French Quarter to South Claiborne Avenue. It stops at all main intersections across St. Charles Avenue, leaving you within walking distance of Audubon Park and Zoo. Expect the entire ride, from Canal Street to Carrollton-Riverbend, to take about an hour (longer during rush hour or on holidays or weekends). Visit the RTA's website (⊕ *www.norta.com*) for updates. The **No. 11 bus** runs the length of Magazine Street up to Audubon Park from Canal Street. It runs every 20 minutes, making stops at five major intersections. The fare is $1.25 for both the streetcar and the bus.

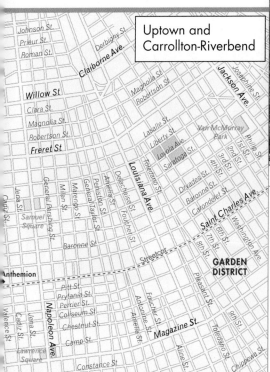

Uptown and Carrollton-Riverbend

6

TOP REASONS TO GO

Ride the streetcar. Take a scenic and leisurely streetcar ride from Canal Street to Audubon Park, ogling the stately mansions that stretch along St. Charles Avenue.

Monkey around in Audubon Park and Zoo. Considered one of the best in the nation, Audubon Zoo offers a wide range of interesting exhibits for visitors of all ages. The adjoining park has beautiful walking trails lined with 100-year-old oaks.

Hang with locals at the Fly. This quieter stretch of Audubon Park is known locally as "the Fly." The levee, a riverside walkway along one side of the park, provides spectacular views of the Mississippi

Explore Carrollton-Riverbend. This bustling neighborhood along Oak Street, Maple Street, and South Carrollton Avenue has restaurants, shops, and popular hangouts for college students and locals.

Shop till you drop. Magazine Street is the city's premier shopping destination.

MAKING THE MOST OF YOUR TIME

You could easily spend two days in this neighborhood: a full day visiting the **Audubon Zoo** and enjoying the park that surrounds it, and another day exploring the boutiques, galleries, and restaurants along **Magazine Street**. If you have extra time, head to **The Fly,** the riverside park on the back side of the zoo, where locals like to picnic and play ball on weekends.

SAFETY

Most of Uptown and Carrollton-Riverbend is safe to walk around during the day and evening. However, take extra care when walking at night in the area between Magazine Street and the river up to Jefferson. Also avoid the area close to the river west of Audubon Park and dark side streets when out late at night.

RIDING THE STREETCAR

View the beautiful mansions and experience the fun local vibe of Uptown via the St. Charles Avenue streetcar, which runs the length of the avenue, from Canal Street right outside of the French Quarter to Carrollton-Riverbend. The relaxing ride takes about an hour and costs $1.25 one-way.

The St. Charles streetcar line runs through Uptown (above) and the CBD (right page, bottom).

If you're coming from the French Quarter, board at Canal and Carondelet. Jump off at Jackson Avenue (a 20-minutes ride) and follow our Garden District Walking Tour (⇨ *see Chapter 1*). Reboard at Louisiana Avenue, which forms the boundary between the Garden District and Uptown. As you approach Louisiana Avenue, the huge white mansion on your left at the intersection was formerly the **Bultman Funeral Home,** whose interiors inspired Tennessee Williams when he was writing his play *Suddenly Last Summer.* It's now a Fresh Market grocery store. Note that unless you have an unlimited day pass ($3) for the streetcar, you'll need to ask for a 25¢ transfer when you pay—otherwise you'll have to pay the full $1.25 (exact change) each time you board.

STREETCAR HISTORY

In the 1900s, streetcars were the most prominent mode of public transit in New Orleans, and by the early 20th century, the city had almost 200 miles of streetcar lines; a ride cost just 5¢. In the 1920s, buses started to overtake the old-fashioned system. Four lines operate today, with plans for expansion under way.

The **Columns Hotel,** built in 1883 as a private home, is on the right after Peniston Street. It's a great place for a cocktail on the grand veranda or for a casual brunch on Sunday. Next, you'll pass the Gothic-style **Rayne Memorial Methodist Church,** built in 1875, one block past the hotel on the left. The 1887 Queen Anne–style **Grant House** up the block was designed by local architect Thomas Sully, with a decorative porch and balcony balustrades.

As you continue, the large avenue at the next stop is Napoleon. The spectacular **Academy of the Sacred Heart,** a private girls' school, is on the right in the next block, past Jena Street. Across the street, the Mediterranean **Smith House** claims one of the most picturesque settings on the avenue. It was built in 1906 for William Smith, president of the New Orleans Cotton Exchange. The **Anthemion,** at 4631 St. Charles Avenue, designed by architect Frank P. Gravely, is an early example of Colonial Revival architecture. The **Brown House,** on the right before Bordeaux Street, is one of the largest mansions on St. Charles Avenue.

Several houses in the next block are turn-of-the-20th-century buildings that emulate an antebellum style. On the left, at No. 4920, is the Colonial Revival **Rosenberg House,** built in 1911. At No. 5120 is the **Milton H. Latter Memorial**

Library, inside a Beaux-Arts mansion. It's one of the few mansions along St. Charles open to the public.

Several blocks ahead, the **Benjamin House,** between Octavia and Joseph streets, is a stunning mansion (circa 1916) with a stone facade designed by the architect Emile Weil. On the next block, past Joseph Street on the right, is the **McCarthy House,** a 1903 Colonial Revival home with ornate columns and flattop doors and windows. The plantation home used in the film *Gone With the Wind* was a set, but it served as inspiration for the columned New Orleans **Tara,** built in 1941, at the corner of Arabella.

As you cross Nashville Avenue, the **Wedding Cake House,** an elaborate Victorian mansion built circa 1896, is on the right. Its most notable feature is the beveled leaded glass in its front door, one of the most beautiful entryways in the city. As you enter the university district, dominating the next block on the left is the neo-Gothic **St. Charles Avenue Presbyterian Church.**

Castles House, on the left after State Street, is in the Colonial Revival style, as is the **St. Charles Avenue Christian Church,** two blocks up on the left. On the right, across from the church, is **Temple Sinai,** the first Reform Jewish congregation in New Orleans. This

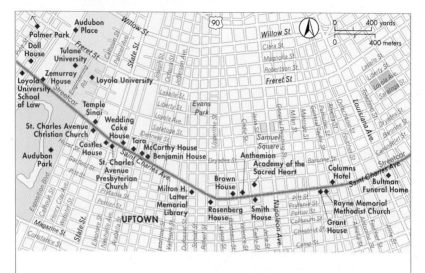

building dates from 1928; the annex on the corner was built in 1970.

Just beyond Calhoun Street, **Loyola University,** on the right, takes up the block after Temple Sinai. **Tulane University,** founded in 1834, is directly beside Loyola. Campuses for both universities extend several blocks off the avenue. On the left, across the avenue from the two universities, is **Audubon Park.**

Back on the streetcar, the heavy stone archway on the right just after Tulane University is the guarded entrance to **Audubon Place.** The private drive has some of the most elegant mansions in the city. **Zemurray House,** the columned white home facing the archway, was built in 1908 by the cotton broker William T. Jay, who sold it to Samuel Zemurray, head of the United Fruit Company. It is now the official residence of Tulane's president. The **Doll House,** a miniature house in the corner yard on the right at Broadway, is said to be the smallest house in New Orleans with its own postal address.

At Broadway, to the left, is the **Loyola University School of Law,** an Italianate building that housed the Dominican Sisters and the college they operated until the 1980s. The street continues several more stops past Broadway along St. Charles until it turns at the Riverbend onto Carrollton Avenue, once the entrance to a former resort town.

You'll travel through the Carrollton-Riverbend neighborhood before reaching the end of the line at **Palmer Park,** where an arts market is held the last Saturday of every month. Reboard the streetcar headed downtown at South Carrolton Avenue and Claiborne Avenue, where the St. Charles Avenue line both begins and ends.

Sightseeing
★★
Dining
★★★
Lodging
★
Shopping
★★★★
Nightlife
★★★

Discover the more residential face of New Orleans in the sprawling Uptown and Carrollton-Riverbend neighborhoods. Just a 30-minute streetcar ride from Canal Street, you'll find blocks of shops on bustling Magazine Street, stunning homes along oak-lined streets, and the first-class Audubon Park and Zoo. Head farther into Uptown and spend a couple of hours walking the length of the levee in Riverbend for stunning views of the Mississippi.

UPTOWN

Updated
by Karen
Taylor-Gist

Uptown encompasses the area upriver from Louisiana Avenue between Tchoupitoulas Street and South Claiborne Avenue, on the west side of the Garden District. Stately mansions line the length of St. Charles Avenue, where you'll likely see colorful Mardi Gras beads hanging from tree limbs throughout the year. Traveling along the avenue from downtown to Uptown provides something of a historical narrative: The city's development unfolded upriver, and the houses grow more modern the farther up you go. Smaller shotgun and Victorian-style homes on side streets display old-world charm, and this family-oriented neighborhood is home to Loyola and Tulane universities. Magazine Street bustles with 6 miles of shops, bars, and restaurants, all the way from the CBD up to Audubon Park.

TOP ATTRACTIONS

FAMILY
Fodor's Choice
★

Audubon Park. Formerly the plantation of Etienne de Boré, the father of the granulated-sugar industry in Louisiana, this large, lush patch of greenery stretches from St. Charles Avenue across Magazine Street to the river. Designed by John Charles Olmsted, nephew of Frederick Law Olmsted (who laid out New York City's Central Park and Asheville's Biltmore Estate), it contains the world-class **Audubon Zoo;** a 1.8-mile track for running, walking, or biking; picnic and play areas; Audubon

Park Golf Course; tennis courts; a swimming pool; horse stables; and a river view. Calm lagoons wind through the park, harboring egrets and other indigenous species. The park and zoo were named for the famous ornithologist and painter John James Audubon, who spent many years working in and around New Orleans. ⊠ *6500 Magazine St., Uptown* ☎ *504/581–4629* ⊕ *www.auduboninstitute.org* ⊠ *Free.*

FAMILY   **Audubon Zoo.** Consistently ranked as one of the top zoos in the nation, the Audubon Zoo presents a wide array of animals in exhibits that mimic their natural habitats. The Louisiana Swamp exhibit re-creates the natural habitat of alligators, including a rare white alligator (technically a leucistic gator), nutrias (large swamp rodents), and catfish; feeding time is always well attended. Among other highlights are the Reptile Encounter, the Komodo dragon exhibit, and new orangutan and elephant exhibits. Several attractions are available for additional fees, including a train tour that departs every 30 minutes from the swamp exhibit. Cool Zoo, a splash park featuring a 28-foot white-alligator slide, bubbling fountains, and splash zones, has one area set aside for toddlers and young children. Gator Run is a lazy river with sand beaches, water cannons, and jumping jets. (Cool Zoo is open weekends in May, then opens daily until mid-August, when it returns to weekends only until Labor Day; separate admission to both the Cool Zoo and Gator Run attractions is $12 for nonmembers.) ⊠ *6500 Magazine St., Uptown* ⊕ *www.auduboninstitute.org* ⊠ *$22.95; combination ticket for zoo and Audubon Aquarium of the Americas, $39.95.*

Loyola University New Orleans. Chartered by the Jesuits in 1912, Loyola University is a local landmark. Its communications, music, and law programs are world-renowned. The Gothic- and Tudor-style Marquette Hall, facing St. Charles Avenue and Audubon Park, provides the backdrop for a quintessential New Orleans photo opportunity. The fourth floor of the neo-Gothic J. Edgar and Louise S. Monroe Library houses the university's Collins C. Diboll Art Gallery, open to the public seven days a week (Monday–Saturday 10–6, Sunday noon–6). ⊠ *6363 St. Charles Ave., Uptown* ⊕ *www.loyno.edu.*

Tulane University. Next to Loyola on St. Charles Avenue, Tulane University's three original buildings face the avenue: **Tilton Hall** (1902) on the right, **Gibson Hall** (1894) in the middle, and **Dinwiddie Hall** (1923) on the left. The Romanesque style, with its massive stone composition and arches, is repeated in several buildings around the quad. More modern campus buildings extend another three blocks to the north, including Newcomb Art Museum, a 3,600-square-foot exhibition facility offering contemporary and historical exhibits (free; Tuesday–Friday 10–5, Saturday 11–4). Tulane offers undergraduate, graduate, and professional degrees in liberal arts, science and engineering, architecture, business, law, social work, medicine, public health, and tropical medicine.

The **Middle American Research Institute and Gallery** (☎ *504/865–5110;* ⊕ *mari.tulane.edu),* located on the third floor of Tulane's Dinwiddie Hall, includes the world's largest documented Guatemalan textile collection and replicas of classic Mayan sculpture. Established in 1924, the institute's collection also includes rare artifacts like poison-dart arrows from Venezuela and shrunken heads from the Brazilian rain forest. On view at the gallery through late 2018 is "Faces of the Maya." The pre-Columbian artifacts are complemented by a collection of books on Latin American culture housed in Tulane's main library (free; weekdays 9–4, appointment recommended). ⊠ *6823 St. Charles Ave., Uptown* ⊕ *www.tulane.edu.*

WORTH NOTING

Anthemion. The emergence of Colonial Revival architecture in the late 19th century was expressive of local weariness with the excesses of the Greek Revival craze that had dominated the mid-century. Anthemion is an excellent example of this return to simplicity. Built in 1896 for the druggist Christian Keppler, it served as the headquarters of the Japanese consulate from 1938 to 1941. ⊠ *4631 St. Charles Ave., Uptown.*

Castles House. The renowned local architect Thomas Sully designed this 1896 Colonial Revival house after the Longfellow House in Cambridge, Massachusetts. The interior has often appeared in the pages of design magazines. It was built for John Castles, president of Hibernia National Bank. ⊠ *6000 St. Charles Ave., Uptown.*

Milton H. Latter Memorial Library. This former private house serves as the most elegant public library in New Orleans. Built in 1907, the Italianate Beaux-Arts mansion was once the home of the silent-movie star Marguerite Clark. The Latter family bought it and donated it to the city as a library in 1948 in memory of their son, who was killed in World War II. An extensive renovation recently restored the home to its former grandeur. ⊠ *5120 St. Charles Ave., Uptown* ☎ *504/596–2625* ⊕ *www. neworleanspubliclibrary.org.*

Orleans Club. This sumptuous mansion was built in 1868 as a wedding gift from Colonel William Lewis Wynn to his daughter. The side building, on the Uptown side of the main building, is an auditorium added in the 1950s. The house is closed to the public, but serves as headquarters to a ladies' social club and hosts many debutante teas and wedding receptions. ⊠ *5005 St. Charles Ave., Uptown.*

CARROLLTON-RIVERBEND

Before becoming part of New Orleans in 1874, this area was a resort town, providing a relaxing getaway with riverfront views. Now the neighborhood is mostly composed of smaller one- and two-story family homes, shady oak-lined streets, and plenty of small restaurants and cafés. With the success of local events, such as the annual Oak Street Po'Boy Festival in October (⊕ *www.poboyfest.com*), the retail strip on Oak Street has blossomed with shops, clothing boutiques, restaurants, and popular bars such as the Maple Leaf, where the Rebirth Brass Band plays every Tuesday night. Nearby Maple Street is a great shopping destination in its own right, attracting the college crowd with an array of bars and cafés. Walk the stretch of the levee from Riverbend back downtown along the river and relax at "the Fly," a popular hangout on the back side of Audubon Zoo, where locals enjoy views of the river while setting up picnics or team sports.

Kids love feeding the giraffes at the Audubon Zoo.

EXPLORING

Arts Market of New Orleans. Spend a morning perusing the craftsmanship of 100 or more artists from all over the region in this open-air market held the last Saturday of each month in beautiful Palmer Park. Vendors include jewelry artists, painters, textile designers, soap makers, and potters. Musicians, a kids' tent, and food stands round out the event. ⊠ *Palmer Park, corner of S. Carrolton and S. Claiborne Aves., Carrollton-Riverbend* ⊕ *www.artsneworleans.org* ✉ *Free.*

Crescent City Farmers Market. Rub shoulders with New Orleans chefs as they rush to pick up fresh vegetables, fish, and meat before their restaurants open. The market caters to both home cooks and professionals who embrace the concept of showcasing local and seasonal ingredients. A new chef is featured each month to prepare delicious lunches. Visitors can indulge in tasty treats like homemade Popsicles, fresh-squeezed juice, and hot-from-the-oven bread, as well as sample the local produce. ⊠ *200 Broadway St., between Leake Ave. and Broadway, Carrollton-Riverbend* ⊕ *www.crescentcityfarmersmarket.org* ✉ *Free.*

MID-CITY AND
BAYOU ST. JOHN

Getting Oriented

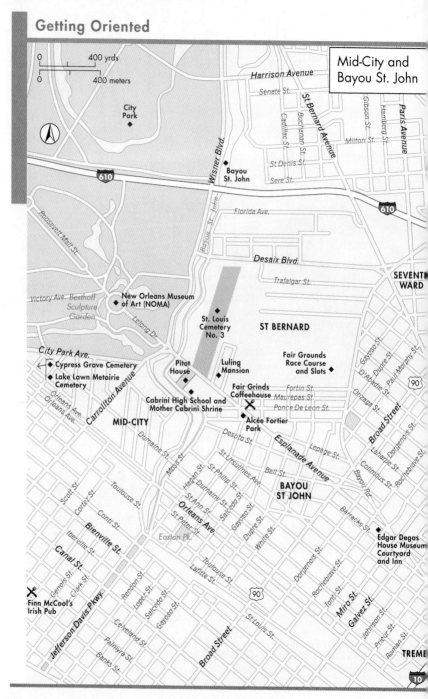

Mid-City and
Bayou St. John

0   400 yrds
0   400 meters

Harrison Avenue
Senate St.

City
Park

St Bernard Avenue

Gibson St.
Hamberg St.
Paris Avenue

Cadillac St.
Buchanan St.

Milton St.

Wisner Blvd.

Bayou
St. John

St Denis St.

Sere St.

Florida Ave.

Roosevelt Mall St.

Bayou St. John

Desaix Blvd.

Trafalgar St.

SEVENTH
WARD

Victory Ave. Besthoff
Sculpture
Garden

New Orleans Museum
of Art (NOMA)

Lelong Dr.

St. Louis
Cemetery
No. 3

ST BERNARD

Fair Grounds
Race Course
and Slots

Gayoso St.
Dupre St.
Paul Morphy St.

City Park Ave.

◆ Cypress Grove Cemetery
◆ Lake Lawn Metairie
Cemetery

Pitot
House

Luling
Mansion

D'Abadie St.

90

Carrollton Avenue

Onzaga St.

Broad Street

Orleans Ave.
Orleans Ave.

Fair Grinds
Coffeehouse

Cabrini High School and
Mother Cabrini Shrine

Fortin St.
Maurepas St.
Ponce De Leon St.

Lahatpe St.
Dorgenois St.
Rochebiave St.

MID-CITY

Dumaine St.

Alcée Fortier
Park

Desoto St.

Esplanade Avenue

Lepage St.

Columbus St.

Moss St.

St Ursulines Ave.

Bayou Rd.

Scott St.

Cortez St.

Toulouse St.

Hagan Ave.
St Philip St.
Dumaine St.
Salcedo St.

Belt St.

BAYOU
ST JOHN

Barracks St.

Conti St.

St Ann St.
Gayoso St.

Bienville St.

Orleans Ave.

Dupre St.
White St.

Edgar Degas
House Museum
Courtyard
and Inn

Iberville St.

St Peter St.

Easton Pk.

Canal St.

Dorgenois St.

Rochebiave St.

Tonti St.

Miro St.
Galvez St.

Genois St.
Clark St.

Rendon St.
Lopez St.
Salcedo St.
Gayoso St.

Toulouse St.

Lafitte St.

90

Johnson St.

✗
Finn McCool's
Irish Pub

Jefferson Davis Pkwy.

Cleveland St.

Prieur St.

Roman St.

Palmyra St.

Broad Street

St Louis St.

TREME

Banks St.

10

GETTING HERE AND AROUND

From downtown there are two easy ways to get into Mid-City: Canal Street or Esplanade Avenue, both of which border the French Quarter. There are two **streetcar** lines that run down Canal Street: one will take you straight down Canal to Metairie Cemetery, and the other will turn down Carrollton Avenue and deposit you right in front of City Park. The **No. 91 Jackson-Esplanade bus,** which you can catch anywhere along Rampart Street in the French Quarter, turns onto Esplanade Avenue, stops near the Degas House, and also takes you right by City Park. The streetcar ride from downtown takes approximately 30 minutes. Allow about 15 minutes for the bus ride down Esplanade. The **Lafitte Greenway** connects Mid-City to the French Quarter via a paved biking and walking path with pleasant city views. The Greenway begins at Basin Street in the French Quarter and ends at the entrance to City Park

MAKING THE MOST OF YOUR TIME

City Park and the Mid-City **cemeteries** are generally open during daylight hours, but the **outdoor patios** of Esplanade Avenue restaurants and cafés stay open well into the night. Allow yourself at least half a day and start in the afternoon, so you can enjoy both activities. **City Park** is one of the largest urban parks in the nation, and you could easily spend much of your time exploring its art collections, hiking trails, vintage carousel, botanical gardens, and gondola rides.

SAFETY

Things can change from cute to creepy in the span of a block or two, so exercise good judgment if you go walking off major streets at night. The areas around Bayou St. John and City Park tend to be safe, especially during daylight hours, but areas closer to Broad Street are rougher, and should be avoided on foot at night. Residential areas surrounding Canal Street and Carrollton Avenue are generally well trafficked and safe.

TOP REASONS TO GO

Explore City Park. This gorgeous and sprawling park is home to dozens of attractions, including a museum, sculpture garden, and amusement park.

Take a cemetery tour. Mid-City has some of the largest, safest, and best-kept cemeteries in New Orleans.

Stroll along Bayou St. John. The grassy banks offer biking and walking trails and splendid views of some of the most historic and lovely homes and landmarks in the city.

QUICK BITES

Fair Grinds Coffeehouse. Just off Esplanade Avenue, Fair Grinds Coffeehouse is the neighborhood spot for fair-trade coffee, tea, and snacks—including vegan treats. There's an upstairs balcony for alfresco dining, and live music at least twice a week. ⊠ *3133 Ponce de Leon St., Bayou St. John* ☎ *504/913–9072* ⊕ *www. fairgrinds.com* ⊟ *No credit cards.*

Finn McCool's Irish Pub. This convivial spot is more than just your average corner bar: it streams European soccer games (opening as early as 7 am to do so) and hosts a popular trivia night on Monday. The kitchen serves sophisticated pub food. ⊠ *3701 Banks St., Mid-City* ☎ *504/486–9080* ⊕ *www.finnmccools.com* ⊟ *No credit cards.*

7

Sightseeing ★★	With their tree-lined streets and avenues, gathering places,
Dining ★	and landmarks, the Mid-City and Bayou St. John neighbor-
Lodging ★	hoods are decidedly more tranquil than their downtown
Shopping ★	counterparts. You're not likely to find "Huge-Ass Beers to
Nightlife ★	Go" or music blaring out of every doorway here. Instead,

you'll find a quieter charm in the gardens, galleries, and lagoons of City Park, in the cemeteries with their elaborately constructed tombs, and on the tree-shaded patios and decks of restaurants and cafés, where you can listen to the church bells keep time as you relax with a cold drink.

Updated by
Cameron
Quincy Todd

Above the French Quarter and below the lakefront, neither Uptown nor quite downtown, Mid-City embraces everything from massive, lush City Park to storefronts along gritty Broad Street. Much of this primarily working-class neighborhood was low-lying swamplands until the late 1800s, and you can still see where the "high ground" was, along the Esplanade Ridge (now Esplanade Avenue). These are the stretches with many of the largest historic houses, churches, and landmarks. Along Carrollton Avenue you can find everything from an old-school Italian ice-cream parlor to strips of inexpensive Central American restaurants. The neighborhood hosts more than a dozen festivals and celebrations a year, from block parties like the Bayou Boogaloo to grand-scale mega-events like the Voodoo Experience. It's easy to figure out which festival is approaching by the bright flags that spring up on people's porches.

MID-CITY

TOP ATTRACTIONS

FAMILY

Fodor'sChoice

★

City Park. Founded in 1854, this 1,300-acre expanse of moss-draped oaks and 11 miles of gentle lagoons is just 2 miles from the French Quarter, but feels like it could be a world apart. With the largest collection of live oaks in the world, including old grove trees that are more than 600 years old, City Park offers a certain natural majesty that's difficult to find in most other urban areas. The art-deco benches, fountains, bridges, and ironwork are remnants of a 1930s Works Progress Administration (WPA) refurbishment and add to the dreamy scenery that visitors enjoy boating and biking through. Within the park are the **New Orleans Museum of Art,** the **Sydney and Walda Besthoff Sculpture Garden,** the **New Orleans Botanical Garden,** the kid-friendly **Carousel Gardens Amusement Park,** a golf course, equestrian stable, sports facilities, and picnic areas. Check the park's website for seasonal activities and special events, such as music festivals, the annual Easter egg hunt, and the eye-popping wonderland that is Celebration in the Oaks between Thanksgiving and New Year's Day. The Morning Call coffee stand, behind the Sculpture Garden, serves hot beignets and café au lait 24/7. Most of the park's offerings are free, but several of the venues inside City Park charge separate admission fees.

7

Open seasonally, the 17-ride **Carousel Gardens Amusement Park** (☎ *504/483–9402; ✉ $4 admission, rides $3 each)* has a New Orleans treasure as its centerpiece: a 1906 carousel (one of only 100 antique wooden carousels left in the country) listed on the National Register of Historic Places. In addition to the cherished "flying horses," the park has rides like the new Musik Express, Rockin' Tug, Coney Tower, Ferris Wheel, Bumper Cars, Monkey Jump, Red Baron miniplane, Scrambler, and Tilt-a-Whirl. The rides here are mostly geared to children, not hard-core thrill seekers, but adults and kids alike enjoy the miniature train that takes passengers on a gentle sightseeing tour through City Park. There are also two 18-hole miniature golf courses, one with a New Orleans theme and one with a Louisiana theme.

The **New Orleans Botanical Garden** (☎ *504/483–9386; ✉ $6)*, opened in 1936 as a Depression-era project of the WPA, is one of the few remaining examples of public garden design from the art-deco period. The garden's collections contain more than 2,000 varieties of plants from all over the world, complemented by sites such as the Conservatory, the Pavilion of the Two Sisters, and the Yakumo Nihon Teien Japanese Garden, as well as theme gardens containing aquatics, roses, native plants, ornamental trees, and shrubs and perennials. The garden showcases three notable talents: New Orleans architect Richard Koch, landscape architect William Wiedorn, and artist Enrique Alférez. Adding a touch of fun, the Historic Train Garden, open on weekends, offers visitors the chance to enjoy baguette-size cars rolling through a miniature version of New Orleans.

City Park is one of the most serene places in all of New Orleans.

Featuring figures and settings from classic children's literature, the whimsical **Storyland** (☎ 504/483–9402; ✉ $4), adjacent to the amusement park, has been a favorite romping ground for generations of New Orleans kids. Youngsters can climb aboard Captain Hook's pirate ship, visit the old lady who lived in a shoe, and journey with Pinocchio into the mouth of a whale. There are more than 25 larger-than-life storybook exhibits in all. ⊠ *Bordered by City Park Ave., Robert E. Lee Blvd., Marconi Dr., and Bayou St. John, Mid-City* ☎ *504/482–4888* ⊕ *www. neworleanscitypark.com.*

FAMILY

Fodor'sChoice

★

New Orleans Museum of Art (NOMA). Gracing the main entrance to City Park since 1911, this traditional fine-arts museum draws from classic Greek architecture, with several modern wings that bring additional light and space to the grand old building. NOMA now has 46 galleries housing an outstanding permanent collection. Made up of nearly 40,000 objects, the installations and exhibits represent historical periods from the Italian Renaissance to the best of the contemporary world. A wealth of American and European art—French, in particular—makes up much of the collection, with works by Monet, Renoir, Picasso, Cornell, and Pollock. Louisiana artists are also well represented, and the museum boasts photography, ceramics, and glassworks from cultures around the globe, plus outstanding holdings in African, pre-Columbian, and Asian art. In addition, the museum offers a year-round schedule of traveling and special exhibitions, events, tours, and public programs.

Henry Moore's handsome *Reclining Mother and Child* greets visitors at the entrance of the **Sydney and Walda Besthoff Sculpture Garden.** Most of the garden's 60-some sculptures, representing some of the

CLOSE UP

Mid-City's Cemeteries

One of Mid-City's biggest attractions is its many cemeteries, which have a haunting beauty. These "cities of the dead" are the final resting places of famous musicians, Storyville madams, voodoo practitioners, politicians, and pirates.

You'll find few if any burials here, though; the dead are in aboveground tombs instead. New Orleans, most of which lies below sea level, has a high water table, which caused (and continues to cause, in some circumstances) buried coffins to pop out of the ground during a heavy rain. Raised graves and vaulted tombs were also an old tradition among the French and Spanish.

Mid-City cemeteries are some of the safest and most-trafficked in the city. Our favorite out here is **St. Louis Cemetery No. 3**, but **Cypress Grove Cemetery** or **Lake Lawn Metairie**

Cemetery are good alternatives. It all depends on what's most convenient.

Located in a less-visited cemetery across from Lake Lawn Metairie, visitors can take a somber pause to remember victims at the **Hurricane Katrina Memorial**

Save Our Cemeteries. This is a great source for historical knowledge, safety info, and tours. ⊠ *Mid-City* ☎ *504/525–3377* ⊕ *www.saveo-urcemeteries.org.*

CEMETERY SYMBOLISM

Most vaults or plots are adorned with symbols, revealing a secret language between the living and dead. An anchor stands for hope, a broken column represents a life cut short, and a broken flower symbolizes a life terminated. Sculpted ivy is a symbol of enduring friendship. Clasped hands stand for unity and love, even after death.

7

biggest names in modern art, were donated by avid local collector Sydney Besthoff. Meandering trails and bridges carry visitors over bayou lagoons and past a fascinating combination of famed traditional sculpture and contemporary works, including major pieces by Jacques Lipchitz, Barbara Hepworth, and Joel Shapiro. The garden is open daily from 10 to 4:45; admission is free. ⊠ *City Park, 1 Collins Diboll Circle, Mid-City* ☎ *504/658–4100* ⊕ *www.noma.org* 🎟 *$12.*

WORTH NOTING

Cypress Grove Cemetery. This expansive and still-used cemetery was founded by the Fireman's Charitable and Benevolent Association in 1840. Over time, as the cemetery expanded, other societies and individuals joined the volunteer firemen in building impressive monuments. Leading architects and craftsmen were called upon to design and build tombs commemorating the lives of many of New Orleans's most prominent citizens. Crafted in marble, granite, and cast iron, tombs at Cypress Grove are among the nation's leading examples of memorial architecture. Of particular note is the Chinese Soon On Tong Association's tomb, which features a grate in front so that visitors can burn prayers written on paper in it. ⊠ *120 City Park Ave., Mid-City.*

Lake Lawn Metairie Cemetery. The largest cemetery in the metropolitan area, known to locals simply as Metairie Cemetery, is the final resting place of nine Louisiana governors, seven New Orleans mayors, three Confederate generals, and musician Louis Prima. Many of New Orleans's prominent families are also interred here in elaborate monuments ranging from Gothic crypts to Romanesque mausoleums to Egyptian pyramids. The arrangement of tombs reflects the cemetery's former life as a horse-racing track, with the tombs arranged around the perimeter and interior. ⊠ *5100 Pontchartrain Blvd., Mid-City* ⊕ *www. lakelawnmetairie.com.*

BAYOU ST. JOHN

Just up Esplanade Avenue from the French Quarter, the Bayou St. John neighborhood is known for its beautiful shady lanes, gorgeous homes, and laid-back vibe. Great restaurants, cafés, and bars dot the landscape, with sidewalk seating and relaxed patios. It's also home to the New Orleans Fairgrounds Race Course and Slots, one of the nation's major horse-racing venues, and the world-famous New Orleans Jazz and Heritage Festival. St. Louis Cemetery No. 3 opens its gates onto Esplanade Avenue, inviting visitors to explore rows of aboveground tombs and mausoleums. At the end of the avenue you'll discover Bayou St. John, the scenic waterway that begins in Mid-City, which meanders through Faubourg St. John and ends at the lakefront. You'll find all sorts of people out enjoying the wide grassy banks—biking, fishing, or just strolling along and admiring the reflection of a sunset on the smooth water.

TOP ATTRACTIONS

Bayou St. John. A bayou is a natural inlet, usually a slow-moving, narrow waterway that emerges from the swamp at one end and joins a larger body of water at the other. This bayou—the only one remaining in New Orleans—borders City Park on the east and extends about 7 miles from Lake Pontchartrain to just past Orleans Avenue. It is named for John the Baptist. June 23 (St. John's Eve, and therefore the day before his feast day) was the most important day in the year for voodoo practitioners, and it was notoriously celebrated on the bayou's banks in the 1800s. The first European settlers in the area, most likely trappers, coexisted with Native Americans here beginning in 1704. Today, the bayou is still a popular destination among New Orleanians, whether for tradition's sake—as is the case for the famed Mardi Gras Indians, who gather here for their annual celebrations—for a festival such as the Bayou Boogaloo in May, or simply for a relaxing afternoon of fishing, canoeing, or picnicking along the grassy banks. Scenic biking and walking trails run alongside the waterway all the way to the lake, where you can watch the graceful old homes of picturesque Moss Street morph into the dazzling waterfront mansions of Bancroft Drive. ⊠ *From the foot of Jefferson Davis Pkwy. to Lakeshore Dr., Bayou St. John.*

Pitot House. One of the few surviving houses that lined the bayou in the late 1700s, and the only Creole colonial–style country house in the city open to the public, Pitot House is named for James Pitot, who bought the property in 1810 as a country home for his family. In addition to being one of the city's most prosperous merchants, Pitot served as New Orleans mayor from 1804 to 1805, the city's first after the Louisiana Purchase, and later as parish court judge. The Pitot House was restored and moved 200 feet to its current location in the 1960s to make way for the expansion of Cabrini High School. It is noteworthy for its stuccoed brick-and-post construction, an example of which is exposed on the second floor. The house is typical of the West Indies style brought to Louisiana by early colonists, with galleries around the house that protect the interior from both rain and sunshine. There aren't any interior halls to stifle ventilation, and the doors are lined up with one another to encourage a cross breeze. The house is furnished with period antiques from the United States, including special pieces from Louisiana. ✉ *1440 Moss St., Bayou St. John* ☎ *504/482–0312* ⊕ *www. louisianalandmarks.org* 🎫 *$10.*

St. Louis Cemetery No. 3. One block from the entrance to City Park, at the end of Esplanade Avenue, stands this cemetery, on an area of high ground along Bayou St. John. It opened in 1854 on the site of an old leper colony. Governor Galvez had exiled the lepers here during the yellow fever outbreak of 1853, but they were later removed to make room for the dead. The remains of Storyville photographer E. J. Bellocq are here, and the cemetery is notable for its neat rows of elaborate aboveground crypts, mausoleums, and carved stone angels. ✉ *3428 Esplanade Ave., Bayou St. John* ⊕ *www.saveourcemeteries.org.*

WORTH NOTING

FAMILY **Alcée Fortier Park.** Situated at Esplanade Avenue and Mystery Street, this tiny sliver of a park was named for the philanthropist and professor Alcée Fortier, who owned much of the surrounding area in the late 19th century and who founded a public school. A neighborhood favorite, the park is almost completely maintained by the efforts of local volunteers, who tend the lush landscaping, which includes palms, caladiums, and azaleas, keep up the collection of whimsical sculptures and art, and make sure the concrete chess tables are ready for game time (complete with baskets of chess pieces). A focal point of the Bayou St. John neighborhood, Alcée Fortier Park is surrounded by a concentration of hip restaurants and neighborhood grocers. ✉ *Esplanade Ave. at Mystery St., Bayou St. John.*

Cabrini High School and Mother Cabrini Shrine. Mother Frances Cabrini, the first American citizen to become a saint (canonized in 1946), purchased the land between Esplanade Avenue and Bayou St. John near City Park in 1905 and built the Sacred Heart Orphan Asylum here. She stayed in the Pitot House, which was on her property until she gave it to the city during construction of the orphanage. In 1959 the institution was converted to a girls' high school in Mother Cabrini's name. Her bedroom here, preserved as it was in her time, is filled with personal effects and maintained as a shrine. Tours of her room and Sacred Heart Chapel are available by appointment. ⊠ *1400 Moss St., Bayou St. John* ☎ *504/483–8690* ⊕ *www.cabrinihigh.com/saint-frances-cabrini-shrine.*

Edgar Degas House Museum, Courtyard, and Inn. The Impressionist Edgar Degas, whose Creole mother and grandmother were born in New Orleans, stayed with his cousins in this house during an 1872 visit to New Orleans, producing 18 paintings and four drawings while here. "This is a new style of painting," Degas wrote in one of the five known letters he sent from New Orleans, explaining that the breakthrough he experienced here led to "better art." Today, this house museum and bed-and-breakfast offers public tours, given by Degas's great-grandnieces, which include the screening of an award-winning film on Degas's family and their sojourn in New Orleans, plus a walk through the historic neighborhood focusing on details from the artist's letters. Feel free to drop by for a look if you're in the vicinity, but check the website or call ahead for event dates or to make an appointment for a full tour. ⊠ *2306 Esplanade Ave., Bayou St. John* ☎ *504/821–5009* ⊕ *www.degashouse. com* ⊠ *$29.*

Fair Grounds Race Course and Slots. The third-oldest racetrack in the country sits just off Esplanade Avenue, among the houses of Bayou St. John. The popular Starlight Racing series, held Friday nights, features live music, DJs, food trucks, a beer garden, and go-go dancers dressed as jockeys. The grounds are also home to the New Orleans Jazz and Heritage Festival. For the clubhouse, be sure to make reservations and be aware that proper attire is required—in this case that means collared shirts, closed shoes, and no shorts. ⊠ *1751 Gentilly Blvd., Bayou St. John* ☎ *504/943–2200 box and restaurant reservations, 504/944–5515 general info* ⊕ *www.fairgroundsracecourse.com* ⊠ *Grandstand free, clubhouse $10* ☉ *Closed May–Oct.*

Luling Mansion. Also called the "Jockey's Mansion," this massive, three-story Italianate mansion is a neighborhood landmark (and now a popular setting for Hollywood film crews). Designed by the prominent New Orleans architect James Gallier Jr., it was built in 1865 for Florence A. Luling, whose family had made a fortune selling turpentine to Union soldiers when they occupied New Orleans during the Civil War. When the Louisiana Jockey Club took over the Creole Race Course (now the Fair Grounds) in 1871, they purchased the mansion and used it as a clubhouse for the next 20-odd years. It is not open to the public. ⊠ *1436–1438 Leda St., Bayou St. John.*

WHERE TO EAT

Updated by Cameron Quincy Todd

New Orleanians are obsessed with food. Over lunch they're likely talking about dinner. Ask where to get the best gumbo, and you'll spark a heated debate among city natives.

Everyone, no matter what neighborhood they're from or what they do for a living, wants a plate of red beans and rice on Monday, has a favorite spot for a roast beef po'boy, and holds strong opinions about the proper flavor for a shaved ice "sno-ball."

The menus of New Orleans's restaurants reflect the many cultures that have contributed to this always-simmering culinary gumbo pot over the last three centuries. It's easy to find French, African, Spanish, German, Italian, and Caribbean influences—and increasingly Asian and Latin American as well. The speckled trout amandine at Antoine's could have been on the menu when the French Creole institution opened in 1840. Across the Mississippi River on the West Bank, Tan Dinh serves fragrant bowls of pho that remind New Orleans's large Vietnamese population of the home they left in the 1970s. And at Compère Lapin, Chef Nina Compton brings expert French and Italian fine-dining traditions to the down-home flavors of her St. Lucia childhood, and of her new home in the Gulf South.

For years New Orleans paid little attention to food trends from the East and West coasts. Recently, however, the city has taken more notice of the "latest things." In Orleans Parish you'll now find gastropubs, gourmet burgers, and numerous small-plate specialists. In a town where people track the crawfish season as closely as the pennant race, no one has to preach the virtues of eating seasonally. New Orleans is still one of the most exciting places to eat in America. There's no danger that will change.

NEW ORLEANS DINING PLANNER

RESERVATIONS

Most restaurants in New Orleans accept reservations, and many popular places are booked quickly, especially on weekend nights. Reservations are always a good idea: we mention them only when they're essential or not accepted. Reserving several weeks ahead is not too far in advance for trips during Mardi Gras, French Quarter Fest, Jazz Fest, and other special events.

WHAT TO WEAR

Unless otherwise noted, restaurants listed in this book allow casual dress. Reviews mention dress only when men are required to wear a jacket or tie. In a luxury restaurant or in one of the old-line, conservative Creole places, dress appropriately.

TIPPING

The standard for tipping in New Orleans is no different from that in the rest of the country—at least 15% or 20%. Sales tax for restaurants is 10%, which means that doubling the tax is a widespread practice.

PRICES

Meals in the city's more upscale restaurants cost about what you'd expect to pay in other U.S. cities. Bargains are found in the more casual restaurants, where a simple lunch or dinner can frequently be had for less than $25. However, even the more expensive restaurants offer fixed-price menus of three or four courses for substantially less than what an à la carte meal costs. Serving sizes are more than generous—some would say unmanageable for the average eater—so many diners order two appetizers rather than a starter and a main course, which can make ordering dessert more practical. Some restaurants offer small- or large-plate options.

WHAT IT COSTS				
	$	$$	$$$	$$$$
Restaurants	under $17	$17–$25	$26–$35	over $35

Restaurant prices in the reviews are the average cost of a main course at dinner or, if dinner is not served, at lunch.

USING THE MAPS

Use the coordinates (✛ 3:F2) at the end of each review to locate properties in each map. The first number after the symbol indicates the map number. Following that is the property's coordinate on the map grid.

RESTAURANT REVIEWS

Listed alphabetically within neighborhood. Restaurant reviews have been shortened. For full information, visit Fodors.com.

THE FRENCH QUARTER

In the city's oldest neighborhood, grand restaurants that opened before the Civil War sit around the corner from contemporary, cutting-edge destinations. The Quarter, as locals call it, is a living neighborhood, and though it's packed with tourists, you'll certainly bump into residents grabbing a cup of coffee or tucking into a po'boy for lunch.

$ ✕ **Acme Oyster House.** A rough-edge classic in every way, this no-frills
SEAFOOD   eatery at the entrance to the French Quarter is a prime source for briny,
FAMILY   chilled Gulf oysters; legendary shrimp, oyster, and roast-beef po'boys;
and tender, expertly seasoned red beans and rice. Even locals can't
resist, although most opt for the less crowded, if less charming, suburban branches (there's one in Metairie). **Known for:** fresh oysters; long
lines; local specialties. ⑤ *Average main: $15* ✉ *724 Iberville St., French
Quarter* ☎ *504/522–5973* ⊕ *www.acmeoyster.com* ✛ *1:D3.*

$ ✕ **Angeline.** Though a relative newcomer to a crowded scene of white-
SOUTHERN   tablecloth bistros in the French Quarter, Angeline stands out for
excellent food, quality service, and relatively fair prices. The brunch
is particularly palate-pleasing, where the elevated Southern flavors of
the menu (renditions of grits, fried chicken, and buttermilk donuts)
really shine. **Known for:** Gulf fish; Southern brunch; fried chicken and
biscuits. ⑤ *Average main: $15* ✉ *1032 Chartres St., French Quarter*
☎ *504/308–3106* ⊕ *www.angelinenola.com* ✛ *1:B4.*

$$$$ ✕ **Antoine's.** Though some people believe Antoine's heyday passed before
CREOLE   the turn of the 20th century, others wouldn't leave New Orleans without at least one order of the original oysters Rockefeller—baked oysters
topped with a parsley-based sauce and bread crumbs. Other notables
on the bilingual menu include *pommes de terre soufflées* (fried potato
puffs), *poisson amadine* or *meuniere* (fish prepared in toasted almond
or brown butter-and-lemon sauce), and baked Alaska. **Known for:** old-
school charm; oysters Rockefeller; baked Alaska. ⑤ *Average main: $36*
✉ *713 St. Louis St., French Quarter* ☎ *504/581–4422* ⊕ *www.antoines.
com* ⊗ *No dinner Sun.* ✛ *1:C3.*

$$$ ✕ **Arnaud's.** This grande dame of classic Creole restaurants still sparkles.
CREOLE   In the main dining room, ornate etched glass reflects light from charm-
Fodor's Choice   ing old chandeliers while the late founder, Arnaud Cazenave, gazes from
★   an oil portrait. **Known for:** Mardi Gras museum; char-grilled oyster
specialties; classic cocktails. ⑤ *Average main: $35* ✉ *813 Bienville St.,
French Quarter* ☎ *504/523–5433* ⊕ *www.arnaudsrestaurant.com* ⊗ *No
lunch Mon.–Sat.* ✛ *1:D3.*

$$$ ✕ **Bayona.** "New World" is the label Louisiana native Susan Spicer
MODERN   applies to her cooking style, the delicious hallmarks of which include
AMERICAN   goat cheese crouton with mushrooms in madeira cream, a Bayona spe-
Fodor's Choice   cialty, and delightfully flavorful vegetable soups, like Caribbean pump-
★   kin or cream of garlic. A legendary favorite at lunch is the sandwich of
smoked duck, cashew peanut butter, and pepper jelly. **Known for:** chef
Susan Spicer; smoked duck sandwich; global flavors. ⑤ *Average main:
$30* ✉ *430 Dauphine St., French Quarter* ☎ *504/525–4455* ⊕ *www.
bayona.com* ⊗ *Closed Sun. No lunch Mon. and Tues.* ✛ *1:C3.*

$$$ ✕ **Bourbon House.** On one of the French Quarter's busiest corners is
CREOLE   Dickie Brennan's biggest and flashiest restaurant yet (he also owns Pal-
ace Café and Dickie Brennan's Steakhouse), and it's a solid hit with
seafood aficionados and—you guessed it—bourbon lovers (there are
five flights to choose from and a vast selection of 90 American whiskeys
to boot). The raw bar is prime real estate, with its sterling oysters on
the half shell, chilled seafood platters, and antique, decorative oyster
plates, but the elegant main dining room is more appropriate for digging

into the Creole catalog—charbroiled oysters, boiled shrimp, and Gulf fish "on the half shell" with lump crab meat. **Known for:** bourbon-milk punch; raw bar; bourbon flights. $ *Average main: $26* ⊠ *144 Bourbon St., French Quarter* ☎ *504/522–0111* ⊕ *www.bourbonhouse. com* ✛ *1:D3.*

$$$ ✕ **Brennan's.** This luxuriously appointed restaurant, located in a gor-
CREOLE geous, salmon-pink, circa-1795 building, closed for a little over a year, then reopened in 2014 to local fanfare. And what's not to love? **Known for:** tourists; Creole brunch; bananas Foster. $ *Average main: $35* ⊠ *417 Royal St., French Quarter* ☎ *504/525–9711* ⊕ *www.bren-nansneworleans.com* ✛ *1:C3.*

$$$ ✕ **Broussard's.** If local restaurants were judged solely by the beauty of
CREOLE their courtyards, Broussard's would certainly be a standout, but the food here is also outstanding. Expect dishes like crispy shrimp toast with pickled okra slaw; Creole crab croquettes; and broiled redfish with a rosemary-and-mustard crust—you won't forget your meal anytime soon. **Known for:** charming courtyard; Sunday jazz; redfish. $ *Average main: $30* ⊠ *819 Conti St., French Quarter* ☎ *504/581–3866* ⊕ *www. broussards.com* ⊘ *No lunch Mon.–Sat.* ✛ *1:C3.*

$$$ ✕ **Cafe Amelie.** There's no shortage of charming courtyards in the
AMERICAN French Quarter, but the candlelit, ivy-covered stone carriageway at Cafe Amelie is one of the most romantic places to get a gourmet meal. The Louisiana-inspired entrées feature hearty portions of lamb steak, pork chops, and fresh seafood. **Known for:** good service; creative cock-tails; romantic setting. $ *Average main: $27* ⊠ *912 Royal St., French Quarter* ☎ *504/412–8965* ⊕ *www.cafeamelie.com* ⊘ *Closed Mon. and Tues.* ✛ *1:B4.*

$ ✕ **Café du Monde.** No visit to New Orleans is complete without a chic-
CAFÉ ory-laced café au lait paired with the addictive, sugar-dusted beignets at
FAMILY this venerable institution. The tables under the green-and-white-stripe
Fodor's Choice awning are jammed with locals and tourists at almost every hour.
★ **Known for:** beignets; café au lait; local landmark. $ *Average main: $3* ⊠ *800 Decatur St., French Quarter* ☎ *504/525–4544* ⊕ *www.cafedu-monde.com* ✛ *1:C4.*

$ ✕ **Central Grocery.** This old-fashioned grocery store creates authentic
DELI muffulettas, a gastronomic gift from the city's Italian immigrants.
FAMILY Made by filling nearly 10-inch round loaves of seeded bread with ham, salami, provolone and Emmentaler cheeses, and olive salad, the muf-fuletta is nearly as popular locally as the po'boy (Central Grocery also sells a vegetarian version). **Known for:** muffulettas; lively setting; cen-tral location. $ *Average main: $8* ⊠ *923 Decatur St., French Quarter* ☎ *504/523–1620* ⊕ *www.centralgrocery.com* ⊘ *Closed Sun. and Mon. No dinner* ✛ *1:C4.*

$ ✕ **Croissant d'Or Patisserie.** In a quiet corner of the French Quarter, you'll
CAFÉ have to look for the quaint Croissant d'Or Patisserie. Once you've found it, you'll understand why locals and visitors return to this col-orful pastry shop for excellent and authentic French croissants, pies, tarts, and custards, as well as an imaginative selection of soups, salads, and sandwiches (don't miss the hot croissant sandwiches with creamy béchamel sauce). **Known for:** breakfast; croissaint sandwiches; authentic

8

French pastries. ⑤ *Average main: $5* ⊠ *617 Ursulines St., French Quarter* ☎ *504/524–4663* ⊕ *www.croissantdornola.com* ⊘ *Closed Tues. No dinner* ✛ *1:B4.*

$$$$ ✕ **Dickie Brennan's Steakhouse.** "Straightforward steaks with a New
STEAKHOUSE   Orleans touch" are the words to live by at this clubby shrine to red meat, the creation of a younger member of the Brennan family of restaurateurs, who also runs Palace Café and the Bourbon House. Start with stellar martinis in the dark cherrywood-paneled lounge, then head back to the cavernous dining room to dig into classic cuts of top-quality beef and seafood. **Known for:** elegant atmosphere; steak; Creole sides. ⑤ *Average main: $36* ⊠ *716 Iberville St., French Quarter* ☎ *504/522–2467* ⊕ *www.dickiebrennanssteakhouse.com* ⊘ *No lunch Sun.–Thurs.* ✛ *1:D3.*

$$$ ✕ **Galatoire's.** With many of its recipes dating to 1905, Galatoire's epito-
CREOLE   mizes the old-style French Creole bistro. Fried oysters and bacon en
Fodor's Choice   brochette are worth every calorie, and the brick-red rémoulade sauce
★   sets a high standard. **Known for:** rémoulade sauce; formal dress; old-school vibes. ⑤ *Average main: $30* ⊠ *209 Bourbon St., French Quarter* ☎ *504/525–2021* ⊕ *www.galatoires.com* ⊘ *Closed Mon.* 🎩 *Jacket required* ✛ *1:D3.*

$ ✕ **Green Goddess.** At this cozy (read: small) restaurant in the heart of
ECLECTIC   the French Quarter, diners are wowed by the inventive and globally inspired cuisine, though the service is a bit eclectic, too. Menus change regularly, but may feature apple cheddar French toast and beet burrata kale salad for lunch, or a bacon sundae with pecan-praline ice cream for dessert. **Known for:** French toast; sandwiches; vegetarian options. ⑤ *Average main: $15* ⊠ *307 Exchange Pl., French Quarter* ☎ *504/301–3347* ⊕ *www.greengoddessrestaurant.com* ⊘ *Closed Mon. and Tues.* ✛ *1:D3.*

$ ✕ **Gumbo Shop.** Even given a few modern touches—like the vegetarian
CREOLE   gumbo offered daily—this place evokes a sense of old New Orleans. The
FAMILY   menu is chock-full of regional culinary anchors: jambalaya, shrimp Creole, rémoulade sauce, red beans and rice, bread pudding, and seafood and chicken-and-sausage gumbos, all heavily flavored with tradition but easy on the wallet. **Known for:** classic Creole food; cheap prices; shabby-chic decor. ⑤ *Average main: $14* ⊠ *630 St. Peter St., French Quarter* ☎ *504/525–1486* ⊕ *www.gumboshop.com* ✛ *1:C4.*

$$$ ✕ **GW Fins.** If you're looking for seafood, you won't be disappointed
SEAFOOD   with GW Fins, which impresses with quality and variety—the bounty of fish species from around the world is among the menu's lures. Chef Tenney Flynn's menu changes daily, depending on what's fresh, but typical dishes have included luscious lobster dumplings, Hawaiian big-eye tuna, and sautéed rainbow trout with spinach, oysters, and shiitake mushrooms. **Known for:** fresh fish; modern setting; creative menu. ⑤ *Average main: $27* ⊠ *808 Bienville St., French Quarter* ☎ *504/581–3467* ⊕ *www.gwfins.com* ⊘ *No lunch* ✛ *1:D3.*

$ ✕ **Hermes Bar.** The allure of Hermes Bar is that you'll have your pick of
CREOLE   the classic dishes that made Antoine's (founded in 1840) famous, without committing to a full-price meal in its austere dining room. Elegant bar snacks such as oysters Rockefeller, shrimp rémoulade, and fried eggplant sticks make just as grand a meal, with the added benefit of a

front-row view of the Bourbon Street crowd. **Known for:** great cocktails; classic small bites; elegant setting. $ *Average main: $13* ⊠ *713 St. Louis St., French Quarter* ☎ *504/581–4422* ⊕ *www.antoines.com* ⊙ *No dinner Sun.* ✢ *1:C3.*

$$ ✕ **Irene's Cuisine.** The walls here are festooned with enough snapshots, garlic braids, and crockery for at least two more restaurants, but it all just adds to the charm of this cozy Italian-Creole eatery. From Irene DiPietro's kitchen come succulent roast chicken brushed with olive oil, rosemary, and garlic; delicious, velvety soups; and fresh shrimp, aggressively seasoned and grilled before they join linguine glistening with herbed olive oil. **Known for:** piano bar; local vibe; long waits. $ *Average main: $20* ⊠ *539 St. Philip St., French Quarter* ☎ *504/529–8811* ⊙ *Closed Sun. No lunch* ✢ *1:B4.*

ITALIAN
FAMILY

$$ ✕ **The Italian Barrel.** Verona-born chef Samantha Castagnetti turns out sumptuous, authentic northern Italian pasta dishes, like fusilli with peas, shallots, and Italian prosciutto in an elegant white cream sauce, alongside meaty mains, such as veal osso buco over decadent polenta, at this recently expanded French Quarter eatery. This is the kind of place that turns first dates into lifelong affairs; you'll feel like you're dining at nonna's house. **Known for:** hearty pasta; affordable wine list; people-watching. $ *Average main: $25* ⊠ *430 Barracks St., French Quarter* ☎ *504/569–0198* ⊕ *www.theitalianbarrel.com* ▭ *No credit cards* ✢ *1:B5.*

ITALIAN

$ ✕ **Johnny's Po-boys.** Strangely enough, good po'boys are hard to find in the French Quarter. Established in 1950, Johnny's compensates for that scarcity with a cornucopia of overstuffed options, even though quality is inconsistent and the prices somewhat inflated for the tourist trade. **Known for:** classic po'boys; roast beef; tourists. $ *Average main: $8* ⊠ *511 St. Louis St., French Quarter* ☎ *504/524–8129* ⊕ *johnnyspoboy. com* ⊙ *No dinner* ✢ *1:D4.*

DELI
FAMILY

8

$ ✕ **Killer Po Boys.** The chefs at this no-frills sandwich stand showcase their creative, globally inspired talents within the traditional French loaf of a po'boy, where you're more likely to see pork belly and smoked salmon on the menu than the typical roast beef and fried seafood standards. What started as a small kitchen in the back of popular Erin Rose bar (where you can still order the sandwiches) is now one of the most reliable places to get a cheap, interesting meal in the Quarter. **Known for:** creative po'boys; vegetarian options; local craft beer. $ *Average main: $11* ⊠ *219 Dauphine St., French Quarter* ☎ *504/462–2731* ⊕ *www. killerpoboys.com* ⊙ *Closed Tues.* ✢ *1:D2.*

DELI

$$ ✕ **Kingfish.** Named after former Louisiana Governor Huey P. Long, who went by the nickname "Kingfish," this stylish French Quarter restaurant pays homage to the Jazz Age, with its pressed-tin ceilings and suspendered bartenders (the excellent craft cocktail list was written by local legend Chris McMillian). **Known for:** snazzy cocktails; good service; small plates. $ *Average main: $22* ⊠ *337 Chartres St., French Quarter* ☎ *504/598–5005* ⊕ *www.kingfishneworleans.com* ▭ *No credit cards* ✢ *1:D3.*

CREOLE

$$$ ✕ **K-Paul's Louisiana Kitchen.** At this comfortable French Quarter café with glossy wooden floors and exposed brick, chef Paul Prudhomme

CAJUN

Mardi Gras Sweet Spotlight: The King Cake

New Orleans is known for lots of local flavor, from pralines and po'boys to beignets and chicory coffee. But for a true taste of Mardi Gras, you can't beat a King Cake.

The origins of the King Cake go back to early-12th-century Europe, when a similar type of cake was baked to represent the arrival of the biblical Three Kings on the 12th day after Christmas. It is thought that French immigrants passed along the tradition to the residents of New Orleans in the late 19th century. Many years and iterations later, the King Cake lives on, and starting on the Epiphany (January 6, the first day of Mardi Gras) through Fat Tuesday (the day before Ash Wednesday), no party is complete without a King Cake at hand.

Traditional King Cakes are a ring-shape, cinnamon-flavored brioche with purple, gold, and green icing for the colors of Mardi Gras. Nowadays King Cakes come in a variety of flavors and fillings, like cream cheese, almond, praline, or chocolate. A small plastic toy baby, said to represent Baby Jesus, is hidden inside the cake. It's tradition that whoever gets the slice with the hidden baby must host the next Mardi Gras party or buy the King Cake for the next celebration.

You can find them all around the area in special bakeries and local grocery stores.

added "Cajun" to America's culinary vocabulary and started the craze for blackening, in which a fish fillet, coated with a thick layer of herbs and spices, is seared until dark. More than three decades later, many still consider a visit to K-Paul's essential for his inventive gumbos, fried crawfish tails, blackened Gulf fish, and sweet potato–pecan pie. **Known for:** Cajun classics; blackened Gulf fish; central location. $ *Average main: $30* ⊠ *416 Chartres St., French Quarter* ☎ *504/596–2530* ⊕ *www.kpauls.com* ☉ *Closed Sun. No lunch Mon.–Wed.* ✦ *1:D3.*

$$$ ✗ **Mr. B's Bistro.** Those who wonder if there really is a New Orleans res-
CREOLE taurant that can properly cater to both tourists and locals need look no
FAMILY farther than Mr. B's. Using as many Louisiana ingredients as possible, the chef offers a hearty veal osso bucco, an irresistible honey-ginger-glazed pork chop, and one of the best barbecue shrimp dishes in the city. **Known for:** French Quarter people-watching; gumbo; pecan pie. $ *Average main: $28* ⊠ *201 Royal St., French Quarter* ☎ *504/523–2078* ⊕ *www.mrbsbistro.com* ✦ *1:D3.*

$$$ ✗ **Muriel's Jackson Square.** Among Jackson Square's many dining spots,
CREOLE Muriel's is easily the most ambitious, in both atmosphere and menu. In the large downstairs rooms, architectural knickknacks and artwork evoke the city's colorful past, while diners indulge in hearty updates of old Creole favorites. **Known for:** entertaining setting; gluten-free options; inventive Creole flavors. $ *Average main: $26* ⊠ *801 Chartres St., French Quarter* ☎ *504/568–1885* ⊕ *www.muriels.com* ✦ *1:C4.*

$$$ ✗ **Nola.** Fans of Emeril Lagasse will want to grab a seat at the food bar
CREOLE overlooking the open kitchen at this French Quarter restaurant. Free-
Fodor's Choice wheeling appetizers are among the big attractions, the standout being
★ "Mama's stuffed chicken wings" with peanut dipping sauce. **Known**

for: stuffed chicken wings; decadent dessert; modern decor. $ *Average main: $28* ✉ *534 St. Louis St., French Quarter* ☎ *504/522–6652* ⊕ *www.emerilsrestaurants.com* ✛ *1:D4.*

$$$

CREOLE

FAMILY

✕ **Palace Café.** Occupying what used to be New Orleans's oldest music store, this Dickie Brennan stalwart is a convivial spot to try some of the more imaginative contemporary Creole dishes, such as andouille-crusted fish, crabmeat cheesecake, and pepper-crusted duck breast with foie gras. Desserts, especially the white-chocolate bread pudding and the homemade ice creams, are luscious. **Known for:** jazz brunch; happy hour; bread pudding. $ *Average main: $27* ✉ *605 Canal St., French Quarter* ☎ *504/523–1661* ⊕ *www.palacecafe.com* ✛ *1:D3.*

$$$

ECLECTIC

✕ **Pelican Club.** Sassy New York flourishes permeate the menu of chef Richard Hughes's smartly decorated, eminently comfortable restaurant in the heart of the French Quarter, but there's still evidence of Hughes's Louisiana origins. The whole crispy flounder with shrimp and diver scallops is decadent, while the rack of lamb with rosemary-pesto crust is almost a spiritual experience. **Known for:** well-heeled locals; Gulf fish; old-school menu. $ *Average main: $32* ✉ *312 Exchange Pl., French Quarter* ☎ *504/523–1504* ⊕ *www.pelicanclub.com* ☽ *No lunch* ✛ *1:D3.*

$

AMERICAN

FAMILY

✕ **Port of Call.** Every night, no matter the weather, people wait for more than an hour outside Port of Call for fist-thick burgers made from freshly ground beef, served with always-fluffy baked potatoes (there are no fries here). A juicy filet mignon is also available. **Known for:** rowdy locals; long waits; great burger. $ *Average main: $14* ✉ *838 Esplanade Ave., French Quarter* ☎ *504/523–0120* ⊕ *www.portofcall-nola.com* ✛ *1:A4.*

$

CREOLE

FAMILY

✕ **Remoulade.** Operated by the owners of the posh Arnaud's, Remoulade is more laid-back and less pricey but serves the same Caesar salad and pecan pie, as well as a few of the signature starters: shrimp Arnaud in rémoulade sauce, baked oysters, turtle soup, and shrimp bisque. "Tasters," or sampler plates of three dishes like gumbo, crawfish pie, and jambalaya, are a steal at $17.50. The marble-counter oyster bar and mahogany cocktail bar date to the 1870s; a dozen oysters shucked here, paired with a cold beer, can easily turn into two dozen, maybe three. **Known for:** shrimp Arnaud; oyster bar; classic cocktails. $ *Average main: $13* ✉ *309 Bourbon St., French Quarter* ☎ *504/523–0377* ⊕ *www.remoulade.com* ✛ *1:C3.*

$$$

CREOLE

✕ **R'evolution.** Superstars rarely start over when they're on top—but celebrity chef Rick Tramonto, best known for his avant-garde creations at Chicago's Tru, headed south when he needed a new challenge. Tramonto hooked up with Louisiana culinary renaissance man John Folse and the two set about remaking the state's creations, combining Folse's deep knowledge of Cajun and Creole food with Tramonto's modern techniques and impeccably high standards. **Known for:** quail three ways; caviar towers; rare wines. $ *Average main: $33* ✉ *Royal Sonesta Hotel, 777 Bienville St., French Quarter* ☎ *504/553–2277* ⊕ *www.revolutionnola.com* ☽ *No lunch Mon.–Thurs. and Sat.* ✛ *1:D3.*

$

CREOLE

✕ **SoBou.** This sleek venture (whose name is short for "South of Bourbon Street") from the Commander's Palace team puts cocktails, beer, and wine front and center. The bar is nearly as big as the dining room.

8

Known for: fish tacos; happy hour; creative cocktails. $ *Average main: $15* ⊠ *W Hotel French Quarter, 310 Chartres St., French Quarter* ☎ *504/552–4095* ⊕ *www.sobounola.com* ✦ *1:D3.*

$ ✕ **Stanley.** Chefs across America are ditching the white tablecloths and
CREOLE applying fine-dining flair to burgers, bar food, and comfort fare. Here
FAMILY chef Scott Boswell takes this tack with the food of Louisiana. **Known for:** eggs Benedict; Caesar salad; prime real estate. $ *Average main: $13* ⊠ *547 St. Ann St., French Quarter* ☎ *504/587–0093* ⊕ *www.stanley-restaurant.com* ▭ *No credit cards* ✦ *1:C4.*

$$ ✕ **Sylvain.** Enjoy the best of contemporary food in an antique setting,
AMERICAN at this sleek gastropub within an 18th-century carriage house. Sylvain celebrates the new and old with an elegant but light touch (look, for example at the "Champagne and fries" starter: a bottle of the finest brut accompanies a plate of hand-cut fries for $50). **Known for:** romantic setting; fried chicken sandwich; great service. $ *Average main: $21* ⊠ *625 Chartres St., French Quarter* ☎ *504/265–8123* ⊕ *www.sylvain-nola.com* ☾ *No lunch Mon.–Thurs.* ✦ *1:C4.*

FAUBOURG MARIGNY, BYWATER, AND TREMÉ

FAUBOURG MARIGNY

The carefully preserved and colorfully painted cottages and shotgun houses of the Faubourg Marigny are home to artists, hipsters, and gay couples. You'll find cool cafés, interesting ethnic options, and neighborhood hangouts with cheap eats. Most travelers make a beeline for Frenchmen Street, a three-block stretch of live-music clubs and bars known as "Bourbon Street for locals."

$ ✕ **Praline Connection.** Down-home cooking in the southern Creole style is
CREOLE the forte of this very Southern restaurant just a few blocks from the French
FAMILY Quarter. The fried or stewed chicken, smothered pork chops, fried chicken livers, and collard greens are definitively executed, and the filé gumbo, peas with okra, and sweet-potato pie are welcome in a neighborhood otherwise in short supply of soul food. **Known for:** Creole favorites; pralines; entertaining staff. $ *Average main: $15* ⊠ *542 Frenchmen St., Faubourg Marigny* ☎ *504/943–3934* ⊕ *www.pralineconnection.com* ✦ *1:A5.*

$$ ✕ **Sukho Thai.** Certainly the most extensive Thai restaurant in the area,
THAI Sukho Thai fits into its arty neighborhood with servers wearing all black and a hip, art-gallery approach to decorating. You can't go wrong with any of the curries, but the fried whole fish with three spicy chili sauces is a showstopper. **Known for:** curries; BYOB; fried whole fish. $ *Average main: $18* ⊠ *2200 Royal St., Faubourg Marigny* ☎ *504/948–9309* ⊕ *www.sukhothai-nola.com* ☾ *Closed Mon.* ✦ *1:A5.*

$ ✕ **Three Muses.** The most eclectic mix of music, food, and people can
ECLECTIC be found on Frenchmen Street, and Three Muses captures everything that makes this vibrant stretch of the Faubourg Marigny worth seeking out. The small-plates menu spans the globe, with charcuterie and cheese plates and standout delicacies like the Korean-style steak bulgogi. **Known for:** live music; romantic evening; cheese plates. $ *Average main: $12* ⊠ *536 Frenchmen St., Faubourg Marigny* ☎ *504/252–4801* ⊕ *www.3musesnola.com* ☾ *Closed Tues. No lunch* ✦ *1:B5.*

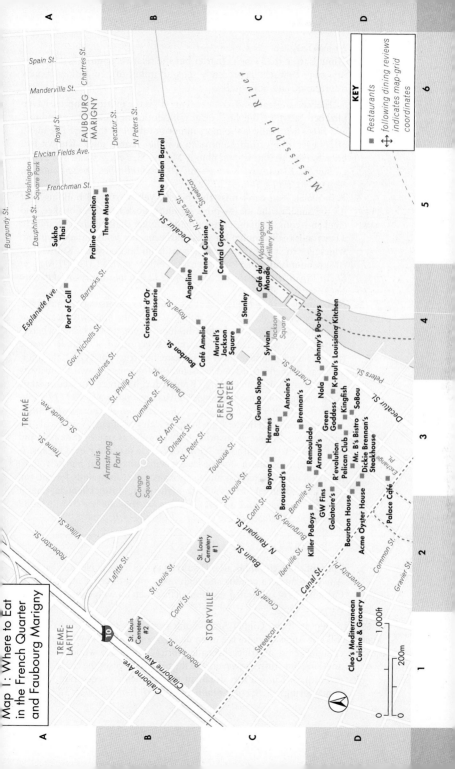

Map 1: Where to Eat in the French Quarter and Faubourg Marigny

KEY

■ Restaurants

✛ following dining reviews indicates map-grid coordinates

Mississippi River

FAUBOURG MARIGNY

TREMÉ

TREMÉ-LAFITTE

STORYVILLE

FRENCH QUARTER

Louis Armstrong Park

Congo Square

St. Louis Cemetery #1

St. Louis Cemetery #2

Washington Square Park

Washington Artillery Park

Jackson Square

Spain St.

Manderville St.

Royal St.

Elysian Fields Ave.

Frenchman St.

Burgundy St.

Dauphine St.

Washington St.

Esplanade Ave.

Barracks St.

Gov. Nicholls St.

Ursulines St.

St. Philip St.

Dumaine St.

St. Ann St.

Orleans St.

St. Peter St.

Toulouse St.

St. Louis St.

Conti St.

Bienville St.

Iberville St.

Canal St.

Chartres St.

Decatur St.

N Peters St.

Bourbon St.

Dauphine St.

Burgundy St.

N. Rampart St.

Basin St.

Crozat St.

Robertson St.

St. Claude Ave.

Tremé St.

Villere St.

Roberston St.

Lafitte St.

St. Louis St.

Conti St.

Claiborne Ave.

University Pl.

Common St.

Gravier St.

Exchange Pl.

Peters St.

Decatur St.

Royal St.

N. Peters St.

Streetcar

Streetcar

Sukho Thai

Praline Connection

Three Muses

The Italian Barrel

Port of Call

Croissant d'Or Patisserie

Angeline

Irene's Cuisine

Central Grocery

Café du Monde

Café Amelie

Muriel's Jackson Square

Stanley

Sylvain

Johnny's Po-boys

K-Paul's Louisiana Kitchen

Gumbo Shop

Hermes Bar

Antoine's

Brennan's

Nola

Green Goddess

SoBou

Kingfish

Remoulade

Arnaud's

R'evolution

Pelican Club

Mr. B's Bistro

Dickie Brennan's Steakhouse

Bayona

Broussard's

GW Fins

Galatoire's

Killer PoBoys

Bourbon House

Acme Oyster House

Palace Café

Cleo's Mediterranean Cuisine & Grocery

1,000ft

200m

BYWATER

Minutes from the French Quarter but still relatively untouched by tourists, edgy Bywater has recently seen an influx of new residents, new restaurants, and new vitality.

$ ✕ **Elizabeth's.** "Real food, done real good" is the motto at hipster-haven
SOUTHERN   Elizabeth's, where the vinyl-print tablecloths look just like grandma's
Fodor's Choice   and breakfast really is the most important meal of the day. The menu
★   offers everything from po'boys to a stellar seared duck. **Known for:**
French toast; praline bacon; Bloody Marys. $ *Average main: $15* ✉ *601 Gallier St., Bywater* ☎ *504/944–9272* ⊕ *www.elizabethsrestaurantnola.com* ☽ *No dinner Sun.* ✛ *3:B5.*

$ ✕ **The Joint.** You can't miss this bright, yellow-striped building, but
SOUTHERN   it's the smell of the meat—pork shoulder, pork ribs, beef brisket, and
FAMILY   chicken—cooking in the custom-made smoker that will draw you in. In
a town not really known for great barbecue, the Joint is the exception, which is why it draws hungry patrons from far and wide. **Known for:** ribs; peanut butter pie; local beer. $ *Average main: $12* ✉ *701 Mazant St., at Royal St., Bywater* ☎ *504/949–3232* ⊕ *www.alwayssmokin.com* ☽ *Closed Sun.* ✛ *3:B6.*

$$ ✕ **N7.** It might seem unlikely that a restaurant specializing in canned fish
TAPAS   would be one of the most romantic places to dine in New Orleans, but
N7 is just that. Once you can find this hidden gem, tucked behind a barely marked large wooden fence on a quiet street off of St. Claude Avenue (there's no telephone number or website; just trust your GPS), the adorable, candlelit courtyard and Parisian bistro interior will whisk you away to a dreamy European evening. **Known for:** habanero-smoked oysters; French wine; romantic date night. $ *Average main: $18* ✉ *1117 Montegut St., Bywater* ☽ *Closed Sun.* ↻ *Reservations not accepted* ✛ *3:B5.*

$ ✕ **Pizza Delicious.** Hipsters, lifelong Bywater residents, and locals far
PIZZA   across town all take great pride in "Pizza D" as one of the only (and
best) places to get authentic New York–style pizza in New Orleans. A tall can of PBR and a slice of cheese will satisfy most, but delve into the specialty pies, pastas, and surprisingly pleasing salads for the full experience. **Known for:** New York–style slices; hipster clientele; Caesar salad. $ *Average main: $15* ✉ *617 Piety St., Bywater* ☎ *504/676–8482* ⊕ *www.pizzadelicious.com* ☽ *Closed Mon.* ✛ *3:B5.*

CBD AND THE WAREHOUSE DISTRICT

The CBD, or Central Business District, is as much about pleasure as work. Amid the modern condos and high-rises, you'll discover many of New Orleans's most celebrated restaurants that keep up with national trends.

CBD

$$$$ ✕ **August.** If the Gilded Age is long past, someone forgot to tell the
MODERN   folks at August, where the main dining room shimmers with masses of
AMERICAN   chandelier prisms, thick brocade fabrics, and glossy woods. Service is
Fodor's Choice   anything but stuffy, however, and the food showcases the chefs' modern
★   techniques. **Known for:** decadent tasting menus; vegetarian options; wine pairings. $ *Average main: $38* ✉ *301 Tchoupitoulas St., Central*

Business District ☎ *504/299–9777* ⊕ *www.restaurantaugust.com* ⊙ *No lunch Sat.–Thurs. (brunch Sun.)* ✛ *2:B4.*

$$$ ✕ **Bon Ton Café.** Bon Ton's opening in 1953 marked the first appearance
CAJUN of a significant Cajun restaurant in New Orleans, and the now-famed crawfish dishes, gumbo, jambalaya, and oyster omelet continue to draw fans. The bustle in the dining room peaks at lunchtime on weekdays, when businesspeople from nearby offices come in droves for turtle soup, eggplant with a shrimp-and-crab étouffée, and warm, sugary bread pudding with whiskey sauce (it packs a serious punch). **Known for:** crawfish; gumbo; turtle soup. ⑤ *Average main: $28* ✉ *401 Magazine St., Central Business District* ☎ *504/524–3386* ⊕ *www.thebontoncafe. com* ⊙ *Closed weekends* ✛ *2:B4.*

$$$ ✕ **Borgne.** In a spacious dining room accented by nautical touches,
SEAFOOD floor-to-ceiling chalkboard panels, and local artwork, you'll find rustic Louisiana seafood dishes with a touch of city sophistication. Named after Lake Borgne in eastern Louisiana, the restaurant honors that area's many Spanish settlers with empanadas and fish à la plancha along with more traditional renditions like the Gulf fish in a bag accompanied by onions, fennel, and crab fat. **Known for:** tapas; business lunches; raw oysters. ⑤ *Average main: $26* ✉ *Hyatt Regency New Orleans, 601 Loyola Ave., Central Business District* ☎ *504/613–3860* ⊕ *www.borgnerestaurant.com* ✛ *2:B2.*

$ ✕ **Cleo's Mediterranean Cuisine & Grocery.** Good things really do come in
MIDDLE EASTERN small packages, like the outstanding falafel you can order at the back of this unpretentious, pocket-size Middle Eastern convenience store outfitted with a handful of tables and chairs. Grab a drink from one of the glass cases, then order from a menu of mouthwatering options, like lamb kebabs and beef gyros. **Known for:** late-night eats; falafel; tabouleh. ⑤ *Average main: $10* ✉ *165 University Pl., Central Business District* ☎ *504/522–4504* ⊕ *www.facebook.com/cleosnola* ✛ *1:D2.*

$$$ ✕ **Compère Lapin.** Those tired of the white-tablecloth restaurants with
FUSION decades-old menus of shrimp rémoulade and redfish renditions (that populate so much of the New Orleans fine dining scene) will be especially pleased with Compère Lapin, a unique and distinctly contemporary ultra-fine dining experience. At the root of Chef Nina Compton's cooking are the comforting flavors and spices of St. Lucian and Italian home kitchens, but presentation and execution of her dishes are that of a top-notch professional chef. **Known for:** sweet potato gnocchi; conch croquettes; inventive cocktails. ⑤ *Average main: $28* ✉ *Old No. 77 Hotel and Chandlery, 535 Tchoupitoulas St., Central Business District* ☎ *504/599–2119* ⊕ *www.comperelapin.com* ✛ *2:B4.*

$$ ✕ **Domenica.** Domenica wows diners with rustic Italian cooking, a rar-
ITALIAN ity in New Orleans's culinary landscape. In the renovated Roosevelt
Fodor's Choice Hotel—a 19th-century landmark—friendly and knowledgeable waiters
★ happily help patrons with lesser-known ingredients, but it doesn't take a lengthy explanation to know that the fresh pastas and wood-fired pizzas are a must. **Known for:** wood-fired pizzas; charcuterie boards; great happy hour. ⑤ *Average main: $20* ✉ *Roosevelt New Orleans Hotel, 123 Baronne St., Central Business District* ☎ *504/648–6020* ⊕ *www. domenicarestaurant.com* ✛ *2:A3.*

8

$$$ ✕ **Drago's.** Since 1969 the Cvitanovich family restaurant has been a
ITALIAN   fixture in Metairie, just a short drive from downtown New Orleans, so
FAMILY   when it was revealed the family would open a second location inside the
Hilton Riverside hotel, locals started salivating and the word quickly
spread. The charbroiled oysters are the absolute must-order (you'll want
extra bread to mop up the toothsome sauce). **Known for:** charbroiled
oysters; local institution; kid-friendly food. $ *Average main: $26* ✉ *Hilton New Orleans Riverside, 2 Poydras St., Central Business District*
☎ *504/584–3911* ⊕ *www.dragosrestaurant.com* ✛ *2:B5.*

$$ ✕ **Grand Isle.** The rustic interior, reminiscent of 1920s and '30s Louisi-
SOUTHERN   ana fish camps, is the perfect backdrop for shrimp gumbo, spicy boiled
shrimp, fresh Gulf fish, cold smoked-and-grilled tuna, and a lemon
icebox pie that will make you fall in love with New Orleans all over
again. Except for freshwater catfish and Canadian mussels, all the seafood comes from the Gulf of Mexico and often straight from the fishermen. **Known for:** fresh Gulf fish; local produce; big crowds. $ *Average
main: $18* ✉ *575 Convention Center Blvd., Central Business District*
☎ *504/520–8530* ⊕ *www.grandislerestaurant.com* ✛ *2:B5.*

$$$$ ✕ **The Grill Room.** With its elegant table settings and canvases depicting
AMERICAN   the lives of British nobility, the Grill Room on the second floor of the
Fodor's Choice   Windsor Court has always been a beacon of class and an elegant set-
★   ting for special occasions (keep your eyes peeled: celebrities in town
for local film shoots often snag tables here). The creative, Cajun- and
Creole-influenced dinner menu allows guests to customize a three- or
five-course tasting dinner, with insightful and unusual wine selections by
sommelier John Mitchell, who draws from a deep cellar with an extensive Bordeaux collection. **Known for:** elegant dining room; tasting dinners; extensive wine list. $ *Average main: $36* ✉ *Windsor Court Hotel,
300 Gravier St., 2nd fl., Central Business District* ☎ *504/523–6000*
⊕ *www.grillroomneworleans.com* ✛ *2:B4.*

$ ✕ **Mother's.** Tourists and locals line up for solid, if unspectacular, down-
CAFÉ   home eats at this island of blue-collar sincerity amid downtown's sea of
glittery hotels. Mother's dispenses baked ham and roast beef po'boys
(ask for "debris" on the beef sandwich and the bread will be slathered
with meat juices and shreds of meat), home-style biscuits and jambalaya,
and chicken and sausage gumbo in a couple of bare-bones yet charming
dining rooms. **Known for:** greasy spoon; big crowds; roast beef debris
po'boys. $ *Average main: $12* ✉ *401 Poydras St., Central Business District* ☎ *504/523–9656* ⊕ *www.mothersrestaurant.net* ✛ *2:B4.*

THE WAREHOUSE DISTRICT

Next to the CBD, in the sprawling Warehouse District, gallery hoppers
and condo dwellers fuel up at trendy bistros and stylish casual eateries.

$ ✕ **Carmo.** Vegan, vegetarian, and gluten-free options abound at this
CARIBBEAN   self-proclaimed "tropical café," which playfully references the cuisines
of Latin America, Southeast Asia, and the Caribbean. Fresh, local, and
organic produce are used to create dishes like *acarajé*, a black-eyed-pea
fritter stuffed with *vatapá* (a cashew, peanut, and coconut paste) or the
Rico sandwich, a breadless creation of grilled plantains, melted cheese,
vegan meat, avocado, salsa fresca, and a tangy secret sauce. **Known
for:** vegan options; Caribbean comforts; fresh juice. $ *Average main:*

Continued on page 136

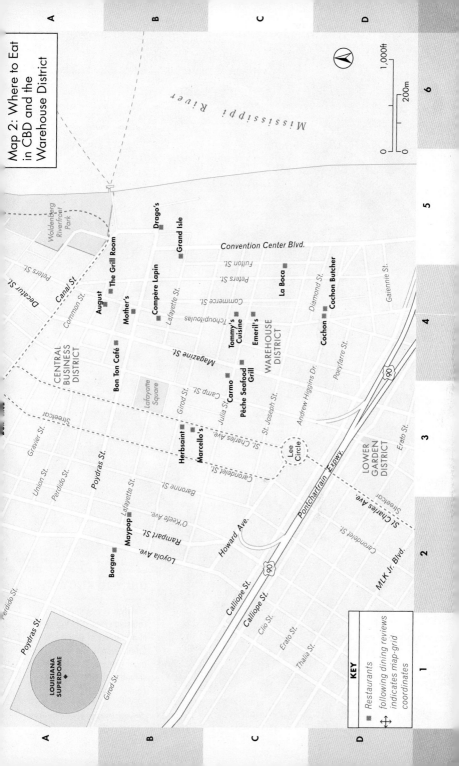

Map 2: Where to Eat in CBD and the Warehouse District

KEY
■ Restaurants
⊕ following dining reviews indicates map-grid coordinates

Mississippi River

Woldenberg Riverfront Park

CENTRAL BUSINESS DISTRICT

WAREHOUSE DISTRICT

LOWER GARDEN DISTRICT

LOUISIANA SUPERDOME

Lafayette Square

Lee Circle

Convention Center Blvd.

Peters St.
Decatur St.
Canal St.
Common St.
Gravier St.
Union St.
Perdido St.
Poydras St.
Lafayette St.
Baronne St.
O'Keefe Ave.
Rampart St.
Loyola Ave.
Girod St.
Howard Ave.
Calliope St.
Clio St.
Erato St.
Thalia St.
Carondelet St.
St. Charles Ave.
MLK Jr. Blvd.
Erato St.
Magazine St.
Camp St.
Julia St.
St. Joseph St.
Andrew Higgins Dr.
Poeyfarre St.
Commerce St.
Tchoupitoulas St.
Fulton St.
Peters St.
Diamond St.
Gaiennie St.
Lafayette St.

Pontchartrain Expwy.
Streetcar
St. Charles Ave. Streetcar

Restaurants:
Drago's
Grand Isle
The Grill Room
August
Mother's
Compère Lapin
Bon Ton Café
Herbsaint
Marcello's
Carmo
Pêche Seafood Grill
Tommy's Cuisine
Emeril's
La Boca
Cochon
Cochon Butcher
Maypop
Borgne

0   1,000ft
0   200m

90

DID YOU KNOW?

Crawfish is a staple in the Louisiana diet. It is found in a number of Cajun and Creole dishes, but it is most commonly boiled and served with potatoes and corn on the cob.

THE CUISINE OF NEW ORLEANS

From humble po' boy shops to white-tablecloth temples of classic Creole cuisine, food is a major reason to visit the Crescent City. People in New Orleans love to eat, and discerning local customers support a multitude of options when it comes to dining. Innovative fine dining restaurants exist alongside more modest eateries serving red beans and rice and boiled crawfish. Whatever the cost, it's hard to find a bad meal in this culinary town.

Given New Orleans's location near the mouth of the Mississippi River and the Gulf of Mexico, it was perhaps inevitable that an outstanding food culture would develop in the area. Farmers grow an abundance of produce—locally prized Creole tomato, okra, strawberries, and chayote (locally know as mirliton)—in the fertile delta soil that surroundes the city and fishermen harvest a wealth of seafood like black drum, speckled trout, shrimp, blue crabs, oysters, and crawfish from the marshes and open waters of the Gulf of Mexico.

As a port city, New Orleans has always been something of a melting pot. The city's native Creole cuisine is a mixture of French, African, and Spanish influences; immigration from Italy and Sicily in the 19th century gave New Orleans its own version of Italian cooking. Plus, there is a lingering influence from an influx of German settlers; more recently, immigrants from Vietnam have brought their culinary traditions to New Orleans and the surrounding parishes.

Creole food is the cooking of the city, while Cajun food evolved from the rural traditions of the plains and swamps of southwest Louisiana. The Acadians, a people of French heritage, arrived in Louisiana after being expelled by the British from parts of Canada (present-day Nova Scotia and surrounding areas) in the 18th century. Like the cuisine of rural France, Cajun cooking is hearty and employs similar cooking techniques such as slow braising and the addition of a roux (a combination of flour and fat), but it features local seafood, game, and produce.

By Robert D. Peyton

(top) A café au lait and beignets served at the renowned Café du Monde.

CLASSIC CREOLE AND CAJUN FOOD

Jambalaya

Oysters Rockefeller

BEIGNETS

Beignets are fried pillows of dough, generally served with powdered sugar (and lots of it!) and steaming cups of café au lait made with New Orleans-style chicory coffee. Beignets are typically consumed for breakfast or for dessert.

ÉTOUFFÉE

Étouffée means "smothered" in French, and the dish can be made with shrimp; chicken; and, most typically, crawfish. The dish is Cajun in origin, but there are Creole versions, as well. As with many Cajun dishes, it starts with a light roux, to which chopped onion, celery, and bell pepper (called "the trinity" in South Louisiana) is added. Some versions contain tomatoes, and the sauce is finished with stock and meat, poultry, or seafood. Crawfish étouffée is best during crawfish season (March–June), but you can find it year-round.

MUFFALETTA

The Muffaletta sandwich was invented at the Central Grocery (923 Decatur St.) by Salvatore Lupo and became popular enough that it can now be found all over town. The sandwich is served on a round loaf that's stuffed with salami, ham, pro-

volone, and a local condiment called olive salad, which typically consists of olives, celery, and pickled peppers. Some restaurants heat the sandwich, but many purists consider that heresy.

OYSTERS ROCKEFELLER

Oysters Rockefeller was invented at Antoine's, the oldest continuously operated restaurant in the United States. The dish, to this day, consists of oysters baked on the half-shell with an anise-scented puree of herbs and bread crumbs. Although the recipe Antoine's uses remains a closely guarded secret, the dish typically contains parsley, chervil, tarragon, and celery leaves. This is a dish that should be ordered while oysters are at their best, between September and April.

JAMBALAYA

Jambalaya is a hearty dish that combines rice with meat, poultry, and/or seafood with a result akin to the Spanish paella. In New Orleans, the dish usually includes tomatoes, giving it a reddish hue. Ingredients can include chicken, andouille, pork, shrimp, crawfish, duck, and even alligator. The requisite "trinity" of onion, celery, and

Shrimp gumbo   Pralines

bell pepper is cooked with or without meat or seafood, and then the rice is added with stock, and the dish is covered to finish.

GUMBO

Gumbo is yet another dish that has both Cajun and Creole variations. It is a thick soup or thin stew that can include almost any meat, poultry, sausage, or seafood found in South Louisiana. Cajuns generally cook the roux for gumbo until it is very dark, giving the dish a nutty flavor, while in New Orleans a lighter roux is employed, and okra and tomatoes are often included. A common ingredient, filé powder (dried, ground sassafras leaves), used as a thickening agent and seasoning, is considered by some as a necessary ingredient for making Cajun and Creole gumbo.

BOUDIN

Boudin is a Cajun sausage that combines rice with pork or other ingredients; some of the best can be found just outside of the city at rural gas stations, where it's frequently eaten as a roadside snack. In restaurants, the stuffing is sometimes removed from its casing, formed into balls, and fried.

TASSO

Tasso is a cured and smoked pork product that is one of the treasures of Acadian charcuterie. It is a highly spiced preparation that is used as a flavor base in many local recipes such as gumbo and red beans. Though it is sometimes called tasso ham, the meat used to prepare it is from the shoulder rather than the leg.

ANDOUILLE

Andouille is a smoked sausage made with both ground and cubed pork and flavored with garlic. It is a variation of a French sausage that in the Cajun interpretation is more highly spiced and aggressively flavored. It appears as an ingredient in many South Louisiana dishes, including gumbo and jambalaya.

PRALINES

Pralines are a sweet patty-shaped Creole treats made with caramelized sugar, cream, butter, and pecans—the latter often sourced from trees that grow locally in great abundance. Modern interpretations include chocolate, peanut butter, and bourbon pralines. Be sure to pronounce it like the locals: "PRAH-line," not "PRAY-line."

$14 ✉ *527 Julia St., Warehouse District* ☎ *504/875–4132* ⊕ *www.caf-ecarmo.com* ⊗ *Closed Sun. No dinner Mon.* ✛ *2:C4.*

$$$

CAJUN

Fodor's Choice

★

✕ **Cochon.** Chef-owned restaurants are common in New Orleans, but this one builds on owner Donald Link's family heritage as he, working with co-owner Stephen Stryjewski (who received a James Beard Award for his work here), prepares Cajun dishes he learned to cook at his grandfather's knee. The interior may be a bit too hip and noisy for some patrons, but the food makes up for it. **Known for:** Cochon du lait; rabbit and dumplings; fried boudin. ⑤ *Average main: $26* ✉ *930 Tchoupitoulas St., Warehouse District* ☎ *504/588–2123* ⊕ *www. cochonrestaurant.com* ✛ *2:D4.*

$

SOUTHERN

Fodor's Choice

★

✕ **Cochon Butcher.** Around the corner from its big brother Cochon, Butcher packs its own Cajun punch with an upscale sandwich menu that dials up the flavor on local classics. With house-cured meats and olive salad, the mufuletta reveals exactly how delicious Italian-Creole can be, though the pork-belly sandwich, with refreshing mint and cucumber, also brings customers back. **Known for:** pork-belly sandwich; to-go treats; delicious cocktails. ⑤ *Average main: $10* ✉ *930 Tchoupitoulas St., Warehouse District* ☎ *504/588–7675* ⊕ *www.cochonbutcher.com* ⊗ *No dinner Sun.* ✛ *2:D4.*

$$$

AMERICAN

✕ **Emeril's.** Celebrity-chef Emeril Lagasse's urban-chic flagship restaurant is always jammed, so it's fortunate that the basket weave–pattern wood ceiling muffles much of the clatter and chatter. The ambitious menu gives equal emphasis to Creole and modern American cooking—try the andouille-crusted drum fish or the barbecue shrimp (one of the darkest, richest versions of that local specialty). **Known for:** top-notch service; barbecue shrimp; decadent desserts. ⑤ *Average main: $30* ✉ *800 Tchoupitoulas St., Warehouse District* ☎ *504/528–9393* ⊕ *www.emer-ilsrestaurants.com* ⊗ *No lunch weekends* ✛ *2:C4.*

$$$

SOUTHERN

Fodor's Choice

★

✕ **Herbsaint.** Chef Donald Link (also of Cochon, Cochon Butcher, and Pêche Seafood Grill) turns out food that sparkles with robust flavors and top-grade ingredients at this casually upscale restaurant. Small plates and starters such as a daily gumbo, charcuterie, and homemade pastas are mainstays. **Known for:** homemade pasta; charcuterie; convivial crowds. ⑤ *Average main: $27* ✉ *701 St. Charles Ave., Warehouse District* ☎ *504/524–4114* ⊕ *www.herbsaint.com* ⊗ *Closed Sun. No lunch Sat.* ✛ *2:B3.*

$$$

LATIN AMERICAN

✕ **La Boca.** Need a break from the bounties of the sea prevalent in New Orleans restaurants? Book a table at this classic Argentine steak house, which moved to a larger space in 2014. **Known for:** malbec; flank steak; grilled provolone. ⑤ *Average main: $27* ✉ *870 Tchoupitoulas St., Warehouse District* ☎ *504/525–8205* ⊕ *www.labocasteaks.com* ⊗ *Closed Sun. No lunch* ✛ *2:C5.*

$$

SOUTHERN

ITALIAN

✕ **Marcello's.** There are two very good reasons to visit Marcello's: comforting Sicilian-American dishes at a reasonable price, and the well-stocked wine store (and cellar) next door, where diners choose from a wide selection of Italian wines to accompany their meal (markups are slightly below regular restaurant prices). Southern Italian food might not scream New Orleans, but the convivial bistro atmosphere, made more picturesque by the passing St. Charles streetcar, will make you

CLOSE UP

Food Glossary

Barbecue shrimp. Shrimp baked in the shell in a blend of olive oil and butter, and seasoned with garlic and other herbs and spices.

Béarnaise. A sauce of egg yolk and butter with shallots, wine, and vinegar, used on meat and fish.

Boudin (pronounced boo- *dan*). A soft Cajun sausage, often spicy, made of pork, rice, and a bit of liver for seasoning.

Bouillabaisse (pronounced *booey-yah-base*). A stew of various fish and shellfish in a broth seasoned with saffron and other spices.

Boulette (pronounced *boo*-let). Minced, chopped, or puréed meat or fish shaped into balls and fried.

Café brûlot (pronounced broo- *loh*). Cinnamon, lemon, clove, orange, and sugar, steeped with strong coffee, then flambéed with brandy and served in special pedestaled cups.

Chicory coffee. The ground and roasted root of a European variety of chicory is added to ground coffee in varying proportions.

Crème brûlée. Literally meaning "burned cream," a custard with a brittle crust of browned sugar.

Dirty rice. In this cousin of jambalaya, bits of meat, such as giblets or sausage, and seasonings are added to white rice before cooking.

Dressed. A po'boy "dressed" contains lettuce, tomato, pickles, and mayonnaise or mustard.

Meunière (pronounced muhn- *yehr*). This method of preparing fish or soft-shell crab entails dusting it with seasoned flour, sautéing it in brown butter, and using the butter with lemon juice as a sauce.

Mirliton (pronounced merl-i- *tawn*). A pale-green member of the squash family, usually identified as a vegetable pear or chayote.

Oysters Bienville (pronounced byen- *veel*). Oysters lightly baked in the shell and topped with a cream sauce flavored with bits of shrimp, mushroom, and green seasonings.

Oysters en brochette (pronounced awn-bro- *shet*). Whole oysters and bits of bacon dusted with seasoned flour, skewered, and deep-fried; traditionally served on toast with lemon and brown butter.

Panéed veal (pronounced pan- *aid*). Breaded veal cutlets sautéed in butter.

Po'boy. A hefty sandwich made with local French bread and any number of fillings: roast beef, fried shrimp, oysters, ham, meatballs in tomato sauce, and cheese are common.

Ravigote (pronounced rah-vee- *gote*). In Creole usage, this is a piquant mayonnaise—usually made with capers—used to moisten crabmeat.

Rémoulade (pronounced ray-moo-lahd). A mixture of olive oil, mustard, scallions, cayenne, lemon, paprika, and parsley, served on cold peeled shrimp or lumps of back-fin crabmeat.

Souffléed potatoes. Thin, hollow puffs of deep-fried potato, produced by two fryings at different temperatures.

Sno-balls. Shaved ice topped with flavored syrup.

Tasso. Smokey cured pork often diced fine and added to dishes as a flavoring.

8

feel part of the neighborhood crowd. **Known for:** wine cellar; grilled artichokes; pork marsala. $ *Average main: $21* ⊠ *715 St. Charles Ave., Warehouse District* ☎ *504/518–6333* ⊕ *www.marcelloscafe.com* ☞ *No lunch weekends* ✛ *2:B3.*

$$$
ASIAN FUSION

✕ **Maypop.** After gaining notoriety for his Southeast Asian–inspired cuisine at Mopho in Mid-City, Chef Micheal Gulotta moved into new territory, with a sophisticated small-bites menu for a downtown crowd. House-made pasta, cured meats, local seafood, and roti bread are accompanied by flavors like ginger, turmeric, and coconut. **Known for:** dim sum; house-made noodles; crispy fried oysters. $ *Average main: $27* ⊠ *611 O'Keefe Ave., Warehouse District* ☎ *504/518–6345* ⊕ *www.maypoprestaurant.com* ✛ *2:B2.*

$$$
SEAFOOD

✕ **Pêche Seafood Grill.** The name implies fish, and that's what you'll find at this modern temple to seafood, the brainchild of nearby Cochon proprietors Donald Link and Stephen Stryjewski. In addition to an airy, modern space enhanced by exposed beams and a wood-burning grill, the dining room has a fascinating history: the building was a former mortuary that claims to have embalmed Confederate president Jefferson Davis on-site. **Known for:** Gulf oysters; raw bar; big crowds. $ *Average main: $28* ⊠ *800 Magazine St., Warehouse District* ☎ *504/522–1744* ⊕ *www.pecherestaurant.com* ⊙ *Closed Sun.* ✛ *2:C4.*

$$
ITALIAN

✕ **Tommy's Cuisine.** The upscale dining rooms here are clubby and festive, the crowd is always interesting, and the menu seamlessly blends Creole and Italian. There are several types of oyster appetizers to choose from, including the signature Oysters Tommy with Romano cheese, pancetta, and roasted red pepper. **Known for:** baked oysters; formal service; lively crowd. $ *Average main: $22* ⊠ *746 Tchoupitoulas St., Warehouse District* ☎ *504/581–1103* ⊕ *www.tommyscuisine.com* ⊙ *No lunch* ✛ *2:C4.*

THE GARDEN DISTRICT

Although a stroll through this quiet enclave of stately antebellum mansions is an essential part of a New Orleans trip, the dining options here are limited, since most of the area is residential. The handful of recommended restaurants, however, are some of the city's most talked about.

$$$
CREOLE

✕ **Commander's Palace.** No restaurant captures New Orleans's gastronomic heritage and celebratory spirit as well as this grande dame of New Orleans fine dining. Upstairs, the Garden Room's glass walls have marvelous views of the giant oak trees on the patio below. **Known for:** turtle soup; jazz brunch; historic gem. $ *Average main: $35* ⊠ *1403 Washington Ave., Garden District* ☎ *504/899–8221* ⊕ *www.commanderspalace.com* ✛ *3:D4.*

$$$
AMERICAN
Fodor's Choice
★

✕ **Coquette.** Every neighborhood needs a hangout, and the dwellers of the Garden District's elegant mansions tend to spend their time at this fabulous corner bistro, enhanced by elaborate chandeliers and a gleaming white-tile floor. The long bar downstairs fuels the lively scene, and the window seats here, looking out on Magazine Street, are always in demand. **Known for:** creative menus; fresh seafood; warm vibe. $ *Average main: $26* ⊠ *2800 Magazine St., Garden District* ☎ *504/265–0421* ⊕ *www.coquettenola.com* ▭ *No credit cards* ⊙ *No lunch Mon.–Thurs.* ✛ *3:D4.*

$$$ ✗**Emeril's Delmonico.** Chef Emeril Lagasse bought the century-old Del-
CREOLE monico restaurant in 1998 and converted it into a large, extravagant
Fodor's Choice restaurant serving some of the most ambitious reinterpretations of clas-
★ sic Creole dishes in town. The atmosphere is lush, with high-ceiling
dining spaces swathed in upholstered walls and super-thick window
fabrics, and the food is decadent. **Known for:** charcuterie; inventive
Creole plates; lavish dining room. ⑤ *Average main: $29* ✉ *1300 St.
Charles Ave., Garden District* ☎ *504/525–4937* ⊕ *www.emerilsrestau-
rants.com* ⊗ *No lunch Sat.–Thurs.* ✛ *3:C4.*

$$ ✗**ROOT.** New Orleans is a dizzying array of culinary creativity, and
MODERN nowhere pushes the boundaries further than ROOT, which serves, for
AMERICAN lack of a better word, "molecular gastronomy" cuisine, the kind of food
created by chefs who grew up admiring Mr. Science as much as Julia
Child, in a fittingly on-trend dining room accented with bright pops of
color. The menu changes frequently but expect to find dishes like hot-
and-sour lemonfish with horseradish "snow," sweet tea fried chicken
wings, and scallops perfumed with actual Cohiba cigar smoke. **Known
for:** molecular gastronomy; adventurous small plates; hip crowd. ⑤ *Average main: $25* ✉ *1800 Magazine St., Garden District* ☎ *504/309–
7800* ⊕ *www.rootnola.com* ⊗ *Closed Sun. and Mon.* ✛ *3:D4.*

$ ✗**Sucré.** Do you have a sweet tooth? If so, make sure to stop in at Sucré,
CAFÉ whether it be for a morning coffee and pastry, a late-night snack (the
FAMILY shop is open till midnight on Friday and Saturday and serves alcohol),
Fodor's Choice or perhaps an afternoon gelato—this stylish sweetshop offers a wide
★ array of irresistible confections. **Known for:** macarons; gelato; chocolate to-go. ⑤ *Average main: $8* ✉ *3025 Magazine St., Garden District*
☎ *504/520–8311* ⊕ *www.shopsucre.com* ✛ *3:D4.*

$ ✗**Turkey and the Wolf.** A young, energetic team adds gourmet touches
AMERICAN (all meat is cured in-house) to over-the-top comfort foods at Turkey
FAMILY and the Wolf: towering fried bologna sandwiches, deviled eggs with
crispy chicken skins, and cheesy melts with peppered dressing. The vibe
is pleasantly divey, a cross between grandma's kitchen and a hipster's
haven. **Known for:** huge sandwiches; long lines; energetic crowd. ⑤ *Average main: $8* ✉ *739 Jackson Ave., Garden District* ☎ *504/218–7428*
⊕ *www.turkeyandthewolf.com* ⊗ *Closed Tues. No dinner Sun.* ✛ *3:D4.*

UPTOWN AND CARROLLTON-RIVERBEND

UPTOWN

The homes in this residential zone range from brightly colored shotguns
to imposing historic mansions. The restaurants also run the gamut:
there are corner po'boy shops and seafood joints, as well as ambitious
bistros. The boutique-lined strip of Magazine Street runs the entire
length of Uptown, and along the way you'll discover everything from
bakeries and sno-ball stands to family eateries and nationally recognized
dining destinations.

$ ✗**Ancora.** Every dish on the short menu here shows an obsessive atten-
ITALIAN tion to detail. The starters prominently feature the sausages and other
FAMILY cured meats that hang inside a glass-walled room in the back. **Known
for:** authentic Italian pizza; neighborhood vibe; house-cured meats.

⑤*Average main: $13* ✉*4508 Freret St., Uptown* ☎*504/324–1636* ⊕*www.ancorapizza.com* ▭*No credit cards* ⊘*No lunch* ✛*3:D3*.

$$ ✕**Atchafalaya.** Even with reservations, expect to wait for weekend
CREOLE   brunch at this Uptown institution, but your taste buds will thank you
later. Locals tend to linger over sultry Creole creations like étouffée
omelets and house-made sausage, a DIY Bloody Mary bar, and jumping
live jazz on Saturday and Sunday. **Known for:** Bloody Mary bar; jazz
brunch; shrimp and grits. ⑤*Average main: $20* ✉*901 Louisiana Ave.,
Uptown* ☎*504/891–9626* ⊕*www.atchafalayarestaurant.com* ⊘*No
lunch Tues. and Wed.* ✛*3:D4*.

$ ✕**Casamento's.** Casamento's has been a haven for Uptown seafood lovers
SEAFOOD   since 1919. Family members still wait tables and staff the immaculate
FAMILY   kitchen in back, while a reliable handful of oyster shuckers ensure that
plenty of cold ones are available for the standing room–only oyster bar.
Known for: neighborhood vibe; fresh oysters; fried seafood. ⑤*Average
main: $8* ✉*4330 Magazine St., Uptown* ☎*504/895–9761* ⊕*www.casa-
mentosrestaurant.com* ⊘*Closed Mon.–Wed. No lunch Sun.* ✛*3:D3*.

$$ ✕**Cavan.** Set back from Magazine Street in a gorgeous converted town
SOUTHERN   house (eating on the large veranda on warm evenings is especially a
treat), the sophisticated menu showcases (mostly) local seafood, as well
as the best East and West Coast oysters. The whole roasted fish and
anything from the raw section of the menu are always good choices.
Known for: whole fish; fresh oysters; charming setting. ⑤*Average main:
$23* ✉*3607 Magazine St., Uptown* ☎*504/509–7655* ⊕*www.cavan-
nola.com* ✛*3:D3*.

$$$ ✕**Clancy's.** Understatement characterizes the mood at locally beloved
CREOLE   Clancy's, and the classy but neutral decor reflects this, though the scene
can get lively. The small bar is usually filled with regulars who know
one another—and tourists who wish they were regulars. **Known for:**
local favorite; extensive wine list; energetic crowd. ⑤*Average main: $28*
✉*6100 Annunciation St., Uptown* ☎*504/895–1111* ⊕*www.clancysne-
worleans.com* ⊘*Closed Sun. No lunch Mon.–Wed. and Sat.* ✛*3:D2*.

$ ✕**Company Burger.** At the Company Burger, you'll have it their way. The
AMERICAN   amazing signature burger comes with two fresh-ground patties, bread-
FAMILY   and-butter pickles, American cheese, and red onions on a freshly baked
Fodor'sChoice   bun. **Known for:** quality burgers; affordable options; no-frills local
★   favorite. ⑤*Average main: $8* ✉*4600 Freret St., Uptown* ☎*504/267–
0320* ⊕*www.thecompanyburger.com* ⊘*Closed Tues.* ✛*3:D3*.

$ ✕**Dat Dog.** No one can leave Dat Dog unhappy. The sprawling stand
AMERICAN   is painted in primary hues, as if the work had been outsourced
FAMILY   to a talented kindergarten class, and the Hawaii shirt–clad staff
Fodor'sChoice   bustle about with the enthusiasm of amateur actors staging a musi-
★   cal. **Known for:** creative hot dogs; rowdy crowds; local draft beers.
⑤*Average main: $8* ✉*5030 Freret St., Uptown* ☎*504/899–6883*
⊕*www.datdog.com* ✛*3:D3*.

$ ✕**Frankie & Johnny's.** If you're trying to find the quintessential New
SEAFOOD   Orleans neighborhood restaurant, look no further. Team pennants,
posters, and football jerseys vie for space on the paneled walls of the
low-ceiling bar and dining room, while a jukebox blares beneath them.
Known for: fresh boiled seafood; local clientele; cold beer. ⑤*Average*

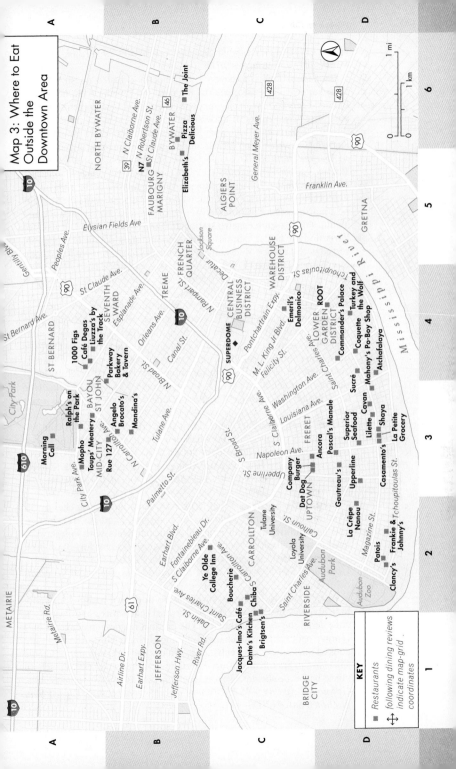

Map 3: Where to Eat Outside the Downtown Area

KEY

■ Restaurants

✦ following dining reviews indicate map-grid coordinates

NORTH BYWATER

BYWATER

■ The Joint

■ Pizza Delicious

■ Elizabeth's

N7

39

46

N Robertson St.

N Claiborne Ave.

St Claude Ave.

FAUBOURG MARIGNY

SEVENTH WARD

TREME

FRENCH QUARTER

ALGIERS POINT

Jackson Square

Decatur

428

428

90

90

General Meyer Ave.

Franklin Ave.

GRETNA

Mississippi River

Elysian Fields Ave

Peoples Ave.

St Claude Ave.

Esplanade Ave.

Orleans Ave.

N Rampart St.

Canal St.

N Broad St.

CENTRAL BUSINESS DISTRICT

WAREHOUSE DISTRICT

SUPERDOME

■ Emeril's

■ Delmonico

ROOT ■

■ Commander's Palace

Turkey and the Wolf ■

■ Coquette

■ Mahony's Po-Boy Shop

■ Atchafalaya

■ Sucré

LOWER GARDEN DISTRICT

Tchoupitoulas St.

Saint Charles Ave.

M. L. King Jr. Blvd.

Felicity St.

Washington Ave.

Louisiana Ave.

Pontchartrain Expy.

1000 Figs ■

Café Degas ■

■ Liuzza's by the Track

Parkway Bakery & Tavern ■

BAYOU ST JOHN

Ralph's on the Park ■

■ Mopho

Toups' Meatery ■

Rue 127 ■

Angelo Brocato's ■

■ Mandina's

Morning Call ■

City Park

MID-CITY

ST JOHN

N Carrollton Ave.

Tulane Ave.

City Park Ave.

Palmetto St.

ST BERNARD

St Bernard Ave.

Gentilly Blvd

610

10

10

10

10

FREERET

■ Pascal's Manale

■ Superior Seafood

■ Lilette

■ Cavan

■ Shaya

■ La Petite Grocery

Napoleon Ave.

Upperline St.

S Claiborne Ave.

S Broad St.

■ Company Burger

■ Dat Dog

■ Ancora

■ Gautreau's

■ Upperline

■ La Crêpe Nanou

■ Casamento's

■ Patois

■ Frankie & Johnny's

■ Clancy's

UPTOWN

Magazine St.

Tchoupitoulas St.

CARROLLTON

Tulane University

Loyola University

Audubon Park

Audubon Zoo

RIVERSIDE

BRIDGE CITY

■ Ye Olde College Inn

■ Boucherie

■ Chiba

■ Jacques-Imo's Café

■ Dante's Kitchen

■ Brigtsen's

Calhoun St.

Saint Charles Ave.

Carrollton Ave.

S Claiborne Ave.

Fontainebleau Dr.

Earhart Blvd.

Dakin St.

River Rd.

Jefferson Hwy.

Earhart Expy.

Airline Dr.

Metairie Rd.

METAIRIE

JEFFERSON

61

61

90

90

1 mi

1 km

A B C D

1 2 3 4 5 6

main: $11 ✉ *321 Arabella St., Uptown* ☎ *504/243–1234* ⊕ *www. frankieandjohnnys.net* ⊹ *3:D2.*

$$$
MODERN
AMERICAN
Fodor's Choice
★

✕ **Gautreau's.** This vine-covered neighborhood bistro doesn't have a sign, but that hasn't stopped the national food media from finding it. Lauded chefs cook with elegant confidence in a classic French style, but with surprising bursts of understated creativity, which can be seen in dishes like seared scallops with parsnip purée and pickled chanterelles. **Known for:** well-heeled locals; hidden gem; caramelized banana split. Ⓢ *Average main: $30* ✉ *1728 Soniat St., Uptown* ☎ *504/899–7397* ⊕ *www.gautreausrestaurant.com* ☾ *Closed Sun. No lunch* ⊹ *3:D3.*

$$
FRENCH

✕ **La Crêpe Nanou.** French chic for the budget-minded is the style at this welcoming neighborhood bistro, where during peak hours there might be a half-hour wait for a table. Woven café chairs on the sidewalk and awnings that resemble metro-station architecture evoke the Left Bank of Paris, and the Gallic focus is also evident in dishes like the filet mignon, served with a choice of several classic French sauces. **Known for:** crepes; moules-frites; classic French vibes. Ⓢ *Average main: $22* ✉ *1410 Robert St., Uptown* ☎ *504/899–2670* ⊕ *www.lacrepenanou.com* ☾ *No lunch Mon.–Sat.* ⊹ *3:D2.*

$$$
SOUTHERN

✕ **La Petite Grocery.** Flower shops sometimes bloom into intimate fine-dining establishments in New Orleans, and this one, with just-bright-enough lighting and a sturdy mahogany bar, has caught on in a big way with the locals. In the kitchen, chef-owner Justin Devillier draws on contemporary American tastes, using Louisiana raw materials whenever he can. **Known for:** blue-crab beignets; neighborhood bistro vibes; celebrity chef. Ⓢ *Average main: $27* ✉ *4238 Magazine St., Uptown* ☎ *504/891–3377* ⊕ *www.lapetitegrocery.com* ☾ *No lunch Mon.* ⊹ *3:D3.*

$$$
MODERN
AMERICAN

✕ **Lilette.** Proprietor-chef John Harris uses French and Italian culinary traditions as springboards for Lilette's inspired dishes. Look for Italian wedding soup, roasted Muscovy duck breast, and fresh crudos. **Known for:** curated wine list; intimate setting. Ⓢ *Average main: $29* ✉ *3637 Magazine St., Uptown* ☎ *504/895–1636* ⊕ *www.liletterestaurant.com* ☾ *Closed Sun.* ⊹ *3:D3.*

$
DELI
FAMILY

✕ **Mahony's Po-Boy Shop.** What happens when a fine-dining chef opens a po'boy joint? You get delicious local shrimp, hand-cut french fries, and nontraditional menu items like chicken livers with coleslaw or fried oysters "dressed" with rémoulade sauce. **Known for:** roast beef; local brews; fried oysters. Ⓢ *Average main: $10* ✉ *3454 Magazine St., Uptown* ☎ *504/899–3374* ⊕ *www.mahonyspoboys.com* ▭ *No credit cards* ⊹ *3:D3.*

$$
ITALIAN

✕ **Pascal's Manale.** Barbecue shrimp is an addictive regional specialty that involves neither a barbecue nor barbecue sauce, and Pascal's is considered the dish's birthplace. The original recipe, introduced a half century ago, remains unchanged: jumbo shrimp, still in the shell, are cooked in a buttery pool enhanced with just the right amount of Creole spice and pepper. **Known for:** entertaining oyster shuckers; old-school vibes; barbecue shrimp. Ⓢ *Average main: $24* ✉ *1838 Napoleon Ave., Uptown* ☎ *504/895–4877* ⊕ *www.pascalsmanale.com* ☾ *Closed Sun. No lunch Sat.* ⊹ *3:D3.*

$$$ ✕ **Patois.** Hidden on a quiet residential corner, this bustling bistro could
FRENCH have been transported directly from Provence. The menu continues the
Fodor's Choice French theme, but with a Louisiana attitude. **Known for:** romantic date
★ night; local produce; French delicacies. ⑤ *Average main: $26* ✉ *6078*
Laurel St., Uptown ☎ *504/895–9441* ⊕ *www.patoisnola.com* ⊟ *No*
credit cards ☉ *Closed Mon. and Tues. No dinner Sun. No lunch Sat.*
and Wed.–Thurs. ✛ *3:D2.*

$$ ✕ **Shaya.** You may think you've been transported to sexy Tel Aviv in
ISRAELI this softly lighted but thoroughly modern dining room set on a hopping
Fodor's Choice stretch of Magazine Street. Here, James Beard Foundation Award–win-
★ ning Chef Alon Shaya's inventive Israeli cooking shines: it is, after all,
the cuisine of his birthplace. **Known for:** lamb ragu hummus; shak-
shouka; wood-burning oven. ⑤ *Average main: $18* ✉ *4213 Magazine*
St., Uptown ☎ *504/891–4213* ⊕ *www.shayarestaurant.com* ✛ *3:D3.*

$$ ✕ **Superior Seafood.** The menu at this Uptown seafood specialist reads
CREOLE like a greatest hits collection from the New Orleans culinary canon:
FAMILY from po'boys and fried green tomatoes on the casual end to stuffed cat-
fish and shrimp andouille brochettes on the fancier side. Brunch might
be the best option here. **Known for:** premium Mardi Gras watching;
seafood staples; high-spirited crowd. ⑤ *Average main: $18* ✉ *4338 St.*
Charles Ave., Uptown ☎ *504/293–3474* ⊕ *www.superiorseafoodnola.*
com ✛ *3:D3.*

$$$ ✕ **Upperline.** For more than 25 years, this gaily colored cottage filled
CREOLE with a museum's worth of regional art has defined New Orleans Creole
Fodor's Choice bistro fare, combining lusty traditional items like dark gumbo or étouf-
★ fée with enough elegance to be worthy of white tablecloths. Boisterous
regulars know their orders before the cocktails even arrive: perhaps
fried green tomatoes with shrimp rémoulade, spicy local shrimp with
jalapeño corn bread, or duck with ginger-peach sauce. **Known for:** fried
green tomatoes with shrimp; roasted duck; historic gem. ⑤ *Average*
main: $29 ✉ *1413 Upperline St., Uptown* ☎ *504/891–9822* ⊕ *www.*
upperline.com ☉ *Closed Mon. and Tues. No lunch* ✛ *3:D3.*

CARROLLTON-RIVERBEND

With Tulane and Loyola universities nearby, it's fitting that the Carrollton-Riverbend neighborhood is filled with casual, affordable, and
on-trend eateries, particularly on busy Maple Street.

$$ ✕ **Boucherie.** Nathanial Zimet's gutsy, down-home cooking, a unique
SOUTHERN blend of Louisiana and contemporary Southern styles, fits right in at its
Fodor's Choice cozy location in a converted Uptown home. The menu here is updated
★ monthly, but it always kicks off with small plates, including every imag-
inable iteration of grits: as fries, cakes, and even crackers. **Known for:**
boudin balls; grits; Krispy Kreme bread pudding. ⑤ *Average main: $21*
✉ *8115 Jeannette St., Carrollton-Riverbend* ☎ *504/862–5514* ⊕ *www.*
boucherie-nola.com ☞ *Brunch only Sun.* ✛ *3:C2.*

$$$ ✕ **Brigtsen's.** Chef Frank Brigtsen's fusion of Creole refinement and
CREOLE Acadian earthiness reflects his years as a Paul Prudhomme protégé,
and his dishes here represent some of the best south Louisiana cooking you'll find anywhere. Everything is fresh, filled with deep, complex flavors, and the menu changes daily. **Known for:** seafood platters;
whimsical dining room; familial vibe. ⑤ *Average main: $29* ✉ *723*

8

Dante St., Carrollton-Riverbend ☎ *504/861–7610* ⊕ *www.brigtsens. com* ⊗ *Closed Sun. and Mon. No lunch* ⊹ *3:C2.*

$$ ✗ **Chiba.** With a chic dining room, late-night hours, and the city's best
SUSHI sushi happy hour, this Oak Street eatery is a favorite dining destination in Carrollton. In addition to creative rolls like the Black and Gold (salmon, avocado, tuna, and cucumber topped with black and gold roe), the restaurant has developed a following for its pillowy steamed buns stuffed with mouthwatering fillings, like duck or chicken katsu. **Known for:** happy hour; steamed buns; creative sushi rolls. $ *Average main: $22* ⊠ *8312 Oak St., Carrollton-Riverbend* ☎ *504/826–9119* ⊕ *www.chiba-nola.com* ⊗ *Closed Sun. No lunch Mon.–Wed.* ⊹ *3:C2.*

$$ ✗ **Dante's Kitchen.** Ask local chefs where they dine on their day off, and
SOUTHERN chances are a good number of them will mention Dante's Kitchen. Chef-owner Eman Loubier, a nine-year veteran of Commander's Palace, prepares seasonal menus for those with a sense of adventure. **Known for:** foodie clientele; chicken-under-a-brick; outdoor patio. $ *Average main: $25* ⊠ *736 Dante St., Carrollton-Riverbend* ☎ *504/861–3121* ⊕ *www.danteskitchen.com* ⊗ *Closed Tues. No lunch Mon. and Wed.–Fri.* ⊹ *3:C2.*

$$ ✗ **Jacques-Imo's Cafe.** Oak Street might look like any other sleepy urban
CREOLE thoroughfare by day, but once the sun sets, the half-block stretch containing Jacques-Imo's Cafe feels like the center of the universe. Prepare for lengthy waits (two hours at times) in the festive bar for a table in the boisterous, swamp-theme dining rooms (fortunately, the bartenders are fast). **Known for:** long lines; entertaining crowds; shrimp-and-alligator sausage cheesecake. $ *Average main: $18* ⊠ *8324 Oak St., Carrollton-Riverbend* ☎ *504/861–0886* ⊕ *www.jacques-imos.com* ⊗ *Closed Sun. No lunch* ⊹ *3:C2.*

MID-CITY AND BAYOU ST. JOHN

Most visitors make their way to Mid-City for Jazz Fest but there's lots happening any time of year. The surrounding dining options include both hip, unpretentious newcomers as well as neighborhood establishments that have been feeding locals affordably for generations.

MID-CITY

$ ✗ **Angelo Brocato's.** Traditional Sicilian gelato, spumoni, cannoli, pas-
CAFÉ tries, and candies are the attractions at this quaint little sweetshop, now
FAMILY over a century old. The crisp biscotti, traditional Sicilian desserts, and the lemon and strawberry ices haven't lost their status as local favorites. **Known for:** tiramisu; authentic gelato; local clientele. $ *Average main: $4* ⊠ *214 N. Carrollton Ave., Mid-City* ☎ *504/486–1465* ⊕ *www.angelobrocatoicecream.com* ⊗ *Closed Mon.* ⊹ *3:B3.*

$ ✗ **Mandina's.** Although New Orleans has many nationally known res-
CREOLE taurants, the locals still frequent their neighborhood favorites. Also
FAMILY known as "the pink house," Mandina's is one such spot, and has been since 1932. **Known for:** turtle soup; large plates; local clientele. $ *Average main: $16* ⊠ *3800 Canal St., Mid-City* ☎ *504/482–9179* ⊕ *www. mandinasrestaurant.com* ⊹ *3:B3.*

$ VIETNAMESE ✕**Mopho.** In general, you'll find the best Vietnamese food in New Orleans at authentic hole-in-the-walls on the city's outskirts, but Mopho is an exception to the rule. At this minimalist, modern space just minutes from City Park, Chef Micheal Gulotta creates elevated dishes based on Vietnamese flavors and locally sourced ingredients. **Known for:** ginger-glazed chicken wings; rice bowls; crispy brussels sprouts. $ *Average main: $13* ✉ *514 City Park Ave., Mid-City* ☎ *504/482–6845* ⊕ *www.mophonola.com* ⊗ *Closed Mon.* ✛ *3:A3.*

$ CREOLE FAMILY ✕**Morning Call.** Once upon a time, there were two famous French Quarter places to get beignets: Café du Monde and Morning Call. Then in 1974, after being open over a century, Morning Call packed up its antique fixtures and relocated to a suburban strip mall. **Known for:** 24-hour dining; beignets; café au lait. $ *Average main: $3* ✉ *City Park Casino, 56 Dreyfous Dr., Mid-City* ☎ *504/300–1157* ⊕ *www.neworleanscitypark.com/in-the-park/morning-call* ✛ *3:A3.*

$$$ CREOLE FAMILY ✕**Ralph's on the Park.** Seasoned restaurateur Ralph Brennan has matched this beautifully renovated historic building with a menu that features innovative twists on contemporary Creole standbys. The culinary staff excel with full-flavored seafood dishes like the Parmesan-fried oysters and a variety of fresh fish. **Known for:** scenic location; old-school service; three-course lunches. $ *Average main: $27* ✉ *900 City Park Ave., Mid-City* ☎ *504/488–1000* ⊕ *www.ralphsonthepark.com* ⊗ *No lunch Mon. and Sat. No dinner Sun.* ✛ *3:A3.*

$$ MODERN AMERICAN ✕**Rue 127.** This diminutive bistro, set back from the street, can be hard to find amid the neighboring bars and casual eateries. Inside, the staff greet you with more enthusiasm than polish, but it only takes a minute to realize that most customers are regulars, and by the first course you'll understand why. **Known for:** rabbit potpie; fresh Gulf fish; neighborhood crowd. $ *Average main: $23* ✉ *127 N. Carrollton Ave., Mid-City* ☎ *504/483–1571* ⊕ *www.rue127.com* ⊗ *Closed Sun. No lunch Mon. and Sat.* ✛ *3:B3.*

$$ CAJUN ✕**Toups' Meatery.** No one can say there were misled by a restaurant called a "meatery." On the menu, you'll find meat, meat, and more meat, from foie gras and charcuterie to a lamb neck with black-eyed-pea salad and tri-tip steak with bordelaise sauce (even the grilled veggies come with a bacon vinaigrette). Chef Isaac Toups, a recent *Top Chef* contestant and crowd favorite, is hardly the only young American chef obsessed with animal flesh, but at this intimate spot with DIY elegance, he adds a Louisiana edge with items like boudin, cracklings, or sides of dirty rice. **Known for:** charcuterie plates; bone marrow; boudin. $ *Average main: $22* ✉ *845 N. Carrollton Ave., Mid-City* ☎ *504/252–4999* ⊕ *www.toupsmeatery.com* ⊗ *Closed Sun. and Mon.* ✛ *3:A3.*

$$ CREOLE FAMILY ✕**Ye Olde College Inn.** A stalwart neighborhood joint, the age-old College Inn occupies a new building after decades in an older, now-razed structure next door. The flat, greasy burgers are still popular, particularly when ordered with french fries and a cold Abita, but the diner fare has been joined by more sophisticated plates. **Known for:** local produce; family-friendly; veal cutlet. $ *Average main: $18* ✉ *3000 S. Carrollton Ave., Mid-City* ☎ *504/866–3683* ⊕ *www.collegeinn1933.com* ⊗ *Closed Sun. and Mon. No lunch* ✛ *3:B2.*

8

BAYOU ST. JOHN

$$
FRENCH
✕ **Café Degas.** Dining at Café Degas is like being at a sidewalk café in Paris, even though the restaurant is completely covered: there's a tree growing through the center of the dining room, and the front windows overlook picturesque Esplanade Avenue. Employees are matter-of-fact, but in a relaxing, European way. **Known for:** romantic setting; authentic French food; pâté and charcuterie. ⑤ *Average main: $20 ⊠ 3127 Esplanade Ave., Mid-City* ☎ *504/945–5635* ⊕ *www.cafedegas.com* ⊗ *Closed Mon. and Tues.* ✛ *3:A4.*

$
CREOLE
✕ **Liuzza's by the Track.** Fried-oyster po'boys drenched in garlic butter, bowls of sweet-corn-and-crawfish bisque, and grilled Reuben sandwiches with succulent corned beef are some of the reasons you might decide to tolerate the poor ventilation in this barroom near the racetrack and Jazz Fest grounds. The Creole chicken and sausage gumbo with shrimp is always good—thin on body, but heavy on spice (the shrimp is cooked to order and can be left out if you have dietary restrictions). **Known for:** barbecue shrimp; people-watching; fried oyster po'boys. ⑤ *Average main: $10 ⊠ 1518 N. Lopez St., Mid-City* ☎ *504/218–7888* ⊕ *www.liuzzasnola.com* ⊗ *Closed Sun.* ✛ *3:A4.*

$
MEDITERRANEAN
✕ **1000 Figs.** Young chef-owner couple Theresa Galli and Gavin Cady, creators of the popular Fat Falafel food truck, opened this cozy Mediterranean café in 2014, serving slightly more sophisticated and hearty versions of the food truck favorites, from overstuffed falafel sandwiches with beet and carrot slaw, to shareable mezze plates. Don't skip the house-made french fries and toum (Middle Eastern creamy garlic sauce). **Known for:** falafel; mezze plates; neighborhood vibe. ⑤ *Average main: $11 ⊠ 3141 Ponce de Leon St., Bayou St. John* ☎ *504/301–0848* ⊕ *www.1000figs.com* ⊗ *Closed Mon.* ☞ *Reservations not accepted* ✛ *3:A4.*

$
CAFÉ
FAMILY
✕ **Parkway Bakery & Tavern.** Former contractor Jay Nix resurrected more than just a dilapidated building when he reopened Parkway: he also brought back to life a dormant community spirit. You can find neighbors and regulars from other parts of the city sinking their teeth into Parkway's roast beef and grilled ham po'boys; some simply wander in for a hot dog and beer at the bar, and to take in the New Orleans nostalgia decorating the walls (President Barack Obama was just one of many famous guests). **Known for:** local scene; long lines; roast beef and fried seafood po'boys. ⑤ *Average main: $9 ⊠ 538 Hagan Ave., Mid-City* ☎ *504/482–3047* ⊕ *www.parkwaypoorboys.com* ⊗ *Closed Tues.* ✛ *3:B3.*

WHERE TO STAY

Updated by
Cameron
Quincy Todd

Before you decide where to stay in New Orleans, put some thought into what you want to do during your visit. Are you interested in history and architecture? Do you want to be where the party is? Are you in town primarily to eat—and to eat well? Do antebellum mansions pique your interest? Do you need to be close to the business district and convention center? New Orleans is a fairly compact town, but if you stay Uptown, you'll need to travel a bit to reach the Quarter. Although most hotels favored by visitors are in the French Quarter, Central Business District (CBD), or Warehouse District, there are also great options farther afield.

The French Quarter is a destination unto itself. With fascinating architecture, vibrant nightlife, chic shopping, and incredible restaurants, you could spend several days without leaving its confines.

Hotels in the CBD, many of them chains, cater to business travelers as well as tourists; most are larger than those in the French Quarter, and have more amenities. Many of the Warehouse District's hotels actually occupy facilities once used to store cotton or other goods. In most cases, thoughtful renovations have kept the original purpose as a design motif, making for an interesting architectural style.

Just across Esplanade Avenue on the north and east of the Quarter is the Faubourg Marigny. Originally a Creole plantation and one of the first "suburbs" of New Orleans, it remains a residential area today, with a bustling nightlife and restaurant scene centered along Frenchmen Street.

To the west, upriver of the city's center, the Garden District and Uptown neighborhoods offer streets lined by the spreading boughs of live oaks, excellent stores, interesting architecture, and more outstanding dining and music venues. You'll find several newer, boutique hotels in the Garden District around St. Charles Avenue.

NEW ORLEANS LODGING PLANNER

RESERVATIONS

Book your room as far in advance as possible—up to a year ahead for Mardi Gras, Jazz Fest, or other special events.

SERVICES

Most hotels have private baths, central heating, air-conditioning, and private phones. More and more major hotels have added Wi-Fi or in-room broadband Internet service, though some chains continue to charge for in-room Wi-Fi. Smaller hotels and bed-and-breakfasts may not have all of these amenities; ask before you book your room.

Hotels that do not have pools may have agreements with nearby health clubs and the like to allow guests to use their facilities for a nominal fee.

Most hotels have parking available, but this can run you as much as $45 a day. Valet parking is usually available at the major hotels. If you park on the street, keep in mind that New Orleans meter attendants are relentless, and ticketing is prevalent for illegally parked vehicles. The minimum fine for a parking ticket is $20.

PRICES

The lodgings we list are the most desirable in each price category, but rates are subject to change. Look for special offers and discounted rates around the holidays and during the heat of summer. Be aware that the cost of lodging may be higher in October (considered peak convention season) and during the July 4 weekend (due to the annual Essence Music Festival). Rates are also high at the end of April and beginning of May during Jazz Fest, but peak during Mardi Gras, when major hotels often will require a three- or four-night minimum stay.

9

WHAT IT COSTS			
$	$$	$$$	$$$$
Hotels	under $150	$150–$224	$225–$300	over $300

Hotel prices are the lowest cost of a standard double room in high season.

WITH KIDS

In the listings, look for FAMILY in the margin, which indicates the property is particularly good for kids.

USING THE MAPS

Throughout the chapter, you'll see mapping symbols and coordinates (3:F2) at the end of each review. The first number after the symbol indicates the map number. Following that is the property's coordinate on the map grid.

WHERE SHOULD I STAY?

NEIGHBORHOOD	VIBE	PROS	CONS
The French Quarter	The tourist-driven main event is action-packed but still charming. Lodging runs from small inns to luxury hotels.	Lots of visitor attractions and nationally acclaimed restaurants. Everything is within walking distance of your hotel.	Crowded, high-traffic area. If you're sound-sensitive, request a room that does not face a main street, or find a hotel away from Bourbon Street.
Faubourg Marigny/ Bywater	Residential area just to the east of the French Quarter with a bohemian feel and fast-growing nightlife scene.	Balanced residential–commercial community. Close to French Quarter nightlife, yet has an eclectic nightlife scene of its own. The area is a more peaceful alternative to the Quarter.	Can be confusing to navigate for newcomers.
CBD and Warehouse District	The Warehouse District is also known as New Orleans's arts district. It's a great area for visitors who want to stay in luxurious high-rise hotels or smaller boutique properties.	Good retail and restaurants, and some of the best galleries and museums in the city. Within walking distance of the French Quarter.	Crowded; traffic can be a problem for pedestrians.
Garden District/ Uptown	Residential, upscale, and fashionable, this neighborhood is a slower-paced alternative to staying downtown.	Beautiful and right on the historic St. Charles Avenue streetcar line. Traffic here is not as heavy as downtown. Excellent shopping opportunities on Magazine Street.	Far from the French Quarter and tourist attractions; must drive or take public transportation.
Mid-City	This is primarily an urban–residential area, with few lodging options.	Many local businesses and mid-price owner-operated restaurants. Home to City Park, one of the largest urban parks in the country.	More challenging for tourists to navigate—some distance from tourist attractions. You'll need a car; public transportation is not convenient.

HOTEL REVIEWS

Listed alphabetically within neighborhood. Hotel reviews have been shortened. For full information, visit Fodors.com.

THE FRENCH QUARTER

$ 🖼 **Astor Crowne Plaza.** A great location within walking distance of
HOTEL everything that counts in the Quarter and downtown comes with a rooftop pool with spectacular views and a great in-house restaurant. **Pros:** convenient location; large rooms; big fitness center and outdoor pool; direct access to streetcar. **Cons:** Bourbon Street is

right next door—too close for some; fees for various Wi-Fi plans. $ *Rooms from: $109* ⊠ *739 Canal St., French Quarter* ☎ *504/962–0500, 877/408–9661* ⊕ *www.astorneworleans.com* ⟲ *693 rooms, 50 suites* ❍| *No meals* ✛ *1:C3.*

$$$$ 📷 **Audubon Cottages.** Seven one- and two-bedroom cottages in the heart
B&B/INN of the French Quarter make up this luxury retreat, affording a wonderful sense of privacy. **Pros:** lovely pool with outdoor lounge and cabanas; private butler service; use of the fitness center at the nearby Dauphine Orleans Hotel. **Cons:** some courtyards are shared. $ *Rooms from: $400* ⊠ *509 Dauphine St., French Quarter* ☎ *504/586–1516* ⊕ *www.auduboncottages.com* ⟲ *7 cottages* ❍| *Breakfast* ✛ *1:C2.*

$ 📷 **Bon Maison Guest House.** It is possible to find quiet, homey accom-
B&B/INN modation on Bourbon Street. **Pros:** on the less touristy end of the Quarter's main drag, but within walking distance of attractions and lots of restaurants; free Wi-Fi; warm welcome from hosts. **Cons:** can be difficult to reserve; minimum three-night stay most of the time; no parking; no breakfast. $ *Rooms from: $140* ⊠ *835 Bourbon St., French Quarter* ☎ *504/561–8498* ⊕ *www.bonmaison.com* ⟲ *4 rooms* ❍| *No meals* ✛ *1:D2.*

$$ 📷 **Bourbon Orleans Hotel.** This hotel's location is about as central as it
HOTEL gets, though the beautiful courtyard and pool provide welcome sanctuary from the loud, 24-hour Bourbon Street action just outside the door. **Pros:** welcome cocktail, complimentary coffee and tea in the lobby, and a free bottle of artesian water in the room; fitness center; Roux restaurant on-site; live entertainment in the on-site bar. **Cons:** lobby level is often crowded; street-facing rooms can be noisy. $ *Rooms from: $179* ⊠ *717 Orleans St., French Quarter* ☎ *504/523–2222* ⊕ *www.bourbonorleans.com* ⟲ *218 rooms, 28 suites* ❍| *No meals* ✛ *1:D2.*

$$ 📷 **Chateau LeMoyne.** Just one block off Bourbon Street, this branch of
HOTEL the Holiday Inn chain is pleasantly distinctive, with spacious rooms occupying a historic 19th-century New Orleans landmark, designed in part by famous architect James Gallier. **Pros:** great location; large, heated saltwater swimming pool; affordable rates; moderately priced authentic Southern breakfast (kids accompanied by adults eat free). **Cons:** some bathrooms are small. $ *Rooms from: $179* ⊠ *301 Dauphine St., French Quarter* ☎ *504/581–1303, 800/465–4329* ⊕ *www.hi-chateau.com* ⟲ *160 rooms, 11 suites* ❍| *No meals* ✛ *1:C3.*

$$ 📷 **Dauphine Orleans.** A great location—within easy walking distance of
HOTEL the action but removed enough to make this a secluded respite—comes with lots of charm. **Pros:** French Quarter architecture; saltwater pool; Tempur-Pedic mattresses; complimentary breakfast, in-room coffee, and bottled water. **Cons:** some rooms require climbing stairs. $ *Rooms from: $160* ⊠ *415 Dauphine St., French Quarter* ☎ *504/586–1800, 800/521–7111* ⊕ *www.dauphineorleans.com* ⟲ *107 rooms, 3 suites* ❍| *Breakfast* ✛ *1:C3.*

$$ 📷 **Four Points By Sheraton French Quarter.** With a heart-of-the-party
HOTEL Bourbon Street location, the most coveted of the well-kept rooms here (especially during Mardi Gras) are the ones with balconies overlooking the street. **Pros:** ideal for those who want to be in the center of the French Quarter action; free Wi-Fi. **Cons:** the high-traffic

9

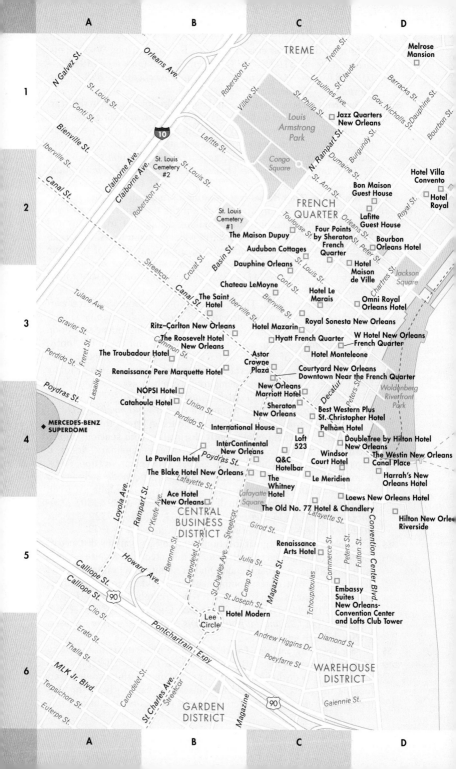

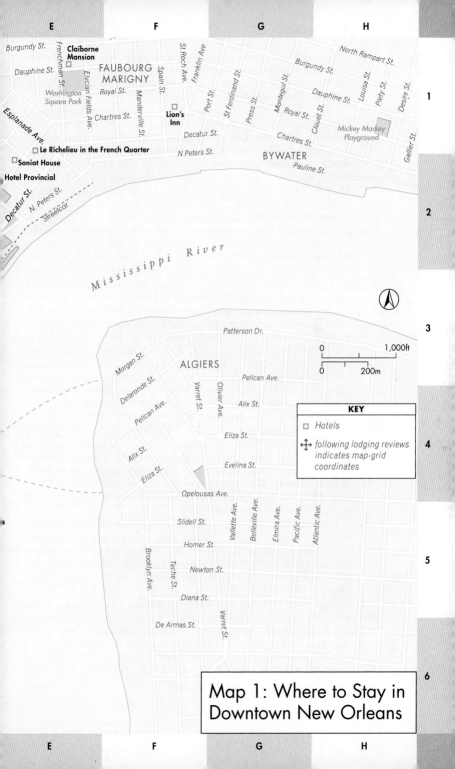

location means the party outside your front door never ends. $ *Rooms from: $214* ✉ *541 Bourbon St., French Quarter* ☎ *504/524–7611, 866/716–8133* ⊕ *www.fourpointsfrenchquarter.com* ⤴ *179 rooms, 7 suites* ⦿| *No meals* ✛ *1:C3.*

$$ 🏨 **Hotel Le Marais.** This contemporary outpost in the heart of the historic
HOTEL   French Quarter has trendy furnishings and a blacklighted lobby that combines urban chic with a voguish New Orleans vibe. **Pros:** modern furnishings; free in-room Wi-Fi; double-paned windows ensure quiet rooms despite location. **Cons:** not for those who want a traditional-looking hotel; no in-hotel restaurant. $ *Rooms from: $159* ✉ *717 Conti St., French Quarter* ☎ *504/525–2300* ⊕ *www.hotellemarais.com* ▭ *No credit cards* ⤴ *66 rooms* ⦿| *Breakfast* ✛ *1:C3.*

$$$$ 🏨 **Hotel Maison de Ville.** A collection of historic town houses and "bach-
HOTEL   elor quarters" make up this charming hotel with a delightfully secluded vibe amid the excitement of the French Quarter. **Pros:** lots of local history; unique rooms; personal and consistent service. **Cons:** slightly worn decor; no on-site restaurant. $ *Rooms from: $315* ✉ *727 Toulouse St., French Quarter* ☎ *504/324–4888* ⊕ *www.maisondeville.com* ⤴ *14 rooms, 1 suite, 1 cottage* ⦿| *Breakfast* ✛ *1:D3.*

$$ 🏨 **Hotel Mazarin.** An enviable French Quarter location combines with
HOTEL   loads of charm, including a picture-perfect courtyard with a fountain
Fodor'sChoice   and guest rooms featuring black-marble floors. **Pros:** complimentary
★   hot breakfast with omelets and waffles; great location; excellent guest service; free welcome cocktail in the 21st Amendment, an on-site, Prohibition-theme bar. **Cons:** rooms facing the street can be noisy; no tubs; no pool. $ *Rooms from: $169* ✉ *730 Bienville St., Downtown* ☎ *504/581–7300, 800/535–9111* ⊕ *www.hotelmazarin.com* ⤴ *102 rooms, 3 suites* ⦿| *Breakfast* ✛ *1:C3.*

$$$ 🏨 **Hotel Monteleone.** One of the grand old hotels of New Orleans, the
HOTEL   Hotel Monteleone dates to 1886 and oozes sophistication, romance,
Fodor'sChoice   and history. **Pros:** great location in the French Quarter; Royal Street
★   shopping; fabulous bar. **Cons:** the lobby and entrance can get crowded. $ *Rooms from: $249* ✉ *214 Royal St., Central Business District* ☎ *504/523–3341, 800/535–9595* ⊕ *www.hotelmonteleone.com* ⤴ *600 rooms, 55 suites* ⦿| *No meals* ✛ *1:C3.*

$$ 🏨 **Hotel Provincial.** This memorably authentic inn feels nicely secluded
HOTEL   yet close to the action. **Pros:** quaint; quiet surroundings (in a residen-tial section of the French Quarter); free Wi-Fi. **Cons:** suites are pricey. $ *Rooms from: $171* ✉ *1024 Chartres St., French Quarter* ☎ *504/581–4995, 800/535–7922* ⊕ *www.hotelprovincial.com* ⤴ *93 rooms, 6 suites* ⦿| *Breakfast* ✛ *1:E2.*

$ 🏨 **Hotel Royal.** Think of a cool big-city boutique hotel, mix in some
HOTEL   authentic New Orleans elegance and a good location, and you've got Hotel Royal. **Pros:** central location; complimentary break-fast; free Wi-Fi; complimentary pralines upon arrival. **Cons:** some rooms are small; no elevator, steps to reach upper floors. $ *Rooms from: $119* ✉ *1006 Royal St., French Quarter* ☎ *504/524–3900, 800/776–3901* ⊕ *www.hotelroyalneworleans.com* ⤴ *43 rooms* ⦿| *No meals* ✛ *1:D2.*

$$ · **Hotel Villa Convento.** This intimate, four-story 1833 Creole town house
HOTEL is located on a quiet street close to the Old Ursuline Convent, yet just
blocks from the Quarter's tourist attractions, shopping, and restaurants.
Pros: located in the quieter residential section of the French Quarter;
true New Orleans flavor; personal service; free Wi-Fi in all rooms; free
limited off-site parking. **Cons:** rooms on the small side; no children
under 10; no pool or fitness center. ⑤ *Rooms from: $165* ✉ *616 Ursu-
lines Ave., French Quarter* ☎ *504/522–1793* ⊕ *www.villaconvento.com*
⇨ *25 rooms* ⑪ *No meals* ✦ *1:D2.*

$$$ · **Hyatt French Quarter.** Airy public spaces, landscaped courtyards, an
HOTEL attractive pool area, and some of the largest guest rooms in the Quarter
create a sense of luxury here. **Pros:** airy and light; right on the edge of
the Quarter but set back from the hubbub of Bourbon Street; outdoor
pool and poolside bar; 24-hour fitness center. **Cons:** slight chain-hotel
feeling; very noisy at check-in and check-out times. ⑤ *Rooms from:
$299* ✉ *800 Iberville St., French Quarter* ☎ *504/586–0800, 800/766–
3782* ⊕ *frenchquarter.hyatt.com* ⇨ *254 rooms* ⑪ *No meals* ✦ *1:C3.*

$$ · **Lafitte Guest House.** In this four-story, 1849 French-style manor house,
B&B/INN each room has different details, from marble fireplaces to four-poster
beds. **Pros:** loads of historic-mansion charm; "mansion rooms" with
balconies are spectacular; updated furnishings. **Cons:** located on a high-
traffic corner of Bourbon Street. ⑤ *Rooms from: $189* ✉ *1003 Bourbon
St., French Quarter* ☎ *504/581–2678, 800/331–7971* ⊕ *www.lafitteg-
uesthouse.com* ⇨ *14 rooms* ⑪ *Breakfast* ✦ *1:D2.*

$$ · **Le Richelieu in the French Quarter.** Guests appreciate the personal
HOTEL friendliness of this old-fashioned, budget-friendly hotel, as well as nice
touches, such as an outdoor saltwater pool—all at a moderate rate in
a great location. **Pros:** good value; affordable on-site parking; close
to the Old Ursuline Convent and the French Market. **Cons:** café open
only for breakfast and lunch; bathrooms are small and dated; no fitness
center; rooms need updating. ⑤ *Rooms from: $160* ✉ *1234 Chartres
St., French Quarter* ☎ *504/529–2492, 800/535–9653* ⊕ *www.leriche-
lieuhotel.com* ⇨ *72 rooms, 15 suites* ⑪ *No meals* ✦ *1:E2.*

$$$ · **The Maison Dupuy.** Seven restored 19th-century town houses just two
HOTEL blocks from Bourbon Street surround one of the Quarter's prettiest
courtyards. **Pros:** quiet, yet still close to French Quarter action; free
Wi-Fi in guest rooms; great pool and courtyard. **Cons:** lobby can be
cramped at check-in; rooms could use updating; crowded during high
season. ⑤ *Rooms from: $239* ✉ *1001 Toulouse St., French Quarter*
☎ *504/586–8000, 800/535–9177* ⊕ *www.maisondupuy.com* ⇨ *187
rooms, 13 suites* ⑪ *No meals* ✦ *1:C2.*

$$ · **Melrose Mansion.** Just steps from the French Quarter, this renovated
B&B/INN Victorian mansion turns on the grandeur with antique furnishings,
hardwood floors, cathedral ceilings, and large chandeliers—and lots
of luxurious, modern conveniences. **Pros:** private and luxurious, with
lots of pampering; renovated property; breakfast included. **Cons:** one
night's stay is charged prior to arrival (special-event policies vary);
guest should use caution when walking around at night. ⑤ *Rooms
from: $169* ✉ *937 Esplanade Ave., French Quarter* ☎ *504/944–2255,*

9

800/650–3323 ⊕ *www.melrose-mansion.com* ↩ *14 rooms, 7 suites* |○| *Breakfast* ✢ *1:D1.*

$$$ ⊞ **New Orleans Marriott Hotel.** This
HOTEL centrally located 41-story skyscraper boasts fabulous views of the Quarter, downtown, and the Mississippi River. **Pros:** centrally located; stunning city and river views. **Cons:** typical chain hotel; lacks charm; charge for Wi-Fi in the rooms (access is free from the lobby). ⑤ *Rooms from: $239* ✉ *555 Canal St., French Quarter* ☎ *504/581–1000, 800/228–9290* ⊕ *www.neworleansmarriott.com* ↩ *1,329 rooms* |○| *No meals* ✢ *1:C4.*

$$$ ⊞ **Omni Royal Orleans Hotel.** One of the more elegant options in the
HOTEL French Quarter, this large white-marble landmark is a replica of the grand 1800s St. Louis Hotel, with columns, gilt mirrors, and magnificent chandeliers—traditional elegance in a central location. **Pros:** old-world grandeur; central location. **Cons:** can be crowded in the lobby and pool areas; daily charge for Wi-Fi. ⑤ *Rooms from: $225* ✉ *621 St. Louis St., French Quarter* ☎ *504/529–5333, 800/843–6664* ⊕ *www.omnihotels.com* ↩ *345 rooms, 26 suites* |○| *No meals* ✢ *1:D3.*

$$$$ ⊞ **Ritz-Carlton New Orleans.** One of the city's most regal hotels sits on
HOTEL Canal Street, with luxurious rooms and suites occupying what was
Fodor's Choice once the Maison Blanche department store. **Pros:** great location for
★ either business or pleasure; modern New Orleans fare at M Bistro; afternoon tea at the hotel is one of the most civilized traditions in the city. **Cons:** sometimes feels a like a chain; rates are among the highest in town. ⑤ *Rooms from: $399* ✉ *921 Canal St., French Quarter* ☎ *504/524–1331* ⊕ *www.ritzcarlton.com* ↩ *527 rooms, 38 suites* |○| *No meals* ✢ *1:B3.*

$$$ ⊞ **Royal Sonesta New Orleans.** Adding a touch of class to its Bourbon
HOTEL Street environs, this French Quarter favorite is soothing from the
Fodor's Choice moment you step into the marbled lobby, where lush plants enhance
★ a cool, serene atmosphere. **Pros:** outstanding service; bustling, cavernous lobby; great balcony views of the Quarter. **Cons:** consistently high occupancy can lead to slow elevator service; rooms facing Bourbon are noisy. ⑤ *Rooms from: $299* ✉ *300 Bourbon St., French Quarter* ☎ *504/586–0300* ⊕ *www.sonesta.com/royalneworleans* ↩ *482 rooms, 35 suites* |○| *No meals* ✢ *1:C3.*

$$ ⊞ **The Saint Hotel.** In the 1909 Beaux-Arts Audubon Building, up-to-
HOTEL the-minute decor really pops in a lobby glittering with chandeliers, atmospheric Carnival photos, and acres of sheer tulle curtains. **Pros:** on the Canal Street streetcar line and parade route; a few blocks from French Quarter action; marble baths; free Wi-Fi. **Cons:** may be too edgy and stark for some guests; lacks traditional New Orleans ambience and charm (part of Marriott's Autograph Collection boutique line).

Haunted Hotels

In New Orleans, reminders of human mortality are never far from view. The city's graves have traditionally been built aboveground, both in keeping with Catholic Latin and French custom and because New Orleans is mostly at or below sea level. Today, walled cemeteries are common tourist destinations. As a port city, New Orleans has always been a boisterous place, where pirates, prostitutes, gamblers, and characters of all stripes could find a comfortable home. The city's reputation as a home for voodoo is well founded; it is the birthplace of legendary voodoo priestess Marie Laveau. Not surprisingly, many of the city's hotels are purportedly home to restless spirits. Guests at the **Dauphine Orleans** (⊠ *415 Dauphine St., French Quarter* ☎ *800/521–7111*) report seeing a dancing woman in the courtyard and the spirit of a patron roaming the grounds, a reminder of the days when there was a brothel here. The grandfather clock in the lobby of the **Hotel Monteleone** (⊠ *214 Royal St., French Quarter* ☎ *800/535–9595*) is said to be haunted by the ghost of

its maker, and in the Garden District's **Columns Hotel** (⊠ *3811 St. Charles Ave., Uptown* ☎ *800/445–9308*), a former owner—who died in 1898—is occasionally still seen by guests. Hurricane Katrina was only the most recent catastrophe to befall New Orleans; yellow fever was a scourge on the city in the 18th and 19th centuries. The **Lafitte Guest House** (⊠ *1003 Bourbon St., French Quarter* ☎ *800/331–7971*) is only one hotel in which victims of the disease are said to linger. Of course you can't talk about the haunted hotels of New Orleans without mentioning the **Bourbon Orleans Hotel** (⊠ *717 Orleans, French Quarter* ☎ *504/523–2222*). Once a ballroom, and then convent, the storied building is said to house apparitions of former tenants, like the Confederate soldier roaming the sixth and seventh floors, and the dancer seen swaying underneath the crystal chandelier in the hotel's ballroom. There are a number of tour operators that cater to those with an interest in the supernatural, but if you stay at the right hotel, you may not need their services.

⑤ *Rooms from: $189* ⊠ *931 Canal St., French Quarter* ☎ *504/522–5400* ⊕ *www.thesainthotelneworleans.com* ▭ *No credit cards* ⇌ *171 rooms* ⫶⊙⫶ *No meals* ✛ *1:B3.*

$$$
B&B/INN
Fodor's Choice
★

⫶⊞⫶ **Soniat House.** Many frequent New Orleans visitors consider these meticulously restored town houses from the 1830s to be the city's finest hotel, with elegant rooms where stunning artwork—including some pieces on loan from the New Orleans Museum of Art—complements polished hardwood floors, Oriental rugs, and American and European antiques. **Pros:** very refined; expert service; timeless elegance. **Cons:** breakfast is delicious, but costs extra; several rooms are accessible by steps only. ⑤ *Rooms from: $245* ⊠ *1133 Chartres St., French Quarter* ☎ *504/522–0570, 800/544–8808* ⊕ *www.soniathouse.com* ⇌ *19 rooms, 10 suites* ⫶⊙⫶ *No meals* ✛ *1:E2.*

$$$
HOTEL

⫶⊞⫶ **W Hotel New Orleans French Quarter.** The many perks here include one of the best locations in the Quarter, rooms designed with funky jazz and tarot-card themes, and balconies that overlook either the courtyard or

Chartres Street. **Pros:** beautiful courtyard and pool; excellent service; lively contemporary decor with a New Orleans flavor. **Cons:** small driveway area can get crowded with valet activity; lines at check-in and check-out. $ *Rooms from: $259* ⊠ *316 Chartres St., French Quarter* ☎ *504/581–1200, 888/627–8260* ⊕ *www.wfrenchquarter.com* ⬳ *97 rooms, 5 suites* †Ⓞ† *No meals* ✛ *1:C3.*

$$$
HOTEL
⊡ **The Westin New Orleans Canal Place.** Views from this large convention hotel are enviable: two-story arched lobby windows overlook the French Quarter, and guest rooms tower over the great bend in the Mississippi River. **Pros:** luxurious rooms and suites; fabulous views of the Mississippi River and the French Quarter; close to shopping. **Cons:** lobby is on the 11th floor of an office tower/shopping mall; hotel has a chain feel; groups can overwhelm common spaces; daily charge for Internet access. $ *Rooms from: $232* ⊠ *100 Iberville St., French Quarter* ☎ *504/566–7006, 800/996–3426* ⊕ *www.starwoodhotels.com/ westin* ⬳ *438 rooms, 40 suites* †Ⓞ† *No meals* ✛ *1:D4.*

FAUBOURG MARIGNY AND TREMÉ

FAUBOURG MARIGNY

$
B&B/INN
⊡ **Claiborne Mansion.** One of the most beautiful places to stay in Faubourg Marigny, the Claiborne Mansion has enormous rooms with high ceilings, canopy beds, polished hardwood floors, and rich fabrics. **Pros:** big rooms; very private and relaxing; within walking distance of several great restaurants and jazz clubs; free Wi-Fi. **Cons:** limited on-site parking. $ *Rooms from: $125* ⊠ *2111 Dauphine St., Faubourg Marigny* ☎ *504/301–1027* ⊕ *www.claibornemansion.com* ⬳ *2 rooms, 5 suites* †Ⓞ† *Breakfast* ✛ *1:E1.*

$
B&B/INN
⊡ **Lions Inn.** Old South room decor adds to the traditional ambience of this bed-and-breakfast, while a swimming pool and hot tub in the private garden offer a welcome escape. **Pros:** gracious owners; private courtyard; lovely neighborhood feel; free Wi-Fi. **Cons:** a 10-minute walk to the Quarter or Frenchmen Street means you may want to take a cab at night; parking is on street. $ *Rooms from: $125* ⊠ *2517 Chartres St., Faubourg Marigny* ☎ *800/485–6846, 504/945–2339* ⊕ *www. lionsinn.com* ⬳ *10 rooms* †Ⓞ† *Breakfast* ✛ *1:F1.*

TREMÉ

$
B&B/INN
⊡ **Jazz Quarters New Orleans.** These charming guesthouses and suites, surrounded by meticulous gardens and furnished with antiques, were once a part of the historic Tremé plantation and are located within walking distance of the French Quarter. **Pros:** not widely known, even among frequent New Orleans visitors; quaint, intimate surroundings; free secure parking; free Wi-Fi. **Cons:** the neighborhood is not the best place to walk around after dark; no breakfast. $ *Rooms from: $135* ⊠ *1129 St. Philip St., Tremé* ☎ *504/523–1372, 800/523–1060* ⊕ *www. jazzquarters.com* ⬳ *5 cottages, 5 suites* †Ⓞ† *No meals* ✛ *1:C1.*

CBD AND THE WAREHOUSE DISTRICT

CBD

$$$ **Ace Hotel New Orleans.** This large, hip hotel is always buzzing with
HOTEL action. **Pros:** good entertainment and dining options on-site; rooftop
pool; sense of character and style. **Cons:** lobby gets loud and crowded
on nights when there are shows; too sceney for some; inconsistent ser-
vice. $ *Rooms from: $269* ⊠ *600 Carondolet St., Central Business Dis-
trict* ☎ *504/900–1180* ⊕ *www.acehotel.com/neworleans* ⥾ *234 rooms*
|◎| *No meals* ✛ *1:B5.*

$$ **Best Western Plus St. Christopher Hotel.** A former office complex from
HOTEL the 1890s offers rooms with exposed-brick walls and basic furnishings
just a block from the French Quarter. **Pros:** good location for the Convention Center and the French Quarter; free Wi-Fi; free Continental
breakfast. **Cons:** bar open Thursday to Saturday only. $ *Rooms from:
$179* ⊠ *114 Magazine St., Central Business District* ☎ *800/645–9312,
504/648–0444* ⊕ *www.stchristopherhotel.com* ▬ *No credit cards*
⥾ *108 rooms* |◎| *Breakfast* ✛ *1:C4.*

$ **The Blake Hotel New Orleans.** In season, the Blake occupies prime real
HOTEL estate on one of the Big Easy's best Carnival corners: the intersection of
St. Charles Avenue and Poydras Street near Lafayette Square. **Pros:** convenient location on the St. Charles Avenue streetcar line; pet-friendly;
free Wi-Fi. **Cons:** busy intersection. $ *Rooms from: $129* ⊠ *500 St.
Charles Ave., Central Business District* ☎ *504/522–9000, 888/211–
3447* ⊕ *www.blakehotelneworleans.com* ⥾ *124 rooms* |◎| *No meals*
✛ *1:C4.*

$$ **Catahoula Hotel.** This charming boutique hotel is a refreshing escape
HOTEL from a run-of-the-mill chain stay. **Pros:** sense of place; comfortable
beds; great lobby for hanging out. **Cons:** rooms are on the small side;
kitchen hours are limited; bar and courtyard get noisy on popular
nights. $ *Rooms from: $177* ⊠ *914 Union St., Central Business Dis-
trict* ☎ *504/603–2442* ⊕ *www.catahoulahotel.com* ⥾ *35 rooms* |◎| *No
meals* ✛ *1:B4.*

$$ **Courtyard New Orleans Downtown Near the French Quarter.** A wrap-
HOTEL around balcony overlooking St. Charles Avenue, a stunning six-story
FAMILY atrium, and some nods to period charm distinguish this family-friendly
CBD hotel. **Pros:** central CBD location; free Wi-Fi. **Cons:** significant
street noise at all hours; balcony rooms are in high demand during
Mardi Gras. $ *Rooms from: $219* ⊠ *124 St. Charles Ave., Central
Business District* ☎ *504/581–9005, 800/321–2211* ⊕ *www.marriott.
com* ⥾ *140 rooms* |◎| *No meals* ✛ *1:C3.*

$$ **DoubleTree by Hilton Hotel New Orleans.** Many of the open, airy rooms
HOTEL offer views of the French Quarter, Canal Street, and the Mississippi
River. **Pros:** close to the French Quarter and riverfront attractions;
across the street from the Insectarium; warm chocolate-chip cookies
upon arrival. **Cons:** chain-hotel vibe. $ *Rooms from: $169* ⊠ *300 Canal
St., Central Business District* ☎ *504/581–1300, 800/222–8733* ⊕ *www.
doubletree.com* ⥾ *367 rooms, 5 suites* |◎| *No meals* ✛ *1:C4.*

$$ **Embassy Suites New Orleans-Convention Center and Lofts Club Tower.** If
HOTEL your primary destination is the Convention Center (three blocks away)
FAMILY or the restaurants, galleries, and museums in the Warehouse District,

9

these suites with bedrooms and separate parlors are a great choice. **Pros:** spacious, well-maintained rooms; friendly service; breakfast included with all rooms; outdoor heated lap pool. **Cons:** a significant distance from the French Quarter. $ *Rooms from: $199* ✉ *315 Julia St., Central Business District* ☎ *504/525–1993, 800/362–2779* ⊕ *www.embassyneworleans.com* 🛏 *280 rooms, 90 Club Suites* ☵ *Breakfast* ✛ *1:C5.*

$$
HOTEL
Fodor's Choice
★

🛏 **Harrah's New Orleans Hotel.** Location, location, location—directly across the street from Harrah's New Orleans Casino, near the Convention Center and Riverfront attractions, close to the Warehouse District, the CBD, and the French Quarter. **Pros:** above-average service; stylish rooms. **Cons:** the hustle and bustle of this part of town mean peace and quiet can be in short supply; casino marketing is ever-present. $ *Rooms from: $175* ✉ *228 Poydras St., at Fulton St., Central Business District* ☎ *504/533–6000, 800/427–7247* ⊕ *www.harrahsneworleans.com* 🛏 *450 rooms* ☵ *No meals* ✛ *1:D4.*

$$$
HOTEL
FAMILY

🛏 **Hilton New Orleans Riverside.** The superb river and city views are hard to beat, and the guest rooms come with all the modern amenities, in close proximity to shops and the casino. **Pros:** well-maintained facilities; hotel runs like a well-oiled machine; great security; two heated outdoor swimming pools. **Cons:** the city's biggest hotel; typical chain service and surroundings. $ *Rooms from: $232* ✉ *2 Poydras St., Central Business District* ☎ *504/561–0500, 855/760–0870* ⊕ *www.hiltonneworleansriverside.com* 🛏 *1,622 rooms, 74 suites* ☵ *No meals* ✛ *1:D5.*

$$$
HOTEL

🛏 **InterContinental New Orleans.** The modern rose-granite structure overlooking St. Charles Avenue has large, well-lighted guest rooms, with contemporary, New Orleans–inspired furnishings. **Pros:** polished service; streetcar is just out front; free Wi-Fi; a good spot to catch the Mardi Gras action. **Cons:** located on one of the city's busiest downtown streets, which can be noisy; large big-box hotel. $ *Rooms from: $239* ✉ *444 St. Charles Ave., Central Business District* ☎ *504/525–5566, 800/424–6835* ⊕ *www.icneworleans.com* 🛏 *484 rooms, including 33 suites* ☵ *No meals* ✛ *1:C4.*

$$
HOTEL

🛏 **International House.** Contemporary style pairs with luxe comforts in guest rooms attractively decorated with modern New Orleans flair. **Pros:** great downtown location near the French Quarter; ideal if you want sophisticated surroundings; atmospheric hotel bar; contemporary vibe with a local accent; great customer service. **Cons:** no pool; hotel faces busy downtown street. $ *Rooms from: $150* ✉ *221 Camp St., Central Business District* ☎ *504/553–9550* ⊕ *www.ihhotel.com* 🛏 *117 rooms, 4 suites* ☵ *No meals* ✛ *1:C4.*

$$$
HOTEL

🛏 **Le Meridien.** This hip property was transformed in 2014 from a W Hotel into Le Meridien (also a Starwood brand). **Pros:** impressive renovation; close proximity to Contemporary Arts Center and the Ogden Museum of Southern Art. **Cons:** a bit far from the Bourbon Street action. $ *Rooms from: $231* ✉ *333 Poydras St., Central Business District* ☎ *504/525–9444* ⊕ *www.lemeridienneworleanshotel.com* 🛏 *410 rooms, 22 suites* ☵ *No meals* ✛ *1:C4.*

$$
HOTEL

🛏 **Le Pavillon Hotel.** One of the most regal hotels downtown offers romantic spaces, attentive service, and high-ceiling, traditionally furnished guest rooms in history-filled surroundings dating to 1907. **Pros:**

elegant French ambience; attentive staff; lovely restaurant. **Cons:** guest rooms could use some updating; not a fit if you're after something contemporary; on a busy street. $ *Rooms from: $189* ✉ *833 Poydras St., Central Business District* ☎ *504/581–3111, 800/535–9095* ⊕ *www. lepavillon.com* ⤴ *219 rooms, 7 suites* ✚ *1:B4.*

$$$ 🏨 **Loews New Orleans Hotel.** One of the friendliest large hotels in the
HOTEL city, this property stands out with stellar service, a Brennan-family restaurant, and bright, oversize rooms. **Pros:** well managed; accessible to everything that counts downtown; friendly service; excellent restaurant and lounge; Keurig coffeemakers in every room; on-site spa; free Wi-Fi. **Cons:** about a 10-minute walk to the French Quarter. $ *Rooms from: $289* ✉ *300 Poydras St., Central Business District* ☎ *504/595–3300, 866/211–6411* ⊕ *www.loewshotels.com/en/new-orleans-hotel* ⤴ *285 rooms, 12 suites* ✚ *No meals* ✚ *1:C4.*

$$ 🏨 **Loft 523.** A good option for chic, loft-style digs, it is so subtle from
HOTEL the outside that you may have trouble finding it among the surrounding buildings. **Pros:** sexy setting; inviting lounge; top-shelf amenities. **Cons:** some guests may be put off by the trendiness of it all; the bar is only open Thursday through Saturday. $ *Rooms from: $199* ✉ *523 Gravier St., Central Business District* ☎ *504/200–6523* ⊕ *www.loft523.com* ⤴ *16 rooms, 2 penthouses* ✚ *No meals* ✚ *1:C4.*

$$ 🏨 **NOPSI Hotel.** One of the city's newest hotels repurposes the New
HOTEL Orleans Public Service Inc. (NOPSI) building, a grand 1920s design, where New Orleanians used to pay their utility bills. **Pros:** good on-site dining and bars; large, newly renovated rooms; friendly and professional staff. **Cons:** rooftop pool area has an odd dress code. $ *Rooms from: $223* ✉ *317 Baronne St., Central Business District* ☎ *844/439–1463* ⊕ *www.nopsihotel.com* ⤴ *217 rooms, 76 suites* ✚ *No meals* ✚ *1:B4.*

$ 🏨 **The Old No. 77 Hotel & Chandlery.** This industrial-chic retreat opened
HOTEL inside a renovated 1854 warehouse which formerly housed the Ambassador Hotel in New Orleans's Central Business District, just four blocks from the buzzing French Quarter. **Pros:** central location that is near the French Quarter but not too close to the noise; stylish vibe; excellent on-site restaurant. **Cons:** some guest rooms don't have windows; lobby can get overcrowded with after-work revelers flocking to the restaurant bar. $ *Rooms from: $107* ✉ *535 Tchoupitoulas St., Central Business District* ☎ *504/527–5271* ⊕ *old77hotel.com* ⤴ *165 rooms* ✚ *No meals* ▤ *No credit cards* ✚ *1:C5.*

$ 🏨 **Pelham Hotel.** This 19th-century building with homey accommoda-
HOTEL tions is close to CBD sights like the Riverwalk and the casino, and offers a less hectic alternative to the convention hotels. **Pros:** centrally located, but far from heavily traveled tourist streets. **Cons:** rooms can be small and some lack windows; no on-site swimming pool or fitness area; noise from downtown traffic. $ *Rooms from: $149* ✉ *444 Common St., Central Business District* ☎ *504/522–4444, 888/856–4486* ⊕ *www. thepelhamhotel.com* ⤴ *60 rooms* ✚ *No meals* ✚ *1:C4.*

$ 🏨 **Q&C Hotelbar.** Intimate and tasteful, this hotel three blocks outside the
HOTEL French Quarter is a good alternative to the megahotels that surround it. **Pros:** feels like a smaller, more intimate property; good bar; two large lobbies. **Cons:** small gym; narrow hallways. $ *Rooms from: $143*

9

⊠ *344 Camp St., Central Business District* ☎ *504/587–9700* ⊕ *www.qandc.com* ⌇ *196 rooms* ⦿ *No meals* ✛ *1:C4.*

$$ 🖼 **Renaissance Pere Marquette Hotel.** On floors named after renowned
HOTEL jazz musicians, large, quiet rooms have soothing colors, comfortable
fabrics, photography by local artists, and oversize marble bathrooms.
Pros: good on-site bar and restaurant; excellent service. **Cons:** location is not especially pedestrian-friendly. ⑤ *Rooms from: $209* ⊠ *817 Common St., Central Business District* ☎ *504/525–1111* ⊕ *www.renaissancehotels.com* ⌇ *272 rooms* ⦿ *No meals* ✛ *1:B3.*

$$$ 🖼 **The Roosevelt Hotel New Orleans.** From its glittering lobby to each
HOTEL beautiful, traditionally furnished guest room, this iconic New Orleans
Fodor's Choice hotel offers a grand experience. **Pros:** exquisite lobby, especially when
★ the holiday decorations are up; location near downtown and French
Quarter; outstanding bar and restaurants; streetcar just outside. **Cons:**
pricey fees for parking and in-room Wi-Fi; rooms aren't as exciting as
other parts of the hotel. ⑤ *Rooms from: $269* ⊠ *123 Baronne St., Central Business District* ☎ *504/648–1200* ⊕ *www.therooseveltneworleans.com* ⌇ *504 rooms, 135 suites* ⦿ *No meals* ✛ *1:B3.*

$$$ 🖼 **Sheraton New Orleans Hotel.** Sheraton Club rooms come with many
HOTEL special amenities, but even the regular guest rooms here are spacious
and well appointed, with contemporary touches and lots of extras. **Pros:**
large hotel with lots of rooms; experienced staff; great service; central
location; rooftop pool and sundeck; recently renovated fitness center.
Cons: typical corporate convention property; lacks the warmth of some
of its competitors; can be crowded during peak season; fee for Wi-Fi in
guest rooms. ⑤ *Rooms from: $244* ⊠ *500 Canal St., Central Business District* ☎ *504/525–2500, 800/325–3535* ⊕ *www.sheratonneworleans.com* ⌇ *1,110 rooms, 53 suites* ⦿ *No meals* ✛ *1:C4.*

$$ 🖼 **The Troubadour Hotel.** This new midsize hotel has a funky, boutique
HOTEL vibe, a great restaurant and rooftop bar, and frequent live, local music.
Pros: large, modern rooms and bathrooms; rooftop bar has great views
of the city; good on-site dining options; close walk to the Quarter. **Cons:**
lobby is small and busy; immediate area around hotel feels remote.
⑤ *Rooms from: $198* ⊠ *1111 Gravier St., Central Business District* ☎ *504/518–5800, 888/858–6652 reservations* ⊕ *www.thetroubadour.com* ⌇ *184 rooms* ⦿ *No meals* ✛ *1:B3.*

$$ 🖼 **The Whitney Hotel.** This stylish European-style boutique hotel, with top-
HOTEL notch service and comfortable rooms, is a great choice if you're looking
to stay away from the Bourbon Street bustle. **Pros:** free Wi-FI; near the
Convention Center, the French Quarter, and the Superdome; rooms come
with coffeemakers and a free bottle of artesian water. **Cons:** located at a
busy downtown intersection; no restaurant on-site. ⑤ *Rooms from: $169* ⊠ *610 Poydras St., Central Business District* ☎ *504/581–4222* ⊕ *www.whitneyhotel.com* ⌇ *93 rooms, 23 suites* ⦿ *No meals* ✛ *1:C4.*

$$$$ 🖼 **Windsor Court Hotel.** Located just four blocks from the French Quarter,
HOTEL this elegant luxury hotel has plenty of upscale amenities—think plush
Fodor's Choice carpeting, marble vanities, and well-appointed dressing areas set in
★ spacious guest rooms. **Pros:** old-world elegance; superior service; location near the French Quarter but not in the thick of it. **Cons:** location
close to casino can mean traffic outside. ⑤ *Rooms from: $355* ⊠ *300*

Gravier St., Central Business District ☎ *504/523–6000, 800/262–2662* ⊕ *www.windsorcourthotel.com* ⟿ *55 rooms, 260 suites, 1 2-bedroom penthouse* ⑪ *No meals* ✛ *1:C4.*

THE WAREHOUSE DISTRICT

$ ▦ **Hotel Modern.** One of the most idiosyncratic and charming hotels in
HOTEL the city delivers a bit of attitude along with its eclectic selection of rooms of all shapes and sizes, from postage-stamp to spacious. **Pros:** on the St. Charles Avenue streetcar line and parade route; hip vibe; friendly service. **Cons:** hallways can be cramped; you're a 20-minute walk from the French Quarter; some rooms are tiny, with small windows; no on-site bar or restaurant. Ⓢ *Rooms from: $129* ✉ *936 St. Charles Ave., Warehouse District* ☎ *504/962–0900, 800/684–9525* ▭ *No credit cards* ⟿ *135 rooms* ⑪ *No meals* ✛ *1:B5.*

$$ ▦ **Renaissance Arts Hotel.** Art lovers looking to stay close to downtown
HOTEL should check out this circa-1910 warehouse-turned-hotel, where huge windows now make for great views from comfortable, spacious, well-designed rooms furnished with a minimalist bent. **Pros:** modern, well-appointed facilities; beautiful artwork; hotel "navigators" serve as personal guides to the city. **Cons:** not suitable for those who want a traditional New Orleans hotel; not convenient to the French Quarter. Ⓢ *Rooms from: $189* ✉ *700 Tchoupitoulas St., Warehouse District* ☎ *504/613–2330* ⊕ *renaissance-hotels.marriott.com* ⟿ *210 rooms, 7 suites* ⑪ *No meals* ✛ *1:C5.*

THE GARDEN DISTRICT

$$ ▦ **Grand Victorian Bed & Breakfast.** This escape from the New Orleans
B&B/INN hoopla more than lives up to its lofty name with well-appointed rooms
Fodor's Choice that evoke old Louisiana through period antiques and distinctive private
★ baths. **Pros:** a block and a half from Commander's Palace Restaurant; elegant; one of the rooms is handicapped accessible; on the St. Charles Avenue streetcar line; free Wi-Fi throughout the house and guest rooms. **Cons:** limited parking; not within easy walking distance of the French Quarter or CBD; usually requires a three-night minimum stay. Ⓢ *Rooms from: $208* ✉ *2727 St. Charles Ave., Garden District* ☎ *504/895–1104, 800/977–0008* ⊕ *www.gvbb.com* ⟿ *8 rooms* ⑪ *Breakfast* ✛ *2:B5.*

$$$ ▦ **Henry Howard Hotel.** A historic mansion recently restored as a chic
HOTEL boutique hotel, rooms have high ceilings, four-poster beds, and modern
Fodor's Choice amenities. **Pros:** large, quiet rooms; friendly staff; a good mix of history
★ and style. **Cons:** no on-site restaurant or gym. Ⓢ *Rooms from: $229* ✉ *2041 Prytania St., Garden District* ☎ *504/313–1577* ⊕ *henryhow-ardhotel.com* ⟿ *18 rooms, 1 penthouse suite* ⑪ *No meals* ✛ *2:B6.*

$$$ ▦ **Pontchartrain Hotel.** A team of local experts recently restored this
HOTEL 1930s hotel to its former glory with inventive decor and excellent dining options. **Pros:** excellent bars and restaurants on-site; lots of style; convenient but quieter part of town. **Cons:** not as much in the immediate walking area as other parts of town; comings and goings of bar patrons makes for a noisy lobby. Ⓢ *Rooms from: $249* ✉ *2031 St. Charles Ave., Garden District* ☎ *504/206–3114* ⊕ *www.thepontchartrainhotel.com* ⟿ *106 rooms* ⑪ *No meals* ✛ *2:B6.*

9

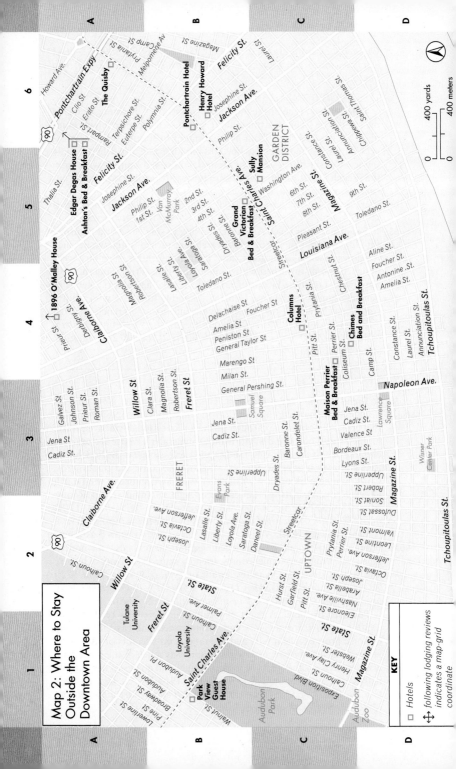

Map 2: Where to Stay Outside the Downtown Area

A | **B** | **C** | **D**

6 | **5** | **4** | **3** | **2** | **1**

Howard Ave.

Pontchartrain Expy

The Quiby

Edgar Degas House
Ashton's Bed & Breakfast

Felicity St.

Jackson Ave.

1896 O'Malley House

Claiborne Ave.

Willow St

Freret St

Jena St

Cadiz St.

Freret St

Willow St

Tulane University

Loyola University

State St.

Saint Charles Ave.

Park View Guest House

Audubon Park

Audubon Zoo

Magnolia St.
Robertson St.

Clara St.

FRERET

Evans Park

Jefferson Ave.

Octavia St.
Joseph St.

Lasalle St.
Liberty St.
Loyola Ave.
Saratoga St.
Danee St.

UPTOWN

Dryades St.

Baronne St.
Carondelet St.

Magnolia St.
Robertson St.

Magazine St.

Pontchartrain Hotel

Henry Howard Hotel

Felicity St.

Magazine St.
Josephine St.

Philip St.

Sully Mansion

GARDEN DISTRICT

Saint Charles Ave.

Grand Victorian Bed & Breakfast

Louisiana Ave.

Columns Hotel

Chimes Bed and Breakfast

Maison Perrier Bed & Breakfast

Napoleon Ave.

Magazine St.

Tchoupitoulas St.

Samuel Square

Lawrence Square

Wisner Center Park

Jena St.
Cadiz St.
Valence St
Bordeaux St.
Lyons St.
Upperline St.
Robert St.
Soniat St.
Dufossat St.
Valmont St.
Leontine St.
Jefferson Ave.
Octavia St.
Joseph St.
Arabella St.
Nashville Ave.
Eleonore St.
State St.
Webster St.
Henry Clay Ave.
Calhoun St.
Exposition Blvd

Delachaise St.   Foucher St.
Amelia St
Peniston St
General Taylor St.
Marengo St.
Milan St.
General Pershing St.

Pitt St.
Perrier St.
Coliseum St.
Camp St.

Chestnut St.
Prytania St.

Aline St.
Foucher St.
Antonine St.
Amelia St.

Constance St.
Laurel St.
Annunciation St.

KEY

☐ Hotels

✛ following lodging reviews indicates a map-grid coordinate

0   400 yards
0   400 meters

$ 🖼 **The Quisby.** This spacious, newly constructed European-style hostel
HOTEL   is a great budget-friendly option, especially during Mardi Gras, when
Fodor's Choice   parades roll right past your window. **Pros:** fun lobby bar; much more
★   than you would expect from a hostel; friendly staff. **Cons:** shared rooms
and bathrooms; single beds. ⑤ *Rooms from: $55* ✉ *1225 St. Charles
Ave., Garden District* ☎ *504/208–4881* ⊕ *www.thequisby.com* ⏎ *30
rooms* ⦿ *No meals* ✛ *2:A6.*

$$ 🖼 **Sully Mansion.** Famous 19th-century architect Thomas Sully built
B&B/INN   this handsome, rambling Queen Anne–style house in 1890. **Pros:** old-
world charm; individualized attention to guests. **Cons:** it's a mile or
so from the French Quarter; most rooms are only accessible by stairs,
though the St. Charles suite is on the first floor; parking is free, but
it's on-street. ⑤ *Rooms from: $158* ✉ *2631 Prytania St., Garden Dis-
trict* ☎ *504/891–0457, 800/364–2414* ⊕ *www.sullymansion.com* ⏎ *8
rooms, 2 suites* ⦿ *Breakfast* ✛ *2:C5.*

UPTOWN

$$ 🖼 **Chimes Bed and Breakfast.** Charming, homey guest rooms all open onto
B&B/INN   the courtyard and have private entrances in this well-appointed B&B.
Fodor's Choice   **Pros:** everything sparkles; just three blocks from the streetcar and Maga-
★   zine Street; laptop and printer for guest use; W-Fi and parking included
with room rate. **Cons:** noise carries easily from room to room; 3 miles
from the French Quarter, which might be too far for some. ⑤ *Rooms
from: $158* ✉ *1146 Constantinople St., Uptown* ☎ *504/899–2621*
⊕ *www.chimesneworleans.com* ⏎ *5 rooms* ⦿ *Breakfast* ✛ *2:C4.*

$ 🖼 **Columns Hotel.** This white-column 1883 Victorian hotel drips with
HOTEL   local charm and is listed on the National Register of Historic Places—
guests especially enjoy the lovely, wide veranda. **Pros:** exquisite architecture; the veranda's perfect for watching the St. Charles Avenue parades
during Mardi Gras; on the streetcar line; complimentary hot breakfast;
live jazz in the ballroom. **Cons:** rooms are large but need updating;
transportation necessary to French Quarter and CBD. ⑤ *Rooms from:
$144* ✉ *3811 St. Charles Ave., Uptown* ☎ *504/899–9308, 800/445–
9308* ⊕ *www.thecolumns.com* ⏎ *20 rooms* ⦿ *Breakfast* ✛ *2:C4.*

$$ 🖼 **Maison Perrier Bed & Breakfast.** Redolent of Southern hospitality and
B&B/INN   historic elegance, this 1890s Victorian mansion is filled with antiques,
local art, and many extra comforts. **Pros:** personalized service; lovely
residential setting; free Wi-Fi. **Cons:** not well located if you prefer to
spend most of your time in the French Quarter; no elevator. ⑤ *Rooms
from: $190* ✉ *4117 Perrier St., Uptown* ☎ *504/897–1807, 888/610–
1807* ⊕ *www.maisonperrier.com* ⏎ *9 rooms* ⦿ *Breakfast* ✛ *2:C4.*

$$ 🖼 **Park View Guest House.** This Victorian guesthouse, steps from the
B&B/INN   streetcar and Audubon Park, adds to the delightful selection of smaller
Uptown lodgings. **Pros:** great park views; easy access to public golf
course; on the St. Charles Avenue streetcar line; good restaurants
nearby; free Wi-Fi. **Cons:** not walkable to downtown or the French
Quarter. ⑤ *Rooms from: $179* ✉ *7004 St. Charles Ave., Uptown*
☎ *504/861–7564* ⊕ *www.parkviewguesthouse.com* ⏎ *22 rooms*
⦿ *Breakfast* ✛ *2:B1.*

9

MID-CITY

$$ 🖼 **Ashton's Bed & Breakfast.** Few details have been overlooked in this
B&B/INN   sumptuous 1861 mansion, where distinctively decorated guest rooms
have a range of beds, including iron-frame, Shaker, and four-poster.
Pros: exquisitely decorated and spacious rooms; nice location not far
from New Orleans City Park; convenient to Jazz Fest. **Cons:** if you
don't have a car, you'll need to take a taxi or city bus to reach the
French Quarter. ⑤ *Rooms from: $190* ✉ *2023 Esplanade Ave., Mid-City* ☎ *504/942–7048, 800/725–4131* ⊕ *www.ashtonsbb.com* ⇆ *8
rooms* ⑩ *Breakfast* ✛ *2:A6.*

$$ 🖼 **Edgar Degas House.** This beautiful property was once home to
B&B/INN   French impressionist Edgar Degas. **Pros:** meticulously maintained
Fodor's Choice   and expertly operated; luxe amenities and extras; on the National
★   Register of Historic Places; close to Jazz Fest. **Cons:** not in the middle
of the action; if you don't have a car, you'll need to catch the city bus
or cab it to the Quarter. ⑤ *Rooms from: $199* ✉ *2306 Esplanade
Ave., Mid-City* ☎ *504/821–5009* ⊕ *www.degashouse.com* ⇆ *9 rooms*
⑩ *Breakfast* ✛ *2:A6.*

$$ 🖼 **1896 O'Malley House.** Best suited for those seeking a less touristy
B&B/INN   New Orleans experience, this elegant B&B near the intersection of
Canal Street and North Carrollton Avenue offers rooms furnished with
antiques and equipped with heavy cypress doors, hardwood floors,
and plush drapery at oversize windows. **Pros:** complimentary snacks,
wine, and beer available; an iPad loaded with information about New
Orleans provided in rooms; walking distance to entertainment and
restaurants; good base for Jazz Fest. **Cons:** roughly 3 miles from the
French Quarter and the Garden District; not for guests wanting to be
in the middle of the action. ⑤ *Rooms from: $155* ✉ *120 S. Pierce St.,
Mid-City* ☎ *504/488–5896, 866/226–1896* ⊕ *www.1896omalleyhouse.
com* ⇆ *8 rooms* ⑩ *Breakfast* ✛ *2:A4.*

NIGHTLIFE AND PERFORMING ARTS

COCKTAIL CULTURE

In the early 1800s the Creole apothecary Antoine Amadie Peychaud ran a pharmacy in the French Quarter. He concocted a cherry-color bitters that is still an essential ingredient of the Sazerac, New Orleans's signature cocktail.

(above) Ingredients for New Orleans's official cocktail, at the Sazerac Bar (top right) Tales of the Cocktail festival (bottom right) The Museum of the American Cocktail

According to legend, Peychaud mixed his bitters with brandy, water, and sugar, then served the drink in a traditional French eggcup called a "coquetier." It wasn't long before English speakers had mangled the French word, calling the drink a "cocktail." It's a good story, except that Peychaud was three years old when the word "cocktail" first appeared in print. But even if the cocktail wasn't invented in New Orleans, no other city has embraced it with more passion. From Peychaud's now-famous bitters to the iconic Hurricane and beyond, New Orleans is home to many of the greatest inventions in cocktail history. In recent years, a new generation of bartenders has reinvigorated the Crescent City's cocktail culture with elaborate techniques and farm-fresh ingredients. —by Todd A. Price

NEW ORLEANS'S OFFICIAL DRINK

Legislators were concerned that giving Louisiana an official cocktail would cause people to associate the state with drinking. Apparently the city of New Orleans was already a lost cause, though, and in 2008 the Sazerac became the official cocktail of New Orleans. It's the only city in the country to have an officially legislated drink.

TOP FIVE ICONIC NEW ORLEANS COCKTAILS

Sazerac: Rye whiskey, Peychaud's bitters, and sugar served in a rocks glass rinsed with absinthe or Herbsaint, a local absinthe substitute

Claim to Fame: Official drink of New Orleans

Best Places to Try One: Column's Hotel Victorian Lounge Bar or French 75

Ramos Gin Fizz: Gin, cream, orange flower water, and lemon and lime juice shaken with an egg white and topped with club soda

Claim to Fame: Huey P. Long's favorite eye-opener

Best Place to Try One: Sazerac Bar at the Roosevelt Hotel

Hurricane: Blend of rum, grenadine, and tropical juices

Claim to Fame: The start of many a lost weekend

Best Place to Try One: Pat O'Brien's

Vieux Carré: Brandy, rye whiskey, sweet vermouth, Bénédictine, and a dash each of Peychaud's and Angostura bitters

Claim to Fame: A perfectly balanced tribute to the French Quarter

Best Place to Try One: Carousel Bar at the Hotel Monteleone, where it was invented

Pimm's Cup: Pimm's No. 1 topped with lemon-lime soda and garnished with a cucumber

Claim to Fame: A British thirst quencher embraced by the Crescent City

Best Place to Try One: Napoleon House

10

Updated by Cameron Quincy Todd

There are many iconic images that come to mind when people think of New Orleans nightlife, including the neon glitz of Bourbon Street and the lone jazzman playing his horn beneath an old French Quarter gas lamp. But this is only the start of what New Orleans nightlife is all about. Whether you're looking for the simple pleasures of a perfectly constructed cocktail with a balcony view or something more adventurous, you've come to the right place.

PLANNING

HOURS

Bars tend to open in the early afternoon and stay open well into the morning hours. Live music usually begins around 6 in a handful of clubs that host early sets, but **things really get going between 9 and 11 pm.** Bear in mind that many venues operate on "New Orleans time," meaning that if a show is advertised to start at 10 pm, it might kick off closer to 11.

If you're a night owl, plenty of clubs have **late-night sets,** some not starting until 1 am.

WHAT TO WEAR

Dress codes are as rare as snow in this city. On any given night in the French Quarter—and especially during the Carnival season—you'll see everything from tuxedos to tutus, T-shirts to fairy wings, and everything in between. Wear whatever is easiest to dance in.

COVER CHARGE VS DRINK MINIMUMS

Many bars on Bourbon Street entice visitors by presenting bands with no cover charge. They make their money by imposing a **one- or two-drink minimum,** with draft beer or soft drinks costing $5 to $8 apiece. In general, prices for beer, wine, and cocktails range from $4 to $9, unless you land in a good neighborhood dive bar, and then the prices can drop by as much as half. Music clubs generally charge a flat cover of between $5 and $20, with the high-end prices usually reserved for nationally touring artists, holidays, and special occasions.

TIPPING THE BAND

Bring cash to live-music clubs; **many bands play for tips alone.** Expect the hat (or the bucket, or the old coffee can, or the empty goldfish bowl) to be passed around once per set.

SAFETY

Although much of New Orleans is safe, it's always a good idea to **keep an eye out and be aware of your surroundings,** especially late at night or if it's readily apparent that you've been hitting the Hurricanes a little too hard. Pickpockets and muggers do exist, but an ounce of prevention in the form of awareness goes a long way toward avoiding any kind of incident. In the French Quarter and downtown it's usually fine to walk from place to place, but if you're traveling through outlying neighborhoods late at night, it's best to take a car or taxi.

EVENT INFO

A great source for concert and event information is **WWOZ,** the jazz and heritage community radio station, which broadcasts worldwide over the Internet at ⊕ *www.wwoz.org.* Local musicians, music historians, and personalities make up the all-volunteer corps of DJs, and they broadcast live 24/7 out of the French Quarter.

For more detailed event listings, check out **Gambit Weekly** (⊕ *www.bestofneworleans.com*), the alternative weekly available free in many bars, cafés, and stores. The **Times-Picayune** (⊕ *www.nola.com*), the city's main newspaper, publishes an entertainment supplement every Friday called Lagniappe. The monthly **OffBeat** (⊕ *www.offbeat.com*) magazine has in-depth coverage of local music and venues and is available at many hotels, stores, and restaurants.

NIGHTLIFE

10

No American town places such a premium on pleasure as New Orleans. From swank hotel lounges and refined jazz halls to sweaty dance clubs and raucous Bourbon Street bars, this city is serious about frivolity—and famous for it. Partying is more than an occasional indulgence in this city—it's a lifestyle. The bars and clubs that pulse with music are the city's lifeblood, and are found in every neighborhood. Like stars with their own gravity, they draw people through their doors to belly up to their bars or head feet-first onto their dance floors. Blues, jazz, funk, R&B, rock, roots, Cajun, and zydeco—there are many kinds of music and nightlife experiences to be had in New Orleans. On any day or night of the year, the city is brimming with musical possibilities.

The French Quarter and Faubourg Marigny are the easiest places to find great music and nightspots. The venues are numerous and all within easy walking distance of one another. In the nearby Warehouse District, New Orleans institutions like Howlin' Wolf, Mulate's, and Circle Bar have been joined by scores of new bars, clubs, and restaurants. Moving upriver through the Garden District and Uptown, you'll find some of the most famous music spots in the city, such as Tipitina's and Maple Leaf. Bywater, Mid-City, and Tremé are residential neighborhoods with fewer commercial strips, but they too have their crown jewels, like Vaughan's, Bullet's, and Rock 'n' Bowl.

FRENCH QUARTER

The old neighborhood, with its Spanish architecture and narrow, French-named streets, is the hub of the Crescent City and remains the beating heart of New Orleans's nightlife. Live music comes at you from all directions—from bars, clubs, concert halls, restaurants, and even from the streets themselves—and many of the neighborhood's restaurants, shops, cafés, and galleries stay open late to accommodate the night crowd. Although mostly fueled by tourists, the French Quarter remains the city's premiere nightlife destination because of its diversity and convenience.

BARS AND LOUNGES

Bar Tonique. An eclectic spot on North Rampart Street, this brick-walled room with private nooks and intimate corner booths looks like a cross between a dive and a lounge on the Riviera. The book-length drinks menu, with everything from pre-Prohibition classics to modern creations, practically recounts the history of the cocktail. The talented staff can turn out any of those offerings with aplomb. ✉ *820 N. Rampart St., French Quarter* ☎ *504/324–6045* ⊕ *www.bartonique.com.*

Bombay Club. A rather swanky lounge for the French Quarter, with leather chairs and dark paneling, covers cocktail history with an encyclopedic menu that starts with drinks from the mid-19th century, and boasts the largest selection of martinis in town. Tucked away from the street in the Prince Conti Hotel, this lair hosts piano players and jazz combos nightly. ✉ *Prince Conti Hotel, 830 Conti St., French Quarter* ☎ *504/577–2237* ⊕ *www.bombayclubneworleans.com.*

Brieux Carre. This pint-sized, colorful microbrewery is making a name for itself as some of the best local beer in the area. There are around nine beers on tap at any given time, often exotic varieties with locally inspired names. A large beer garden and outdoor patio in the back is the brewery's best feature. ✉ *2115 Decatur St., French Quarter* ☎ *504/304–4242* ⊕ *www.brieuxcarre.com.*

Fodor's Choice
★
Cane and Table. With its elegant, understated Caribbean decor, dim lighting, and low volumes, this rum house is a refreshing relief from the general chaos of the neighborhood. The friendly barkeeps boast about "ProtoTiki Cocktails" (specialty rum drinks with modern twists), but there's a sophisticated list of Spanish wines to choose from as well. The space offers a large marble bar, charming courtyard out back, and small tables for intimate dining. Come for the cocktails and atmosphere, but don't miss out on the food: the menu combines Caribbean and Southern culinary traditions, and the dishes are inventive and intensely flavorful. ✉ *1113 Decatur St., French Quarter* ☎ *504/581–1112* ⊕ *www.caneandtablenola.com.*

Carousel Bar. A favorite New Orleans drinking destination since 1949, the revolving bar has served the likes of Tennessee Williams, Truman Capote, and Ernest Hemingway. A recent renovation added extra space for a second bar, more tables, and a stage that hosts free shows by local musicians Wednesday through Saturday. ⊠ *Hotel Monteleone, 214 Royal St., French Quarter* ☎ *504/523–3341* ⊕ *www.hotelmonteleone.com.*

Cat's Meow. Before you see it, you'll hear this Bourbon Street landmark, New Orleans's most popular karaoke bar. Given an ideal corner location, the bar's tall doors and windows oHAHAHAHpen onto two streets, luring undergrads, conventioneers, and bachelorette parties to hit the dance floor and grab the mic. High-energy MCs and DJs keep the night spinning along, but get on the sign-up sheet early if you want a chance at French Quarter fame. ⊠ *701 Bourbon St., French Quarter* ☎ *504/523–2788* ⊕ *www.catskaraoke.com.*

Chart Room. Unpretentious even by New Orleans standards, this little dive not far from Canal Street draws a good number of locals from the Quarter and beyond for inexpensive drinks and wide-open doorways that offer table seating just off the sidewalk. ⊠ *300 Chartres St., French Quarter* ☎ *504/522–1708.*

Cosimo's. Few tourists make their way to this hip neighborhood hangout, in a far corner of the Lower Quarter. A short flight of stairs leads to a darts and billiards room. Quirky wagon wheel–shape ceiling fans, ample windows, and a friendly vibe make it a low-key place to wind down. Food options include pizzas, burgers, and Cosimo's famous fried green beans. ⊠ *1201 Burgundy St., French Quarter* ☎ *504/522–9715.*

Fodor's Choice
★
French 75. This is a must-visit for any who love to submerge themselves in old-time elegance. Adjoining Arnaud's, the classic New Orleans Creole restaurant, this dark-wood bar is complete with leather-backed chairs and imposing columns. The bartenders work magic with their encyclopedic knowledge of cocktails and arsenal of ingredients. Be sure to venture upstairs to the Germaine Wells Mardi Gras Museum (free), a slightly bizarre showcase for memorabilia and ball gowns worn by the original owner's daughter. ⊠ *813 Bienville St., French Quarter* ☎ *504/523–5433* ⊕ *www.arnaudsrestaurant.com/french-75.*

10

Kerry Irish Pub. This well-worn favorite has a pool table, a jukebox stocked with the Pogues and Flogging Molly, and, of course, Guinness on draft. A small stage at the back hosts Irish musicians, singer-songwriters, and R&B or jazz musicians nightly with no cover charge. It's one of the last venues for Irish music in the Quarter. ⊠ *331 Decatur St., French Quarter* ☎ *504/527–5954.*

Fodor's Choice
★
Lafitte's Blacksmith Shop. Perhaps the most photographed building in the Quarter after the St. Louis Cathedral, this 18th-century blacksmith shop was once a front for the eponymous pirate's less legitimate business ventures—or so says local legend. Today, it's an atmospheric piano bar with a rustic, candlelit interior and a small outdoor patio shaded by banana trees. Despite the addition of a few flat-screen TVs, a drink here just after sundown, under the soft glow of candles, lets you slip back in time for an hour or so. ⊠ *941 Bourbon St., French Quarter* ☎ *504/593–9761* ⊕ *www.lafittesblacksmithshop.com.*

Molly's at the Market. Grab a perch almost any time of day at one of the best-known and most popular bars along the far stretch of Decatur Street, where you'll find perfect pints of Guinness, generously poured cocktails, and gregarious bartenders. From a window seat, you can watch the crowds of shop-goers, sightseers, and all-day revelers. Everyone from politicians to punk rockers eventually drifts though these doors. ⊠ *1107 Decatur St., French Quarter* ☎ *504/525–5169* ⊕ *www.mollysatthemarket.net.*

> **ONE FOR THE ROAD**
>
> Although bottles and glasses are officially banned on the street, New Orleans is one of the few places where it's legal to carry a drink in public. Ready to move on? Ask the bartender for a "go cup."

Fodor's Choice ★ **Napoleon House Bar and Café.** It's a living shrine to what may be called the semiofficial New Orleans school of decor: faded grandeur. Chipped wall paint, diffused light, and a tiny courtyard with a trickling fountain and lush banana trees create a timeless escapist mood. The house specialty is a Pimm's Cup (here they top Pimm's No. 1 with lemonade and 7-Up). This vintage restaurant and watering hole has long been popular with writers, artists, and other free spirits, although today most customers are tourists. But even locals who don't venture often into the French Quarter will make an exception for Napoleon House. ⊠ *500 Chartres St., French Quarter* ☎ *504/524–9752* ⊕ *www.napoleonhouse.com.*

Old Absinthe House. In its 200-year history, this low-key oasis with its famous marble absinthe fountain has served guests including Oscar Wilde, Mark Twain, Franklin Roosevelt, and Frank Sinatra. It's now mostly frequented by tourists and casual local characters who appreciate a good brewski or cocktail to go. Thousands of business cards stapled to the wall serve as interesting wallpaper. ⊠ *240 Bourbon St., French Quarter* ☎ *504/523–3181* ⊕ *www.ruebourbon.com/ old-absinthe-house.*

Pat O'Brien's. Sure, it's touristy, but there are reasons Pat O's has been a must-stop on the New Orleans drinking trail since Prohibition. Friendly staff, an easy camaraderie among patrons, and a signature drink—the pink, fruity, and extremely potent Hurricane, which comes with a souvenir glass—all make this French Quarter stalwart a pleasant afternoon diversion. There's plenty of room to spread out, from the elegant side bar and piano bar that flank the carriageway entrance to the lush (and in winter, heated) patio. Expect a line on weekend nights, and if you don't want your glass, return it for the deposit. ⊠ *718 St. Peter St., French Quarter* ☎ *504/525–4823* ⊕ *www.patobriens.com.*

Patrick's Bar Vin. Dapper Patrick Van Hoorebeek holds court at his wine bar in a clubby atmosphere of dark wood and red upholstery. Wines by the glass are the specialty, but there's also an excellent selection of cocktails and beers, including Van Hoorebeek's own Belgian brew. Major oenophiles can rent personal wine lockers. Only a few steps from Bourbon Street, Bar Vin feels like another world. It opens at noon on Friday to catch the lunch crowd. ⊠ *730 Bienville St., French Quarter* ☎ *504/200–3180* ⊕ *www.patricksbarvin.com.*

GAY BARS AND CLUBS

Bourbon Pub. It's impossible to miss this 24-hour video bar at the corner of St. Ann and Bourbon streets, especially in early evenings, when the doors are open and the dance crowd spills into the street. There's usually a cover charge on Friday and Saturday nights after 10 pm; Sunday afternoon is devoted to vintage videos by assorted gay icons. ⊠ *801 Bourbon St., French Quarter* ☏ *504/529–2107* ⊕ *www.bourbonpub.com.*

Café Lafitte in Exile. This Bourbon Street stalwart attracts a somewhat older and very casual group of gay men. The second floor has a pool table, pinball machine, and wraparound balcony with a bird's-eye view of the lively street scene below. Sunday afternoon, when the oldies spin and the paper-napkin confetti flies, is especially popular. ⊠ *901 Bourbon St., French Quarter* ☏ *504/522–8397* ⊕ *www.lafittes.com.*

Corner Pocket. Filmmaker John Waters reportedly counts the Pocket as a New Orleans favorite, and with skinny, tattooed strippers on the bar and an inebriated drag queen emcee, it's easy to see why. Sleazy fun on a good night, but keep your wits about you. ⊠ *940 St. Louis St., French Quarter* ☏ *504/568–9829* ⊕ *www.cornerpocket.net.*

The Golden Lantern. The Lower Quarter has become a lot more upscale since this neighborhood gay haunt's heyday, but (the officially named) Tubby's Golden Lantern soldiers on. The bartender's whim determines the music, the drinks are strong, and happy hour runs from noon to 8 pm Monday and Tuesday, and from 8 am to 8 pm every other day. The bar is best known as ground zero for the annual Southern Decadence drag parade, when a throng gathers out front for the kickoff. ⊠ *1239 Royal St., French Quarter* ☏ *504/529–2860.*

Good Friends. With its tasteful decor and reasonable volume level, this is a slightly more upscale, sedate alternative to the blasting disco bars down the street. The Queen's Head Pub on the second floor, open weekends, has darts, a wraparound balcony, and respectable martinis. Brush up on your show tunes at the popular Sunday afternoon piano sing-along. ⊠ *740 Dauphine St., French Quarter* ☏ *504/566–7191* ⊕ *www.goodfriendsbar.com.*

Napoleon's Itch. The only gay bar in New Orleans that's also attached to a large hotel, this narrow space is in the heart of St.-Ann-and-Bourbon gay central; it's a must-visit during the annual Southern Decadence festival. The comfy sofas and handsome bartenders are a plus, and the crowd tends to be a bit dressier than at similar venues. ⊠ *Bourbon Orleans Hotel, 734 Bourbon St., French Quarter* ☏ *504/237–4144.*

Oz. A spacious dance club that mainly attracts young gay men also draws straight men and women, largely because of the scarcity of good dance floors in the French Quarter. It's open around the clock and tends to peak very late. ⊠ *800 Bourbon St., French Quarter* ☏ *504/593–9491* ⊕ *www.ozneworleans.com.*

Parade Disco. High-energy disco is the rule at this dance club above the Bourbon Pub. If it gets to be too much, a quieter back bar and a balcony offer respite. The crowd is mostly male and young, but women are welcome. ⊠ *801 Bourbon St., above Bourbon Pub, French Quarter* ☏ *504/529–2107* ⊕ *www.bourbonpub.com.*

10

MUSIC CLUBS

B.B. King's Blues Club. This mid-South chain fits in well on Decatur Street, where its casual bar fare and consistent live music attracts a wide range of tourists. Music starts at noon on weekdays and as early as 9 am on weekends, and sets continue well into the night. Bar grub is Southern comforts like barbecue ribs and fried chicken. ⊠ *1104 Decatur St., French Quarter* ☎ *504/934–5464* ⊕ *www.bbkings.com/new-orleans.*

Davenport Lounge. These swanky digs in the Ritz-Carlton are home to their namesake, Jeremy Davenport, an old-school crooner in the mold of Sinatra and Crosby. With a hot trumpet, Davenport plays Wednesday through Saturday and draws a mixed crowd of visitors and locals to the swinging dance floor. ⊠ *The Ritz-Carlton, New Orleans, 921 Canal St., French Quarter* ☎ *504/524–1331* ⊕ *www.ritzcarlton.com.*

Fritzel's European Jazz Pub. An old-school gem in the midst of Bourbon Street's many venues with bad cover bands, this Dixieland music club, built in the style of the old jazz halls, has tight rows of seating close to the stage and floating barmaids. Drinks cost a little more, but there's never a cover charge. Shows nightly. ⊠ *733 Bourbon St., French Quarter* ☎ *504/586–4800* ⊕ *www.fritzelsjazz.net.*

House of Blues. Despite its name, blues rarely makes the bill at this Decatur Street link in the national chain. The midsize venue embraces rock, country, soul, funk, and world music, and it's one of the city's most reliable destinations for national touring acts. The adjoining restaurant hosts a popular gospel brunch. The **Parish,** a more intimate offshoot upstairs from the main house, books edgier, up-and-coming groups. ⊠ *225 Decatur St., French Quarter* ☎ *504/310–4999* ⊕ *www. houseofblues.com/neworleans.*

The Jazz Playhouse. Serious music lovers converge on this intimate lounge with a modern aesthetic. Top-notch local jazz and brass acts like the Glenn David Andrews Band and the Brass-A-Holics are a refreshing change from the loud rock and blues cover bands that have become the Bourbon Street norm. There are multiple sets of local talent daily between 5 pm and midnight. There's no cover, but you can pay $20 in advance for guaranteed preferred seating. ⊠ *Royal Sonesta Hotel, 300 Bourbon St., French Quarter* ☎ *504/553–2299* ⊕ *www.sonesta.com.*

One Eyed Jack's. This former Toulouse Street theater hosts rock bands, as well as local up-and-comers, '80s nights, and even the occasional female arm-wrestling competition. The 19th-century saloon interior provides an appropriately decadent backdrop for Fleur de Tease, the resident burlesque troupe. ⊠ *615 Toulouse St., French Quarter* ☎ *504/569–8361* ⊕ *www.oneeyedjacks.net.*

Palm Court Jazz Café. Banjo player Danny Barker immortalized this restaurant in his song "Palm Court Strut." Traditional New Orleans jazz is presented in a timeless setting with tile floors, exposed-brick walls, and a handsome mahogany bar. There are decent creature comforts here; regional cuisine is served, and you can sit at the bar and rub elbows with local musicians. A wide selection of records and CDs are available for sale. ⊠ *1204 Decatur St., French Quarter* ☎ *504/525–0200* ⊕ *www. palmcourtjazzcafe.com.*

FAMILY
Fodor's Choice
★

Preservation Hall. At this cultural landmark founded in 1961, a cadre of distinguished New Orleans musicians, most of whom were schooled by an ever-dwindling group of elder statesmen, nurture the jazz tradition that flowered in the 1920s. There is limited seating on benches—many patrons end up squatting on the floor or standing in back—and no beverages are served, although you can bring your own drink in a plastic cup. Nonetheless, legions of satisfied music lovers regard an evening at this all-ages venue as an essential New Orleans experience. Cover charge is $15 (cash only), and $20 for Friday and Saturday performances. The price can be a bit higher for special appearances. A limited number of advanced "Big Shot" tickets ($35–$50) guarantee you a seat and let you skip the line. ⊠ *726 St. Peter St., French Quarter* ☎ *504/522–2841* ⊕ *www.preservationhall.com.*

FAUBOURG MARIGNY, BYWATER, AND TREMÉ

FAUBOURG MARIGNY

Frenchmen Street in the Marigny is the hottest music strip in town, and is also known for its food and street life. Much of Frenchmen's activity is within a three-block area (between Decatur and Dauphine streets), where fun-seekers crawl bars and people-watch on the sidewalk. Some clubs along this strip charge a $5–$10 cover for music, but many charge nothing at all. Along St. Claude Avenue a diverse cluster of bars and clubs offers everything from brass-band jams to death metal to experimental, avant-garde indie rock.

BARS AND LOUNGES

AllWays Lounge & Theatre. This lounge-theater combo has become one of the centerpieces of the local indie, avant-garde, and art scenes. Evoking 1930s Berlin, the lounge has a black-and-red color scheme and frayed-at-the-edges art-deco aesthetic. Musicians, burlesque dancers, clowns, artists, and jacks-of-all-trades take to the stage here most nights of the week. Meanwhile, in the back of the house, the 100-seat AllWays Theatre hosts weekend plays and other performances. ⊠ *2240 St. Claude Ave., Faubourg Marigny* ☎ *504/218–5778* ⊕ *www.theallwayslounge.net.*

Checkpoint Charlie's. This bustling corner bar draws young locals who shoot pool and listen to blues and rock, whether live or from the jukebox—24 hours a day, seven days a week. Weekends often feature hard rock, punk, and metal bands. There's also a paperback library, a menu of bar grub, and even a fully functioning laundromat. ⊠ *501 Esplanade Ave., Faubourg Marigny* ☎ *504/281–4847.*

Mag's 940. This friendly gay bar hosts special events ranging from country western line-dance lessons to burlesque and drag shows. There's a big-screen TV for games and a large selection of vodkas and top-shelf bourbons. It proclaims itself "the cleanest bar in New Orleans."⊠ *940 Elysian Fields Ave., Faubourg Marigny* ☎ *504/948–1888.*

The Maison. This historic building—with a sprawling three-story floor plan, interior balconies, a terrific kitchen, plus multiple bars, stages, and dance floors—has become one of Frenchmen Street's most popular destinations. Live music every night of the week (normally with no cover) make it inviting, and the managers skillfully weave local and touring

10

Continued on page 186

by Alison Fensterstock
and Jennifer Odell

Above and opposite, French Quarter jazz clubs, Maison Bourbon and Preservation Jazz Hall.

NEW ORLEANS NOISE

The late local R&B star Ernie K-Doe once said, "I'm not sure, but I think all music comes from New Orleans." He wasn't far off. The Crescent City has crafted American music for hundreds of years—from Jelly Roll Morton's Storyville jazz piano to the siren sound of Louis Armstrong's genre-defining trumpet; from Little Richard's first French Quarter rock 'n'roll recording session to Lil Wayne's hip-hop domination.

Right, New Orleans' musical legend, Louis Armstrong.

THE SOUNDS OF THE BIG EASY

JAZZ

The roots of New Orleans jazz reach back to the 17th century, when slaves sang traditional songs in Congo Square. As their African and Caribbean poly-rhythms blended with European styles, new sounds were born.

In the Storyville red-light district in 1895, cornetist Buddy Bolden played what is considered to be the first jazz. It was a march-meets-syncopation sound that drew from the city's numerous fraternal and societal brass marching bands, from ragtime, and from blues.

Pianist Jelly Roll Morton, who also got his start playing in Storyville's bordellos, helped transition ragtime into jazz with his more flamboyant playing style. In 1915 he published the first jazz composition, "Jelly Roll Morton Blues."

But it was the cornet and trumpet players of the day who really sounded off. Joe "King" Oliver, Louis Armstrong's mentor, changed his cornet's sound by holding a plunger over the bell. Sidney Bechet revolutionized soloing with his radical fingering. Louis Armstrong made jazz a phenomenon with his skill, improvisational style, and showmanship. These men were the originators of New Orleans Dixieland, which rapidly spread across the nation and was itself transformed—here and elsewhere—through the decades.

Today, young New Orleans musicians benefit from the work of contemporary jazz players and educators like pianist Ellis Marsalis. His students have included Terence Blanchard, Donald Harrison, Jr., and Nicholas Payton, as well as his own talented sons: Wynton (trumpet), Branford (sax), Delfeayo (trombone), and Ellis III (drums).

LISTEN TO: King Oliver, Louis Armstrong, Sidney Bechet, Jelly Roll Morton, Kid Ory, Donald Harrison, Jr., Nicholas Payton, Trombone Shorty, Christian Scott.

GO TO: Preservation Hall and Palm Court Jazz Café (traditional; French Quarter). Snug Harbor and the Blue Nile (contemporary; Faubourg Marigny).

EXPERIENCE IT: during ranger-led talks and walks at the Jazz National Historic Park (www.nps.gov/jazz).

Far left, clockwise from left, jazz at Bourbon Street, Jelly Roll Morton, Louis Armstrong. Below right, Zydeco accordionist. Left, Soul Rebel Brass Band.

BRASS BANDS

To lay down those 2/4 and 4/4 rhythms, traditional New Orleans Dixieland was greatly influenced by the format of the city's brass bands: trumpet or coronet for melody; clarinet for countermelody and harmony; trombone to emphasize the chord-change notes; banjo (later replaced by guitar); tuba (later, the piano); and drums.

In the 1970s and '80s, young brass bands like Rebirth and Dirty Dozen updated the traditional rollicking drum-and-horn street parade sound with funk and hip-hop. Now they're the elder statesmen of a thriving scene.

LISTEN TO: Hot 8, Stooges, Rebirth, Soul Rebels.
GO SEE: Rebirth at the Maple Leaf (Tues., Uptown); Soul Rebels at Le Bon Temps Roulé (most Thurs., Uptown).
EXPERIENCE IT: at the Backstreet Cultural Museum (www.backstreetmuseum. org), with artifacts from the Mardi Gras Indian, brass band, and second-line traditions.

CAJUN AND ZYDECO

Most purveyors of plaintive French-language balladry and squeeze-box and fiddle-driven dancehall rhythms play a few hours outside of the city. But some bands, like the Grammy-nominated Lost Bayou Ramblers, do make their way into *la ville*. The same is true of zydeco, accordion and washboard-driven music that evolved from the rural black-Creole sounds and urban R&B.

LISTEN TO: Cajun—Beausoleil, Feufollet, Pine Leaf Boys, Les Freres Michot, Savoy Family Cajun Band. Zydeco—Clifton Chenier, Chubby Carrier, Terrance Simien, Rockin' Dopsie Jr.
GO TO: For Cajun, Mulate's the Original Cajun (Warehouse District); dba (the Marigny). For zydeco, Bruce Daigrepont's Sunday *fais do do* at Tipitina's (Uptown). Every Thursday Rock 'n' Bowl (Mid-City) books Cajun, zydeco, and swamp pop.
EXPERIENCE IT: at mid-June's Louisiana Cajun-Zydeco Festival (www.jazzand heritage.org/cajun-zydeco) in the French Quarter.

Above, performers at Congo Square, New Orleans, Jazz Fest.
Below, Allen Toussaint.
Top right, Dr. John.
Below right, Partners-N-Crime.

SOUL AND R&B

In the 1950s and '60s, producers like Allen Toussaint and Dave Bartholomew laid the groundwork for rock 'n' roll with funky, groove-based R&B that captured the gritty, fun-loving rhythm of New Orleans.

LISTEN TO: Professor Longhair, Fats Domino, Irma Thomas, Ernie K-Doe, Allen Toussaint, Neville Brothers, Dr. John, Guitar Lightnin' Lee, Little Freddie King.

GO SEE: Veterans like Al "Carnival Time" Johnson and Ernie Vincent still perform around town, most often at festivals, but occasionally at the Rock 'n' Bowl, dba, or neighborhood bars.

BOUNCE AND HIP-HOP

The danceable, hard-driving party rap known as bounce originated in New Orleans housing projects and neighborhood bars in the late 1980s. In the 1990s, No Limit and Cash Money Records put New Orleans hip-hop on the map.

LISTEN TO: Big Freedia, Truth Universal, Partners-N-Crime, Mystikal, Juvenile, Lil' Wayne

GO SEE: Big-name acts like Juvenile and Mystikal play at the House of Blues (the Quarter) or the Arena (CBD). Look for bounce performers and hip-hop artists at Republic (Warehouse District) and other small rock venues around town.

SECOND LINES AND JAZZ FUNERALS

Second line parade in the French Quarter.

If you encounter a marching band parading down the streets of New Orleans, chances are it's a second line, a type of parade historically associated with jazz funerals. The term second line refers specifically to the crowd that marched behind the "first line" of the brass band and family of the deceased. During the early 20th century, the New Orleans second line served an important community function; African Americans were not allowed to buy insurance, so they formed mutual-aid societies—called Social Aid and Pleasure Clubs—to help members through tough times. The tradition continues to this day; different Social Aid and Pleasure Clubs parade in all neighborhoods of the city every weekend of the year, outside of the hottest summer months. If you get wind of an authentic second line, go, but use caution. Stick to the safer-looking streets, and be prepared to make an exit if things start to get edgy.

The website www.blogofneworleans. com posts routes and schedules for the weekend's second lines.

Sylvester Francis has spent the better part of a lifetime documenting second-line parades and jazz funerals; his **Backstreet Cultural Museum** (*1116 St. Claude Ave., Tremé, 504/522–4806, www. backstreetmuseum.org*) is a repository of second-line mementos and tons of photographs. Open Tuesday through Saturday.

"Uncle" Lionel Batiste of the Tremé Brass Band.

JAZZ AND HERITAGE FESTIVAL

Above, crowds and performers at Jazz Fest. Opposite page, Mr. Okra vending truck.

A sprawling, rollicking celebration of Louisiana music, food, and culture, Jazz Fest is held annually the last weekend in April and the first weekend in May at the historic Fair Grounds Race Course. The grounds reverberate with rock, Cajun, zydeco, gospel, rhythm and blues, hip-hop, folk, world music, country, Latin, and, yes, traditional and modern jazz. Throw in world-class arts and crafts, exhibitions and lectures, and an astounding range of local food, and you've got a festival worthy of America's premiere party town.

Over the years, Jazz Fest lineups have come to include mainstream performers—Bruce Springsteen, Tom Petty, and Eric Clapton topped the bill in recent years—but at its heart the festival is about the hundreds of Louisiana musicians who live, work, and hone their chops in the Crescent City. Many New Orleans musicians are still recovering from the effects of Hurricane Katrina, and Jazz Fest is their chance to show a huge, international audience that the music survives.

HISTORY

Veterans of the first Jazz Fest, which took place in 1970 in what's now Armstrong Park, talk about it with the same awe and swagger of those who rolled in the mud at Woodstock in 1969. The initial lineup included such legendary performers as Mahalia Jackson, Duke Ellington, Fats Domino, The Meters, and the Olympia Brass Band, who played for a small audience of about 350 people, approximately half the number of performers and production staffers it took to put the event on. In 2006 the first post-Katrina festival drew an estimated 300,000 to 350,000 people from all over the world and showcased the talents of some 6,000 performers, artisans, and chefs. Many of the musicians who performed at the first Jazz Fest came back to play the emotional 2006 festival. In 2014 the festival welcomed more than 430,000 attendees.

Official Logo of Jazz and Heritage Festival.

MUSIC

Each of the 12 stages has its own musical bent. The Congo Square stage hosts hip-hop and world music, the Fais-Do-Do stage specializes in Cajun and zydeco performers, fans of traditional jazz head for the Economy Hall Tent, and everyone spends at least a few minutes in the Gospel Tent soaking up the exuberant testimony.

FOOD

Cooks from all over Louisiana turn out dishes both familiar (shrimp po'boys and jambalaya) and exotic (alligator sausage, anyone?). Favorites include gumbo, soft-shell-crab, cochon de lait po'boys, and Crawfish Monica, a creamy pasta dish. Beer and wine are available, but hard liquor is taboo.

CRAFTS

Craft areas at Jazz Fest include Contemporary Crafts, near the Gospel Tent, which sells wares from nationwide artists; the Louisiana Marketplace, near the Fais-Do-Do stage and Louisiana Folklife Village, which showcase area folk art; and a Native American Village, which spotlights indigenous culture. Surrounding the Congo Square stage are stands with African and African-influenced artifacts items. ■TIP→ **Many artists have a spot for only part of the fest; ask about their schedule before putting off any purchases.**

A tent beside Economy Hall sells CDs by festival performers, as well as other New Orleans and Louisiana artists; nearby is the official merchandise, including limited-edition Jazz Fest posters, which range in price from about $70 for a numbered silkscreen to several hundred dollars for a signed and numbered remarque print. In the Books Tent, local authors sign works on Louisiana music and culture. ■TIP→ **You don't need to bring a lot of cash. ATMs are located throughout the site.**

JAZZ FEST TIPS

■ Book hotels as early as possible.

■ Thursdays on the second weekend are the least-packed day, and a local favorite.

■ You can purchase a full program once you arrive at the festival, with detailed schedules and maps, or tear the "cubes" out of the *Gambit* weekly paper, *Offbeat* monthly, or the *Times-Picayune's* weekly Lagniappe pullout. Free iPhone apps are also available.

■ Don't stress out trying to catch all the big names; inevitably, the obscure local musicians provide the most indelible Jazz Fest memories.

■ For a break from the heat and sun (plus air-conditioned indoor restrooms), visit the Grandstand, which hosts exhibits, cooking demonstrations (often with free samples), musician interviews, and an oyster bar.

■ Longtime fest goers bring flags to let friends know where they're located. These make great markers when trying to find your friends in the crowd.

■ Cool, casual, and breathable fabrics, along with a wide-brim hat and plenty of sunscreen, are your best bets for the long day outdoors. Wear comfortable shoes, and ones that can get dirty. The grounds are a racetrack, after all, and by the end of Jazz Fest the ground is a mix of dust, straw, mud, and crawfish shells.

DJs into their lineup of parties and events. ⊠ *508 Frenchmen St., Faubourg Marigny* ☎ *504/371–5543* ⊕ *www.maisonfrenchmen.com.*

Mimi's. A popular local hangout, this two-story nightspot perches on the corner of Franklin and Royal streets with a wraparound balcony and big windows that stay open most evenings. Downstairs is a bar with table seating, couches, and a pool table, while upstairs is home to a tapas-style kitchen and dance floor. Due to permit issues, live music is intermittent, but entertainment and local personalities are big here every night. ⊠ *2601 Royal St., Faubourg Marigny* ☎ *504/872–9868* ⊕ *mimismarigny.com.*

Phoenix. This lounge bills itself as a "Leather/Levi Neighborhood Alternative Bar," and that's a pretty apt description. The downstairs bar is a popular Marigny nightspot, with a calendar of special events and themed parties, including the International Mr. Leather Contest. The upstairs bar, called The Eagle, is notorious for its "anything goes" atmosphere. ⊠ *941 Elysian Fields Ave., Faubourg Marigny* ☎ *504/945–9264* ⊕ *www.neworleansphoenix.com.*

R Bar. Behind the tinted windows of this corner bar, find a red-vinyl-clad hipster hangout and stylish social hub with a throwback ambience. In addition to crawfish boils on Friday afternoons (in season), the place runs offbeat specials—on Monday night, for example, 10 bucks gets you a shot and a haircut—and it's prime real estate on costume holidays like Mardi Gras and Halloween. ⊠ *Royal St. Inn, 1431 Royal St., Faubourg Marigny* ☎ *504/948–7499* ⊕ *www.royalstreetinn.com.*

MUSIC CLUBS

Fodor'sChoice
★

d.b.a. At this southern outpost of a popular pair of bars in Brooklyn and Manhattan's East Village, the selection of drinks—including international and craft beers on tap, bourbons and scotches, and obscure tequilas, all listed on chalkboards above the bar—is reason enough to visit. Live music most nights and the Marigny's best people-watching in a narrow cypress-lined room make it a neighborhood favorite. ⊠ *618 Frenchmen St., Faubourg Marigny* ☎ *504/942–3731* ⊕ *www.dbaneworleans.com.*

Siberia Lounge. Live music at this dimly lighted St. Claude staple club ranges from punk rock to Balkan folk music. Other attractions are the daily drink specials, late night perogies, and selection of hard-to-find Slavic brews and malts. Early shows are usually free. ⊠ *2227 St. Claude Ave., Faubourg Marigny* ☎ *504/265–8855* ⊕ *www.siberialounge.com.*

> **FRENCHMEN STREET PERSONALITIES**
>
> Street life on Frenchmen can be as entertaining as anything going on inside the clubs and bars. Artists and brass bands gather on corners and in doorways on most weekends and turn intersections and sidewalks into impromptu, open-air galleries, boutiques, and dance parties. A poet selling custom love sonnets typed up on a vintage typewriter and a shopping cart–turned–mechanical bull with built-in music and smoke machine are just some of the rarities you'll encounter on an average night.

Snug Harbor. This intimate club with a sometimes-steep cover charge is one of the city's best rooms to soak up modern jazz. It is the home base of such esteemed talent as vocalist Charmaine Neville, who plays every Monday, and pianist-patriarch Ellis Marsalis (father of Wynton and Branford). The dining room serves good local food but is best known for its burgers. ⊠ *626 Frenchmen St., Faubourg Marigny* ☎ *504/949–0696* ⊕ *www.snugjazz.com.*

Fodor's Choice
★

The Spotted Cat. Jazz, old-time, and swing bands perform nightly at this rustic club right in the thick of the Frenchmen Street action. Sets start at 4 pm on weekdays and 2 pm on weekends. Drinks cost a little more at this cash-only destination, but there's never a cover charge and the entertainment is great—from the popular bands to the cadres of young, rock-step swing dancers. ⊠ *623 Frenchmen St., Faubourg Marigny* ⊕ *www.spottedcatmusicclub.com.*

BYWATER

Perhaps the edgiest local scene in New Orleans can be found in Bywater, home to a dozen low-key bars. Past the corner of Royal and Franklin streets a smattering of watering holes cater to a varied crowd. As an added incentive to explore this neighborhood, local idol Kermit Ruffins (of *Treme* fame) plays in Bywater and the Seventh Ward some nights.

BARS AND LOUNGES

Fodor's Choice
★

Bacchanal Fine Wine & Spirits. In the far reaches of Bywater, Bacchanal is part wineshop, part bar, part music club—and one hundred percent neighborhood hangout. Among the wine racks in this old building are two big round tables, as well as seating in the courtyard and a spacious new bar upstairs that serves beer and liquor. You can have a bottle uncorked on the premises or order by the glass. The kitchen supplies gourmet cheese plates and small, tasty dishes that go well with the wine selections—osso buco, mussels, and confit chicken leg are among the best. Local bands play seven nights a week. ⊠ *600 Poland Ave., Bywater* ☎ *504/948–9111* ⊕ *www.bacchanalwine.com.*

BJ's Lounge. This gritty corner bar is a beloved neighborhood joint. Most weekends it hosts music, like Little Freddie King, who blows the top off the place. ⊠ *4301 Burgundy St., Bywater* ☞ *Cash only.*

10

Country Club New Orleans. A mixed crowd enjoys an elegant retreat from the hustle and bustle of the city in this handsome 19th-century Bywater mansion. The interior restaurant, bar, and parlor rooms underwent a total renovation in 2016, and decor has a trippy Palm Springs vibe, with plenty of glitter and neon. The outdoor pool and deck bar hidden away behind lush vegetation and high walls is especially popular with the gay crowd. Pool access requires a small fee, and towels and lockers are available. ⊠ *634 Louisa St., Bywater* ☎ *504/945–0742* ⊕ *www. thecountryclubneworleans.com.*

Parleaux Beer Lab. At the first microbrewery in the Bywater, you can spend your time discussing hops and malts with other enthusiasts, or just relax in the large backyard while enjoying the best of local food truck fare. The community-oriented space often hosts special events like fund-raisers, multicourse dinners, and outdoor yoga classes. ⊠ *634 Lessups St., Bywater* ☎ *504/702–8433* ⊕ *www.parleauxbeerlab.com.*

MUSIC CLUBS

Vaughan's. Legendary Thursday night live music sets (served up with free red beans and rice late in the evening) are the big draw at this ramshackle place in Bywater's farthest reaches. At other times, the place is an exceptionally friendly neighborhood dive. ⊠ *800 Lesseps St., at Dauphine St., Bywater* ☎ *504/947–5562.*

TREMÉ

Tremé, which has found new popularity in the wake of the HBO series, is one of the oldest musical neighborhoods in the nation. Largely residential, Tremé is home to some great local nightclubs and music venues. Be careful traveling after dark, however, as the neighborhood remains rough.

MUSIC CLUBS

Bullet's Sports Bar. For a real taste of New Orleans, drop by on a Thursday night, when Kermit Ruffins is playing. Not just the soul of the city, but the soul food, too, emerges as Kermit and friends serve up their famous barbecue and fixin's in between sets. Featured in the HBO series *Treme*, Bullet's has become something of a New Orleans hot spot, but remember that if the neighborhood around the bar looks a little scary, that's because it *is* a little scary. Use caution when traveling here, but be prepared for a warm and welcoming musical experience when you arrive. ⊠ *2441 A.P. Tureaud Ave., Tremé.*

Candlelight Lounge. This small, old-school joint draws a crowd on Monday for jazz by Corey Henry and Friends (and free red beans and rice), and local brass bands most other nights of the week. Uncle Lionel Batiste, a club fixture of legendary proportions, has sadly passed away, but the lively music and local atmosphere are still the same. We recommend taking a cab out here. ⊠ *925 N. Robertson St., Tremé* ☎ *504/906–5877.*

OFF THE BEATEN PATH

Kermit's Tremé Mother-in-Law Lounge. Local personality and jazz legend Kermit Ruffins now reigns at this brightly covered club that once belonged to R&B singer Ernie K-Doe. The club is a jewel of the Tremé neighborhood, hosting the best of local talent in jazz and blues nightly. The kitchen serves popular New Orleans cuisine. Look forward to the occasional cameo from Kermit himself. The neighborhood's a bit dodgy, so take a cab. ⊠ *1500 N. Claiborne Ave., Tremé* ☎ *504/814–1819* ⊕ *www.kermitstrememotherinlawlounge.com.*

CBD AND WAREHOUSE DISTRICT

CBD

The Central Business District (CBD) is mostly quiet at night, but you can find some terrific nightspots closer to Canal Street and the French Quarter.

BARS AND LOUNGES

Loa. In voodoo tradition, *loa* are the divine spirits, and this bar just off the lobby of the chic International House Hotel certainly strives for an extraordinary experience with its modern, upscale decor. Well-heeled downtown professionals mingle with an international crowd gathering for the evening to sip on inventive, high-end cocktails created by the friendly bartenders here. A new apéritif hour from 4 to 5 Thursday through Saturday includes a tasting of one of the delicious signature cocktails. ✉ *International House Hotel, 221 Camp St., Central Business District* ☎ *504/553–9550* ⊕ *www.ihhotel.com.*

Piscobar. Hidden on a small CBD side street, this chic little bar serves both inventive and traditional cocktails crafted from the Peruvian spirit, Pisco. The inner courtyard is divine for a sunset drink, and the hotel now operates an equally charming rooftop bar as well. ✉ *Catahoula Hotel, 914 Union St., Central Business District* ☎ *504/603–2442* ⊕ *www.catahoulahotel.com.*

Rusty Nail. Nestled in between the overhead highway and a series of converted 18th-century warehouses, this discreet neighborhood bar can be difficult to find. With live music most nights of the week, a great selection of scotches, a gorgeous renovated patio, frequent visits by food trucks, and even the occasional play reading, it's worth firing up the GPS to get here. ✉ *1100 Constance St., Central Business District* ☎ *504/525–5515* ⊕ *www.rustynailnola.com.*

The Sazerac Bar. One of the most famous bars in Louisiana, this art-deco gem and slinger of fine libations has a pedigree that dates back to the mid-19th century. Drawn to the signature Sazerac cocktail and Ramos gin fizz, a famous and intriguing clientele has graced this hotel bar over the years, including Governor Huey P. Long, who in the 1930s built a 90-mile highway between New Orleans and the state capital, just so, many believe, he could get directly to the hotel lounge for his signature drink. ✉ *Roosevelt Hotel, 123 Baronne St., Central Business District* ☎ *504/648–1200* ⊕ *www.therooseveltneworleans.com.*

Victory. Amid the city's drab business district hides another entry in the growing list of craft cocktail bars. Named for Daniel Victory, one of the city's best mixologists (and an owner), it draws a young professional crowd to its dimly lit, vaguely industrial space for drinks that push the boundaries of traditional cocktails. A cozy room in the back is available for private parties and intimate sipping. ✉ *339 Baronne St., Central Business District* ☎ *504/522–8664* ⊕ *www.victorynola.com.*

CASINOS

Harrah's New Orleans Casino. Commanding the foot of Canal Street, where it anchors a cluster of restaurants and clubs, this Beaux-Arts–style casino is the largest in the South. Try your luck at one of the 3,800 slot machines, 20 poker tables, and every other game of chance that you can imagine. There's an upscale steak house and a club in the middle of the gaming floor. Valet parking is available. ✉ *8 Canal St., Central Business District* ☎ *504/533–6000, 800/427–7247* ⊕ *www.harrahsneworleans.com.*

WAREHOUSE DISTRICT

With its many apartment buildings converted from 19th-century warehouses and cotton mills as backdrop, the Warehouse District has become a real draw for locals and visitors alike with numerous bars, restaurants, and clubs that cater to hip professionals. It's also home to the contemporary-arts scene, with dozens of galleries arranged throughout the district that host their own series of parties and celebrations.

Enjoying New Orleans Music with Your Kids

Bourbon Street's entertainment options are largely off-limits to children, but younger music fans need not feel excluded. Dozens of options exist outside of barrooms and traditional clubs, and several of the most prestigious clubs offer all-ages shows.

Preservation Hall and **Palm Court Jazz Café**, both legendary jazz venues, welcome underage patrons. **Tipitina's** and **Howlin' Wolf** occasionally host all-ages shows as well (see listings in this chapter). Around **Jackson Square**, talented street musicians perform most days

of the week, and the **French Market** hosts a regular series of concerts as well as a separate busking stage for local and visiting performers to play for tips. The **Louisiana Music Factory,** an excellent New Orleans music store, regularly hosts in-store performances (⇨ see Shopping). And kids are always welcome at the free shows staged by the National Park Service's **New Orleans Jazz Historical Park**, both at the park's visitor center (⇨ see the French Quarter) and at the shows Tuesday through Saturday afternoon in the French Market.

BARS AND LOUNGES

Ernst Cafe. Ernst has been operating as a bar since the first years of the 20th century, and the classic interior and upstairs balcony provide a welcome respite for conventioneers, lawyers from nearby firms, and service-industry folks winding down from shifts at area hotels. The classic menu includes local bar-food staples like fried green tomatoes, po'boys, wraps, and burgers. ⊠ 600 S. Peters St., Warehouse District ☎ 504/525–8544 ⊕ www.ernstcafe.co.

MUSIC CLUBS

Circle Bar. Like something out of a Tim Burton film, this teetering old Victorian house that straddles the concrete jungles of downtown and the Warehouse District hides one of the coolest indie-rock clubs in the city. Scenesters descend on the recently renovated venue around 10 pm, but earlier in the evening this is a laid-back neighborhood haunt. Pull on your skinny jeans, so that you can squeeze into the room that holds what might be the world's tiniest stage. ⊠ 1032 St. Charles Ave., Warehouse District ☎ 504/588–2616 ⊕ www.circlebarneworleans.com.

Howlin' Wolf. This New Orleans favorite has long been a premier venue and anchor of the Warehouse District club and music scene. With a great corner location in a converted warehouse, they host larger rock, funk, blues, Latin, and hip-hop shows nearly every night on the main stage. Meanwhile, a side bar called The Den books intimate events and popular weekly parties like Brass Band Sundays. ⊠ 907 S. Peters St., Warehouse District ☎ 504/529–5844 ⊕ www.thehowlinwolf.com.

Mulate's. Across the street from the Convention Center, this large venue seats 400, and the dance floor quickly fills with couples twirling and two-stepping to authentic Cajun bands from the countryside. Regulars love to drag first-timers to the floor for impromptu lessons. The home-style

Cajun cuisine is acceptable, but what matters is the nightly music. ✉ *201 Julia St., Warehouse District* ☏ *504/522–1492* ⊕ *www.mulates.com.*

Republic. Part of the new generation of music venues in the Warehouse District, this rock club retains the rough-timbered feel of the cotton-and-grain warehouse it used to be. The club books touring hip-hop stars and rock bands as well as local acts, and DJs take over the sound system late at night for popular dance parties. ✉ *828 S. Peters St., Warehouse District* ☏ *504/528–8282* ⊕ *www.republicnola.com.*

THE GARDEN DISTRICT

Near downtown and right on the streetcar line, the Garden District is relatively easy to reach and offers numerous options for dining and going out, especially along St. Charles Avenue, the main thoroughfare. Running parallel, just a few blocks toward the river, Magazine Street is another corridor rich with restaurants, bars, and nightspots. St. Charles Avenue tends to offer a more upscale and elegant version of nightlife, with historic venues and a touch of haute couture, while Magazine Street caters to a younger crowd of students and young professionals looking for vibrant neighborhood hangouts, beer gardens, and sidewalk cafés.

BARS AND LOUNGES

The Avenue Pub. Beer lovers from around the globe make a beeline to this 24-hour neighborhood joint with pressed-tin ceilings. Boasting the best beer selection in New Orleans, the bar hosts a regular schedule of tastings and special events. The whiskey selection also ranks among the top in town. Sip your pint on the wraparound balcony upstairs, where you can watch streetcars roll past on St. Charles Avenue. ✉ *1732 St. Charles Ave., Garden District* ☏ *504/586–9243* ⊕ *www.theavenuepub.com.*

Barrel Proof. This dimly lit whiskey bar is popular with the local service industry crowd. The bar boasts more than 250 types of the spirit, and the kitchen serves a menu of meat and cheese dishes that pair well with whiskey sipping. ✉ *1201 Magazine St., Garden District* ☏ *504/299–1888* ⊕ *www.barrelproofnola.com.*

The Bulldog. The postcollege set claims most of the seats on the beautiful brick patio here, with its views of the Magazine Street bustle and a fountain made from dozens of beer taps. The dog-friendly venue bills itself as "Uptown's International Beer Tavern," and it backs up that boast with 50 different brews on tap and more than 100 bottles. Solid bar food keeps patrons well fueled, but during crawfish season, boiled mudbugs from the seafood market across the street are the preferred fare. ✉ *3236 Magazine St., Garden District* ☏ *504/891–1516* ⊕ *bulldog.draftfreak.com.*

Garden District Pub. Just down the block from some of Magazine Street's finest boutiques, you'll find this neighborhood haunt that, with its exposed-brick walls and a copper-top bar, exudes the ambience of a 19th-century pub, complete with Sazeracs and absinthe on a terrific drinks menu. It's a great place to end a day of exploring or to get the evening started, while mingling among neighborhood denizens. ✉ *1916 Magazine St., Garden District* ☏ *504/267–3392* ⊕ *www.gardendistrictpub1916.com.*

10

Hot Tin. The view from this hip penthouse bar is unbeatable, but if you can't get a seat outside, curl up in a plush booth under the plated tin ceiling and enjoy the Tennessee Williams-inspired memorabilia filling the walls. Even the cocktails are served in antique glassware. ✉ *The Pontchartrain Hotel, 2031 St. Charles Ave., Garden District* ☎ *504/323–1500* ⊕ *www.hottinbar.com.*

Parasol's Restaurant & Bar. Roast beef po'boy devotees genuflect at the mention of this friendly hole-in-the-wall, which for more than 60 years has served the sloppy sandwiches along with Guinness on tap. The annual St. Patrick's Day block party at Parasol's spills out into the surrounding lower Garden District neighborhood; it's grown so large that police have had to erect barricades to keep traffic out—or to keep the revelers in. ✉ *2533 Constance St., Garden District* ☎ *504/302–1543.*

Tracey's. This cavernous sports bar and neighborhood pub comes with a backstory. The owners used to manage Parasol's, a nearby dive famous for its roast beef po'boys. When new owners at Parasol's forced them out, they took their recipe and most of their regulars around the corner to this larger location on Magazine Street. And, well, now the neighborhood has two great bars with stellar roast beef po'boys. ✉ *2604 Magazine St., Garden District* ☎ *504/897–5403* ⊕ *www.traceysnola.com.*

UPTOWN AND CARROLLTON-RIVERBEND

UPTOWN

Uptown is rich in clubs, although they are far less concentrated here than downtown. They tend to be tucked down residential side streets or scattered along one of the main drags, and they mostly cater to the large populations of college students and young professionals who dwell in this part of town. Many are local institutions and ever-popular destinations for music lovers drawn to the beats of funk, brass, blues, and rock.

BARS AND LOUNGES

Bar Frances. This bar's casual elegance is readily apparent during its popular happy hour, when Francophiles can enjoy pork rillette, chicken liver mousse, and $4 Chartruese cocktails. A small patio of bistro tables looks out onto Freret Street. ✉ *4525 Freret St., Uptown* ☎ *504/371–5043* ⊕ *www.barfrances.com.*

Fodor's Choice
★
Columns Hotel's Victorian Lounge Bar. An old-fashioned or a Sazerac on the expansive front porch, shaded by centuries-old oak trees, overlooking the St. Charles Avenue streetcar route alongside Uptown gentry decked out in preppy attire, ranks as one of New Orleans's most traditional experiences. Built in 1883 as a private home, the Columns has been the scene of TV ads, movies, and plenty of weddings. The interior scenes of Louis Malle's *Pretty Baby* were filmed here. The Victorian Lounge, with its restored period decor and a fireplace, has a decaying elegance marred only by the television above the bar. There's a great happy hour, too, with live jazz combos playing Monday through Friday. ✉ *3811 St. Charles Ave., Uptown* ☎ *504/899–9308* ⊕ *www.thecolumns.com.*

Cooter Brown's. This rambling tavern across from the Mississippi River levee boasts 400 different bottled beers and 45 on tap. That, along with the excellent cheese fries and an oyster bar, makes it a favorite haunt of students from nearby Tulane and Loyola universities, along with nostalgic alums. ⊠ *509 S. Carrollton Ave., Uptown* ☎ *504/866–9104* ⊕ *www.cooterbrowns.com.*

Cure. This pioneer of the revitalized Freret Corridor, one of the city's first serious cocktail bars, adds a touch of urban chic to a historic neighborhood. A doorman welcomes guests into a converted fire station with 20-foot ceilings and a lovely patio. Knowledgeable bartenders use a breathtaking arsenal of liquor to push the boundaries of what a drink can be. Take note that even in August, men must wear long pants on Thursday, Friday, and Saturday, and baseball caps are not allowed at any time. ⊠ *4905 Freret St., Uptown* ☎ *504/302–2357* ⊕ *www.curenola.com.*

Fodor'sChoice ★ **Delachaise.** A long, slender room with plush banquettes in a charming sliver of a building on a busy stretch of St. Charles Avenue looks as if it were air-dropped straight from Paris. Offering a carefully chosen (and reasonably priced) selection of beer, spirits, and wines by the glass, the menu also includes upscale small plates, such as frog legs, frites fried in goose fat, and house-made paté. ⊠ *3442 St. Charles Ave., Uptown* ☎ *504/895–0858* ⊕ *www.thedelachaise.com.*

F&M Patio Bar. For college kids and grown-ups reliving their youth, an all-nighter in New Orleans isn't complete until you've danced on top of a pool table at this classic hangout. There's a loud jukebox, a popular photo booth, and a late-night kitchen (it fires up around 7 pm and keeps serving until early morning). The tropical-themed patio can actually be peaceful at times. You'll need to get here by car or taxi. ⊠ *4841 Tchoupitoulas St., Uptown* ☎ *504/895–6784* ⊕ *www.fandmpatiobar.com.*

The Kingpin. Deep-red walls and a velvet Elvis lend this Uptown spot a touch of kitsch, but the friendly atmosphere, a jukebox stocked with vintage soul and modern rock, and a young, fun crowd keep people coming back nightly. It's a frequent destination for food trucks and a favorite place to cheer on the city's beloved Saints. ⊠ *1307 Lyons St., Uptown* ☎ *504/891–2373.*

St. Joe's. A young, Uptown professional crowd packs this narrow bar known for its blueberry mojitos and religious-themed decor. The narrow front bar has more crosses than a Catholic church; the back patio, strung with Chinese lanterns and decorated with statues of Asian deities, is a "Caribbean Zen temple," in the owner's words. ⊠ *5535 Magazine St., Uptown* ☎ *504/899–3744* ⊕ *stjoesbar.com.*

Sovereign Pub. No need to book a ticket to the United Kingdom when this cozy bar so faithfully re-creates a British pub. Even the daily newspapers come from the other side of the pond. Accordingly, you can count on a well-poured pint and warm company. ⊠ *1517 Aline St., Uptown* ☎ *504/899–4116.*

MUSIC CLUBS
Le Bon Temps Roulé. Local acts from a wide range of genres—including the Soul Rebels with their standing Thursday-night gig—shake the walls of this ramshackle Magazine Street nightspot. The music normally gets

started after 10 pm. Pool tables and a limited bar-food menu keep the crowd, including plenty of students from nearby Tulane and Loyola universities, occupied until the show starts. ⊠ *4801 Magazine St., Uptown* ☏ *504/895–8117.*

Tipitina's. Rub the bust of legendary New Orleans pianist Professor Longhair (or "Fess") inside this Uptown landmark named for one of the late musician's popular songs. The old concert posters on the walls read like an honor roll of musical legends, both local and national. The midsize venue boasts an eclectic and well-curated calendar, particularly during the weeks of Jazz Fest. The long-running Sunday afternoon Cajun dance party still packs the floor. Although the neighborhood isn't dangerous, it's far enough out of the way to require a cab trip. ⊠ *501 Napoleon Ave., Uptown* ☏ *504/895–8477* ⊕ *www.tipitinas.com.*

CARROLLTON-RIVERBEND

Farther uptown than Uptown, the Carrollton-Riverbend area is a favorite among students at Loyola and Tulane universities and is home to citywide favorites like the famous Maple Leaf club, which hosts live music every night of the week. Around the corner, Carrollton Station is a more laid-back option, with bands on weekends and some weeknights. Uptown bars tend to warm up with after-work crowds and then play late into the night.

BARS AND LOUNGES

Oak Wine Bar and Bistro. The dark windows give no hint of the sleek, modern lounge inside. This sophisticated spot for grown-ups to mingle over glasses of wine and gourmet nibbles draws professionals from Uptown and the nearby suburbs. Jazz and folk musicians perform Friday and Saturday. ⊠ *8118 Oak St., Carrollton-Riverbend* ☏ *504/302–1485* ⊕ *www.oaknola.com.*

MUSIC CLUBS

Carrollton Station. This cozy neighborhood bar keeps unfolding the farther back you go—from the front bar to the stage to the backyard. The regular schedule of live music emphasizes local roots, rock, and acoustic acts. It's two blocks off the Carrollton streetcar line and close to the Oak Street commercial district. ⊠ *8140 Willow St., Carrollton-Riverbend* ☏ *504/865–9190* ⊕ *www.carrolltonstation.com.*

Fodor's Choice **Maple Leaf.** The phrase "New Orleans institution" gets thrown around a
★ lot, but this place deserves the title. It's wonderfully atmospheric, with pressed-tin walls and a lush tropical-themed patio, and it's also one of the city's best venues for blues, New Orleans–style R&B, funk, zydeco, and jazz. On Sunday afternoons, the bar hosts the South's longest-running poetry reading. Rebirth Brass Band's standing Tuesday gig is a show everyone should see, and Joe Krown starts his set around 10:30 pm. It's a long haul from the French Quarter, but worth the trip, especially if combined with a visit to one of the restaurants clustered near this commercial stretch of Oak Street. ⊠ *8316 Oak St., Carrollton-Riverbend* ☏ *504/866–9359* ⊕ *www.mapleleafbar.com.*

MID-CITY AND BAYOU ST. JOHN

MID-CITY

A quick streetcar ride up Canal from downtown, this mostly residential area around City Park is almost like a small town. Its neighborhood joints are unknown to most tourists, but the area has lots to offer if you know where to look. Venues are spread out, so a car or taxi is recommended at night.

BARS AND LOUNGES

Finn McCool's Irish Pub. Created by devoted soccer fans from Belfast, this popular and expansive neighborhood bar beams in European games via satellite. Pool and darts tournaments are a regular feature as well, and the kitchen serves tasty pub fare. On Monday night, there's popular and competitive trivia. If you happen to be in town for St. Patrick's Day, don't miss their rollicking daylong festival. ⊠ *3701 Banks St., Mid-City* ☎ *504/486–9080* ⊕ *www.finnmccools.com.*

Twelve Mile Limit. This neighborhood joint might be off the beaten path, but it's worth the trip for its unlikely combination of an innovative cocktail menu and…barbecue. This place compares favorably to swanky wine and cocktail bars like Cure or the Delachaise, yet it offers a decidedly down-home vibe with its pulled pork and brisket, its run-down exterior (a contrast with the nicely done interior), and reasonable prices. ⊠ *500 Telemachus St., Mid-City* ☎ *504/488–8114.*

MUSIC CLUBS

Banks Street Bar and Grill. This comfortable Mid-City nightspot has become one of the city's most reliable venues for local music, with live shows—sometimes several a night—every day of the week. The bill of fare leans toward blues and funk. There is no cover charge for music. ⊠ *4401 Banks St., Mid-City* ☎ *504/486–0258* ⊕ *www.banksstreetbarandgrill.com.*

Chickie Wah Wah. Right on the Canal Street streetcar line, this neighborhood music club is unassuming from the outside but hosts some of the city's most popular acts. With happy hour and early evening sets and a covered patio, this destination is a favorite among low-key New Orleanians who aren't into late nights. ⊠ *2828 Canal St., Mid-City* ☎ *504/304–4714* ⊕ *www.chickiewahwah.com.*

FAMILY **Rock 'n' Bowl.** Down-home Louisiana music, rockabilly, R&B, and New Orleans swing in a bowling alley? Go ahead: try not to have fun. This iconic venue has a terrific lineup of music Wednesday through Saturday. Thursday is Cajun, Zydeco, and Swamp Pop Night, when some of the best musicians from rural Louisiana take the stage. The new Front Porch Grill serves burgers made from grass-fed Louisiana beef. ⊠ *3000 S. Carrollton Ave., Mid-City* ☎ *504/861–1700* ⊕ *www.rocknbowl.com.*

Treo. This large cocktail bar lets patrons sprawl out in the courtyard, barroom, and upstairs art gallery. The drinks menu extends from the best of the classics to inventive new concoctions from the friendly bartenders, and the gallery hosts exhibits of local talent each month. The kitchen serves coastal Italian cuisine. Located in a more desolate pocket of Mid-City, it's best to take a cab at night. ⊠ *3835 Tulane Ave., Mid-City* ☎ *504/304–4878* ⊕ *www.treonola.com.*

10

BAYOU ST. JOHN

Winding around the bayou and the surrounding blocks, you'll find one of the city's prettiest and quietest neighborhoods. A few solid bars offer entertainment and cheap cocktails, but if you want to really do like the locals, get a go cup and sit along the water.

BARS AND LOUNGES

Bayou Beer Garden. Claim a seat on the sprawling multilevel outdoor patio at this low-key neighborhood pub and sip a pint from the great selection of beers. Multiple TVs show the big game, and the bar occasionally hosts live music. Next door, and sharing an adjoining courtyard, a slightly more sophisticated sister property has opened as a wine garden. The wine garden offers gourmet meat and cheese boards and popular wines on tap. ⊠ *326 N. Jefferson Davis Pkwy., Mid-City* ☎ *504/302–9357* ⊕ *www.bayoubeergarden.com.*

Pal's. Tucked away in a quiet residential neighborhood, this hipster hangout updated a neighborhood bar with the kind of carefully designed run-down vibe that might make Tom Waits smile. All the details are there, down to the soft-core porn on the restroom walls. ⊠ *949 N. Rendon St., Bayou St. John* ☎ *504/488–7257.*

PERFORMING ARTS

For a relatively small city, New Orleans has a remarkably vibrant and varied performing-arts community. While there are many traditional performance venues around town, one of the most exciting movements in recent years is the fringe theater action along Saint Claude Avenue, in the Bywater neighborhood. The annual Fringe Theater Festival brings pop-up performances, but there are also some permanent venues as well.

CLASSICAL MUSIC

Friends of Music. This organization brings superior performers from all over the world to Tulane University's Dixon Hall. Concerts take place approximately once a month, and tickets usually cost $30 to $35. ⊠ *Willow St. entrance, Tulane University, Uptown* ☎ *504/895–0690* ⊕ *www.friendsofmusic.org.*

Louisiana Philharmonic Orchestra. The always good, sometimes excellent LPO now holds court at the recently restored Orpheum Theater while continuing to perform at Tulane and Loyola university auditoriums, and at local churches. There's also a concert series in parks around town during the spring months. ⊠ *1010 Common St., Suite 2120, Central Business District* ☎ *504/523–6530* ⊕ *www.lpomusic.com.*

New Orleans Center for Creative Arts (*NOCCA*). Wynton Marsalis and Harry Connick Jr. are just two of the better-known alumni of this prestigious high school. NOCCA hosts some fine student and faculty shows at its modern Faubourg Marigny campus, and The NOCCA Stage Company presents top-notch performances by visiting jazz, classical, dance, and theater artists. The focus is on emerging talent, and tickets usually sell out fast. ✉ *2800 Chartres St., Bywater* ☎ *504/940–2787* ⊕ *www.nocca.com.*

Trinity Artist Series. Gratifying concerts of all types—solo, choral, orchestral, and chamber—fill the vaulted interior of Trinity Episcopal Church most Sunday evenings. Organized by local organist Albinas Prizgintas, the series features both local and regional artists, though the occasional star passes through. Admission is free, and a relaxed, enjoyable evening is assured. And if you're fortunate enough to be in town the right weekend in late March or early April, don't miss "Bach Around the Clock," a 29-hour performance marathon that features everything from the eponymous composer's fugues and variations to classic rock hits arranged for organ. ✉ *1329 Jackson Ave., Garden District* ☎ *504/522–0276* ⊕ *www.trinityartistseries.com.*

DANCE

New Orleans Ballet Association. The city's prestigious dance organization has returned to the lavishly renovated Mahalia Jackson Theater with a full schedule. Performances also take place at other venues, including Freda Lupin Memorial Hall at NOCCA. ✉ *1419 Basin St., Tremé* ☎ *504/522–0996* ⊕ *www.nobadance.com.*

FILM

New Orleans Film Festival. Cinephiles can get their fix during this juried festival in October, which brings an influx of indie and film culture to town and commandeers screens at venues throughout the city. The Film Society, which presents the annual festival, also hosts screenings year-round, a French film fest, themed film series, and a gala. ✉ *New Orleans* ☎ *504/309–6633* ⊕ *www.neworleansfilmsociety.org.*

The Theatres At Canal Place. This first-run and art-house minimultiplex has five screens of premium viewing in the upscale Canal Place shopping center, on the edge of the French Quarter. A renovation added deluxe leather seating as well as a full-service gourmet café and bar that offers wait service for in-theater dining and cocktails. ✉ *Canal Place, 333 Canal St., French Quarter* ☎ *844/462–7342* ⊕ *www.the-theatres.com.*

Zeitgeist Multidisciplinary Arts Center. Working with volunteer staff and a shoestring budget, Zeitgeist founder and filmmaker Rene Broussard established this funky and eclectic space as a venue for experimental theater. It later developed into the city's center for alternative cinema, though it continues to stage live performances as well. ✉ *1618 Oretha Castle Haley Blvd., Uptown* ☎ *504/352–1150* ⊕ *www.zeitgeistnola.org.*

10

OPERA

Marigny Opera House. An elegant, whitewashed building on a quiet residential street, this "Church of the Arts" has been hosting the Marigny Opera Ballet since 2014. Besides highly coveted private events and weddings, the House also hosts New Orleans Opera Association productions, other plays, and mostly classical music. ✉ *725 St. Ferdinand St., Bywater* ☎ *504/948–9998* ⊕ *www.marignyoperahouse.org.*

New Orleans Opera Association. Returning to the Mahalia Jackson Theater for the Performing Arts and the Placido Domingo Stage, the October–April opera season generally showcases three operas, as well as a small handful of special events. Opera on Tap is an innovative series bringing performances to area pubs. ✉ *New Orleans* ☎ *514/529–2278, 504/529–3000* ⊕ *www.neworleansopera.org.*

THEATER

AllWays Lounge and Theatre. From contemporary burlesque to Brecht's *Threepenny Opera*, the Allways provides an enticing array of avant-garde theater and performance art. It's hip, sly, and always provocative. ✉ *2240 St. Claude Ave., Faubourg Marigny* ☎ *504/218–5778* ⊕ *www. theallwayslounge.net.*

Saenger Theatre. Reopened for the 2013 season after a massive, multiyear renovation and restoration effort, the Saenger hosts a Broadway in New Orleans series as well as national headliners. The theater, built in 1927, has impressive ceiling decorations, a chandelier that came from a château near Versailles, and Italian baroque–style flourishes. ✉ *143 N. Rampart St., Tremé* ☎ *504/525–1052* ⊕ *www.saengernola.com.*

Southern Repertory Theater. This well-established theater company specializes in original, first-rate contemporary theater productions. It stages premiers by regional and international playwrights and hosts a variety of community workshops and classes. Performances are held at various venues around town. ✉ *6221 S. Claibourne Ave., Suite 310, Warehouse District* ☎ *504/522–6545* ⊕ *www.southernrep.com.*

SHOPS AND SPAS

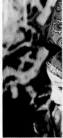

Updated by
Cameron
Quincy Todd

The Crescent City's shopping is as eclectic as its music, food, and culture. In local boutiques and specialty stores, you'll find everything from rare antiques to novelty T-shirts, artwork, jewelry, fashion, and foods that represent the city's varied flavors. Up and down Magazine Street and throughout the French Quarter, you'll spot old-world influences intersecting with modern trends, making it easy for even the most discerning shopper to find something new to treasure.

New Orleanians have a deep love for their city and its culture. For shoppers, this translates into pride-centric merchandise, including jewelry and clothing bearing city emblems, such as the fleur-de-lis—the stylized iris design associated with New Orleans since its early days—and Mardi Gras masks, black-and-gold Saints symbols, and humorous statements about political issues and local personalities. Residents strongly support local entrepreneurs, and there are many homegrown stores selling locally made goods.

Make sure to pay attention to some of the city's artwork. Posters designed around Jazz Fest and other special events, for example, often become collector's items. In the thriving arts districts, you'll find contemporary works by local artists alongside renowned names in the art world. The sounds of New Orleans—Dixieland, contemporary jazz, rhythm and blues, Cajun, zydeco, rap, hip-hop, and the unique bounce beat—are available in music stores, such as Louisiana Music Factory and Peaches Records, and at live-music venues including Preservation Hall, Snug Harbor, and House of Blues. Bookstores stock a plethora of local books on photography, history, cooking, and folklore. Clothing stores focus on items that wear well in New Orleans's often intense heat and humidity, with styles ranging from the latest runway fashions to vintage frocks and styles by local designers.

WHAT'S WHERE

The Crescent City's main shopping areas are the **French Quarter,** with narrow, picturesque streets lined with antiques shops, art galleries, and gift, fashion, and home decor stores; the **Central Business District (CBD)** and the **Warehouse District,** best known for contemporary art galleries and cultural museums; and **Magazine Street,** the city's 6-mile boutique strip filled with designer clothing, accessories, locally made jewelry, antiques shops, art galleries, and specialty stores. Magazine Street stretches from the CBD to the Uptown area. Nearby, the **Carrollton-Riverbend** neighborhood is another hot spot for finding women's clothing, jewelry, and bookstores.

> **PRIDE IN BLOOM**
>
> The fleur-de-lis, historically an emblem of French royalty, has long been a symbol of New Orleans. Since Hurricane Katrina, however, locals have elevated the fleur-de-lis into a symbol of pride and recovery. You can find creative examples all over the city, worked into jewelry, artwork, candles, glassware, T-shirts, and even tattoos.

SHOPPING PLANNER

OPENING HOURS

Head to the French Quarter and Magazine Street for some of the best locally owned shops and art galleries in the city. Unlike big malls and chain stores, most of the independent boutiques tend to keep bankers' hours, from about 10 am to 5 or 6 pm, so plan your shopping excursions accordingly. Some stores are open seven days a week, but most of Magazine Street and the French Quarter's smaller shops are closed on Sunday. Some stores are open on weekends, but closed Monday. It's best to call ahead if you're aiming to visit a certain location.

FINDING UNIQUE GIFTS

Bring home a taste of New Orleans. Some of the Crescent City's best souvenirs are the edible kind. For pralines, head to the French Quarter to either **Aunt Sally's** (⌧ *810 Decatur St.*), where a box of six starts around $15, or to **Laura's Candies** (⌧ *331 Charles St.*). After your visit to **Café du Monde** (⌧ *800 Decatur St., French Quarter*), dust the powdered sugar off your shirt and grab a box of beignet mix ($3.59) to pack in your suitcase. **Sucré** (⌧ *3025 Magazine St., Garden District*) sells artisanal chocolates with New Orleans flavors, such as bananas Foster and chicory.

To re-create the city's Creole flavor in your own kitchen, be sure to pick up a few cookbooks. In recent years, some of the city's top chefs have produced beautiful books with cooking tips, travelogues, and memories of home, as well as lots of recipes. Don't miss Chef Donald Link's first book, *Real Cajun,* which won the James Beard Award, and his more recent *Down South,* both packed with gorgeous photography and mouthwatering recipes. Iconic restaurants like **Brennan's, Galatoire's,** and **Tujague's** publish their own cookbooks of century-old favorites. And fans of Chef Susan Spicer's Bayona and Mondo restaurants will want to look for her *Crescent City Cooking*. For an amazing selection of cookery and books about New Orleans' culinary heritage, including hard-to-find titles and local favorites, stop by **Kitchen Witch Cookbooks** (⊠ *1452 N. Broad St., Mid-City*).

For wearable souvenirs with a Crescent City sense of humor, head to **Dirty Coast** (⊠ *5631 Magazine St. and 713 Royal St.*) and **Fleurty Girl** (⊠ *632 St. Peter St. and 3117 Magazine St.*) These locally owned boutiques offer T-shirts and other clothing with New Orleans–theme slogans and snazzy graphics.

For souvenirs that go beyond the typical, visit the gift shops inside New Orleans's many museums and cultural institutions. The stores, which help support these organizations' missions, are typically open to shoppers without paying museum admission. The gift shop within the **New Orleans Museum of Art** (⊠ *1 Collins C. Diboll Circle, Mid-City*), for example, has a wealth of books on art, photography, and Louisiana cooking, as well as scarves, puzzles, and locally made crafts, such as jewelry by New Orleans designer Mignon Faget. The **Ogden Museum of Southern Art** (⊠ *925 Camp St., Warehouse District*) includes the beautifully curated Center for Southern Craft and Design store, where you'll find ceramics, glasswork, jewelry, and books on and by Southern artists. The store at the **Historic New Orleans Collection** 's (⊠ *533 Royal St., French Quarter*) gift shop is the place to find such items as a reproduction of a 1916 Louisiana railroad map or a *NOVA* documentary DVD on Hurricane Katrina, as well as many other maps, prints, photos, and publications on Louisiana history. The **Aquarium of the Americas** (⊠ *1 Canal St., French Quarter*), the **Audubon Insectarium** (⊠ *423 Canal St., French Quarter*), and the **Audubon Zoo** (⊠ *6500 Magazine St., Uptown*), all part of the Audubon Nature Institute, have gift shops stocked with colorful, quirky, educational, and fun items for children and adults.

FRENCH QUARTER

Browsing through the French Quarter is as much a cultural experience as a shopping excursion. Royal Street, known for its antiques stores, is great for a stroll and some window-shopping. Along both Royal and Chartres streets, you'll find clusters of high-end art galleries displaying traditional, contemporary, and New Orleans–centric works. Many stores sell decorative Carnival masks that range from simple feather-and-ceramic styles that go for about $10 apiece to handcrafted, locally made varieties that carry much heftier price tags. Jewelry stores feature estate and antique jewelry alongside contemporary creations. Souvenir shops are around every corner, especially as you approach the heavily trafficked areas near the river. If your energy lags, plenty of cafés, coffee shops, candy stores, and bistros are there to provide a boost.

Antiques shops are one of New Orleans's specialties.

SHOPPING CENTERS AND MARKETS

French Market. Vendors have been selling their wares on this spot since 1791, making it one of the oldest public marketplaces in the country. Today, the French Market includes a large flea market, small produce stands, and retail shops. For the daily flea market, dozens of vendors set up tables inside and outside the covered pavilion, selling inexpensive jewelry, sunglasses, handbags, T-shirts, curios, and food items, like spice mixes and hot sauces. The market generally is open daily from about 8 to 7, but hours can vary depending on the weather. ⊠ *1200 block of N. Peters St., French Quarter* ☎ *504/522–2621* ⊕ *www.frenchmarket.org.*

Jax Brewery. A historic factory building that once produced Jax beer now holds a mall filled with local shops and a few national chain stores, like Chico's, along with a food court and balcony overlooking the Mississippi River. Shops carry souvenirs, clothing, books, artwork, and more, with an emphasis on New Orleans–themed items. The mall is open daily. On hot summer days, it's an air-conditioned refuge. ⊠ *600 Decatur St., French Quarter* ☎ *504/566–7245* ⊕ *jacksonbrewerybar.com.*

ANTIQUES AND COLLECTIBLES

Brass Monkey. This small, charming shop specializes in Limoges boxes with design motifs ranging from small red beans—a favorite food in New Orleans—to baby carriages. It also has antique walking sticks, Venetian glass, and English Staffordshire porcelain. ⊠ *407 Royal St., French Quarter* ☎ *504/561–0688.*

French Antique Shop. One of the largest collections of European crystal and bronze chandeliers in the country glitters over gilded mirrors, 18th- and 19th-century hand-carved marble mantels, French and Continental furniture, porcelain, and objets d'art in this shop, which originally opened in 1947 and is run by the second generation of its founding family. ⊠ *225 Royal St., French Quarter* ☎ *504/524–9861* ⊕ *www.gofrenchantiques.com.*

Harris Antiques. Locals and visitors alike are drawn to this shop for its two floors of 19th-century paintings, 18th- and 19th-century French and English furniture, large mirrors, bronze sculptures, and chandeliers. ⊠ *233 Royal St., French Quarter* ☎ *504/523–1605* ⊕ *www.harrisantiques.com.*

James H. Cohen & Sons Inc. Pick up a piece of history in this shop, opened in 1898, which sells many one-of-a-kind antique firearms, swords, and currency, including coins from as early as 319 BC. There are also obsolete bank notes, jewelry made from rare coins, and collectibles such as antique opera glasses. ⊠ *437 Royal St., French Quarter* ☎ *504/522–3305, 800/535–1853* ⊕ *www.cohenantiques.com.*

Keil's Antiques. Leave yourself plenty of time to browse the three floors of 18th- and 19th-century French and English furniture, chandeliers, estate jewelry, art, statuary, and other furnishings. The shop, run by the fourth generation of the family that founded it in 1899, is a favorite stop for interior designers. ⊠ *325 Royal St., French Quarter* ☎ *504/522–4552* ⊕ *www.keilsantiques.com.*

Fodor'sChoice **Lucullus.** With a focus on the art of food—preparing it, serving it, and
★ savoring it—Lucellus is named after an ancient Roman known for his luxurious banquets. The store is filled mainly with items from the 18th and 19th centuries: antique French tables, English china, cooking and serving utensils, linens, lighting, food-related art, snuff boxes, and more, including oddities like Lady Sarah Churchill's picnic set. The shop is owned by Patrick Dunne, author of *Epicurean Collector*. ⊠ *610 Chartres St., French Quarter* ☎ *504/528–9620* ⊕ *www.lucullusantiques.com.*

Moss Antiques. This store specializes in French and English antiques from the early 19th century, including jewelry, wooden boxes, furniture, porcelain oyster plates, sculpture, objets d'art, walking sticks, and silver services. ⊠ *411 Royal St., French Quarter* ☎ *504/522–3981* ⊕ *www. mossantiques.com* ☉ *Closed Sun.*

Fodor's Choice ★ **M.S. Rau.** Antiques lovers may want to set aside several hours to marvel at the extensive collection here. Rare pieces, such as furniture from royal families, join 18th- and 19th-century French, American, and English antiques, sterling silver, statuary, fine art, and jewelry in this 30,000-square-foot store, which opened in 1912. ⊠ *630 Royal St., French Quarter* ☏ *504/523–5660, 888/557–2406* ⊕ *www.rau-antiques.com.*

Royal Antiques. French, English, and Continental antique furniture and Biedermeier pieces can be found alongside chandeliers, sconces, trumeau mirrors, accessories, and estate jewelry in this shop, which was founded in 1899. ⊠ *309 Royal St., French Quarter* ☏ *504/524–7033* ⊕ *www.royalantiques.com.*

Secondline Arts and Antiques. This 8,000-square-foot retail wonderland is filled with interesting antiques, light fixtures, salvaged items, and art. The store's selection of salvaged elements, mostly from old New Orleans houses, and art from emerging local artists, allows shoppers to take home a unique piece of the city. A night market stays open in the courtyard until 10 pm weekdays and midnight on weekends. The shop also rents bicycles by the hour, day, or week, and runs bicycle tours. ⊠ *1209 Decatur St., French Quarter* ☏ *504/875–1924* ⊕ *www.secondlinenola.com.*

Vintage 329. An essential stop for memorabilia collectors. Vintage 329 carries items autographed by celebrities, such as a framed photo signed by Gene Autry, a music sheet autographed by Fred Astaire and Ginger Rogers, a guitar signed by the Allman Brothers, concert posters, costume jewelry, and signed first editions. New items arrive every week. ⊠ *329 Royal St., French Quarter* ☏ *504/525–2262.*

Waldhorn & Adler. Founded in 1881, one of the city's oldest antiques stores specializes in French, Italian, and English furniture from the 18th, 19th, and early 20th centuries. It also carries new and estate jewelry. ⊠ *343 Royal St., French Quarter* ☏ *504/581–6379* ⊕ *www.waldhornadlers.com* ⊗ *Closed Mon.*

Whisnant Galleries. Antique weapons and armor are the real eye-catchers here, with pieces from the Gothic to the art-deco period, but the shop also carries a large selection of antique furniture, lighting, and mirrors; paintings from the 18th, 19th, and 20th centuries; pre-Columbian, Chinese, African, and ethnic art and jewelry; religious items; objets d'art; and statuary. ⊠ *343 Royal St., French Quarter* ☏ *504/524–9766* ⊕ *www.whisnantgalleries.com.*

ART GALLERIES

Fodor's Choice ★ **A Gallery for Fine Photography.** The rare books and photography here include works from local artists like Josephine Sacabo and Richard Sexton; luminaries such as E. J. Bellocq, Ansel Adams, and Henri Cartier-Bresson; and contemporary giants, including Annie Leibovitz, Walker Evans, Helmut Newton, and Herman Leonard. ⊠ *241 Chartres St., French Quarter* ☏ *504/568–1313* ⊕ *www.agallery.com.*

Angela King Gallery. Gallery owner Angela King renovated an 1850s jewelry store into a modern gallery that exhibits oil paintings, prints, and metal and cast-glass sculptures from about 25 contemporary artists. ✉ *241 Royal St., French Quarter* ☎ *504/524–8211* ⊕ *www. angelakinggallery.com.*

Artist's Market. This co-op of regional artists showcases a wide variety of works, including handmade masks, photography focusing on New Orleans personalities and scenery, ceramics, blown glass, paintings, wrought-iron architectural accents, turned-wood bowls and vases, prints, jewelry, beads, and more. ✉ *1228 Decatur St., French Quarter* ☎ *504/561–0046* ⊕ *www.artistsmarketnola.com.*

SHOPPING TOUR

Local art-and-antiques shopping consultant **Macon Riddle** (☎ *504/899–3027* ⊕ www.neworleansantiquing.com) conducts half- and full-day personalized shopping expeditions by appointment. She can sometimes gain access to antiques warehouses not normally open to the public.

Elliott Gallery. Pioneers of modern and contemporary art are represented, with a large selection of prints and paintings by Marc Chagall, Picasso, and others. ✉ *540 Royal St., French Quarter* ☎ *504/523–3554* ⊕ *www. elliottgallery.com.*

Great Artists' Collective. More than 50 regional artists display their works in this double-shotgun house in the middle of the French Quarter. You'll find paintings, metalwork mirrors, a vast array of earrings, blown glass, ceramics, wood sculptures, handmade clothing, hats, ironwork, masks, and vignettes in oyster shells. ✉ *815 Royal St., French Quarter* ☎ *504/525–8190* ⊕ *www.greatartistscollective.com.*

Harouni Gallery. David Harouni, a favorite local artist, offers his take on neo-Expressionism in his paintings of faces, figures, and streetscapes, created in this gallery-studio space. ✉ *933 Royal St., French Quarter* ☎ *504/299–4393* ⊕ *www.harouni.com.*

Kurt E. Schon, Ltd. In a hushed art-museum atmosphere, this gallery, with its well-educated staff, showcases high-end European paintings from the 18th and 19th centuries. ✉ *510 St. Louis St., French Quarter* ☎ *504/524–5462* ⊕ *www.kurteschonltd.com* ⊘ *Closed Sun.*

La Belle Galerie & the Black Art Collection. Global themes from Russian art to African American experiences in music, history, and culture are portrayed through limited-edition graphics, photographs, posters, paintings, furniture, ceramics, textiles, and sculpture. ✉ *309 Chartres St., French Quarter* ☎ *504/529–5538.*

Michalopoulos. Local artist James Michalopoulos showcases his abstract visions of New Orleans's architecture, street scenes, and personalities in oil paintings, lithographs, prints, posters, and serigraphs. ✉ *617 Bienville St., French Quarter* ☎ *504/558–0505* ⊕ *www.michalopoulos.com.*

Rodrigue Studios. One of Louisiana's most successful artists, George Rodrigue (1944–2013) is best known for his series featuring the Blue Dog, which has become a local icon. But it's the images of his Cajun ancestors in stylized Acadiana settings that got the most praise from art critics. His work is available in original paintings and signed and numbered silkscreen prints, mixed media, and sculpture. ⊠ *730 Royal St., French Quarter* ☎ *504/581–4244* ⊕ *www.georgerodrigue.com.*

BOOKS

Dauphine Street Books. New and used books focus on local history, the arts, modern fiction, and out-of-print works, including a fine selection of antiquarian books and obscure titles. ⊠ *410 Dauphine St., French Quarter* ☎ *504/529–2333* ⊘ *Closed Wed.*

Fodor'sChoice **Faulkner House Books.** Named for ★ William Faulkner, who rented a room here in 1925, this bookstore is designated a National Literary Landmark. It specializes in first editions, rare and out-of-print books—mostly by Southern authors—but also carries new titles. The store keeps thousands of additional books at an off-site warehouse and hosts an annual Words & Music Festival that salutes Faulkner and new Southern writers and musicians. ⊠ *624 Pirate's Alley, French Quarter* ☎ *504/524–2940* ⊕ *www.faulknerhouse.net.*

Librairie Book Shop. Set up like a library with well-stocked shelves of old, new, and hard-to-find volumes, this spot carries one of the Quarter's largest selections of local books, posters, and postcards. ⊠ *823 Chartres St., French Quarter* ☎ *504/525–4837.*

> **DID YOU KNOW?**
>
> Literary legends like Tennessee Williams, William Faulkner, Truman Capote, and Anne Rice called New Orleans home for at least part of their lives, and a number of other writers still work in and write about the city. Because of this literary heritage, bookstores give local authors optimum shelf space.

CLOTHING

Fodor'sChoice **Fleurty Girl.** Owned by the ebullient Lauren Thom, Fleurty Girl—its ★ name is a play on "fleur-de-lis"—is the place to go for New Orleans apparel, home decor, and gifts. The store is known for its T-shirts displaying the humorous catchphrases and iconography of local culture and New Orleans Saints pride. There's affordable jewelry, children's books, colorful rain boots, Carnival-themed gear, and fleurs-de-lis in every imaginable form. There's also a location in the Garden District, at 3117 Magazine Street. ⊠ *632 St. Peter St., French Quarter* ☎ *504/304–5529* ⊕ *www.fleurtygirl.net.*

Perlis Clothing French Quarter. A smaller version of the locally owned Perlis boutique on Magazine Street, this shop such items as polo shirts and neckties with crawfish logos, as well as everything from Hawaiian shirts to boxer shorts printed with images of Tabasco products and New Orleans themes. ⊠ *Jax Brewery, 600 Decatur St., Suite 104, French Quarter* ☎ *504/523–6681* ⊕ *www.perlis.com.*

Fodor'sChoice **Trashy Diva Boutique.** New Orleans–based designer Candice Gwinn puts ★ a retro-romantic spin on the women's fashions she creates. Inspired by styles from the 1940s to the 1950s, the Trashy Diva line includes

GLUTTONY TO GO

There are lots of treats to sample while you're in the Big Easy, but you don't have to eat them all while you're here. Many of the city's famous tastes come in easy-to-pack (or ship) forms. In the French Quarter, you can pick up classic pralines at **Aunt Sally's Praline Shop** or **Laura's Candies**. Don't forget some beignet mix and chicory coffee to re-create the breakfasts you've enjoyed at **Café du Monde**. All of the city's bookstores and many gift shops are stocked with a variety of cookbooks by local chefs and tomes about local tastes. In the Garden District, **Sucre** sells artisanal chocolates with New Orleans flavors, such as bananas Foster and chicory.

dresses, blouses, skirts, coats, jewelry, and upscale shoes with vintage flair and modern fit. The Trashy Diva lingerie shop, located at 712 Royal Street, features corsets and romantic evening wear. An expansive Trashy Diva shoe, clothing, and lingerie boutique is also located in the 2000 block of Magazine Street. ⊠ *537 Royal St., French Quarter* ☎ *504/522–4233* ⊕ *www.trashydiva.com.*

United Apparel Liquidators. Label-loving locals as well as celebrities in town shooting movies are known to shop at this designer clothing liquidator. The tiny boutique is busting with deeply discounted apparel, shoes, and accessories by major designers, such as Marni, Balenciaga, Michael Kors, Phillip Lim, and Prada. Contemporary lines, such as Serfontaine Denim, Steven Alan, Yigal Azrouel, and Alexander Wang, have also been spotted on the racks. The stylish, friendly, and eminently helpful sales staff has created a loyal cult of frequent shoppers. ⊠ *518 Chartres St., French Quarter* ☎ *504/301–4437* ⊕ *www.shopual.com.*

Violet's. Girly girls rule at this boutique, which caters to the softer side of feminine dress, featuring skirts, sexy blouses, handbags, jewelry, and accessories, with styles ranging from contemporary to retro romantic. ⊠ *808 Chartres St., French Quarter* ☎ *504/569–0088.*

FOOD

Aunt Sally's Praline Shop. Satisfy your sweet tooth with an array of pralines, made while you watch. The traditional version is concocted from cane sugar spiked with pecans, but other flavors include chocolate, café au lait, and even bananas Foster. You can also buy hot sauce, prepackaged muffuletta mix, and Bourbon Street glaze, as well as art and books about New Orleans, zydeco CDs, and logo cups and aprons. ⊠ *French Market, 810 Decatur St., French Quarter* ☎ *504/524–3373, 800/642–7257* ⊕ *www.auntsallys.com.*

Café du Monde. This open-air café and New Orleans landmark serves café au lait (half coffee, half hot milk) and beignets (holeless doughnuts sprinkled liberally with powdered sugar). Take-home products from the café include prepackaged chicory coffee and beignet mix, coffee mugs, and posters depicting the spot. The café's store across the street also sells logo T-shirts, aprons, and other souvenirs. Another branch is in the CBD, at the Outlet Collection at Riverwalk. ✉ *800 Decatur St., French Quarter* ☎ *504/525–4544, 800/772–2927* ⊕ *www.cafedumonde.com.*

Evans Creole Candy Factory. The aroma of candy cooking will draw you in to this sweets shop, established in 1900. You'll find a variety of pralines, pecan logs, and New Orleans's own Cuccia Chocolates, as well as coffee and gift baskets. ✉ *848 Decatur St., French Quarter* ☎ *504/522–7111, 800/637–6675.*

Laura's Candies. In the candy-making business since 1913, this shop sells sweet pralines as well as chocolate specialties—including its signature Mississippi mud, made with milk or dark chocolate laced with caramel. ✉ *331 Chartres St., French Quarter* ☎ *504/525–3880, 800/992–9699* ⊕ *www.laurascandies.com.*

New Orleans School of Cooking and Louisiana General Store. Learn how to make a roux and other Louisiana cooking techniques at this school that's inside a renovated 1800s molasses warehouse. Lessons are seasoned with history and tales of the state's famous cuisine. The general store stocks all kinds of regional spices, condiments, sauces, snacks, gift baskets, and cookbooks. ✉ *524 St. Louis St., French Quarter* ☎ *504/525–2665, 800/237–4841* ⊕ *www.neworleansschoolofcooking.com.*

Tabasco Country Store. Named for the famous Louisiana-produced hot sauce, this store also offers spices, cookbooks, New Orleans–themed clothing and aprons, kitchen accoutrements, ties, posters, pewter items, and more. ✉ *537 St. Ann St., French Quarter* ☎ *504/539–7900* ⊕ *www.nolacajunstore.com.*

HOUSEWARES

NOLA Boards. Gorgeous wooden cutting boards, expertly crafted from Louisiana Sinker Cypress and branded with the signature NOLA BOARDS logo, make great gifts to lug home. Husband-and-wife team Mandy Simpson and Daren Sumrow design and create these wood pieces, as well as custom countertops and furniture. The shop sells boards ranging from coasters to cheese boards to large butcher blocks, and also carries smaller household gifts from local vendors. There's a second location Uptown at 4304 Magazine Street. ✉ *519 Wilkinson St., Suite 105, French Quarter* ☎ *504/435–1485* ⊕ *www.nolaboards.com.*

JEWELRY AND ACCESSORIES

Currents Fine Jewelry. Owners Terry and Sylvia Weidert create a variety of chic, art deco–inspired designs in 14- and 18-karat gold and platinum. ✉ *627 Royal St., French Quarter* ☎ *504/522–6099* ☉ *Closed Sun.*

Dashka Roth Contemporary Jewelry and Judaica. The handmade contemporary jewelry on display here is the work of designer Dashka Roth and 80 other artists. The store sells necklaces, rings, and bracelets as well as contemporary Judaica, including kiddush cups, mezuzahs, menorahs, and dreidels. The store is closed for all Jewish holidays. ✉ *332 Chartres St., French Quarter* ☎ *504/523–0805, 877/327–4523* ⊕ *www.dashkaroth.com.*

FodorsChoice
★ **Fifi Mahony's.** Anyone with a passion for playing dress-up and a flair for the dramatic will love this place filled with custom wigs, wild accessories, makeup, and hair products. The shop provides essential resources for Mardi Gras and Halloween costumes as well as ample creative advice. ⊠ *934 Royal St., French Quarter* ☎ *504/525–4343* ⊕ *www.fifimahonys.com.*

Goorin Brothers. From fedoras to flat caps, you'll find hats of every style and shape at this national chain with a local sensibility, including straw toppers perfect for strolling the streets of the French Quarter. Another branch, at 2127 Magazine Street, offers custom millinery for those looking for a personal fit. ⊠ *709 Royal St., French Quarter* ☎ *504/523–4287* ⊕ *www.goorin.com.*

Krewe du Optic. Luxury sun and optical frames crafted by local designer Stirling Barrett have been featured by celebrities, beauty magazines, and garnered enough national attention to open a new outpost in Manhattan's Soho. This flagship store features custom fittings, a sunroom, courtyard, and espresso bar. ⊠ *809 Royal St., French Quarter* ☎ *504/407–2925* ⊕ *www.krewe.com.*

NOLA Couture. Preppy motifs and New Orleans pride are the twin hallmarks of this line of locally designed accessories. You'll find belts, neckties, pet leashes, wallets, hats, headbands, bags, glassware, and totes emblazoned with tiny Crescent City symbols—fleurs-de-lis, sno-balls, pelicans, hurricane swirls, streetcars—all in repeat patterns. They're the perfect gift for the prepster in your life. There is also a location Uptown, at 3308 Magazine Street. ⊠ *Jackson Sq., 528 St. Peter St., French Quarter* ☎ *504/875–3522* ⊕ *www.nolacouture.com.*

Porter Lyons. The cuff bracelets, pendants, and other fine jewelry at this chic, minimalist boutique have a distinctly funky yet simplistic style. The store also carries scents, candles, and other small gifts. ⊠ *631 Toulouse St., French Quarter* ☎ *504/518–4945* ⊕ *www.porterlyons.com.*

Quarter Smith. Gemologist and gold- and silversmith Ken Bowers designs contemporary jewelry in gold, silver, and platinum and carries a selection of antique pieces. ⊠ *535 St. Louis St., French Quarter* ☎ *504/524–9731* ⊕ *www.quartersmith.com* ⊘ *Closed Sat.–Mon.*

Sterling Silvia. Silvia and Juan Asturias operate this business near the French Market, where Silvia's fleur-de-lis and flower-inspired designs share space with other silver jewelry from Chile, Mexico, Indonesia, Russia, Thailand, and elsewhere. There are also coral pieces, gift items, ceramic dolls, and more. ⊠ *41 French Market Pl., French Quarter* ☎ *504/299–9225* ⊕ *www.sterlingsilvia.com.*

MASKS

Mask Gallery. Artist Dalili fabricates his intricate but wearable masks out of leather at a workstation in the front of the store. There also are masks made by other local artists, as well as Venetian and feather versions, pewter sculptures, jewelry, and figurines. ⊠ *738 Royal St., French Quarter* ☎ *504/523–6664* ⊕ *www.neworleansmask.com.*

MARDI GRAS SHOPPING BLITZ

The best way to experience the joys of Carnival is to go in costume. To assemble the perfect get-up, start at the top, with a custom-made wig from Fifi Mahony's on Royal Street in the French Quarter. Feel free to turn to the store's expert staff for all manner of advice, from how to properly apply glitter eye shadow and false eyelashes to how to pull off Lady Gaga's platinum bow-tied hairdo. For the rest of your outfit, stroll down to the French Market, where you can find cheap sunglasses, feather boas, and all sorts of other accessories, or continue to the **Artist's Market,** where there are masks you'll want to keep long after Mardi Gras has faded into Lent. For a one-stop costume experience, travel to Magazine Street and **Funky Monkey** for costumes, stockings, wigs, and accessories, or the **Encore Shop,** where you can choose from affordable ball gowns, suits, and more. Mardi Gras is all about having fun. So dress the part, enjoy the sardonic humor of the Carnival krewes, and have a ball.

Maskarade. A large selection of Mardi Gras masks range from locally made funky crafts to handmade Venetian creations, as well as custom designs and a large selection of affordable masks under $50. ⊠ *630 St. Ann St., French Quarter* ☎ *504/568–1018* ⊕ *www.themaskstore.com.*

NOVELTIES AND GIFTS

Erzulie's Authentic Voudou. If the food, music, and architecture of New Orleans hasn't yet cast its spell on you, this voodoo shop might do the trick. Altars display good-luck charms and other ritual items, as well as spell kits, elixirs and potions, body-care products, voodoo dolls, gris-gris bags, and gift items. Tarot readings also are available. ⊠ *807 Royal St., French Quarter* ☎ *504/525–2055, 866/286–8368* ⊕ *www. erzulies.com* ☉ *Closed Tues. and Wed.*

Esoterica Occult Goods. Calling itself "the one-stop shop for all your occult needs," this store is a great place to pick up potions, gris-gris bags, jewelry, spell kits, incense, altar and ritual items, as well as books on magic and the occult arts. Tarot readings are also available. ⊠ *541 Dumaine St., French Quarter* ☎ *504/581–7711, 866/581–7711* ⊕ *www.onewitch.com.*

Forever New Orleans. It's all about the Crescent City in this small shop filled with New Orleans–themed items, including glassware adorned with pewter fleurs-de-lis, affordable jewelry that boasts local icons, stationery, tiles, clocks, ceramics, framed crosses, charms, bottle stoppers, frames, candles, cookbooks, and more. This is a great place to pick up upscale souvenirs and gifts. ⊠ *700 Royal St., French Quarter* ☎ *504/586–3536.*

Idea Factory. At this fun little shop, wood becomes art at the hands of craftspeople who carve functional clocks, clipboards, and jewelry boxes, as well as whimsical whirligigs, hand-carved board games, puzzles, kaleidoscopes, and toys, proving that not all playthings need to be plugged in. ✉ *924 Royal St., French Quarter* ☎ *504/524–5195, 800/524–4332* ⊕ *www.ideafactoryneworleans.com.*

Nadine Blake. New Orleans native Nadine Blake worked in interior design in New York before moving home and setting up shop. Her delightful store reflects her varied travels and eclectic interests with quirky gifts, gorgeous design books, handmade note cards, vintage furniture, and a slew of cool whatnots. ✉ *1036 Royal St., French Quarter* ☎ *504/529–4913* ⊕ *www. nadineblake.com.*

> ### HEALTHY JAVA
>
> Local coffee brands like Community, French Market, Luzianne, and Café Du Monde add up to 30% chicory to their coffee, which gives it a bitter quality that some people like (it also served to stretch out coffee supplies during past shortages). Chicory is caffeine-free and reportedly helps control blood sugar, reduce cholesterol, and boost bone-mineral density, and may be good for your liver.

Rendezvous Inc. A throwback to the days of Southern belles, this shop on Jackson Square has linens and lace, ranging from christening outfits for babies to table runners, napkins, women's handkerchiefs, and more. It also offers a charming array of antiques and reproductions, such as perfume bottles, tea sets, fleurs-de-lis, and crosses. ✉ *Jackson Sq., 522 St. Peters St., French Quarter* ☎ *504/522–0225* ⊕ *www.rendezvouslinens.com.*

Santa's Quarters. It's Christmas year-round at this shop, which displays a diverse range of traditional and novelty ornaments and decorations, Santa Clauses of all kinds, and a host of Louisiana-themed holiday items. ✉ *1025 Decatur St., French Quarter* ☎ *888/334–7527* ⊕ *www. santasquarters.com.*

What's New. Everything in this store carries a New Orleans theme, making it a great place to buy souvenirs people will actually want to keep, including fleur-de-lis–covered flasks, decorative pillows, nightlights with shades made from photographs of city scenes, glassware, ceramics, jewelry, and other works by local artists. ✉ *French Market, 824 Decatur St., French Quarter* ☎ *504/586–2095* ⊕ *www.whatsnew-nola.com.*

SPA AND BEAUTY

Bourbon French Parfums. Opened in 1843, this old world–style shop offers about three dozen fragrances for men and women, including a 200-year-old formula for men's cologne. It will custom-blend perfumes for individuals based on assessments of body chemistry, personality, and scent preferences. The shop also sells perfume bottles and toiletries. ✉ *805 Royal St., French Quarter* ☎ *504/522–4480* ⊕ *www. neworleansperfume.com.*

Fodor's Choice ★ **Hové Parfumeur, Ltd.** A must for perfume lovers, this store has been creating fragrances since 1931. Scented oils, soaps, sachets, and potpourri have been made on-site for four generations and are sold all over the world. There are dozens of fragrances for men and women, as well as bath salts, anti-aging treatments, massage and body oils, antique shaving and dressing-table accessories, as well as new and antique perfume bottles. ✉ *434 Chartres St., French Quarter* ☎ *504/525–7827* ⊕ *www. hoveparfumeur.com.*

TOYS

FAMILY **Little Toy Shop.** For more than 50 years, this has been the stop for a mix of New Orleans souvenirs, miniature die-cast metal cars (from the Model T to the Hummer), character lunchboxes, puppets, plastic animals, and collectible Madame Alexander dolls. There is a second location in the French Quarter at 513 St. Ann Street. ✉ *900 Decatur St., French Quarter* ☎ *504/522–6588* ⊕ *www.littletoyshopnola.com.*

FAUBOURG MARIGNY AND BYWATER

FAUBOURG MARIGNY

A mostly residential neighborhood with a vibrant nightlife scene, the Marigny is filled with restaurants and bars on or around Frenchmen Street and the St. Claude Avenue Arts District. A scattering of shops and outdoor vendors stay open late into the evening, perfect for a quick browse as you explore the neighborhood's music scene.

ANTIQUES AND COLLECTIBLES

LA46 General Store & Vintage Market. A curated collection of vintage goods ranges from kitschy knickknacks and vintage toys to chic retro furniture, and many props and costumes for the nearby St. Claude theaters. On the second Saturday of each month, the shop hosts evening events with live music. ✉ *2232 St. Claude Ave., Faubourg Marigny* ☎ *504/220–5177* ⊕ *www.louisiana46.com* ☽ *Closed Sun..*

MUSIC

Louisiana Music Factory. A favorite resource for New Orleans and regional music—new and old—the Louisiana Music Factory has records, tapes, CDs, DVDs, sheet music, and books, as well as listening stations, music-oriented T-shirts, original art, and a stage that hosts frequent live concerts. ✉ *421 Frenchmen St., Faubourg Marigny* ☎ *504/586–1094* ⊕ *www.louisianamusicfactory.com.*

WINE

Faubourg Wines. This charming shop is packed with both fine and affordable wines, as well as select gourmet ciders and beers. For a $2 corkage fee, imbibers can enjoy purchases at a curtained window alcove or sidewalk bistro table. The shop provides glasses, and sells fresh bread and cheese selections from Bellegarde Bakery and St. James Cheese Co. Free wine tastings are usually held on Wednesdays from 6 to 8 pm. ✉ *2805 St. Claude Ave., Faubourg Marigny* ☎ *504/342–2217* ⊕ *www. faubourgwines.com.*

BYWATER

The few stores in this mostly residential neighborhood reflect the area's bohemian spirit, selling unique and locally made products. If you're planning to browse the Bywater, though, bring along a map or a knowledgeable local, as the shops are sparse. There are, however, plenty of cafés and restaurants for refueling.

ANTIQUES AND COLLECTIBLES

Bargain Center. Inside this funky muraled storefront on a busy Bywater corner, you'll find thrifted art, clothing, furniture, and knickknacks ranging from junk to vintage treasures, as well as some local arts and crafts. ⊠ *3200 Dauphine St., Bywater* ☎ *504/948–0007.*

A RELAXING SCENT

Take home the scents of New Orleans with soaps, sprays, candles, and perfumes in sweet olive or vetiver. The latter was a staple in proper Creole households, where it was used to keep moths away from fabrics and add a pleasant scent to bed linens and clothing stored in armoires. The oil extracted from the roots of this grass is popular with aromatherapy enthusiasts, who claim the scent relieves stress and increases energy.

NOVELTIES AND GIFTS

Island of Salvation Botanica. Owned by voodoo priestess Sallie Ann Glassman and located inside the New Orleans Healing Center, this mystical shop specializes in voodoo religious supplies (candles, herbs, tinctures, books, incense), as well as Haitian and world art. Glassman also offers crystal-ball readings by appointment, while other staff members do psychic visions and tarot card readings. ⊠ *New Orleans Healing Center, 2372 St. Claude Ave., Suite 100, Bywater* ☎ *504/948–9961* ⊕ *www.islandofsalvationbotanica.com.*

CBD AND WAREHOUSE DISTRICT

CBD

The Central Business District is filled with large hotels, national chain stores, and a few high-end and locally owned boutiques that cater to a loyal clientele.

SHOPPING CENTERS AND MARKETS

The Shops at Canal Place. This high-end shopping center focuses on national chains, including Saks Fifth Avenue, Michael Kors, Anthropologie, Banana Republic, Coach, J.Crew, Lululemon, and BCBG Max Azria. But the mall also includes quality local shops, such as Jean Therapy denim boutique, Wehmeier's leather goods, and Saint Germain shoes. A highlight is the Mignon Faget jewelry store, which carries the renowned local designer's full line of upscale, Louisiana-inspired creations. ⊠ *333 Canal St., Central Business District* ☎ *504/522–9200* ⊕ *www.theshopsatcanalplace.com.*

CLOTHING

Fodor's Choice ★ **Rubensteins.** One of the city's premier men's stores has been selling high-end suits, tuxedos, casual wear, and made-to-measure apparel since 1924. Brands range from Brioni and Zegna to Ralph Lauren, Prada, and Hugo Boss. ⊠ *102 St. Charles Ave., Central Business District* ☎ *504/581–6666* ⊕ *www.rubensteinsneworleans.com* ⊘ *Closed Sun.*

JEWELRY AND ACCESSORIES

Adler's. This century-old, locally owned jewelry store carries upscale watches, engagement rings, gemstone jewelry, wedding gifts, top-of-the-line china, silver, crystal, and more. ⊠ *722 Canal St., Central Business District* ☎ *504/523–5292, 800/925–7912* ⊕ *www.adlersjewelry.com.*

Clock and Watch Shop. Master clockmaker Josef Herzinger repairs and restores all types of new, vintage, and antique watches and clocks at his two-story shop. He also sells more than several brands of new watches and clocks, ranging from miniature and mantel styles to large grandfather clocks. ⊠ *824 Gravier St., Central Business District* ☎ *504/525–3961* ⊕ *www.clockwatchshop.com* ⊘ *Closed weekends.*

Meyer the Hatter. One of the South's largest hat stores has been in operation for more than a hundred years and is currently run by the fourth generation of the Meyer family. A favorite of locals and out-of-towners, the shop carries a large selection of fedoras, tweed caps, Kangols, cowboy hats, and just about any type of topper you can put on your head. ⊠ *120 St. Charles Ave., Central Business District* ☎ *504/525–1048, 800/882–4287* ⊕ *www.meyerthehatter.com* ⊘ *Closed Sun.*

WAREHOUSE DISTRICT

In the vibrant Warehouse District, museums and art galleries abound, showcasing works from local, regional, and nationally known artists. Julia Street in particular is a destination for art lovers—it's packed with galleries, many of them owned by artists. The *Times-Picayune* newspaper and its website, NOLA.com, publish detailed listings of exhibition openings. The events are generally accompanied by wine and hors d'oeuvres and sometimes live music. The galleries' days of operation can vary, so it's best to confirm gallery hours; many owners are happy to set up appointments.

SHOPPING CENTERS AND MARKETS

The Outlet Collection at Riverwalk Marketplace. Built in what was once the International Pavilion for the 1984 World's Fair, the Outlet Collection at Riverwalk is an upscale outlet mall with shops such as Neiman Marcus Last Call, Johnston & Murphy Factory Store, and outlets for Coach, Forever 21, Carter's Babies and Kids, Chico's, and Steve Madden. Outside the mall is Spanish Plaza, the scene of frequent outdoor concerts and special events. ⊠ *500 Port of New Orleans Pl., Warehouse District* ☎ *504/522–1555* ⊕ *www.riverwalkneworleans.com.*

ART GALLERIES

Ariodante. Mostly local and Gulf Coast artists are represented in this gallery, featuring high-end and reasonably priced contemporary crafts and fine art, including jewelry, blown glass, sculpture, furniture, photography, paintings, ceramics, and decorative accessories. ✉ *535 Julia St., Warehouse District* ☎ *504/524–3233* ⊕ *www. ariodantegallery.com.*

FodorśChoice **Arthur Roger Gallery.** One of the most respected local galleries has compiled a must-see collection of contemporary artwork by Lin Emery, Jacqueline Bishop, and Willie Birch, as well as national names such as glass artist Dale Chihuly and the film director and photographer John Waters. ✉ *432–434 Julia St., Warehouse District* ☎ *504/522–1999* ⊕ *www.arthurrogergallery.com.*

★

Callan Contemporary. This sleek gallery specializes in contemporary sculpture and paintings from both local and internationally renowned artists, including Pablo Atchugarry, Eva Hild, Raine Bedsole, Key-Sook Geum, Adrian Deckbar, and Sibylle Peretti. ✉ *518 Julia St., Warehouse District* ☎ *504/525–0518* ⊕ *www.callancontemporary. com* ⊗ *Closed Sun. and Mon.*

FodorśChoice **Center for Southern Craft and Design store.** You don't have to pay admission to enter this part of the Ogden Museum of Southern Art, where you can buy ceramics, glasswork, decorative pieces, books, scarves, and jewelry by Southern artists. The museum itself is filled with contemporary and folk paintings, mixed-media artworks, photography, and sculpture. ■**TIP**➔ **Live music and after-hours events are held on Thursday.** ✉ *925 Camp St., Warehouse District* ☎ *504/539–9650* ⊕ *www.ogdenmuseum.org* ⊗ *Closed Tues.*

★

George Schmidt Gallery. History—and New Orleans's rich past in particular—is the passion of artist George Schmidt. His gallery displays and sells paintings and narrative art, from small-scale monotypes to mural-size depictions of historic moments. He also sells signed and numbered prints of his work. ✉ *626 Julia St., Warehouse District* ☎ *504/592–0206* ⊕ *www.georgeschmidt.com* ⊗ *Closed Sun. and Mon.*

Jonathan Ferrara Gallery. Cutting-edge art with a message is the focus of this gallery's monthly exhibits. Contemporary paintings, photography, mixed-media artworks, sculpture, glass, and metalwork by local and international artists are displayed. ✉ *400A Julia St., Warehouse District* ☎ *504/522–5471* ⊕ *www.jonathanferraragallery.com.*

LeMieux Gallery. Gulf Coast artists from Louisiana to Florida display art and high-end crafts here, alongside work by the late New Orleans abstract artist Paul Ninas. ✉ *332 Julia St., Warehouse District* ☎ *504/522–5988* ⊕ *www.lemieuxgalleries.com* ⊗ *Closed Sun.*

FAMILY **New Orleans Glassworks and Printmaking Studio.** One of the South's largest glassblowing and printmaking studios has a viewing room where visitors can watch glassblowers at work. The gallery also displays and sells functional and decorative art and sculptures. ✉ *727 Magazine St., Warehouse District* ☎ *504/529–7279* ⊕ *www.neworleansglassworks.com* ⊗ *Closed Sun.*

Octavia Art Gallery. This gallery space features a number of established, mid-career, and emerging local and international artists who work in a variety of media. The gallery also shows works by 20th-century masters such as Andy Warhol, Keith Haring, and Alex Katz. ✉ *454*

Julia St., Warehouse District ☎ *504/309–4249* ⊕ *www.octaviaartgallery.com* ☉ *Closed Sun. and Mon.*

Soren Christensen. More than 30 local, national, and international artists working in a diverse range of media and aesthetics showcase their talents at this gallery. Popular artists include Gretchen Weller Howard, Steven Seinberg, Karen Scharer, and Audra Kohout. ⊠ *400 Julia St., Warehouse District* ☎ *504/569–9501* ⊕ *www.sorengallery.com* ☉ *Closed Sun. and Mon.*

CLOTHING

Friend. A boutique in the lobby of the Ace Hotel features local and small designers of hip, unique menswear. Small gifts and accessories from other local shops are also available. Next door, the Marfa-born Freda boutique sells women's clothes. ⊠ *Ace Hotel New Orleans, 600 Carondolet St., Suite 120, Warehouse District* ☎ *504/342–2162* ⊕ *www.friendneworleans.com.*

Wehmeiers. Exotic leathers—especially American alligator, lizard, and South African ostrich—become fashionable men's and women's belts, boots, shoes, handbags, wallets, briefcases, and even golf bags at this 50-year-old store. ⊠ *The Shops at Canal Place, 333 Canal St., Warehouse District* ☎ *504/383–7120* ⊕ *www.wehmeiers.com.*

FOOD, WINE, AND SPIRITS

Wine Institute of New Orleans. This hybrid institute, best known as "WINO," is part wine school, part wine store, and part high-tech wine-tasting experience. Walk around with a glass and sample this shop's more than 120 wines, available to taste for a fee by the ounce, half glass, or full glass using Enomatic serving systems (the machines resemble a soda fountain or beer taps). Buy the wines you like by the bottle, or just continue to taste to your heart's content—just make sure you keep tabs on your credit card tally, as it's easy to get carried away. Charcuterie, artisanal cheese, and other small plates are also on offer. The Thursday-evening wine-tasting classes fill up quickly, so plan ahead if you are interested. ⊠ *610 Tchoupitoulas St., Warehouse District* ☎ *504/324–8000* ⊕ *www.winoschool.com.*

THE GARDEN DISTRICT AND MAGAZINE STREET

A winding, 6-mile strip of kitsch, commerce, funk, and fashion, Magazine Street is a shopper's mecca, a browser's paradise, and a perch for prime people-watching. It meanders from Uptown through the Garden District to downtown. Young professionals, college students, and hipsters flock to the area's funky vintage shops, cafés, boutiques, restaurants, and casual bars. Clothing stores here run from on-trend casual wear to vintage and consignment goods to high-end designer apparel. The street houses mostly locally owned stores, but there are also a few chains like American Apparel, Design Within Reach, and Free People. Antiques and home furnishing shops also are scattered throughout.

If you're in town for Mardi Gras, buy a mask at one of the city's many costume shops.

City buses provide transportation to and along Magazine Street, and streetcars travel St. Charles Avenue, which is a short walk away. Walking the 6-mile length of Magazine is possible, but some blocks have more stores than others, and you're better off making a plan and deciding your focus beforehand. If you're looking for a clothing-driven shopping experience, for example, try the blocks farther west, between Nashville and Jefferson avenues, where there are a number of stores carrying designer labels. Between Jackson Avenue and Felicity Street, to the east, you'll find a stretch of shops selling eco-friendly attire and accessories, menswear, and home decor. The blocks between Louisiana and Washington avenues are filled with popular restaurants, bars, and boutiques. Detailed maps are available from the Magazine Street Merchants Association.

Magazine Street Merchants Association. The Magazine Street Merchants Association publishes a free brochure with maps and descriptions of the myriad stores, galleries, restaurants, and shops that line the city's boutique strip; it's available in hotels and stores, or you can request or download one from the association's website. ⊠ *New Orleans* ☎ *504/342–4435* ⊕ *www.magazinestreet.com.*

ANTIQUES AND COLLECTIBLES

As You Like It Silver Shop. Everything you'd want in silver is available here, with a bounty of discontinued, hard-to-find, and obsolete American sterling-silver tea services, trays, and flatware. Victorian pieces, art-nouveau and art-deco items, and engraved pillboxes round out the selection. The store also offers monogramming, repair, and sterling-silver pattern identification. ⊠ *3033 Magazine St., Garden District* ☎ *800/897–6915* ⊕ *www.asyoulikeitsilvershop.com* ⊘ *Closed Sun.*

La Belle Nouvelle Orleans. In this eclectic shop, industrial lighting and reclaimed building materials mix with European antique furniture, artwork, porcelain, sculpture, and oddities from the 18th to 20th century. An open-air patio outfitted with garden benches, fountains, and other outdoor decor is linked to the main showroom by a warehouse-type gallery stacked almost floor to ceiling with furniture, salvaged doors, and other architectural items. ⊠ *2112 Magazine St., Garden District* ☎ *504/581–3733* ⊕ *www.labellenouvelle.com* ⊘ *Closed Sun.*

Magazine Antique Mall. If you are easily overwhelmed, you should take a deep breath before you walk into this expansive shop, where every possible inch of counter and shelf space is filled with antiques and vintage goods. You will find an array of costume and fine jewelry, vintage photographs, antique clocks, home decor, glassware, clothing, silver, furniture, china and ceramics, and a variety of other collectibles from a number of vendors. ⊠ *3017 Magazine St., Garden District* ☎ *504/896–9994.*

ART GALLERIES

Derby Pottery. Fragments of wrought ironwork and other architectural details form the inspiration for many of Mark Derby's beautiful pottery pieces, from mugs and vases to handmade Victorian reproduction tiles. His clocks and plaques, fashioned from reproductions of New Orleans's historic art-deco water-meter covers, have earned cult popularity, and his reproductions of letter tiles found on Crescent City street corners can be spotted all over town. ⊠ *2029 Magazine St., Garden District* ☎ *504/586–9003* ⊕ *www.derbypottery.com* ⊘ *Closed Sun.*

RHINO Contemporary Crafts Co. The name of this shop stands for Right Here In New Orleans, which is where most of the artists involved in this upscale co-op live and work. You'll find original paintings in a variety of styles, metalwork, sculpture, ceramics, glass, functional art, jewelry, fashion accessories, and artwork made from found objects. The gallery also holds art classes for children and adults. ⊠ *2028 Magazine St., Garden District* ☎ *504/523–7945* ⊕ *www. rhinocrafts.com.*

Thomas Mann Gallery I/O. Handmade jewelry by local artist Thomas Mann, known for his "technoromantic" pins, earrings, bracelets, and necklaces (often featuring industrial-style hearts), is showcased here, alongside work by a changing slate of other artists. The result is an eclectic mix of contemporary jewelry, housewares, sculpture, and unique gifts—the "I/O" stands for "Insight-full Objects." ⊠ *1810 Magazine St., Garden District* ☎ *504/581–2113, 800/875–2113* ⊕ *www. thomasmann.com* ⊘ *Closed Sun.*

BOOKS

Garden District Book Shop. This small store at the Rink boutique shopping center is packed with works of history, fiction, and cookbooks by local, regional, and national authors; it was the first stop on novelist Anne Rice's book tours when she lived in New Orleans. Autographed copies and limited editions of her titles are usually in stock, and the store hosts frequent author events. ⊠ *The Rink, 2727 Prytania St., Garden District* ☎ *504/895–2266* ⊕ *www.gardendistrictbookshop.com.*

> **LOOKING FOR LAGNIAPPE**
>
> A *lagniappe* (pronounced LAN-yap), a little something extra, is a tradition in New Orleans, whether it's getting a free taste of fudge at the candy store, free whipped cream on your latte, or an unexpected balloon animal from the clowns who entertain visitors on Jackson Square.

CLOTHING

Defend New Orleans. The stylish, minimalist designs on the T-shirts, sweatshirts, tanks, and baseball caps at this shop focus on a love for the city and its spirit. Many proceeds go to nonprofits and community organizations. An additional store can be found at the Ace Hotel New Orleans (*600 Carondelet St.*) in the Warehouse District. ⊠ *1101 First St., Garden District* ☎ *504/941–7010* ⊕ *www.defendneworleans.com.*

Funky Monkey. Popular with local college students, this clothing exchange mixes new, used, and vintage apparel for men and women with hipster T-shirts, handmade costumes, and lots of quirky accessories—all at affordable prices. ⊠ *3127 Magazine St., Garden District* ☎ *504/899–5587* ⊕ *www.funkymonkeynola.com.*

Green Serene. This store is for women who love clothing that reflects their values as well as their style. The boutique sells only clothes and accessories made by environmentally friendly means. Owner Jamie Menutis has an expert eye for sourcing chic, affordable dresses, shirts, skirts, and pants made with organic cotton, soy silk, hemp, alpaca, and other eco-fabrics, including—and this is something you should really feel—surprisingly soft recycled plastics. Cool, locally made tote bags, candles, and other accessories are also in keeping with the green theme. ⊠ *2041 Magazine St., Garden District* ☎ *504/252–9861.*

Tchoup Industries. This shop represents a new movement in local, ethically sourced products with a distinct New Orleans stamp imprinted on them. Handmade shoulder bags, backpacks, fanny packs, and dopp kits are fashioned from locally grown or repurposed durable and waterproof materials. ⊠ *115 Saint Mary St., Garden District* ☎ *504/872–0726* ⊕ *www.tchoupindustries.com.*

FOOD

Sucré. Elaborate confections on display in the window lure Magazine Street strollers inside this pastel-painted café and shop. The sweets live up to their colorful surroundings: artisanal chocolates, pillowy marshmallows, French *macarons*, and other treats crafted by executive pastry chef Tariq Hanna and his team are among the best in the city. You can buy chocolates individually, mix and match to create your own box, or purchase a preassembled box organized by theme. ⊠ *3025 Magazine St., Garden District* ☎ *504/520–8311* ⊕ *www.shopsucre.com.*

HOUSEWARES

Fodor's Choice
★

perch. Eclectic, feminine, and contemporary, this store's home furnishings are the sort you'd find in a high-end architectural magazine. If you love the look but don't have the decorating gene, the staff provide interior design services. ⊠ *2844 Magazine St., Garden District* ☎ *504/899–2122* ⊕ *www.perch-home.com* ☽ *Closed Sun.*

Spruce Eco-Studio. Even if you aren't looking for environmentally friendly furniture and accessories, this chic home-decor store is worth a visit for its carefully chosen collection of Jonathan Adler ceramics and lamps, John Robshaw bedding, and Greenform outdoor items. The owner has a sharp eye for design, and an environmental consciousness that makes going green seem smart and easy. ⊠ *2043 Magazine St., Garden District* ☎ *504/265–0946* ⊕ *www.sprucenola.com* ☽ *Closed Sun.*

JEWELRY

Gogo Jewelry. You'll find yourself in a good mood after spending just a few minutes in this store surrounded by Gogo Borgerding's brightly colored jewelry designs. Her vibrant cuff bracelets, made of sterling silver and anodized aluminum, are the store's signature pieces. The boutique also carries her sterling-silver necklaces, rings, and other items, as well as works by a few other artists. A quirky blend of kitsch and high-end, the shop also features offbeat items like paint-by-number sets and taxidermy. ⊠ *2036 Magazine St., Suite A, Garden District* ☎ *504/529–8868* ⊕ *www.ilovegogojewelry.com* ☽ *Closed Sun.*

MUSIC

Peaches Records. This locally owned music shop specializes in vinyl as well as CDs, with a focus on New Orleans rap, hip-hop, and bounce. You'll also find jazz, gospel, classic soul, and a few music accessories, along with the record store's signature apparel. ⊠ *4318 Magazine St., Garden District* ☎ *504/282–3322* ⊕ *www.peachesrecordsandtapes.com.*

NOVELTIES AND GIFTS

Lionheart Prints. Local designer Liz Maute Cook is known for her witty and whimsical hand-printed greeting cards, sold in this shop alongside her signature apparel, paper goods, and other curated small gifts. The shop also holds workshops on letterpress printing and

11

other crafts. ✉ *3312 Magazine St., Garden District* ☎ *504/267–5299* ⊕ *www.lionheartprints.com.*

SPA AND BEAUTY

Fodor's Choice ★ **Aidan Gill for Men.** Merging the attentiveness of a spa with the old-world charm of a barbershop, this high-end men's salon caters to guys who prefer getting a hot-towel shave and a haircut while enjoying a whiskey. The front of the store is devoted to manly diversions, with shaving sets, contemporary and New Orleans–theme cuff links, pocket knives, wallets, bow ties (a specialty), grooming products for face and hair, and gifts. The store has a second location at 550 Fulton Street in the Warehouse District. ✉ *2026 Magazine St., Garden District* ☎ *504/587–9090* ⊕ *www.aidangillformen.com.*

UPTOWN AND MAGAZINE STREET, WITH CARROLLTON-RIVERBEND

Clothing boutiques, home-decor stores, contemporary art galleries, and trendy restaurants, many housed in turn-of-the-20th-century cottages, are scattered throughout the area near Tulane and Loyola universities. Reflecting the neighborhood's family-friendly vibe, you'll find something for every age: toys and novelties, locally made jewelry, books, artwork, and Crescent City–centric T-shirts. The Uptown end of Magazine Street, a popular haunt for college students and young professionals, is a main shopping drag. On Maple Street, boutiques cover about six blocks, from Carrollton Avenue to Cherokee Street, and in the Riverbend, they dot the streets behind a shopping center on Carrollton Avenue. Oak Street, a burgeoning boutique corridor and one of the city's up-and-coming dining destinations, has several of the city's newest cafés and restaurants, serving everything from barbecue to sushi.

UPTOWN

ANTIQUES AND COLLECTIBLES

Kevin Stone Antiques & Interiors. Unusual European antiques, most from the 17th, 18th, and early 19th centuries, fill this shotgun house; the collection includes many large, very ornate pieces from the Louis XIV and XV eras. The inventory ranges from small decorative bowls and sconces to grand pianos and armoires. ✉ *3420 Magazine St., Uptown* ☎ *504/891–8282, 504/458–7043* ⊕ *www.kevinstoneantiques.com.*

ART GALLERIES

Carol Robinson Gallery. This two-story Uptown house features contemporary paintings and sculpture by U.S. artists, with a special nod to those from the South, including Jere Allen, David Goodman, Nell C. Tilton, and Jean Geraci. ✉ *840 Napoleon Ave., at Magazine St., Uptown* ☎ *504/895–6130* ⊕ *carolrobinsongallery.net.*

Cole Pratt Gallery. Contemporary paintings and sculptures by more than 40 Southern artists are displayed in this modern space. Opening receptions are held the first Saturday of every month. ✉ *3800 Magazine St., Uptown* ☎ *504/891–6789* ⊕ *www.coleprattgallery.com.*

Nuance/Louisiana Artisans Gallery. Local and regional blown-glass artists are represented in this Riverbend neighborhood studio, which also carries an eclectic mix of jewelry, pewter, ceramics, lamps, T-shirts, and more. ✉ *728 Dublin St., Uptown* ☎ *504/865–8463* ⊕ *www.nuanceglass.com* ☉ *Closed Sun.*

BOOKS

Octavia Books. The building's contemporary architecture stands out, and the attractive layout inside invites customers to leisurely browse a selection with an emphasis on architecture, art, and fiction as well as books of local interest. The store hosts frequent book signings. ✉ *513 Octavia St., Uptown* ☎ *504/899–7323* ⊕ *www.octaviabooks.com.*

CLOTHING

Jean Therapy. Popular for its diverse range of denim brands—the store carries more than 100 styles of jeans for men and women—this busy shop also offers a small collection of tops, jackets, and accessories, as well as T-shirts emblazoned with New Orleans slogans and local lingo. There's another branch in the CBD, at the Shops at Canal Place, 333 Canal Street. ✉ *5505 Magazine St., Uptown* ☎ *504/897–5535* ⊕ *www.jeantherapy.com.*

Perlis. The first floor of this venerable New Orleans retail institution is devoted to outfitting men with classic suits (white linen and seersucker are very popular), sportswear, shoes, ties, and accessories, as well as the store's signature crawfish-logo polo shirts. The second floor is filled with dressy, casual, and formal wear for women. ✉ *6070 Magazine St., Uptown* ☎ *504/895–8661* ⊕ *www.perlis.com* ☉ *Closed Sun.*

FOOD AND WINE

Southern Food and Beverage Museum gift shop. The Southern Food and Beverage Museum documents and celebrates Southern culinary heritage, so its gift shop, of course, carries some of the best cookbooks from the South. It also has a food-related and New Orleans–centric gifts, cooking utensils, and vintage and modern cocktail tools and manuals. ✉ *1504 Oretha Castle Haley Blvd., Uptown* ☎ *504/569–0405* ⊕ *www.southernfood.org.*

St. James Cheese Company. Inspired by cheese shops in Europe, the stock here includes massive wheels and wedges of Gruyère, Brie, cheddar, blue, and exotic cheeses from around the globe. Owners Danielle and

HISTORY AND COMMERCE

The shops of the Riverbend neighborhood are easily reached by a St. Charles Avenue streetcar. The line runs parallel to Magazine Street, all the way from Canal Street to the Riverbend. The leisurely ride takes you through the Garden District neighborhood, with its historic mansions, to Audubon Park, and Tulane and Loyola universities. At the corner where St. Charles meets Carrollton, step off the streetcar for a bite at the famous Camellia Grill or ride a few blocks down to Oak Street for a coffee and a croissant at Breads on Oak, one of the best bakeries in the city (✉ *8640 Oak St.*).

11

Richard Sutton pride themselves on the select inventory, which also includes specialty meats and a variety of great foodie gifts, such as cutting boards, preserves, pastas, cutlery, crackers, and more. Sandwiches and salads are served daily, making this a popular, and crowded, spot at lunchtime. ✉ *5004 Prytania St., Uptown* ☎ *504/899–4737* ⊕ *www. stjamescheese.com.*

JEWELRY AND ACCESSORIES

Fleur D'Orleans. Silver jewelry adorned with the fleur-de-lis is the main attraction here, but you'll also find items that carry other New Orleans icons such as crowns, masks, hearts, and architectural details. In addition to jewelry, the store sells handbags, handmade paper, glassware, wood and ceramic boxes, batik scarves, ironwork, and more. Another location is at 818 Chartres Street, in the French Quarter. ✉ *3701-A Magazine St., Uptown* ☎ *504/899–5585* ⊕ *www. fleurdorleans.com* ☽ *Closed Sun.*

Fodor'sChoice
★
Mignon Faget. Mignon Faget is the most famous jewelry designer in New Orleans, and her upscale sterling-silver and 14k-gold collections reflect her love and fascination with botany, nature, architecture, and the city's culture. Elements of bamboo, fleurs-de-lis, honey bees, red beans, and iron balconies have all been inspirations. Faget studied sculpture at Newcomb College at Tulane University and started out as a fashion designer in 1969, but she quickly gave up clothing to focus exclusively on jewelry. Her work has been featured in museums and shops around the world, but her biggest fan club remains right here in New Orleans, where her pieces are instantly recognized. In addition to her boutique on Magazine Street, she has a gallery at the Shops at Canal Place. ✉ *3801 Magazine St., Uptown* ☎ *504/891–2005* ⊕ *www.mignonfaget.com.*

LINGERIE

Basics Underneath. The ladies here are focused on ridding the world of sagging bra straps and overflowing cups. With a sharp eye for measurement, the staff specialize in finding the right fit, whether it's something for work or for a more romantic occasion. The store also carries sleepwear and gifts. Next door, at 5515 Magazine Street, is Basics Swim and Gym, a fitness and swimwear boutique from the same owners. ✉ *5513 Magazine St., Uptown* ☎ *504/894–1000* ⊕ *www.basicsunderneath.com* ☽ *Closed Sun.*

NOVELTIES AND GIFTS

Aux Belles Choses. This dreamy cottage of French and English delights has richly scented soaps, vintage and new linens, antique enamelware, collectible plates, and decorative accessories. ✉ *3912 Magazine St., Uptown* ☎ *504/891–1009* ⊕ *www.abcneworleans.com.*

Dirty Coast. T-shirts and bumper stickers with the phrase "Be a New Orleanian. Wherever you are" deeply resonated with displaced residents after Hurricane Katrina. Since then, locals leave it to this shop's shirts, stickers, and hats to both satirize ("New Orleans: So far behind, we're ahead") and celebrate local culture in a clever way. The store has a second location at 713 Royal Street, in the French Quarter. ✉ *5631 Magazine St., Uptown* ☎ *504/324–3745* ⊕ *www.dirtycoast.com.*

Hazelnut. Founded by stage and television actor Bryan Batt (he played Salvatore Romano on *Mad Men*) and his partner, Tom Cianfichi, this jewel box of a shop carries gorgeous home accessories and gifts, including New Orleans–themed toile frames, decorative items, stemware, tableware, accent furniture, frames, and more. ⊠ *5515 Magazine St., Uptown* ☎ *504/891–2424* ⊕ *www.hazelnutneworleans.com* ⊗ *Closed Sun.*

Orient Expressed Imports. Imported porcelain, vases, ceramics, jewelry, and the store's own line of smocked children's clothing are popular gift items. The shop also has a showroom of home furnishings, including accent furniture, lamps, and antique accessories. ⊠ *3905 Magazine St., Uptown* ☎ *504/899–3060* ⊕ *www.orientexpressed.com* ⊗ *Closed Sun.*

Scriptura. The Italian-leather address books, fancy journals, hand-decorated photo albums, specialty papers, custom stationery, handmade invitations, and high-quality fountain pens sold here are fitting tributes to the art of handwriting. The store also creates gorgeous stationery with New Orleans themes. ⊠ *5423 Magazine St., Uptown* ☎ *504/897–1555* ⊕ *www.scriptura.com* ⊗ *Closed Sun.*

SHOES

Victoria's Shoes. Jimmy Choo, Giuseppe Zanotti, Hoss Intropia, and Marni are just a few of the high-end brands available here. The boutique also carries handbags and jewelry. ⊠ *4858 Magazine St., Uptown* ☎ *504/265–8010.*

SPA AND BEAUTY

Belladonna Day Spa. This haven of relaxation offers the usual day-spa services—pedicures, manicures, massages, facials, etc.—while the gift shop area, called "retail therapy," features decorative housewares, pajamas, and high-end bath and body products. ⊠ *2900 Magazine St., Uptown* ☎ *504/891–4393* ⊕ *www.belladonnadayspa.com.*

TOYS

FAMILY **Magic Box.** This toy shop, beloved by both children and adults, sells the kind of items you won't find in big-box stores. While they do carry popular toys by LEGO and Playskool, the emphasis is on independent brands. You'll find everything from baby toys to play items for older children to party games for adults. The staff go above and beyond with customer service, and can help with shipping and assembly. ⊠ *5508 Magazine St., Uptown* ☎ *504/899–0117* ⊕ *www.magicboxneworleans.com.*

CARROLLTON-RIVERBEND

BOOKS

Blue Cypress Books. At this shop, college students, locals, and visitors alike sift through the crowded shelves and tables of used and rare books in all genres, including children's. The shop also sells postcards and small locally themed gifts by the register. ⊠ *8126 Oak St., Carrollton-Riverbend* ☎ *504/352–0096* ⊕ *www.bluecypressbooks.com.*

CLOTHING

Angelique. This upscale women's clothing store provides on-trend apparel, shoes, and accessories from contemporary labels such as Diane von Furstenberg, Halston Heritage, Vince, Red Valentino, and Alice & Olivia. An Angelique shoe boutique is located at 5421 Magazine Street, and a children's store is at 5519 Magazine Street. ⊠ *7725 Maple St., Carrollton-Riverbend* ☎ *504/866–1092* ⊙ *Closed Sun.*

C. Collection. Geared toward fashion-forward college students, this store resembles a sorority-house closet jammed with hip, flirty, affordable clothes, shoes, handbags, and accessories, ranging from casual to dressy, by brands such as Kensie and Tulle. ⊠ *8141 Maple St., Carrollton-Riverbend* ☎ *504/861–5002* ⊕ *www.ccollectionnola.com* ⊙ *Closed Sun.*

Encore Shop. This high-end resale shop supports the local symphony orchestra by selling previously owned designer clothes, from casual to formal wear, as well as shoes, handbags, and jewelry. The shop also sells consignment items. ⊠ *7814 Maple St., Carrollton-Riverbend* ☎ *504/861–9028* ⊕ *www.lpovolunteers.org/encore-shop* ⊙ *Closed Sun. and Mon.*

Gae-Tana's. Racks are filled with a mix of natural fabrics and stylish but comfortable clothing that stay on trend. The combination makes this shop a favorite stop for fashion-conscious mature women as well as college students looking for skirts, jeans, shorts, dresses, blouses, casual shoes, handbags, and jewelry. ⊠ *7732 Maple St., Carrollton-Riverbend* ☎ *504/865–9625* ⊕ *www.gaetanas.com* ⊙ *Closed Sun.*

Swap. You're as likely to find designer duds by Diane von Furstenberg and Dolce & Gabbana as Ann Taylor and J.Crew on the racks of this upscale consignment store. New consignors come in every day, adding fresh inventory. A children's store, Swap for Kids (*7722 Maple Street*), is next door, offering junior clothing and accessories, maternity apparel, strollers, diaper bags, and high-end accessories. A second women's store is at 5530 Magazine Street. ⊠ *7716 Maple St., Carrollton-Riverbend* ☎ *504/304–6025* ⊕ *www.swapboutique.com* ⊙ *Closed Sun.*

Yvonne LaFleur. Although the clothes may be stylish and contemporary, this beloved local boutique's approach is decidedly old-world elegance. Owner Yvonne LaFleur custom-designs hats for all occasions, and her store is always infused with the soft scent of her signature perfume line. The romantic fashions here run the gamut from casual dresses and flirty skirts to lingerie, ball gowns, and a whole room filled with bridal dresses in a variety of styles. ⊠ *8131 Hampson St., Carrollton-Riverbend* ☎ *504/866–9666* ⊕ *www.yvonnelafleur.com* ⊙ *Closed Sun.*

JEWELRY

Symmetry Jewelers. Designer Tom Mathis creates custom wedding and engagement rings and other in-house designs and also repairs jewelry. The shop also stocks a variety of contemporary designs by local, national, and international jewelry artists. ⊠ *8138 Hampson St., Carrollton-Riverbend* ☎ *504/861–9925, 800/628–3711* ⊕ *www.symmetryjewelers.com* ⊙ *Closed Sun. and Mon.*

MID-CITY

This neighborhood isn't known as a shopping destination. However, the store inside the New Orleans Museum of Art (NOMA) is worth a stop for anyone interested in art-related gifts or souvenirs. Small wine shops in the area also provide perfect companions for picnics in City

Park or along Bayou St. John. A streetcar runs along Canal Street and then down North Carrollton Avenue, ending at City Park Avenue, near the park and art museum.

FOOD, WINE AND SPIRITS

Pearl Wine Co. This wine-and-spirits shop is connected to Pearl Bar next door, and you can grab a bottle here and enjoy it at the bar. Besides wine, the store also has a well-stocked spirits selection with a wide array of Scotches, bourbons, vodkas, and tequilas. The shop also offers tastings and frequent wine classes that take participants on virtual wine tours around the world. ⊠ *American Can Company, 3700 Orleans Ave., Suite C, Mid-City* ☎ *504/483–6314* ⊕ *www.pearlwineco.com.*

Swirl. Swirl specializes in inexpensive, everyday wines. The cozy neighborhood spot also has a wine bar that's a comfortable place to sip and learn about different vintages. Organized with colorful signs describing the bottles, including a "Cheap and Tasty" designation, the store also has a small selection of cheeses and gifts. ⊠ *3143 Ponce de Leon St., Mid-City* ☎ *504/304–0635* ⊕ *www.swirlnola.com* ☼ *Closed Sun.*

NOVELTIES AND GIFTS

The GOOD Shop. This unassuming storefront within a coffee shop is a great stop for gifts with a socially conscious spin: every purchase of a handcrafted candle, soap, jewelry item, or T-shirt sold here goes towards a specific charity or relief effort. The boutique also sells goods from beloved local brands like Tchoup Industry bags, Smoke Perfume, and Zeko jewelry. ⊠ *4201 Canal St., Mid-City* ☎ *504/264–2478.*

New Orleans Museum of Art gift shop. Stocked with art and photography books, children's items, puzzles, jewelry, and locally made crafts, this gift shop is well worth a visit, even if you're not browsing the museum's exhibits. The shop has its own cookbook, as well as items created exclusively for it by local favorite jewelry designer Mignon Faget. You don't have to pay museum admission to enter the shop; just say you are shopping at the front desk, and you will receive a special pass. ⊠ *1 Collins C. Diboll Circle, Mid-City* ☎ *504/658–4116* ⊕ *www.noma.org* ☼ *Closed Mon.*

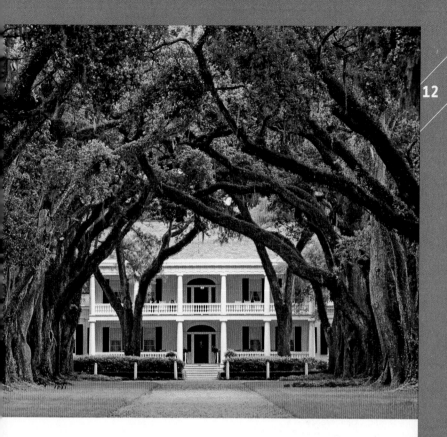

SIDE TRIPS FROM
NEW ORLEANS

WELCOME TO SIDE TRIPS FROM NEW ORLEANS

TOP REASONS TO GO

★ **Take a swamp tour:** Get to know the wetlands surrounding New Orleans on a boat ride. The area is home to alligators, snakes, nutrias, and more.

★ **Visit quirky Abita Springs:** Head to the home of the Abita brewery for an afternoon trip, and check out the Abita Mystery House museum.

★ **Jam to Cajun and zydeco music:** Ensembles of fiddles, accordions, and guitars produce eminently danceable folk music, with songs sung in a mélange of English and Cajun French. Zydeco, closely related to Cajun music, adds washboard and drums to the mix to create an R&B-infused jumping rhythm.

★ **Marvel at plantation homes:** Stately homes will have you reenacting your favorite scenes from *Gone with the Wind*; some are beautifully preserved, others lie in ruin alongside bayous, testifying to the clash between old and new.

Baton Rouge, the state's capital and second-largest city, is about an hour and a half west of New Orleans. Plantation homes are scattered between the two cities, within a two-hour drive if you take the scenic Great River Road. Lafayette, about two hours west of New Orleans via Interstate 10, is a good post for exploring Cajun Country. Smaller Cajun towns surround the small city in all directions.

1 Abita Springs. This quirky town is an easy day trip from New Orleans. Part of the drive is on a 30-mile causeway over Lake Pontchartrain.

2 Plantation Country. Take a journey into the past and see some of the South's most beautiful antebellum

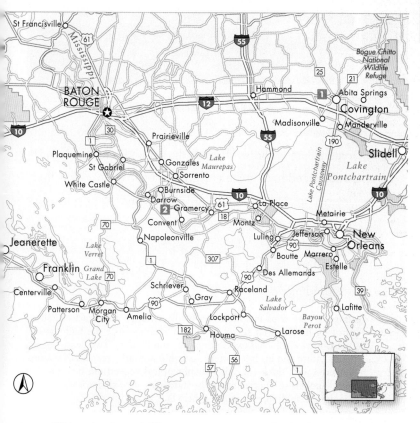

homes. Within an hour's drive of New Orleans you will see dozens of plantation homes in various states of repair scattered along either side of the Mississippi, heading west toward the state's capital, Baton Rouge. The views these days also include sights of the heavy industry scattered along the river west of New Orleans.

3 Cajun Country. French Louisiana, spread across the bayous, rice fields, and canebrakes to the west of New Orleans, is famous for two things: its food (jambalaya and blackened fish) and its music (Cajun and zydeco). You'll also find excellent antiques shopping and many natural and historical sights. Here you'll find much of

what the Big Easy has to offer, but in a family-friendly, small-town setting.

Updated
by Karen
Taylor-Gist

New Orleans has never been a typical old Southern city. But look away to the west of town, and you can find that antebellum world evoked by the term "Dixieland," which was coined here in the early 19th century. Anyone with an interest in the history of the Old South or a penchant for picturesque drives along country roads should spend at least half a day along the winding Great River Road, which the romantic ruins of plantation homes share with restored manors.

Popular day trips include tours of the swamps and brackish, slow-moving bayous that surround New Orleans—once the highways of the Choctaw, Chickasaw, Chitimacha, and Houma. Two centuries ago Jean Lafitte and his freebooters easily hid in murky reaches of swamp, covered with thick canopies of subtropical vegetation; it's said that pirate gold is still buried here. The state has a wild alligator population of about 2 million, and most of them laze around in these meandering tributaries and secluded backwaters of south Louisiana.

A variety of tour companies take groups to swampy sites a half hour to two hours away from the city center. Guides steer you by boat through still waters, past ancient gnarled cypresses with gray shawls of Spanish moss, explaining the state's flora and fauna and the swamp traditions of the trappers who settled here. *For swamp tour operators, see Cajun Encounters.*

South Louisiana, the center of the Cajun population, is decidedly French in flavor. In small communities along the coast and in the upland prairie, Cajun French is still spoken, though just about everyone also speaks English. After a hard day's work fishing or working crawfish ponds, rural residents of Cajun Country often live up to the motto "*Laissez les bons temps rouler!,*" or "Let the good times roll!"

PLANNING

WHEN TO GO

Spring and fall are especially full of small-town, family-friendly festivals celebrating local food and culture. Cooler temperatures make late September and October a good time for plantation exploring and swamp tours as well, but it's also the tail end of hurricane season. In December, plantation homes are decked out for the holidays, and seasonal bonfires glow along the river.

ABOUT THE RESTAURANTS

Part of the considerable charm of the region west of New Orleans is the Cajun food, popularized in the 1970s and early 1980s by Cajun chef Paul Prudhomme, a native of Opelousas. This is jambalaya, crawfish pie, and filé gumbo country, and nowhere else on Earth is Cajun food done better than where it originated. Cajun food is often described as the robust, hot-peppery country kin of Creole cuisine. It's a cuisine built upon economy—heavy on the rice and the sauces, lighter on the meats—and strongly influenced by African and French cooking traditions. Indigenous sea creatures turn up in étouffées, bisques, and pies, and you can find jambalaya, gumbo, and blackened fish on almost every Acadian menu. Alligator meat is a great favorite, as are sausages like andouille and boudin (stuffed with a spicy pork-and-rice dressing). Cajun food is very rich, and portions tend to be ample. Biscuits and grits are breakfast staples, and many an evening meal ends with bread pudding.

Cajun cuisine extends beyond Cajun Country itself and into many of the restaurants along River Road. North of Baton Rouge, however, in St. Francisville, more typical Southern fare prevails. Here you will still find po'boys and sometimes gumbo, but barbecue is more common than boudin. ⇨ *For descriptions of many Cajun foods, see Chapter 8.*

ABOUT THE HOTELS

Some of the handsome antebellum mansions along River Road are also bed-and-breakfasts, allowing visitors to roam the stately rooms during the day and then live out the fantasy of spending the night there in a big four-poster or canopied bed. The greatest concentration of accommodations in Cajun Country is in Lafayette, which has an abundance of chain properties as well as some bed-and-breakfasts. Charming B&Bs are also abundant in other nearby towns, including St. Francisville, which is considered one of the best B&B towns in the South.

Restaurant and hotel reviews have been shortened. For full information, visit Fodors.com.

WHAT IT COSTS			
	$	**$$**	**$$$**	**$$$$**
Restaurants	under $16	$16–$22	$23–$30	over $30
Hotels	under $90	$90–$120	$121–$150	over $150

Restaurant prices are the average cost of a main course at dinner or, if dinner is not served, at lunch. Hotel prices are the lowest cost of a standard double room in high season.

ABITA SPRINGS

45 miles north of New Orleans.

Tiny Abita Springs, north of Lake Pontchartrain, is notable for three things: artesian spring water, Abita beer, and an oddball institution known as the Abita Mystery House. It's a fun day trip from New Orleans.

EXPLORING

Abita Brewing Company. Head out to Abita Springs to see where this popular beer is made—the area has long been known for its artesian spring water, which is used in brewing. Half-hour guided tours, $5, run Wednesday, Thursday, and Sunday 2–3 pm, Friday 1–3 pm, and Saturday 10:30 am–3 pm. Tours include four brew samplings. Note that closed-toe shoes need to be worn on all tours. ⊠ *166 Barbee Rd., Covington ✛ On the line between Abita Springs and Covington* ☎ *985/893–3143* ⊕ *www.abita.com.*

Abita Mystery House. Artist John Preble's strange vision—sort of a Louisiana version of the Watts Towers of Los Angeles—is an obsessive collection of found objects (combs, old musical instruments, paint-by-number art, and taxidermy experiments gone horribly awry) set in a series of ramshackle buildings, including one covered in mosaic tiles. This museum is truly odd and entertaining, but not for clutter-phobes. Ask Preble if you can see his studio, where he creates paintings of green-eyed Creole beauties. ⊠ *22275 Hwy. 36, at Grover St.* ☎ *985/892–2624* ⊕ *www.abitamysteryhouse.com* 🎟 *$3.*

WHERE TO EAT

$$
AMERICAN
✕ **Abita Brew Pub.** Abita's original brewery is now the setting for meals chosen from a surprisingly lengthy menu of pasta, salads, burgers, and entrées like jambalaya, barbecue ribs, and pecan-crusted catfish. These dishes all go well with the beer—a full selection of Abita on tap, including seasonal brews. **Known for:** Abita on tap; hearty pub fare; Southern flavors. Ⓢ *Average main: $17* ⊠ *72011 Holly St.* ☎ *985/892–5837* ⊕ *www.abitabrewpub.com* ۝ *Closed Mon.*

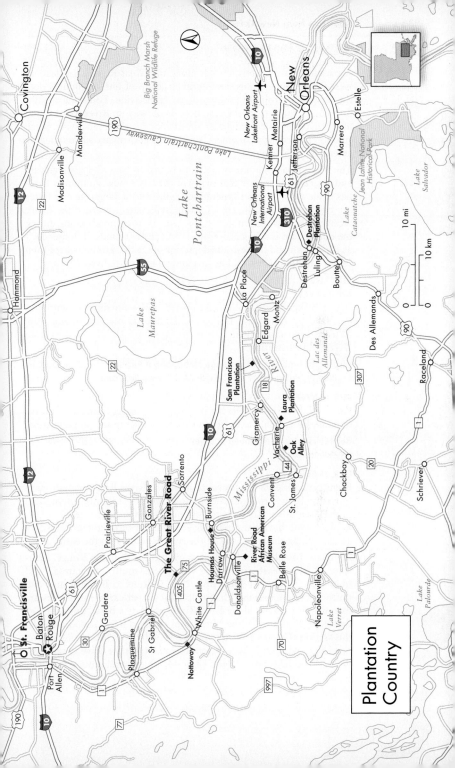

Plantation Country

PLANTATION COUNTRY

A parade of plantations unfolds along the Great River Road leading west from New Orleans, and another group of fine old houses dots the landscape around the town of St. Francisville. Louisiana plantation homes range from the grandiose Nottoway on River Road to the humbler, owner-occupied Butler Greenwood near St. Francisville. Some sit upon an acre or two; others, such as Rosedown, are surrounded by extensive, lush grounds.

The River Road plantations are closely tied to New Orleans's culture and society: it was here that many of the city's most prominent families made their fortunes generations ago, and the language and tastes are historically French. The St. Francisville area, on the other hand, received a heartier injection of British-American colonial culture during the antebellum era, evinced in the landscaped grounds of homes such as Rosedown and the restrained interior of Oakley House, where John James Audubon, the ornithologist and painter, once lived.

GETTING HERE AND AROUND

AIR TRAVEL

Baton Rouge Metropolitan Airport, 7 miles north of downtown, is served by American, Delta, and United. Louis Armstrong New Orleans International Airport is off Interstate 10, 20 minutes from Destrehan Plantation.

Airport Information Baton Rouge Metropolitan Airport (*BTR*). ⊠ *9430 Jackie Cochran Dr., Baton Rouge* ☎ *225/355–0333* ⊕ *www.flybtr.com.*

BUS TRAVEL

Greyhound Southeast Lines has frequent daily service from New Orleans to Baton Rouge and Lafayette, and limited service to surrounding areas.

Bus Information Greyhound Southeast Lines. ☎ *800/231–2222* ⊕ *www. greyhound.com.*

CAR TRAVEL

From New Orleans the fastest route to the River Road plantations is Interstate 10 west to Interstate 310 to Exit 6 (River Road). Alternatives to the Great River Road are to continue on either Interstate 10 or U.S. 61 west; both have signs marking exits for various plantations. Route 18 runs along the west bank of the river, Route 44 on the east.

Interstate 10 and U.S. 190 run east–west through Baton Rouge. Interstate 12 heads east, connecting with north–south Interstate 55 and Interstate 59. U.S. 61 leads from New Orleans to Baton Rouge and north. Ferries across the Mississippi cost $1 per car; most bridges are free. Route 1 travels along False River, which is a blue "oxbow lake" created ages ago when the Mississippi changed its course and cut off this section. The drive along Interstate 10 will take a little more than an hour from New Orleans to Baton Rouge. Expect the drive to take two hours if you take either Route 18 or 44, which wind around the river.

TIMING

Don't try to visit every plantation listed here—your trip will turn into a blur of columns. If you can, spend the night at one of the plantations, such as Oak Alley or Nottoway, and then tour the region. Oak Alley and Laura plantations are just a few miles from each other and provide a nice contrast in architectural styles and approaches. St. Francisville is a weekend trip in its own right. If you're visiting from New Orleans and are pressed for time, then Destrehan, one of the state's oldest plantations, might fit the bill; it's 23 miles from the city.

TOURS

Allons à Lafayette. Guided tours of the River Road plantations and swamp tours are available for groups of 15 or more from this company, based in Lafayette. Tours of Cajun areas are also available. ☎ *800/264–5465* ⊕ *www.allonsalafayette.com.*

Cajun Encounters Tour Co. From Cajun Encounters you can get guided tours to Oak Alley and Laura Plantations, as well as personal tours of Honey Island Swamp, even one that's at night. ☎ *866/928–6877, 504/834–1770* ⊕ *www.cajunencounters.com.*

VISITOR INFORMATION

Baton Rouge Area Convention and Visitors Bureau. ✉ *359 Third St., Baton Rouge* ☎ *225/383–1825, 800/527–6843* ⊕ *www.visitbatonrouge.com.*

Louisiana Visitor Information Center. ✉ *702 River Rd., Baton Rouge* ☎ *225/219–1200* ⊕ *www.crt.state.la.us.*

West Feliciana Parish Tourist Commission. ✉ *11757 Ferdinand St., St. Francisville* ☎ *225/635–4224, 800/789–4221* ⊕ *www.stfrancisville.us.*

THE GREAT RIVER ROAD

Between New Orleans and Baton Rouge, beautifully restored antebellum plantations along the Mississippi are filled with period antiques, evoking tales of Yankee gunboats and the ghosts of former residents. Industrial plants share the scenery now, and the man-made levee, constructed in the early 20th century in an attempt to keep the mighty Mississippi on a set course, obstructs the river views that plantation residents once enjoyed. Still, you can park your car and climb up on the levee to survey a stretch of the wide, muddy river.

Between the Destrehan and San Francisco plantations you will drive through what amounts to a deep bow before the might of the Mississippi: the Bonnet Carré Spillway is a huge swath of land set aside specifically to receive the river's periodic overflow, thus protecting New Orleans, 30 miles downriver.

The Great River Road is also called, variously, Route (or LA) 44 and 75 on the east bank of the river and Route (or LA) 18 on the west bank. "LA" and "Route" are interchangeable; we use "Route" throughout this chapter. Alternatives to the Great River Road are Interstate 10 and U.S. 61; both have signs marking exits for various plantations. All the plantations described are listed on the National Register of Historic Places, and some of them are B&Bs. Plantation touring can take anywhere from an hour to two days, depending upon how many houses you want to see—and how much talk of moonlight and magnolias you'd like to hear.

EXPLORING

Destrehan Plantation. The oldest intact plantation in the lower Mississippi Valley is a simple West Indies–style house, built in 1787–90 by a free man of color and typical of the homes built by the earliest planters in the region. It is notable for the hand-hewn cypress timbers used in its construction and for the insulation in its walls, made of *bousillage,* a mixture of horsehair, Spanish moss, oyster shells, and mud. A costumed guide leads a 45-minute tour through the house, which is furnished with period antiques. Also explore the grounds, where there are several smaller structures and massive oak trees borne down by their weighty, old branches. Demonstrations of crafts such as weaving, barrel-making, or open-hearth cooking bring the period to life, and an annual fall festival with music, crafts, and food is held the second weekend in November. ⊠ *13034 River Rd., Destrehan* ✛ *23 miles west (upriver) of New Orleans* ☎ *985/764–9315, 877/453–2095* ⊕ *www. destrehanplantation.org* 🖃 *$20.*

Houmas House. Majestic 200-year-old oaks surround this classic-looking, white-pillared Louisiana plantation house, which is actually two buildings of quite different styles joined together. In 1770, Alexander Latil built the smaller rear house in the French–Spanish Creole style that was becoming popular in New Orleans. The Greek Revival mansion was added to the grounds in 1828 by Wade Hampton, who eventually connected the two structures with an arched carriageway. ⊠ *40136 Hwy. 942, ½ mile off Rte. 44, Darrow* ✛ *58 miles west of New Orleans* ☎ *225/473–9380* ⊕ *www.houmashouse.com* 🖃 *Guided home and garden tour $24.*

Laura Plantation. This is a more intimate and better-documented presentation of Creole plantation life than any other property on River Road. The narrative of the guides is built on first-person accounts, estate records, and original artifacts from the Locoul family, who built the simple, Creole-style house in 1805. Laura Locoul, whose great-grandparents founded the estate, wrote a detailed memoir of plantation life, family fights, and the management of slaves. The information from Laura's memoir and the original slave cabins and other outbuildings (workers on the plantation grounds lived in the cabins into the 1980s) provide rare insights into slavery in south Louisiana. The plantation gift shop stocks a large selection of literature by and about slaves and slavery in southern Louisiana and the United States. Senegalese slaves at Laura are believed to have first told folklorist Alcée Fortier the tales of Br'er Rabbit; his friend, Joel Chandler Harris, used the stories in his Uncle Remus tales. ⊠ *2247 Hwy. 18 (River Rd.), Vacherie* ✛ *57 miles west of New Orleans* ☎ *225/265–7690, 888/799–7690* ⊕ *www. lauraplantation.com* 🖃 *$20.*

Fodor's Choice
★

Nottoway. The South's largest plantation house is a dramatic monument to antebellum grandeur. Built in 1859, the mansion is Italianate in style, with 64 rooms, 22 columns, and 200 windows. The crowning achievement of architect Henry Howard, it was saved from destruction during

Nottoway Plantation

the Civil War by a Northern officer (a former guest of the owners, Mr. and Mrs. John Randolph). An idiosyncratic, somewhat rambling layout reflects the individual tastes of the original owners and includes a grand ballroom, famed in these parts for its crystal chandeliers and hand-carved columns. You can stay here overnight, and a formal restaurant serves breakfast, lunch, and dinner daily. The plantation is 2 miles north of its namesake, the town of White Castle (you'll understand how the town got its name when you see the vast, white mansion, which looks like a castle). ✉ *31025 Hwy. 1, White Castle* ✛ *30 miles northwest of Madewood, 75 miles west of New Orleans* ☎ *225/545–2730, 866/527–6884* ⊕ *www.nottoway.com* ✉ *$20.*

Oak Alley. The most famous of all the antebellum homes in Louisiana is a darling of Hollywood, having appeared in such major movies as *Interview with the Vampire* and *Primary Colors*, as well as smaller movies and television productions. Built between 1837 and 1839 by Jacques T. Roman, a French Creole sugar planter from New Orleans, Oak Alley is an outstanding example of Greek Revival architecture. The 28 gnarled oak trees that line the drive and give the columned plantation its name were planted in the early 1700s by an earlier settler. A guided tour introduces you to the grand interior of the manor, furnished with period antiques. Be sure to take in the view from the upper gallery of the house and to spend time exploring the expansive grounds. A number of late-19th-century cottages behind the main house provide simple overnight accommodations, and a restaurant is open daily from 8:30 am to 3 pm. ✉ *3645 River Rd. (Hwy. 18), Vacherie* ✛ *3 miles west of*

San Francisco Plantation stands out for its over-the-top "Steamboat Gothic" exterior.

Laura Plantation, 60 miles west of New Orleans ☎ *225/265–2151, 800/442–5539* ⊕ *www.oakalleyplantation.com* ✉ *$22.*

River Road African American Museum. The contributions of African Americans in Louisiana's rural Mississippi River communities come to light through exhibits that explore their cuisine, the Underground Railroad, free people of color, and the rural roots of jazz. ⊠ *406 Charles St., Donaldsonville* ☎ *225/474–5553* ⊕ *www.africanamericanmuseum.org* ✉ *$5.*

San Francisco Plantation. An intriguing variation on the standard plantation style, with galleries resembling the decks of a ship, the San Francisco Plantation seems to have inspired a new architectural term: "Steamboat Gothic." The house, completed in 1856, was once called "St. Frusquin," a pun on a French slang term, *sans fruscins,* which means "without a penny in my pocket"—the condition its owner, Valsin Marmillion, found himself in after paying exorbitant construction costs. Valsin's father, Edmond Bozonier Marmillion, had begun the project, and according to lore, his design for the house was inspired by the steamboats he enjoyed watching along the Mississippi. Upon his father's death, Valsin and his German bride, Louise von Seybold, found themselves with a plantation on their hands. Unable to return to Germany, Louise brought German influence to south Louisiana instead. The result was an opulence rarely encountered in these parts: ceilings painted in trompe-l'oeil, hand-painted toilets with primitive flushing systems, and cypress painstakingly rendered as marble and English oak. Tour guides impart the full fascinating story on the 45-minute tour through the main house. An authentic one-room schoolhouse and a slave cabin have been installed on the grounds, which you can tour at your leisure. Louisiana novelist Frances Parkinson Keyes used the site as the model for her novel *Steamboat Gothic.* ⊠ *2646 River Rd., Garyville* ✛ *18 miles west of Destrehan Plantation, 35 miles west of New Orleans* ☎ *985/535–2341, 888/322–1756* ⊕ *www.sanfranciscoplantation.org* ⌂ *$17.*

WHERE TO EAT

$
SOUTHERN
✕ **B&C Seafood.** This small shop and restaurant serves some of the tastiest seafood gumbo around River Road (and there's plenty of competition). Try a dash of hot sauce and a sprinkle of filé, or sample the alligator burgers; finish with a scoop of rich, dense bread pudding. **Known for:** exotic meats; seafood to-go; bread pudding. ⑤ *Average main: $11* ⊠ *2155 Rte. 18, beside Laura Plantation, Vacherie* ☎ *225/265–8356* ⊗ *Closed Sun.*

$$$$
CAJUN
✕ **Latil's Landing Restaurant.** Set in the rear wing of Houmas House Plantation, Latil's Landing is furnished with period antiques and reproductions that put you in the mood for its French cuisine with Louisiana influence—a mélange of traditional ingredients with contemporary cooking techniques and flavors. Try the foie gras or curried pumpkin and crawfish bisque. **Known for:** antique furnishings; traditional Creole flavors; foie gras. ⑤ *Average main: $38* ⊠ *Houmas House Plantation, 40136 Hwy. 942, Darrow* ☎ *225/473–9380, 888/323–8314.*

$
SOUTHERN
✕ **Spuddy's Cajun Foods.** Midway between Laura and Oak Alley plantations, downtown Vacherie is short on sights but long on flavor, thanks in no small part to this down-home lunchroom. Photos and murals on the walls tell tales of local history, while po'boys, jambalaya, and fried catfish fill the tables. **Known for:** local flavor; homemade sausages; jambalaya. ⑤ *Average main: $10* ⊠ *2644 Hwy. 20, Vacherie* ☎ *225/265–4013* ⊗ *Closed weekends. No dinner Sat.–Thurs.*

$
CAJUN
✕ **Wayne Jacob's Smokehouse Restaurant.** LaPlace is known as the andouille capital of the world, and the spicy, smoky, Cajun-style sausage is deservedly popular here. In this butcher shop that doubles as a functional, straightforward restaurant for weekday lunches, you can get andouille in burgers, in gumbo, made into chips for dipping, or worked into white beans and rice. **Known for:** andouille sausage; Sunday jazz brunch; comfort food. ⑤ *Average main: $13* ⊠ *769 W. Fifth St., Laplace* ☎ *985/652–9990* ⊕ *www.wjsmokehouse.com* ⊗ *No dinner.*

WHERE TO STAY

$$$$
B&B/INN
▥ **Houmas House B&B.** Experience the luxurious and beautiful grounds of this plantation house in one of 21 rooms in newly built cottages that face a row of oak trees about a block away from the plantation house. **Pros:** breakfast and a tour of the mansion are included in the nightly rate; beautiful grounds. **Cons:** noise from nearby street can get loud in front rooms. ⑤ *Rooms from: $350* ⊠ *40136 Hwy. 942, Darrow* ☎ *225/473–9380* ⊕ *www.houmashouse.com* ⮐ *21 rooms* ⦿| *Breakfast.*

$$$$
B&B/INN
▥ **Madewood B&B.** Expect gracious hospitality, lovely antiques, and canopied beds in both the 21-room main house and Charlet House, a smaller structure on the plantation grounds that holds three of the inn's eight guest rooms. **Pros:** quiet; beautiful; staying here is like stepping back in time—though with Wi-Fi and other modern amenities. **Cons:** some may find it too quiet; no TV; dinner is a group affair. ⑤ *Rooms from: $265* ⊠ *4250 Rte. 308, Napoleonville* ☎ *985/369–7151* ⊕ *www. madewood.com* ⮐ *8 rooms* ⦿| *Some meals.*

$$$$
B&B/INN

📶 **Nottoway B&B.** At the largest antebellum plantation in the South, you can wander around the grounds at night, sit on the upstairs balcony and watch the ships go by on the river, and enjoy other Southern pastimes. **Pros:** sleeping in history. **Cons:** with so many rooms and a busy schedule of tours and events, this isn't the place to get away from it all. ⑤ *Rooms from: $219* ✉ *31025 Hwy. 1, White Castle* ☎ *225/545–2730, 866/527–6884* ⊕ *www.nottoway.com* ⌚ *40 rooms, 2 suites* ⑩ *Breakfast.*

$$$$
B&B/INN

📶 **Oak Alley B&B.** These 100-year-old one- and two-bedroom cottages on Oak Alley Plantation's grounds, just beyond the shadow of the big house, combine country charm (brass beds and antiques or reproductions) with practical and useful amenities. **Pros:** spectacular sunrise views from the levee in front of the plantation; serene quiet; charming rooms with comfortable beds and amenities. **Cons:** few nearby options for supplies and food (although the chef can make dinners ahead of time, to be delivered to your cottage during the day). ⑤ *Rooms from: $165* ✉ *3645 River Rd. (Rte. 18), Vacherie* ☎ *225/265–2151, 800/442–5539* ⊕ *www.oakalleyplantation.com* ⌚ *8 cottages* ⑩ *Breakfast.*

ST. FRANCISVILLE

25 miles north of Baton Rouge on U.S. 61.

A cluster of plantation homes all within a half-hour drive, a lovely, walkable historic district, renowned antiques shopping, and a wealth of comfortable B&Bs draw visitors and locals from New Orleans to overnight stays in St. Francisville. The town is just a two-hour drive from New Orleans, so it's also possible to make this a day trip.

St. Francisville's historic district, particularly along Royal Street, is dotted with markers identifying basic histories of various structures, most of them dating to the late 18th or early 19th century. The region's Anglo-Protestant edge, in contrast to the staunchly French-Catholic tenor of the River Road plantations, is evident in the prominent **Grace Episcopal Church,** on a hill in the center of town and surrounded by a peaceful, Spanish moss–shaded cemetery. A smaller (and older) Catholic cemetery is directly across a small fence from the Episcopal complex.

EXPLORING

**OFF THE
BEATEN
PATH**

Angola Museum. The 18,000 acres that make up the notorious Angola prison are a half-hour drive from St. Francisville, at the dead end of Highway 66. With a prison population of about 6,000 inmates, this is one of the largest prisons in the United States. Nicknamed "The Farm," Angola was once a working plantation, with prisoners for field hands. Now it produces 4 million pounds of vegetables each year, which feed 11,000 inmates across the state. The prison has been immortalized in countless songs and several films and documentaries, including *Dead Man Walking* and *Angola Prison Rodeo—the Wildest Show in the South.* The latter film is based on the prison's biannual rodeo in April and October, which offers visitors a rare look inside the grounds of the prison. Inmates set up stands where they sell their

Dropping in on a jam session is a must-do in Cajun Country.

arts and crafts during the rodeo. A small museum outside the prison's front gate houses a fascinating, eerie, and often moving collection of photographs documenting the people and events that have been a part of Angola. Items such as makeshift prisoner weapons and the electric chair used for executions until 1991 are also on display. ⊠ *Hwy. 66* ☎ *225/655–2592* ⊕ *www.angolamuseum.org* ⊠ *Free.*

The Myrtles. A 110-foot gallery with Wedgwood-blue cast-iron grillwork makes a lovely setting for the weddings and receptions frequently held at the Myrtles. The house, built around 1796, has elegant formal parlors with rich molding and faux-marble paneling. Because the upper floor is used as a bed-and-breakfast, the scope of the daytime guided tour is limited. The house is reputedly haunted, and fun mystery tours, held at night, are more of a draw than daytime tours (reservations are a good idea). ⊠ *7747 U.S. 61* ✛ *About 1 mile north of downtown St. Francisville* ☎ *225/635–6277, 800/809–0565* ⊕ *www.myrtlesplantation.com* ⊠ *$15 daytime tours, $15 mystery tours.*

OFF THE
BEATEN
PATH
Audubon State Historic Site and Oakley Plantation House. John James Audubon did a major portion of his *Birds of America* studies in this 100-acre park, and the three-story Oakley Plantation House is where Audubon tutored the young Eliza Pirrie, daughter of Mr. and Mrs. James Pirrie, who owned the house. The simple—even spartan—interior contrasts sharply with the extravagances of many of the River Road plantations and demonstrates the Puritan influence in this region. The grounds, too, recall the English penchant for a blending of order and wilderness in their gardens. You must follow a short path to reach the house from the parking lot. A state-run museum at the start of the path provides

an informative look at plantation life as it was lived in this region 200 years ago. ⊠ *11788 LA Hwy. 965 ✛ 2 miles south of St. Francisville off U.S. 61* ☎ *225/635–3739, 888/677–2838* ⊕ *www.crt.state.la.us* ⊠ *Park and plantation tour $10.*

Fodor's Choice
★

Rosedown Plantation and Gardens. The opulent, beautifully restored house at Rosedown dates from 1835. The original owners, Martha and Daniel Turnbull, spent their honeymoon in Europe; Mrs. Turnbull fell in love with the gardens she saw there and had the land at Rosedown laid out even as the house was under construction. She spent the rest of her life lovingly maintaining some 28 acres of exquisite formal gardens. The State of Louisiana owns Rosedown, and the beauty of the restored manor, including the furniture (90% of which is original), can be appreciated on a thorough hour-long tour led by park rangers. Be sure to allow ample time for roaming the grounds after the tour. ⊠ *12501 Hwy. 10, off U.S. 61* ☎ *225/635–3332, 888/376–1867* ⊕ *www.crt.state.la.us* ⊠ *$12.*

WHERE TO EAT AND STAY

$$
AMERICAN

✕ **The Magnolia.** This low-key and unassuming restaurant turns into a St. Francisville hot spot on Friday and Saturday nights. During the day, locals and tourists flock to "the Mag" for sandwiches, pizza, steaks, and Southern and Mexican dishes. **Known for:** live music on Friday nights; cocktails; Mexican flavors. ⑤ *Average main: $17* ⊠ *5689 Commerce St.* ☎ *225/635–6528* ⊕ *www.themagnoliacafe.net* ⊘ *Closed Sun. No dinner Mon.–Wed.*

$$
B&B/INN

⛨ **Barrow House Inn.** Fittingly located on St. Francisville's historic Royal Street, these two old houses hold some of the most comfortable bed-and-breakfast accommodations in the area, with antique furnishings in most of the rooms. **Pros:** good location in downtown St. Francisville; comfortable atmosphere; friendly staff. **Cons:** if you don't like antiques, you may feel as if you're in a museum or your grandmother's home. ⑤ *Rooms from: $115* ⊠ *9779 Royal St.* ☎ *225/635–4791* ⊕ *www.top-teninn.com* ⊅ *3 rooms, 4 suites* ⊚ *Breakfast.*

$$$$
B&B/INN

⛨ **The Myrtles.** If you don't mind a deep legacy of hauntings, you'll enjoy these character-filled guest rooms on the second floor of the plantation house and in a couple of outlying buildings, all filled with antiques and most with four-poster beds. **Pros:** historic property oozes atmosphere; ghost hunters' paradise. **Cons:** feels like it's in the middle of nowhere; easily spooked travelers might want to stay elsewhere. ⑤ *Rooms from: $200* ⊠ *7747 U.S. 61* ☎ *225/635–6277, 800/809–0565* ⊕ *www.myrtlesplantation.com* ▭ *No credit cards* ⊅ *14 rooms, 2 suites* ⊚ *Breakfast.*

CAJUN COUNTRY

French Louisiana, lying amid the bayous, rice fields, and canebrakes to the west of New Orleans, has become famous in the rest of the country for its food—"jambalaya and a crawfish pie and filé gumbo," as Hank Williams put it—and its rollicking Cajun and zydeco music. The Cajun culture has its roots far from these parts in the present-day Canadian provinces of Nova Scotia and New Brunswick, where French settlers colonized a region they called "l'Acadie" at the start of the 17th century.

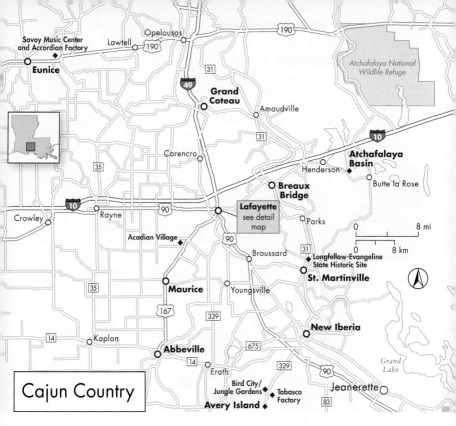

Cajun Country

After the British seized control of the region in the early 18th century, the French were expelled. Henry Wadsworth Longfellow described their exile in his epic poem "Evangeline." Many Acadians eventually settled in 22 parishes of southwestern Louisiana. Their descendants are called "Cajun," a corruption of "Acadian"; some continue the traditions of the early French settlers, living by fishing and fur trapping.

Cajun culture is decidedly rural, rooted in a smattering of tiny towns and in the swamps and bayous that wind among them. Driving from one village to the next, antiques shoppers and nature lovers alike will find a whole lot to love. Live oaks with ragged gray buntings of Spanish moss form canopies over the bottle-green bayous. Country roads follow the contortions of the Teche (pronounced *tesh*), the state's longest bayou, and meander through villages where cypress cabins rise up out of the water on stilts and moored fishing boats and canoe-like pirogues scarcely bob on the sluggish waters. At the centers of these same villages are wonderful bakeries, historic churches, fresh oyster bars, and regional antiques for sale in small, weathered shops.

Many visitors to this region are surprised to hear the dialect for the first time. Cajun French is an oral tradition in which French vocabulary and grammar encounter the American accent, and it differs significantly

Acadian
Cultural
Center **10**

Acadian Village ..**1**

Acadiana Center
for the Arts **5**

Acadiana Park
Nature Station ...**7**

Alexandre
Mouton House
and Lafayette
Museum **3**

Cathedral of St.
John the
Evangelist **2**

Lafayette
Courthouse **4**

Lafayette Science
Museum **6**

Paul and Lulu
Hilliard
University
Art Museum **9**

Vermilionville ...**8**

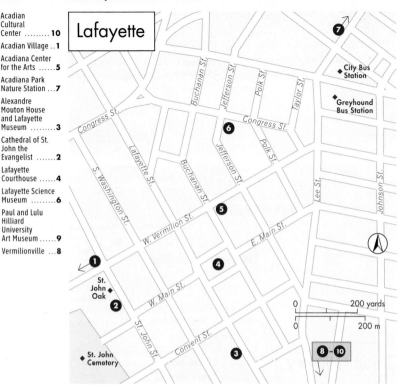

from what is spoken in France. English is also spoken throughout Cajun Country, but you will hear Gallic accents and see many signs that read "Ici on parle français" (French spoken here).

GETTING HERE AND AROUND

BUS TRAVEL

Greyhound has numerous daily departures from New Orleans to Lafayette. The trip takes three to three and a half hours.

Bus Information Greyhound. ☎ 800/231–2222 ⊕ www.greyhound.com.

CAR TRAVEL

Interstate 10 runs east–west across the state and through New Orleans. Take Interstate 10 west to the Lafayette exit, 136 miles from New Orleans. The interstate route takes about two hours and 15 minutes. Return to New Orleans via U.S. 90, down through Houma, for scenic stopovers. This route will take about three hours.

TRAIN TRAVEL

Amtrak connects New Orleans and Lafayette via the *Sunset Limited*. Trains make the three- to four-hour scenic trip each way once daily.

Train Amtrak. ☎ 800/872–7245 ⊕ www.amtrak.com.

VISITOR INFORMATION

Contacts Lafayette Convention and Visitors Commission. ☎ *337/232–3737,
800/346–1958* ⊕ *www.lafayettetravel.com.* **St. Martin Parish Tourist Commission.** ☎ *888/565–5939* ⊕ *www.cajuncountry.org.* **St. Landry Parish Tourist
Commission.** ☎ *877/948–8004, 337/948–8004* ⊕ *www.cajuntravel.com.*

LAFAYETTE

136 miles west of New Orleans.

Lafayette (pronounced lah-fay-
ette), with a population of about
130,000 (the largest city in Cajun
Country), is a major center of
Cajun life and lore. It's an interesting and enjoyable city, with some
worthwhile historical and artistic
sights. The simulated Cajun villages at **Vermilionville** and **Acadian
Village** provide evocative intro-
ductions to the traditional Cajun
way of life. Excellent restaurants
and B&Bs make Lafayette a good
jumping-off point for exploring the
region. In recent years the city has
had an infusion of new restaurants
and nightclubs—particularly downtown.

MURALS

There are several outdoor murals
by the local artist Robert Dafford
in the center of Lafayette, including a 100-foot-wide Louisiana
swamp scene titled *Till All That's
Left is a Postcard,* across from
Dwyer's Café. Another work, titled
Ex-Garage and full of splashy cars
and TVs with vignettes of Cajun
life, is on the Jefferson Tower
Building. The reflections in the
bumpers of the cars reveal area
musicians and traditions.

EXPLORING

Acadiana Center for the Arts. This multicultural arts center hosts exhibits,
musical performances, lectures, and children's programs. Film screenings are occasionally held at the in-house movie theater. ✉ *101 W.
Vermilion St.* ☎ *337/233–7060* ⊕ *www.acadianacenterforthearts.org.*

Acadian Cultural Center. A unit of the National Park Service, the center
traces the history of the area through numerous audiovisual exhibits
on food, music, and folklore. Be sure to watch the introductory film,
which is a dramatization of the Expulsion of the Acadians (1755–1764),
when the British deported the descendants of French settlers in the
maritime provinces of Canada to the 13 colonies. Clips from the 1929
silent movie *Evangeline* (a fictional account based on the Longfellow
poem about an Acadian girl's search for her lost love) are incorporated into the presentation—film buffs will love it. Ranger-guided boat
tours of Bayou Vermilion take place March through June and September through November in a traditional Cajun boat. ✉ *501 Fisher Rd.*
☎ *337/232–0789* ⊕ *www.nps.gov/jela* ☒ *Free.*

FAMILY **Acadiana Park Nature Station.** Naturalists are on hand in the interpre-
tive center at this three-story cypress structure, which overlooks a
150 acres of nature trails and natural forest. The northern section
includes a managed butterfly habitat. The focus here is on environmental education. Free guided tours are offered on weekends by
request. Make reservations for a guided evening hike on the last

Saturday of the month ($2.14 per person). ⊠ *1205 E. Alexander St.* ☎ *337/291–8448* ⊕ *www.naturestation.org* ☙ *Free.*

Alexandre Mouton House and Lafayette Museum. Built in 1800 as the *maison dimanche,* or "Sunday house" (a town house used when attending church services) of town founder Jean Mouton, this galleried town house with a mid-19th-century addition now preserves local history. It was later home to Alexandre Mouton (1804–1885), the first Democratic governor of Lousiana. The older section is an excellent example of early Acadian architecture and contains artifacts used by settlers. The main museum features Civil War–era furnishings and memorabilia and an exhibit on Mardi Gras. ⊠ *1122 Lafayette St.* ☎ *337/234–2208* ⊕ *www.lafayettemuseum.com* ☙ *$5.*

Cathedral of St. John the Evangelist. This Dutch Romanesque structure with Byzantine touches was completed in 1916 (construction began in 1912). In the cemetery behind the church are aboveground tombs that date back to 1820; interred here are town founder Jean Mouton, Civil War hero General Alfred Mouton, General Alfred Gardiner, and Cidalese Arceneaux. Next to the cathedral is a nearly 500-year-old St. John Oak, one of the charter members of the silent but leafy Louisiana Live Oak Society. ⊠ *515 Cathedral St.* ☎ *337/232–1322* ⊕ *www. saintjohncathedral.org.*

Lafayette Courthouse. The courthouse contains an impressive collection of more than 2,000 historical photographs of life in the Lafayette area. There are images of famous politicians such as Dudley LeBlanc and Huey Long working the stump, and scenes from the Great Mississippi Flood of 1927. ⊠ *800 S. Buchanan St.* ☎ *337/233–0150.*

FAMILY **Lafayette Science Museum.** This sparkling natural-history museum includes changing exhibitions and lots of fun hands-on science for kids. The most popular permanent attraction is the planetarium, outfitted with high-definition digital equipment. ⊠ *433 Jefferson St.* ☎ *337/291–5544* ⊕ *www.lafayettesciencemuseum.org* ☙ *$5.35.*

OFF THE BEATEN PATH **Acadian Village.** Most of the structures at this re-creation of an early-19th-century bayou settlement were moved here to construct a representative "village." They actually represent a broad range of Acadian architectural styles, and the rustic general store, smithy, and chapel are replicas. The park is on 10 wooded acres, with a meandering bayou crisscrossed by wooden footbridges. Each house is decorated with antique furnishings. The weeks before Christmas bring "Noel Acadien au Village," with evening-only hours, musicians, food, and buildings covered in festive lights. ⊠ *200 Greenleaf Dr., south of downtown* ☎ *337/981–2364, 800/962–9133* ⊕ *www.acadianvillage.org* ☙ *$8.*

Paul and Lulu Hilliard University Art Museum. Inside a gleaming glass box built in 2003, this museum on the campus of the University of Louisiana at Lafayette features world-class works, including 150 paintings and collages by Henry Botkin and a Louisiana collection including artists Elemore Morgan Jr., George Rodrigue, and Hunt Slonem. ⊠ *710 E. St. Mary Blvd.* ☎ *337/482–2278* ⊕ *hilliardmuseum.org* ☙ *$5.*

FAMILY **Vermilionville.** Directly behind the Acadian Cultural Center, this living-history village re-creates the early life of the region's Creoles, Cajuns, and Native Americans, focusing on the late 1700s to 1890. On select days, visitors can see a blacksmith demonstration or watch weavers at work. There are exhibits in 19 Acadian-style structures, including a music hall where live Cajun or zydeco music is played on weekend afternoons. A large, rustic restaurant serves Cajun classics. Check ahead for live demonstrations from the on-site cooking school. ⊠ *300 Fisher Rd., off Surrey St.* ☏ *337/233–4077, 866/992–2968* ⊕ *www.vermilionville.org* ⌂ *$10.*

WHERE TO EAT

$$$ ✕ **Café Vermilionville.** This 19th-century inn with crisp white linens and
CAJUN   old brick fireplaces serves French and Cajun dishes to a well-dressed crowd. Among the specialties are Gulf fish Acadian and grilled duck breast. **Known for:** special-occasion dinners; old-fashioned service; fine dining. ⑤ *Average main: $30* ⊠ *1304 W. Pinhook Rd.* ☏ *337/237–0100* ⊕ *www.cafev.com* ⊗ *Closed Sun.*

$$ ✕ **Crawfish Time.** From roughly December through June, when Louisiana
SOUTHERN   crawfish are in season, local families pack in to partake in the outrageous abundance. Order from the menu—including crawfish, oysters, and a few sides like sausage links and boiled potatoes, plus cold beer—in the simple, stripped-down dining room filled with big tables. **Known for:** crawfish; seafood picnics; drive-through window. ⑤ *Average main: $20* ⊠ *2019 Verot School Rd.* ☏ *337/988–2645* ⊕ *www.lacrawfishtime. com* ▭ *No credit cards* ⊗ *Closed June–Nov. No lunch weekends.*

$ ✕ **Johnson's Boucaniere.** This *boucaniere* (Cajun French for smokehouse)
SOUTHERN   is run by the next generation of the family that operated the iconic Johnson's Grocery in Eunice, Louisiana, which closed in 2005. It's a laid-back, friendly place with a refreshing blend of tradition and modern style. **Known for:** boudin sausages; Cajun-style barbecue; local vibe. ⑤ *Average main: $10* ⊠ *1111 St. John St.* ☏ *337/269–8878* ⊕ *www. johnsonsboucaniere.com* ⊗ *Closed Sun. and Mon.*

$$ ✕ **Prejean's.** In this cypress house decorated with swamp trees and a
CAJUN   large stuffed alligator at the entrance, people gather over red-and-white-
Fodor's Choice   check tablecloths to chow down on some local classics: crawfish and
★   alligator sausage cheesecake, Cajun duckling, or any of the kitchen's four distinctive gumbos. Grilled seafood provides some lighter options. **Known for:** crawfish étouffée; boudin sausage; live music. ⑤ *Average main: $21* ⊠ *3480 N.E. Evangeline Throughway* ☏ *337/896–3247* ⊕ *www.prejeans.com.*

$ ✕ **T-Coon's Café.** This often-busy diner serves a hearty Cajun breakfast
CAJUN   and lunch, which feature daily specials such as smothered rabbit, catfish court boulion, or crawfish omelets. The Southern fare also includes fried chicken and seafood dishes. **Known for:** Cajun flavors; comfort food; fried chicken. ⑤ *Average main: $10* ⊠ *1900 W. Pinhook Rd.* ☏ *337/233–0422* ⊕ *www.tcoons.com* ⊗ *No dinner.*

WHERE TO STAY

$$$$ ▥ **Buchanan Lofts.** These five rooms inside a refurbished building that once
B&B/INN   was the first department store in Lafayette are like seriously stylish apartments—each has a different layout, but they're all quite spacious, with floor-to-ceiling windows, lots of exposed brick, and streamlined, minimalist

furnishings. **Pros:** close to everything downtown; huge rooms filled with stylish furnishings. **Cons:** not much local character. $ *Rooms from: $180* ✉ *403 S. Buchanan St.* ☎ *337/534–4922* ⊕ *www.buchananlofts.com* ⌨ *5 rooms* ⊗ *No meals.*

$$ ⌂ **Doubletree by Hilton Lafayette.** In
HOTEL this large high-rise quite close to Interstate 10, near the business district, traditional furnishings outfit the standard rooms, and the riverside rooms overlook the Bayou Vermilion. **Pros:** typical Hilton amenities; location is convenient for sightseeing; comfy beds. **Cons:** reservations are hard to come by if there's a wedding or event; halls can be loud when the hotel is full. $ *Rooms from: $109* ✉ *1521 W. Pinhook Rd.* ☎ *337/235–6111, 800/445–8667* ⊕ *www.hilton.com* ⌨ *327 rooms* ⊗ *No meals.*

CREOLE VS. CAJUN

Cajun cuisine relies on locally available ingredients, including pork, seafood, smoked meats, yams, and rice. Creole cuisine is more cosmopolitan, incorporating French, Spanish, Italian, African, and French Caribbean influences. Most Cajun and Creole dishes include the "holy trinity" of sautéed celery, bell pepper, and garlic or onion as a base, but Creole dishes, like their French counterparts, are defined by their sauces. Examples include shrimp Creole, crawfish bisque, and oysters Rockefeller.

$$$ ⌂ **Mouton Plantation.** In the 19th-century Mouton Plantation, this quiet
B&B/INN hotel features 11 rooms with early Acadian antiques. **Pros:** pretty grounds; glass of wine and house tour included in rates. **Cons:** rooms can be a little stuffy. $ *Rooms from: $140* ✉ *338 N. Sterling St.* ☎ *337/233–7816* ⊕ *www.moutonplantation.com* ⌨ *11 rooms* ⊗ *Breakfast.*

$$$ ⌂ **T'Frere's House.** Built circa 1890 of native cypress and handmade bricks,
B&B/INN some rooms in the Acadian-style "Little Brother's House" are furnished with French and Louisiana antiques while others are more modern. **Pros:** charming decor; owners like to feed their guests well. **Cons:** it feels a bit far from everything; not a good option if you're on a diet. $ *Rooms from: $129* ✉ *1905 Verot School Rd.* ☎ *337/984–9347, 800/984–9347* ⊕ *www.tfrereshouse.com* ⌨ *8 rooms, 1 suite* ⊗ *Breakfast.*

NIGHTLIFE AND PERFORMING ARTS

Pick up a copy of the *Times of Acadiana* to find listings for *fais-do-dos*, zydeco dances, and other events. The free weekly is available online and in hotels, restaurants, and shops.

Blue Moon Saloon. This cottage doesn't look like much from the street, but after you pay your cover at the garden gate, you'll soon find yourself on a large covered deck packed with a young crowd dancing to the hottest local Cajun, zydeco, and roots music acts. The owner also rents out a whole two-bedroom house, which easily sleeps six and includes a full kitchen and a library/study; it costs $600 a night. ✉ *215 E. Convent St.* ☎ *337/234–2422* ⊕ *www.bluemoonpresents.com.*

El Sid O's. This family-run zydeco club hosts music on Friday and Saturday nights. Sid Williams manages the club, and his brother's band, Nathan and the Zydeco Cha-Chas, perform frequently—as does

Nathan's son's band, Lil Nathan and the Zydeco Big Timers. ⊠ *1523 N. St. Antoine St.* ☎ *337/235–0647.*

Randol's. This good Cajun restaurant is also a "salle de danse," with music and dancing nightly. ⊠ *2320 Kaliste Saloom Rd.* ☎ *337/981–7080, 800/962–2586* ⊕ *www.randols.com.*

FESTIVALS

ArtWalks. Downtown galleries are open and the streets are hopping during this popular event, held on the second Saturday of each month. ⊠ *Lafayette* ☎ *337/291–5566* ⊕ *www.downtownlafayette.org.*

Downtown Alive! For the last 30 years, on Friday evenings from mid-March through June and from September through November, dancing crowds converge on downtown Lafayette, where bands play an open-air stage. ⊠ *Jefferson St. at Main St.* ☎ *337/291–5566* ⊕ *www. downtownlafayette.org.*

Festival Acadiens et Creoles. This huge music-and-food fest is held mid-October in Girard Park. The admission's free, the food's outstanding— but the music is the best thing about it all. ⊠ *Lafayette* ☎ *337/232–3737, 800/346–1958* ⊕ *www.festivalsacadiens.com.*

Festival International de Louisiane. Taking place on the last weekend of April, this free music festival may rival the New Orleans Jazz and Heritage Festival; it fills the streets with entertainers, artisans, and chefs from French-speaking nations and communities. ⊠ *Lafayette* ☎ *337/232–8086* ⊕ *festivalinternational.org.*

Mardi Gras. The biggest bash in this neck of the woods is in February or March (depending on when Lent occurs). About a dozen parades take to the streets over a couple of weeks, culminating on "Fat Tuesday," and a festive atmosphere fills the city. ⊠ *Lafayette* ⊕ *www.lafayettetravel.com.*

SHOPPING

ANTIQUES

Sans Souci Fine Crafts Gallery. If you are looking for authentic Louisiana crafts, you've come to the right place. Pottery, furniture, items made out of gourds, metal and wood, and corn-husk dolls and jewelry are all created by members of the Louisiana Crafts Guild, headquartered here. ⊠ *219 E. Vermilion St.* ☎ *337/266–7999* ⊕ *www.louisiana-crafts.org* ☉ *Closed Mon.*

FOOD

Don's Specialty Meats & Grocery. Fill your cooler with boudin, cracklins, stuffed pork chops, quail, and a variety of sausages. There's another location at 104 Highway 726 in Carencro, also just outside Lafayette. ⊠ *730 I-10 S. Frontage Rd., Scott* ☎ *337/234–2528, 337/896–6370 Carencro* ⊕ *www.donsspecialtymeats.com.*

Poupart's Bakery. The fresh French bread and pastries made here are outstanding. The shop also sells specialty sauces and preserves, as well as king cakes, available during the Carnival season. ⊠ *1902 W. Pinhook Rd.* ☎ *337/232–7921* ⊕ *www.poupartsbakery.com* ☉ *Closed Mon.*

EUNICE

20 miles southwest of Opelousas.

As home to some of Cajun music's most prominent proponents and establishments, tiny Eunice lays claim to some heft within the Cajun music world. Saturday is the best time to visit: spend the morning at a jam at the Savoy Music Center; at midday move on for dancing at Fred's Lounge; end the day at the Rendez-Vous des Cajuns variety show, in Eunice's Liberty Theatre.

EXPLORING

Eunice Depot Museum. This museum, in a former railroad depot, contains modest exhibits on Cajun culture, including music and Mardi Gras celebrations. ⌧ *220 S. C. C. Duson Dr.* ☎ *337/457–6540, 337/457–2565* ▧ *Free.*

Prairie Acadian Cultural Center. Part of the Jean Lafitte National Historical Park, this impressive center has well-executed exhibits tracing the history and culture of the Prairie Acadians, whose lore and customs differ from those of the Bayou Acadians south of Lafayette. Food, crafts, and music demonstrations are held on Saturday. ⌧ *250 W. Park Ave.* ☎ *337/457–8499* ⊕ *www.nps.gov/jela/prairie-acadian-cultural-center-eunice.htm* ▧ *Free.*

Fodor'sChoice ★   **Savoy Music Center and Accordion Factory.** Part music store, part Cajun accordion workshop, proprietor Marc Savoy's factory turns out about five specialty accordions a month for people around the world. On Saturday morning, accordion players and other instrumentalists head here for jam sessions, and musicians from all over the area drop in. ⌧ *Hwy. 190 ⊹ 3 miles east of town* ☎ *337/457–9563* ⊕ *www.savoy-musiccenter.com* ▧ *Free.*

NIGHTLIFE AND PERFORMING ARTS

Fred's Lounge. This place is hopping on Saturday from about 9 am until about 2 pm—or for as long as the Cajun band jams and dancers crowd the tiny dance floor. A regular radio broadcast (on KVPI 1050 AM) captures the event. Drive north from Eunice on Route 13 to reach the tiny town of Mamou. ⌧ *420 6th St., Mamou* ☎ *337/468–5411* ▧ *Free.*

Rendez-Vous des Cajuns. In addition to showcasing the best Cajun and zydeco bands, this two-hour variety program presents local comedians and storytellers and even a "Living Recipe Corner." The show, mostly in French, has been dubbed the "Cajun Grand Ole Opry"; it's held every Saturday at 6 pm in a 1924 movie house and is broadcast on local radio and TV. ⌧ *Liberty Center for the Performing Arts, 200 W. Park Ave., at 2nd St.* ☎ *337/457–7389* ▧ *$5.*

Southwest Louisiana Zydeco Music Festival. The town of Plaisance, on the outskirts of Opelousas, holds this event in a bean field on the Saturday before Labor Day. A parade, accordion contest, and zydeco breakfast are all part of the festivities. ⌧ *Opelousas* ☎ *337/290–6048* ⊕ *www.zydeco.org.*

12

EVENTS

Courir de Mardi Gras. The area surrounding Eunice is the major stomping ground for an annual event, Courir de Mardi Gras, French for "Fat Tuesday Run," which takes place on Mardi Gras Day. Costumed horseback riders dash through the countryside, stopping at farmhouses along the way to shout, *"Voulez-vous recevoir cette bande de Mardi Gras?"* ("Do you wish to receive the Mardi Gras krewe?") The answer is always yes, and the group enlarges and continues, gathering food for the street festivals that wind things up. ⊠ *Eunice.*

BREAUX BRIDGE

10 miles northeast of Lafayette, 20 miles southeast of Grand Coteau.

During the first full weekend in May the Crawfish Festival draws more than 100,000 visitors to this little dyed-in-the-wool Cajun town on Bayou Teche. The town has attracted a small arts community and has traded its honky-tonks for B&Bs, antiques shops, and restaurants.

Chamber of Commerce. You can pick up a city map and information at the Chamber of Commerce, at the foot of the bridge that gives Breaux Bridge its name, about ½ mile south of Interstate 10. ⊠ *314 E. Bridge St.* ☎ *337/332–5406* ⊕ *www.breauxbridgeacc.com.*

WHERE TO EAT AND STAY

$ ✕ **Poche's.** Order your authentic Cajun cooking at the counter of this
CAJUN   butcher shop and lunchroom, then eat in or take away. The daily specials will always stick to your ribs. **Known for:** cracklings; lunch counter; stuffed chicken. ⑤ *Average main: $8* ⊠ *3015 Main Hwy., 2 miles from center of Breaux Bridge* ☎ *337/332–2108* ⊕ *www.poches.com.*

$$ ⌂ **Bayou Cabins.** These cozy one- and two-bedroom cabins are right on
B&B/INN   a main drag, but with their homey decor and shade from the property's many trees—and with some featuring porches facing Bayou Teche—they feel rustic and have personality galore. **Pros:** socializing with guests and locals in the café. **Cons:** you can hear the busy road nearby. ⑤ *Rooms from: $100* ⊠ *100 W. Mills Ave.* ☎ *337/332–6158* ⊕ *www.bayoucabins. com* ☉ *Café closed Mon. and Tues.* ➟ *14 rooms* ⦿| *Breakfast.*

$$$ ⌂ **Maison des Amis.** In this 19th-century house on the bank of Bayou
B&B/INN   Teche, rooms have either queen- or full-size beds covered with luxuri-
Fodor's Choice   ous linens and pillows and private bathrooms with claw-foot tubs.
★   **Pros:** bayou views; steps from downtown Breaux Bridge. **Cons:** breakfast is provided at a nearby restaurant, where you may have to wait. ⑤ *Rooms from: $125* ⊠ *111 Washington St.* ☎ *337/507–3399* ⊕ *www. maisondesamis.com* ➟ *4 rooms* ⦿| *Breakfast.*

NIGHTLIFE

La Poussière. This ancient Cajun honky-tonk has live music on Saturday nights and Sunday afternoons. ⊠ *1301 Grand Point Ave.* ☎ *337/332– 1721* ⊕ *www.lapoussiere.com.*

Alligators Up Close: Swamp Tours

The bayous, swamps, and rivers of south Louisiana's wetlands present a tantalizingly unfamiliar landscape to many visitors, and the best way to get acquainted is by boat. Tour operators offer convenient departure times and hotel pickups in New Orleans. Most use airboats or pontoon boats, but—depending on the size of the group—a bass boat might be used. Anticipate one to two hours on the water and 45 minutes to two hours' commute time to and from New Orleans. Prices are generally around $20 per person. Expect to see nutrias, members of the rodent family that resemble beavers in appearance and size; egrets, white, long-necked herons with flowing feathers; turtles; and the occasional snake. During the warmer months, alligator sightings are common. Many of the guides use either chicken or marshmallows to attract them. Plant life includes Spanish moss, cypresses, water oaks, and water hyacinths (members of the lily family). In the summer months be prepared for the heat and humidity—and don't forget insect repellent and a hat.

Cajun Country Swamp Tours. These tours are led by guide Walter "Butch" Guchereau, who was born, raised, and still lives on the banks of Bayou Teche in Breaux Bridge. An experienced outdoorsman with a degree in zoology and biology, Guchereau uses Cajun crawfish skiffs for his tours to make them environmentally unobtrusive. His son Shawn also leads tours. ✉ *1209 Rookery Rd., Breaux Bridge* ☎ *337/319–0010* ⊕ *www.cajuncountryswamptours.com* 🖃 *$20.*

McGee's Swamp Tours. Boats take passengers out daily for 1½-hour tours of the Atchafalaya Basin. Tour times are contingent upon the presence of at least four passengers. McGee's is a 25-minute drive east of Lafayette. The company also organizes canoe and airboat trips, sunset tours, and photography excursions. ✉ *1337 Henderson Levee Rd., Henderson* ⌖ *From I–10, Exit 115 at Henderson, turn left on Rte. 352 (1 block south of the highway) and follow it more than 2 miles east over Bayou Amy; turn right atop the levee onto Levee Rd.* ☎ *337/228–2384* ⊕ *www.mcgeesswamptours.com* 🖃 *Tours $20–$50.*

ATCHAFALAYA BASIN

5 miles northeast of Breaux Bridge, 12 miles east of Lafayette.

The Atchafalaya Basin is an eerily beautiful 800,000-plus-acre swamp wilderness, the storybook version of mystical south Louisiana wetlands. Boating enthusiasts, bird-watchers, photographers, and nature lovers are drawn by vast expanses of still water, cypresses rising out of the marsh and dripping with Spanish moss, and blue herons taking flight. The basin is best viewed from one of the tour boats on its waters, but it's possible to explore around its edges on the 7 miles of Henderson's Levee Road (aka Route 5; Exit 115 off Interstate 10), which provides several opportunities to cross the levee and access swamp tours, bars, and restaurants on the other side.

CLOSE UP

Cajun and Zydeco Music

It's 9 am on a typical Saturday morning in the Cajun prairie town of Mamou, and Fred's Lounge (⇨ *Nightlife and Performing Arts in Eunice*) is already so full that people are spilling out the door. Inside, Cajun singer Donald Thibodeaux gets a nod from the radio announcer, squeezes his accordion, and launches into the "Pine Grove Blues." Oblivious to the posted warning that reads "This is not a dance hall," the packed bar begins to roll. Fred's Lounge may not be a "formal" dance hall, but plenty of dancing is done here; it gets especially lively during Mamou's Mardi Gras and July 4 celebrations. And every Saturday morning for more than 40 years, live Cajun radio shows have been broadcast from the late Fred Tate's lounge. Things get revved up at 8 am and keep going till 1 pm, and the show is aired on Ville Platte's KVPI radio (1050 AM).

Music has been an integral expression of Cajun culture since early Acadian immigrants unpacked stringed instruments and gathered in homes for singing and socializing. *"Fais-do-do"* (pronounced *fay*-doh-doh) is what mothers would murmur to put their babies to sleep as the fiddlers tuned up before one of these house parties. With the growth of towns, most of the fais-do-dos were supplanted by dance halls, but the name stuck. Accordions, steel guitars, and drums were added

and amplified to be heard over the noise of crowded barrooms.

Cajun music went through some lean years in the 1940s and '50s, when the state attempted to eradicate the use of the Cajun-French language, but today Cajun music is enjoyed at street festivals and restaurants such as Randol's and Prejean's, which serve equal portions of seafood and song. These places not only keep the music and dance tradition alive, but also serve as magnets for Cajun dance enthusiasts from around the world.

Zydeco, the dance music of rural African Americans of south Louisiana, is closely related to Cajun music, but with a slightly harder, rock-influenced edge. The best place to find the music is in one of the roadside dance halls on weekends. Modern zydeco and Cajun music both feature the accordion, but zydeco tends to be faster and uses heavy percussion and electric instruments; electric guitars and washboards (called a *frottoir*), largely absent from Cajun music, are staples. Zydeco bands often play soul- and R&B-inflected tunes sung in Creole French.

Dance is the universal language of Cajun Country, but don't worry if you're not fluent—there's always someone happy to lead you around the floor and leave you feeling like a local.

ST. MARTINVILLE

15 miles south of Breaux Bridge.

St. Martinville, along winding Bayou Teche, is the heart of Evangeline country. It was founded in 1761 and became a refuge for Acadians expelled from Nova Scotia as well as royalists who escaped the guillotine during the French Revolution. Known as Petit Paris, this little town was once the scene of lavish balls and operas, and you can still see the original old opera house on the central square. St. Martinville is tucked away from the state's major highways and misses much of the tourist traffic. It's a tranquil and historically interesting stop, although neighboring towns are better for dining and nightlife. The St. Martinville Tourist Information Center is across the street from the Acadian Memorial and African American Museum.

EXPLORING

Acadian Memorial. A video introduction, a wall of names of Acadian Louisiana refugees, and a huge mural relate the odyssey of the Acadians. Behind the small heritage center containing these memorials, an eternal flame and the coats of arms of Acadian families pay tribute to their cultural and physical stamina. ⊠ *121 S. New Market St.* ☎ *337/394–2258* ⊕ *www.acadianmemorial.org* ✉ *$3, includes admission to African American Musuem* ☉ *Closed Sun. and Mon.*

African American Museum. This museum traces the African and African American experience in southern Louisiana. Videos, artifacts, and text panels combine to create a vivid, disturbing, and inspiring portrait of a people. It is an ambitious and refreshing counterpoint to the sometimes sidelined references to slavery and its legacy. ⊠ *125 New Market St.* ☎ *337/394–2233* ✉ *$3, includes admission to Acadian Memorial* ☉ *Closed Sun. and Mon.*

Longfellow-Evangeline State Historic Site. Shaded by giant live oaks draped with Spanish moss, this 157-acre park has picnic tables and pavilions and early Acadian structures. The on-site museum traces the history of the Acadians and their settlement along the Bayou Teche in the early 1800s. The modest house was built in 1815 of handmade bricks, and it contains Louisiana antiques. An hour-long tour includes many interesting details about life on the plantation. ⊠ *1200 N. Main St. (Rte. 31)* ✛ *½ mile north of St. Martinville* ☎ *337/394–3754, 888/677–2900* ⊕ *www.crt.state.la.us/louisiana-state-parks/historic-sites/longfellow-evangeline-state-historic-site* ✉ *$4.*

St. Martin de Tours. The mother church of the Acadians and one of the country's oldest Catholic churches, this 1836 building was erected on the site of an earlier church. Inside is a replica of the Lourdes grotto and a baptismal font said to have been a gift from Louis XVI. Emmeline Labiche, who may have inspired Henry Wadsworth Longellow's poem "Evangeline," is buried in the small cemetery behind the church. ⊠ *133 S. Main St.* ☎ *337/394–6021* ⊕ *www.saintmartindetours.org.*

WHERE TO STAY

$$$

B&B/INN

🛏 **Old Castillo Bed and Breakfast.** Comfortable rooms with hardwood floors and the odd early Louisiana antique occupy a two-story red-brick building that in the early 1800s was an inn for steamboat passengers and a gathering place for French royalists. **Pros:** right by a number of attractions; friendly staff; delicious breakfast. **Cons:** downstairs rooms are a bit noisy; decor is a little dated. ⑤ *Rooms from: $125* ⊠ *220 Evangeline Blvd.* ☎ *337/394–4010* ⊕ *www.oldcastillo.com* ⇆ *7 rooms* ⏐◎⏐ *Breakfast.*

NEW IBERIA

10 miles south of St. Martinville.

The hub of lower Cajun Country is second only to Lafayette as an arts-and-culture draw. Grand homes of sugarcane planters dominate the residential section of Main Street, just off Bayou Teche, pointing to a glorious past as the center of a booming sugar industry. Park downtown or stay in one of the numerous B&Bs and you can easily walk to the bayou, restaurants, art galleries, and shops in the historic business district. Downtown stretches eight blocks east and west on Main Street (Route 182) from the intersection of Center Street (Route 14). The Shadows-on-the-Teche plantation home is at this intersection and is a good place to park.

EXPLORING

Bayou Teche Museum. The story of New Iberia's Spanish colonial roots and the role of Bayou Teche in helping nurture Cajun culture are on display in this small, well-organized museum, housed in a historic building that was once a grocery. Interactive exhibits cover the area's history, its colorful characters, and its culture. The museum's interior layout is based on the snakelike curves of Bayou Teche itself. ⊠ *131 Main St.* ☎ *337/606–5977* ⊕ *www.bayoutechemuseum.org* ⊠ *$5.*

Conrad Rice Mill. The country's oldest rice mill that's still in operation, dating from 1912, produces distinctive wild pecan rice. Tours are conducted on the hour between 10 am and 3 pm. The adjacent **Konriko Company Store** sells Cajun crafts and foods. ⊠ *307–309 Ann St.* ☎ *337/364–7242, 800/551–3245* ⊕ *www.conradricemill.com* ⊠ *Mill $4.*

Shadows-on-the-Teche. One of the South's best-known plantation homes was built on the bank of the bayou for the wealthy sugar planter David Weeks in 1834. In 1917 his descendant William Weeks Hall conducted one of the first historically conscious restorations of a plantation home, also preserving truckloads of documents that helped explain day-to-day life here. The result is one of the most fascinating tours in Louisiana. Weeks Hall willed the property to the National Trust for Historic Preservation in 1958, and each year the trust selects a different historical topic to emphasize. Surrounded by 2.5 acres of lush gardens and moss-draped oaks, the two-story rose-hue house has white columns, exterior staircases sheltered in cabinetlike enclosures, and a pitched roof pierced by dormer windows. The furnishings are 85% original to the house. ⊠ *317 E. Main St.* ☎ *337/369–6446, 877/200–4920* ⊕ *www.shadowsontheteche.org* ⊠ *$10.50 house and gardens; $8.50 gardens only.*

AVERY ISLAND

9 miles southwest of New Iberia.

The Louisiana coastline is dotted with "hills" or "domes" that sit atop salt mines, and Avery Island is one of these. They are covered with lush vegetation, and because they rise above the surface of the flatlands, they are referred to as islands.

Avery Island is the birthplace of Tabasco sauce, which pleases the Cajun palate and flavors many a Bloody Mary.

EXPLORING

Bird City. The bird sanctuary on the southeast edge of Jungle Gardens is sometimes so thick with egrets that it appears to be blanketed with snow. The largest egret colony in the world (20,000) begins nesting here in February or March, and offspring remain until the following winter. Herons and other birds find refuge here as well. ⊠ *Hwy. 329.*

FAMILY **Jungle Gardens.** This 170-acre garden has trails through stands of wisteria, palms, lilies, irises and ferns, and offers a lovely perspective on southern Louisiana wilderness. Birdlife includes white egrets and Louisiana herons, and there's also a 900-year-old statue of Buddha. These gardens belonged to Edward Avery McIlhenny, the son of the Tabasco company's founder, who brought back plants from his travels: lotus and papyrus from Egypt, bamboo from China. You can park your car at the beginning of the trails and strike out on foot, or drive through the gardens and stop at will. ⊠ *Hwy. 329* ☏ *337/369–6243* ⊕ *www.junglegardens.org* 🏷 *$8, $12.50 with Tabasco Visitors Center.*

Tabasco Factory. Tabasco was invented by Edmund McIlhenny in the mid-1800s, and the factory is still presided over by the McIlhenny family. Tabasco is sold all over the world, but it is aged, distilled, and bottled only here, on Avery Island (these days the peppers themselves are mostly grown in Central and South America). You can take a self-guided factory tour that lasts about an hour and a half and highlights the production process along with conservation efforts on the island. The Jungle Gardens and Bird City are adjacent. ⊠ *Hwy. 329* ☏ *337/373–6129, 800/634–9599* ⊕ *www.tabasco.com* 🏷 *$5.50, $12.50 with Jungle Gardens.*

ABBEVILLE

15 miles south of Lafayette.

Abbeville has a number of historic buildings and three pretty village squares anchoring the center of downtown. It's a good stop for pleasant walks and for oysters on the half shell, a local obsession. The town sponsors the annual Giant Omelet Festival each November, and some 5,000 eggs go into the concoction. Abbeville is also the base for Steen's Cane Syrup.

Vermilion Parish Tourist Commission. You can pick up information about the town of Abbeville and the entire parish at the Vermillion Parish Tourist Commission. Many buildings in Abbeville's 20-block Main Street district are on the National Register of Historic Places. ⊠ *1905 Veterans Memorial Dr.* ☏ *337/898–6600* ⊕ *www.mostcajun.com.*

EXPLORING

St. Mary Magdalen Catholic Church. This fine Romanesque Revival building built in 1920 has stunning stained-glass windows. ⊠ *300 Père Megret St.* ☏ *337/893–0244* ⊕ *www.stmarymagdalenparish.org.*

WHERE TO EAT

$$ ✕ **Dupuy's Oyster Shop.** This small and simply furnished restaurant has SEAFOOD been serving oysters in the same location since 1869. Seafood platters feature seasonal catches. **Known for:** fresh Gulf oysters; po'boys;

seafood platters. ⑤ *Average main: $18* ⊠ *108 S. Main St.* ☎ *337/893–2336* ⊕ *www.dupuysoystershop.com* ⊟ *No credit cards* ⊙ *Closed Sun. and Mon. No lunch Sat.*

$ ✕ **Richard's Seafood Patio.** Cross the Vermilion River on a vintage draw-
CAJUN   bridge and continue down a winding country road to find this classic Cajun "seafood patio," a no-frills dining room serving immense
quantities of boiled crawfish, shrimp, and crabs. There's a full menu
of fried and grilled items—and cold beer. **Known for:** low-key setting;
fresh shellfish; long waits. ⑤ *Average main: $15* ⊠ *1516 S. Henry St.*
☎ *337/893–1693* ⊟ *No credit cards* ⊙ *Closed Sun.*

MAURICE

10 miles north of Abbeville, almost 11 miles south of Lafayette.

Maurice is considered the gateway to Vermilion Parish, and lies between
Lafayette and Abbeville. Many overlook this small town, but it's worth
the stop for Hebert's Specialty Meats' world-famous turducken and the
Maurice Flea Market.

WHERE TO EAT

$ ✕ **Hebert's Specialty Meats.** A visit to Cajun country is not complete with-
CAJUN   out a stop at Hebert's. This butcher shop is one of several contenders
claiming credit for inventing turducken—a turkey stuffed with a duck
that's been stuffed with a chicken. **Known for:** turducken; andouille
sausage; boudin. ⑤ *Average main: $14* ⊠ *8212 Maurice Ave. (Rte. 167)*
☎ *337/893–5062* ⊕ *www.hebertsmaurice.com.*

SHOPPING

Maurice Flea Market. From fine antiques to slightly rusted kitchen utensils, this is a treasure-hunter's paradise. Be prepared to spend more than
an hour at this store. ⊠ *9004 Maurice Ave. (Rte. 167)* ☎ *337/898–2282*
⊙ *Closed Sun.–Tues.*

TRAVEL SMART
NEW ORLEANS

GETTING HERE AND AROUND

New Orleans fills an 8-mile stretch between the Mississippi River and Lake Pontchartrain. Downtown includes the French Quarter, the Central Business District (CBD), the Warehouse District, Tremé, and the Faubourg Marigny. Uptown includes the Garden District, Audubon Park, and Tulane and Loyola universities, as well as the Carrollton and Riverbend neighborhoods.

It's best to know your location relative to the following thoroughfares: Canal Street (runs from the river toward the lake), St. Charles Avenue (runs uptown from Canal), Interstate 10 (runs west to the airport, east to Slidell), and LA Highway 90 (takes you across the river to the West Bank). Coming from the airport, to get to the CBD, exit Interstate 10 at Poydras Street near the Louisiana Superdome. For the French Quarter, look for the Vieux Carré exit. If approaching from the east on Interstate 10, take the Canal Street exit for the CBD or the Orleans Avenue exit for the French Quarter.

Canal Street divides the city roughly into the Uptown and downtown sections (though the CBD and Warehouse District, considered part of downtown, actually lie just upriver from Canal). Keeping a visual on the Superdome is the surest way to know where the CBD is; the French Quarter lies just to the southeast of it over Canal Street.

Streets that start in the French Quarter and cross over Canal Street change names as they go upriver. For example, Decatur Street becomes Magazine Street and Royal Street becomes St. Charles Avenue. Addresses begin at 100 on either side of Canal Street, and begin at 400 in the French Quarter at the river.

▌ AIR TRAVEL

Flying time is 3 hours from New York, 2 hours 30 minutes from Chicago, 1 hour 40 minutes from Dallas, and 4 hours from Los Angeles. Book early for popular times such as Mardi Gras and Jazz Fest.

Airline Security Issues Transportation Security Administration. ⊕ *www.tsa.gov.*

AIRPORTS
The major gateway to New Orleans is Louis Armstrong New Orleans International Airport (MSY), 15 miles west of the city in Kenner. There's an airport exit off Interstate 10. Plan for about 30–45 minutes travel time from downtown New Orleans to the airport (longer at rush hour). An alternative route is Airline Drive, which will take you directly to the airport from Tulane Avenue or the Earhart Expressway. Be prepared for stoplights and possible congestion.

Airport Information Louis Armstrong New Orleans International Airport (*MSY*). ☎ 504/303–7500 ⊕ *www.flymsy.com.*

GROUND TRANSPORTATION
SHUTTLE BUSES
Shuttle-bus service to and from the airport and downtown hotels is available through Airport Shuttle New Orleans, the official ground transportation of Louis Armstrong International Airport. You can purchase tickets at the Airport Shuttle ticket booths throughout the first-level Baggage Claim area. To return to the airport, call 24 hours ahead of your scheduled departure. The cost one-way to the CBD is $24 per person, and the trip takes about 40 minutes.

The Regional Transit Authority of New Orleans and Jefferson Transit (JeT) of Jefferson Parish offer buses to and from the airport daily. The RTA's Airport Express offers nine daily departures to downtown. The last leaves at 7 pm from the Departures Level. The trip down Airline Drive to Elk Place and Canal Street, just outside the French Quarter, takes about 45 minutes. Heading to the airport, the last bus leaves downtown at 5:45 pm. Fare is $1.50. JeT's express bus, $2, takes about 50 minutes to follow Airline Drive into the city. On weekdays, it goes downtown and to Mid-City; on weekends, it stops in Mid-City only. From the airport, catch the E2 Airport line on the second level near the Delta counter in the median. Airport-bound buses leave every 30–35 minutes from Loyola and Tulane avenues downtown, next to the main branch of the New Orleans Public Library, and from the corner of Tulane and Carrollton avenues in Mid-City. The last bus leaves at 6:52 pm from Tulane and Loyola, 9:49 pm from Tulane and Carrollton. Uber and Lyft offer transportation from the airport. Meet app-based ride services in the Ground Transportation Center.

Contacts Airport Shuttle New Orleans.
☎ 504/522–3500, 866/596–2699 ⊕ www.airportshuttleneworleans.com. **Jefferson Transit.** ☎ 504/818–1077 ⊕ www.jefferson-transit.org/e2airport.php.

TAXIS

A cab ride to or from the airport and Uptown or downtown costs $36 for up to two passengers. For groups of three or more, the rate is $15 per person. Pickup is on the lower level, outside the baggage-claim area. There may be an additional charge for extra baggage. ⇨ *See Taxi Travel for taxi companies and contact information.*

▮ BIKE TRAVEL

Biking is a good option for getting around New Orleans, especially in Faubourg Marigny.

Contacts Bicycle Michael's. ✉ 622 Frenchmen St., Faubourg Marigny ☎ 504/945–9505 ⊕ www.bicyclemichaels.com. **Bullfrog Bike Tours.** ✉ 214 Decatur St., across from House of Blues, French Quarter ☎ 504/619–4162, 877/734–8687 ⊕ neworleans.bullfrogbiketours.com.

▮ BOAT TRAVEL

BY FERRY

The ferry ride across the river to Algiers is an experience in itself, affording great views of the river and the New Orleans skyline, as well as the heady feeling of being on one of the largest and most powerful rivers in the world. Pedestrians enter near Spanish Plaza and the Riverwalk shopping area and board the Canal Street Ferry from above. Bicycles board from below on the left of the terminal; cars are no longer allowed on the ferry. The trip to Algiers takes about 5 minutes. On weekdays, ferries leave on the quarter-hour and three-quarter-hour from the east bank (New Orleans), and on the hour and half hour from the West Bank (Algiers). Ferries run from 6 am to 9:45 pm Monday through Thursday, from 6 am to 11:45 pm on Friday; 10:30 am to 11:45 pm Saturday, and from 10:30 am to 9:45 pm on Sunday. Be sure to check return times with the attendants if you are crossing in the evening—it's no fun to be stranded on the other side. There are wheelchair-accessible restrooms on the ferry.

Information Canal Street Ferry. ✉ *Bottom of Canal St., at Convention Center Blvd.* ☎ 504/309–9789 ⊕ www.norta.com.

▮ BUS AND STREETCAR TRAVEL

GETTING AROUND BY BUS AND STREETCAR

Within New Orleans, the Regional Transit Authority (RTA) operates a public bus and streetcar (not "trolley") system with interconnecting lines throughout the city. The buses are generally clean and on time, and run regularly from about 6 am to about 9 pm, later on some routes. Smoking, eating, and drinking are prohibited on RTA vehicles. Buses are wheelchair accessible, as are the Canal Street, Riverfront, and Loyola Avenue streetcar lines; the St. Charles Avenue streetcars are not.

ROUTES

The Riverfront streetcar covers a 2-mile route along the Mississippi River, connecting major sights from the end of the French Quarter (Esplanade Avenue) to the New Orleans Convention Center (Julia Street). Eight stops en route include the French Market, Jackson Brewery, the Aquarium of the Americas, Canal Place, Fulton Street entertainment area, The Riverwalk, Woldenberg Park, and the Hilton Hotel. This streetcar operates daily from 6 am until 11:30 pm, every 20 minutes during peak hours.

The historic streetcars of St. Charles Avenue run along St. Charles Avenue from Common Street to the Riverbend at Carrollton Avenue roughly every 10 minutes for most of the day. From Riverbend, this line continues along Carrollton Avenue to Claiborne Avenue in Mid-City. Streetcar service on St. Charles Avenue runs almost 24 hours a day.

A third streetcar line runs along Canal Street from the river near Harrah's Casino to either City Park or to the cemeteries. Going from Harrah's Casino to the cemeteries, it passes every 16 minutes. As it gets closer to City Park, it passes every 30 minutes. The Canal Street line operates from 7 am to about 1 am, with longer waits after midnight.

The newest streetcar line, which opened in early 2013, runs along Loyola Avenue, with stops in the CBD and French Quarter, then heads eastward into Tremé, the Faubourg Marigny, and Bywater. It departs from the Union Passenger Terminal every 20 minutes between 6 am and 11:30 pm, heads to the French Market Station, and makes stops at Canal Street and Harrah's Casino. Stops in Tremé, Marigny, and Bywater are every 30 minutes.

COSTS

Bus and streetcar fare is $1.25 exact change plus 25¢ for transfers. Unlimited passes, valid on both buses and streetcars, cost $3 for 1 day, $9 for 3 days, and $55 for 31 days. The daily passes are available from streetcar and bus operators; 3-day and 31-day passes are available at many local hotels and at most Walgreens.

Bus and Streetcar Information RTA. ☎ 504/248–3900 ⊕ www.norta.com.

TICKET/PASS	PRICE
Single Fare	$1.25
One-day Jazzy Pass	$3
Three-day Jazzy Pass	$9
Thirty-one-day Jazzy Pass	$55

▌ CAR TRAVEL

CAR RENTALS

If you plan to stick to the highly touristed areas of New Orleans, you may want to keep it simple and use taxis, ride-share services, streetcars, and the airport shuttle. However, if you plan to travel beyond the French Quarter and the Garden District, renting a car is a good idea.

If you decide to rent a car, rates in New Orleans begin at around $45 per day ($250 per week) for an economy car with air-conditioning, automatic transmission, and unlimited mileage. Prices do not include local tax on car rentals, or other surcharges, which can add another 15%–20% to your cost. All major agencies, including Avis, Budget, Hertz, Enterprise, and National Car Rental, have outlets in New Orleans.

GASOLINE

Gas stations are not plentiful within the city of New Orleans. The downtown area is particularly short on stations; head for Rampart Street if you need gas while downtown. If you're in Uptown, you'll find stations along Carrollton Avenue.

PARKING

Meter maids and tow trucks are plentiful everywhere, especially in the French Quarter. Avoid spaces at unmarked corners: less than 15 feet between your car and the corner will result in a ticket. Watch for temporary "no parking" signs, which pop up along parade routes and during film shoots. The SP + Parking and

Premium Parking websites can help you find lots and garages around town.

Garages Premium Parking. ☎ *844/236-2011* ⊕ *premiumparking.com.* **SP + Parking.** ☎ *504/525-5476* ⊕ *neworleansparking. spplus.com.*

FROM NEW ORLEANS TO	ROUTE	DISTANCE
Atchafalaya Basin	I-10	124 miles
Avery Island	I-10, U.S. 90	140 miles
Baton Rouge	I-10	80 miles
Breaux Bridge	I-10, U.S. 31	130 miles
Lafayette	I-10	136 miles
St. Francisville	I-10, U.S. 61	105 miles
Oak Alley	U.S. 61, La. 44	55 miles
Opelousas	I-10, U.S. 190	135 miles
San Francisco Plantation	U.S. 44	35 miles

ROAD CONDITIONS

Surface roads in New Orleans are generally bumpy, and potholes are common, thanks to the city's swampy, shifting terrain and extensive live-oak roots. Along St. Charles Avenue, use caution when crossing over the neutral ground (median); drivers must yield to streetcars and pedestrians along this route. Afternoon rush hour affects New Orleans daily, and backups on Interstate 10 can start as early as 3 pm.

▌TAXI TRAVEL

Cabs are metered at $3.50 base fare (up to two passengers, plus $1 for each additional passenger), then $2 per mile. If you're trying to hail a cab in New Orleans, try Decatur Street, Canal Street, or major hotels in the Quarter or the CBD. Otherwise, call.

During Mardi Gras it can be extremely difficult to get a cab or ride-share; plan an alternate way to get home (or enjoy the party until public transportation starts up again in the morning).

Taxi Companies **United Cabs.** ☎ *504/522-9771* ⊕ *www.unitedcabs.com.* **Veterans.** ☎ *504/367-6767.* **White Fleet-Elks Elite Cab Co.** ☎ *504/822-3800.* **Yellow-Checker Cab.** ☎ *504/525-3311.*

▌TRAIN TRAVEL

Three major Amtrak lines travel to and from New Orleans Union Passenger Terminal. The *Crescent*, operating daily, runs to and from New York and Washington, D.C., via Atlanta. Also daily, the *City of New Orleans* runs to and from Chicago via Memphis. Running three times weekly, the *Sunset Limited* runs to and from Los Angeles via Tucson and Houston.

Information Amtrak. ☎ *800/872-7245* ⊕ *www.amtrak.com.* **Union Passenger Terminal.** ✉ *1001 Loyola Ave.* ☎ *504/528-1612.*

TRAIN ROUTE	SERVES	APPROX. COST
City of New Orleans	Chicago	$135
Crescent	New York	$165
Sunset Limited	Los Angeles	$200

ESSENTIALS

▌ CHILDREN IN NEW ORLEANS

The Louisiana Children's Museum, the Audubon Zoo, and the Insectarium often have activities that are both educational and fun. Sites such as ⊕ *new-orleans. macaronikid.com* and ⊕ *neworleanskids. com* can help you find what's happening while you're in town.

Be sure to plan on visiting the French Quarter, but avoid Bourbon Street. Things are out in the open, whether you plan to see them or not. In the evening, Bourbon Street quickly becomes overloaded with large, noisy, and drunk crowds.

If you're renting a car, don't forget to arrange for a car seat when you reserve.

Local Information New Orleans Convention & Visitors Bureau. ✉ *2020 St. Charles Ave., Garden District* ☎ *800/672–6124, 504/566–5011* ⊕ *www.neworleanscvb.com.*

▌ DAY TOURS AND GUIDES

Given the variety of perspectives available in New Orleans, a package tour can be a good option, especially for first-time visitors. Highlights will likely include the French Quarter and Riverwalk, with daytime visits to spots like the Audubon Zoo, the Garden District, and possibly a plantation or swamp tour.

BUS TOURS

Several local tour companies give two- to four-hour city bus tours that include the French Quarter, the Garden District, Uptown, and the lakefront. Prices range from $30 to $70 per person. Both **Gray Line** and **New Orleans Tours** offer a longer tour that combines a two-hour city tour by bus with a two-hour steamboat ride on the Mississippi River.

New Orleans Tours leads city, swamp, and plantation tours, as well as steamboat cruises. **Tours by Isabelle,** the oldest tour company in New Orleans (operating since

1979), runs city, swamp, plantation, and combination swamp–plantation tours.

For visitors interested in seeing the scope of the impact of the 2005 storm and keeping the local economy in motion, **Gray Line** and **Tours by Isabelle** both offer tours of Hurricane Katrina damage and recovery. For the more personal experience, choose **Tours by Isabelle.**

PLANTATION TOURS

Full-day plantation tours by bus from New Orleans, which include guided tours through one of three antebellum plantation houses along the Mississippi River, are offered by **Gray Line** and **New Orleans Tours.**

Tours by Isabelle includes a stop for lunch in its full-day plantation package that traces the history of the Cajun people. (The cost of lunch isn't included.) Also available is the Grand Tour: a daylong minibus tour that includes a visit to one plantation, lunch in a Cajun restaurant, and a two-hour boat tour of the swamps via either a speedy airboat or a peaceful bayou pontoon boat, with a Cajun trapper and raconteur.

RIVERBOAT CRUISES

The **New Orleans Steamboat Company** offers narrated riverboat cruises up and down the Mississippi, complete with a jazz band, on the steamboat *Natchez,* an authentic paddle wheeler. Ticket sales and departures for the *Natchez* are at the Toulouse Street Wharf behind Jackson Brewery.

New Orleans Paddle Wheels has a Mississippi River cruise aboard the *Creole Queen.* Highlighting the port and French Quarter, this cruise leaves daily from the Riverwalk. There is also an evening jazz dinner cruise from 7 to 9 (boarding at 6:30 pm, which is also when the band starts playing and the cash bar opens); tickets are available for dinner (a Creole buffet) and the cruise, or just the cruise and live music. The company also offers a cruise to Chalmette Battlefield, the site of the Battle of New Orleans, which provides an opportunity to learn about the 1815 battle, and tour the battlefield. The ticket office is at the Poydras Street Wharf near the Riverwalk.

SPECIAL-INTEREST TOURS

Macon Riddle's Let's Go Antiquing offers personalized shopping itineraries of the city's antiques stores, galleries, or boutiques based on your interests and preferences (not all tours are about antiques).

The **New Orleans School of Cooking**, in the heart of the French Quarter, offers classes on Cajun and Creole cuisine. Visit the website for details about class schedules and rates.

SWAMP TOURS

Exploring an exotic Louisiana swamp and traveling into Cajun country are highlights for many visitors. Dozens of swamp-tour companies are available. Check at your hotel or the visitor center for a complete listing. *Many do not provide transportation from downtown hotels, but those listed below do.* Full-day tours often include visiting a plantation house.

WALKING TOURS

Free hour-long walking tours along the Mississippi River levee, with a discussion of the interaction between the river and the city, are given Tuesdays through Saturdays at 9:30 am by rangers of the **Jean Lafitte National Historical Park and Preserve**. Tickets are available at the Jean Lafitte Park's French Quarter Visitor Center starting at 9 am on the morning of the tour. Check the National Park Service website for details. Tickets are free, but tours are limited to 25 people. Two-hour general history tours, beginning at the 1850 House on Jackson Square, are given Tuesday through Sunday at 10:30 and 1:30 by **Friends of the Cabildo**.

Friends of the Cabildo also offers more unusual geographic tours, including the Irish Channel and the vibrant South Market District, where you'll see a mix of new construction, historic preservation, and adaptive reuse of buildings, along with music history tours.

Several specialized walking tours conducted by knowledgeable guides on specific aspects of the French Quarter and the Garden District are also available; **Tours by Isabelle** and **Historic New Orleans** are two reputable companies.

The cemeteries of New Orleans fascinate many people because of their unique aboveground tombs. **Save Our Cemeteries** conducts guided walking tours of St. Louis No. 1 as well as Lafayette No. 1. Generally, reservations are required.

Voodoo- and spiritual-themed tours are popular in New Orleans, and several companies, including **Haunted History Tours, Historic New Orleans,** and **New Orleans Spirit Tours** all have spooky options to choose from.

Contact Information Friends of the Cabildo. ☎ *504/523-3939* ⊕ *www.friendsofthecabildo.org.* **Gray Line.** ☎ *800/233-2628, 504/569-1401* ⊕ *www.graylineneworleans.com.* **Haunted History Tours.** ☎ *888/644-6787, 504/861-2727* ⊕ *www.hauntedhistorytours.com.* **Historic New Orleans Walking Tours.** ☎ *504/947-2120* ⊕ *www.tourneworleans.com.* **Honey Island Swamp Tours.** ☎ *985/641-1769* ⊕ *www.honeyislandswamp.com.* **Jean Lafitte Swamp and Airboat Tours.** ☎ *800/445-4109, 504/689-4186* ⊕ *www.jeanlafitteswamptour.com.* **Let's Go Antiquing.** ☎ *504/899-3027* ⊕ *www.neworleansantiquing.com.* **New Orleans Paddle Wheels.** ☎ *800/445-4109, 504/529-4567* ⊕ *www.creolequeen.com.* **New Orleans School of Cooking.** ✉ *524 St. Louis St.* ☎ *800/237-4841, 504/208-5320* ⊕ *www.neworleansschoolofcooking.com.* **New Orleans Spirit Tours.** ☎ *504/314-0806* ⊕ *www.spirittoursneworleans.com.* **New Orleans Steamboat Company.** ☎ *800/233-2628, 504/569-1401* ⊕ *www.steamboatnatchez.com.* **New Orleans Tours.** ☎ *504/592-1991* ⊕ *www.notours.com.* **Save Our Cemeteries.** ☎ *504/525-3377* ⊕ *www.saveourcemeteries.org.* **Tours by Isabelle.** ☎ *877/665-8687, 504/398-0365* ⊕ *www.toursbyisabelle.com.*

GAY AND LESBIAN TRAVEL

New Orleans has a large gay and lesbian population throughout the metropolitan area. The most gay-friendly neighborhood is the French Quarter, followed by the Faubourg Marigny, just outside the Quarter.

The website ⊕ *frenchquarter.com* has an LGBTQ section including an interactive map of entertainment locations and an events calendar.

Throughout the year there are a number of gay festivals. The biggest is Southern Decadence, held Labor Day weekend. The city also has gay-friendly guesthouses and B&Bs, particularly along Esplanade Avenue.

Ambush, a local newspaper published twice monthly, provides a list of current events in addition to news and reviews. You can find this publication at many gay bars.

HEALTH

The intense heat and humidity of New Orleans in the height of summer can be a concern for anyone unused to a semitropical climate. Pace yourself to avoid problems, particularly dehydration. Pollen levels can be extremely high, especially in April and May. Know your own limits and select indoor activities in the middle of the day; you'll find the locals doing the same thing.

MONEY

Prices throughout this guide are given for adults. Substantially reduced fees are almost always available for children, students, and senior citizens.

ATMs can easily be found on Decatur, Royal, and Chartres streets, close to Canal, at most gift shops, and in most bars in the French Quarter. These machines generally have high fees. As anywhere, use common sense when withdrawing cash and be aware of your surroundings. If getting cash at night, try to use machines in more populated areas.

ITEM	AVERAGE COST
Cup of Coffee	$3
Glass of Wine	$7–$10
Glass of Beer	4–$6
Po'boy	$8–$12
One-Mile Taxi Ride	$3.50 plus $2 per mile
Museum Admission	$12–$27

PACKING

New Orleans is casual during the day and casual to slightly dressy at night. A few restaurants in the French Quarter require men to wear a jacket and tie at dinner. Take comfy walking shoes.

In winter you'll want a coat or warm jacket, especially for evenings, which can be downright cold. In summer pack for hot, sticky weather, but be prepared for borderline-glacial air-conditioning, and bring an umbrella in case of sudden thunderstorms. Leave the plastic raincoats behind (they're extremely uncomfortable in high humidity). In addition, pack a sun hat and sunscreen, even for strolls in the city—the sun can be fierce.

Insect repellent will come in handy if you plan to be outdoors on a swamp cruise or dining alfresco in the city; mosquitoes come out in full force after sunset in warm weather.

SAFETY

New Orleans has long drawn unwelcome attention for its high crime rate. The New Orleans Police Department regularly patrols the French Quarter, and tourists are seldom the target of major crimes. Still, common sense is invaluable.

Know where you're going or ask the concierge at your hotel about the best route. In the French Quarter, particularly if you're on foot, stay on streets that are heavily populated. In other areas of the city it is often advisable to drive or take a taxi. High-end neighborhoods and derelict properties adjoin one another throughout New Orleans, making aimless strolling a bad idea outside the Quarter. Try to stick to the recommended walks and areas in this book, and be aware of your surroundings.

Call a taxi or ride-share service late at night or when the distance is too great to walk; this is even more important if you've been drinking.

▌ TAXES

A local sales tax of 10% applies to all goods and services purchased in Orleans Parish, including food. Taxes outside Orleans Parish vary and are slightly lower. Due to a state revitalization program, art sold in designated "cultural districts" is exempt from state or local sales tax. Most businesses whose wares are tax-free have signs pointing this out, but be sure to ask if it's unclear.

Louisiana was the first state in the United States to grant a sales-tax rebate to foreign shoppers. Look for shops, restaurants, and hotels that display the distinctive tax-free sign, and ask for a voucher for the 10% sales tax tacked on to the price of many products and services. Present the vouchers and receipt with your plane ticket and passport at the tax rebate office at the Louis Armstrong New Orleans International Airport, in the main lobby of Terminal C, and you can receive up to $500 in cash back. If the amount redeemable is more than $500, a check for the difference will be mailed to your home address. Call the airport refund office for complete information.

Contact Airport Refund Office. ☎ 504/467–0723 ⊕ www.louisianataxfree.com.

▌ TIPPING

A standard restaurant tip is 20%; if you truly enjoyed your meal and want to reward good service, then consider more. If you use the services of the concierge, a tip of $5 to $10 is appropriate, with an additional gratuity for special services or favors. Always keep a few dollar bills on hand—they'll come in handy for tipping bellhops, doormen, and valet parking attendants, and for rewarding the many fine street musicians who entertain day and night.

▌ VISITOR INFORMATION

For general information and brochures, contact city and state tourism bureaus. The New Orleans Convention & Visitors Bureau's website is a comprehensive resource for trip planning, hotel and tour booking, and shopping in the city; you can also download brochures, coupons, walking tours, and event schedules, as well as find links to other helpful websites. The Louisiana Office of Tourism offers the same with a statewide focus.

Contacts Louisiana Office of Tourism. ☎ 800/677–4082 ⊕ www.louisianatravel.com. **New Orleans Convention & Visitors Bureau.** ☎ 800/672–6124, 504/566–5011 ⊕ www.neworleanscvb.com.

ONLINE RESOURCES
The Louisiana Department of Culture, Recreation and Tourism's website gives a general overview of tourism in Louisiana.

New Orleans Online provides basic trip planning and travel tools. The city's official site has updates on local issues and government affairs.

The Volunteer Louisiana Commission's website (⊕ www.volunteerlouisiana.gov) has a section about opportunities to volunteer while on vacation called "Voluntourism" that can link you up with numerous opportunities.

The website of the *Gambit* weekly newspaper does a good job of representing varying perspectives on life in the city, with a comprehensive events calendar.

The French Quarter website gives great links to event, lodging, and parking information, as well as an interactive French Quarter map. And for that something extra, Experience New Orleans has links to a blog, podcast, and fun video tours, in addition to the standard tourist sites.

For general information about events, hotels, and restaurants, check the official New Orleans travel site, ⊕ *www.neworleans.com*. For Louisiana music coverage (plus other entertainment news), *OffBeat* magazine's website is a good bet, as is the radio station WWOZ, which streams online and maintains a music calendar. Everything you need to know about the New Orleans Jazz & Heritage Festival can be found at its website. A site devoted entirely to Mardi Gras, Mardi Gras New Orleans, includes histories, parade schedules, and other specific Mardi Gras information.

For arts happenings around town, the Arts Council of New Orleans website has a calendar of art, music, dance, film, theater, literature, and culinary events in the city. The site also includes an artist directory and other resources.

All About Louisiana The Louisiana Department of Culture, Recreation and Tourism. ⊕ *www.crt.state.la.us*.

All About New Orleans City of New Orleans. ⊕ *www.nola.gov*. Experience New Orleans. ⊕ *www.experienceneworleans.com*. Frenchquarter.com. ⊕ *www.frenchquarter. com*. Neworleans.com. ☎ 800/476-1651 ⊕ *www.neworleans.com*. New Orleans Online. ⊕ *www.neworleansonline.com*.

Music, Festivals, and Events Arts Council of New Orleans. ⊕ *www.artsneworleans. org*. Mardi Gras New Orleans. ⊕ *www. mardigrasneworleans.com*. New Orleans Jazz & Heritage Festival. ☎ 504/558-6100 ⊕ *www.nojazzfest.com*. OffBeat Magazine. ☎ 504/944-4300 ⊕ *www.offbeat.com*. WWOZ. ☎ 504/568-1239 ⊕ *www.wwoz.org*.

Periodicals Gambit. ☎ 504/486-5900 ⊕ *www.bestofneworleans.com*. The New Orleans Advocate. ✉ 840 St. Charles Ave. ☎ 504/636-7400 ⊕ *www.theadvocate. com/new_orleans*. The Times-Picayune. ☎ 800/925-0000 ⊕ *www.nola.com*.

INDEX

A

Abbeville, *38, 259–260*
Abita Brew Pub ✕, *234*
Abita Brewing Company, *234*
Abita Mystery House, *234*
Abita Springs, *230, 234*
Academy of the Sacred Heart (Uptown), *101*
Acadian Cultural Center, *247*
Acadian Memorial, *257*
Acadian Village, *38, 248*
Acadiana Center for the Arts, *247*
Acadiana Park Nature Station, *247–248*
Ace Hotel New Orleans ⌂, *159*
Acme Oyster House ✕, *120*
Adler's (shop), *50, 216*
African American Museum, *257*
Aidan Gill for Men (spa), *223*
Air travel, *20, 236, 262–263*
Alcée Fortier Park, *115*
Alexander Mouton House and Lafayette Museum, *248*
Alligators, *255*
AllWays Lounge & Theatre, *177, 198*
Ancora ✕, *139–140*
Angela King Gallery, *206*
Angeline ✕, *120*
Angelique (shop), *226–227*
Angelo Brocato's ✕, *144*
Angola Museum, *242–243*
Anthemion, *101*
Antoine's ✕, *120*
Aquarium of the Americas, *27*
Arnaud's ✕, *120*
Ariodante (gallery), *216–217*
Art for Art's Sake (festival), *35*
Arthur Roger Gallery, *217*
Artist's Market, *206*
ArtWalks, *251*
As You Like Silver Shop, *219–220*
Ashton's Bed & Breakfast ✕, *166*
Astor Crowne Plaza ⌂, *150–151*
Atchafalaya ✕, *140*
Atchafalaya Basin, *255*
Audubon Aquarium of the Americas, *27, 43*
Audubon Butterfly Garden and Insectarium, *43*
Audubon Clubhouse Café ✕, *98*
Audubon Cottages ⌂, *151*

Audubon Park, *27, 102*
Audubon Place, *102*
Audubon State Historic Site and Oakley Plantation House, *243–244*
Audubon Zoo, *27, 99*
August ✕, *128–129*
Aunt Sally's Praline Shop, *208*
Aux Belles Choses (shop), *225*
Avenue Pub, *191*
Avery Island, *38, 258–259*

B

B.B. King's Blues Club, *176*
B&C Seafood ✕, *241*
Bacchanal Fine Wine & Spirits (bar), *187*
Backstreet Cultural Museum, *60, 73*
Banks Street Bar and Grill, *195*
Bar Frances, *192*
Bar Tonique, *172*
Bargain Center (shop), *215*
Barrel Proof (bar), *191*
Barrow House Inn ⌂, *244*
Bars and lounges, *172–174, 177, 186, 187, 188–189, 190, 191–193, 194, 195, 196*
Basics Underneath (shop), *225*
Basketball, *24*
Bayona ✕, *120*
Bayou Beer Garden, *196*
Bayou Cabins ⌂, *253*
Bayou St. John, *19, 114–116*
nightlife and the arts, 196
restaurants, 109, 146
safety, 109
Bayou Teche Museum, *258*
Beauregard-Keyes House, *48, 50*
Bed and breakfasts, *151, 155–156, 157, 158, 161, 163, 165, 166, 238–239, 241, 242, 244, 249–250, 253, 257*
Belladonna Day Spa, *226*
Benjamin House, *101*
Best Western Plus St. Christopher Hotel ⌂, *159*
Bicycle travel, *263*
Bird City, *259*
BJ's Lounge, *187*
Blaine Kern's Mardi Gras World at Kern Studios, *27, 60, 84*
Blake Hotel New Orleans, The ⌂, *159*
Blue Cypress Books (shop), *226*
Blue Moon Saloon, *250*

Boat and ferry travel, *36, 263*
Bombay Club, *172*
Bon Maison Guest House ⌂, *151*
Bon Ton Café ✕, *129*
Books and movies about New Orleans, *25*
Borgne ✕, *129*
Boucherie ✕, *143*
Bourbon French Parfums (shop), *213*
Bourbon House ✕, *120–121*
Bourbon Orleans Hotel ⌂, *151*
Bourbon Pub (gay bar), *175*
Bourbon Street, *45*
Brass Monkey (shop), *203*
Breaux Bridge, *38, 253*
Brennan's ✕, *121*
Brevard House, *91*
Brieux Carre (bar), *172*
Brigtsen's ✕, *143–144*
Broussard's ✕, *121*
Brown House, *101*
Buchanan Lofts ⌂, *249–250*
Buckner Mansion, *93*
Bulldog, The (bar), *191*
Bullet's Sports Bar, *188*
Bultman Funeral Home, *100*
Bus tours, *266*
Bus travel, *20, 263–264*
Cajun Country, 246
Plantation Country, 236
Bywater, *18, 70–73, 187–188, 215*

C

C. Collection (shop), *227*
Cabildo, *45*
Cabrini High School and Mother Cabrini Shrine, *115–116*
Cafe Amelie ✕, *121*
Café Cake ✕, *67*
Café Degas ✕, *146*
Café des Amis ✕, *38*
Café du Monde ✕, *41, 121, 208–209*
Café Lafitte in Exile (gay bar), *175*
Café Vermilionville ✕, *249*
Cajun Country, *38, 231, 244–260*
Cajun Country Swamp Tours, *255*
Cajun music, *181, 184, 230, 252, 256*
Callon Contemporary (gallery), *217*

Canal Street, *50*
Candlelight Lounge, *188*
Cane and Table (bar), *172*
Car travel, *20, 264–265*
Cajun Country, 246
Plantation Country, 236
Carmo ✕, *130, 136*
Carol Robinson Gallery, *223*
Carousel Bar, *173*
Carousel Gardens Amusement Park, *111*
Carrollton-Riverbend, *19, 97–106, 143–144, 194*
Carrollton Station (club), *194*
Casamento's ✕, *140*
Catahoula Hotel ⊞, *159*
Cat's Meow (bar), *173*
Cavan ✕, *140*
CBD and Warehouse District, *18, 77–86*
hotels, 159–163
nightlife and the arts, 188–191
restaurants, 79, 128–130, 136, 138
safety, 79
shopping, 215–218
walking tours, 32–33
Celebration in the Oaks, *35*
Cemeteries, *22, 73, 89, 92, 109, 113, 114, 115*
Center for Southern Craft and Design Store, *217*
Central Grocery ✕, *121*
Chamber of Commerce (Breaux Bridge), *253*
Chart Room (bar), *173*
Chateau LeMoyne ⊞, *151*
Checkpoint Charlies (bar), *177*
Chess, *47*
Chiba ✕, *144*
Chickie Wah Wah (club), *195*
Children, attractions for, *27, 266*
hotels, 49
nightlife and the arts, 190
Chimes Bed & Breakfast ⊞, *165*
Christ Church Cathedral, *93*
Christopher Porché-West Galerie, *71*
Churches and cathedrals
Abbeville, 259
French Quarter, 46, 47, 48, 62–63
Garden District, 93
Lafayette, 248
St. Francisville, 242
St. Martinville, 257
Tremé, 76
Warehouse District, 86

Circle Bar, *190*
City Park, *27, 109, 111*
Claiborne Mansion ⊞, *158*
Clancy's ✕, *140*
Cleo's Mediterranean Cuisine & Grocery ✕, *120*
Climate, *21, 233*
Clock and Watch Shop, *216*
Cochon ✕, *136*
Cochon Butcher ✕, *136*
Cocktails, *37, 169*
Cole Pratt Gallery, *223–224*
Coliseum Square Park, *91*
Colonel Short's Villa, *93*
Columns Hotel ⊞, *101, 165*
Columns Hotel Victorian Lounge Bar, *192*
Commander's Palace ✕, *138*
Company Burger ✕, *140*
Compère Lapin ✕, *129*
Congo Square, *74*
Conrad Rice Mill, *258*
Contemporary Arts Center, *84*
Cooter Brown's (bar), *192–193*
Coquette ✕, *138*
Corner Pocket (gay bar), *175*
Cosimo's (bar), *173*
Costs, *13, 268*
Country Club New Orleans, *187*
Courir de Mardi Gras, *38, 253*
Courtyard New Orleans Downtown Near the French Quarter ⊞, *159*
Crawfish Time ✕, *249*
Credit cards, *13*
Crescent City Farmers' Market, *85*
Crescent Park, *71–72*
Croissant d'Or Patisserie ✕, *121–122*
Cure (bar), *193*
Currents Fine Jewelry (shop), *209*
Cypress Grove Cemetery, *113*

D

d.b.a. (club), *186*
Dance, *197*
Dante's Kitchen ✕, *144*
Dashka Roth Contemporary Jewelry and Judaica (shop), *209*
Dat Dog ✕, *140*
Dauphine Orleans ⊞, *151*
Dauphine Street Books, *207*
Davenport Lounge, *176*
Defend New Orleans (shop), *221*
Delachaise (bar), *193*
Derby Pottery (gallery), *220*

Destrehan Plantation, *238*
Dickie Brennan's Steakhouse ✕, *122*
Dirty Coast (shop), *225*
Discount passes, *36*
Dixie, *64*
Dr. Bob, *72*
Doll House, *102*
Domenica ✕, *129*
Don's Specialty Meats & Grocery, *251*
DoubleTree by Hilton Hotel New Orleans ⊞, *159*
DoubleTree by Lafayette ⊞, *250*
Downtown Alive! (festival), *251*
Drago's ✕, *130*
Drink & Learn: The Cocktail Tour, *37*
Dupuy's Oyster Shop ✕, *259–260*

E

Easter, *34*
Edgar Degas House Museum, Courtyard and Inn ⊞, *116, 166*
Eiffel Society, *93*
1850 House, *50*
1896 O'Malley House ⊞, *166*
El Sid-o's (club), *250–251*
Elizabeth's ✕, *128*
Elliot Gallery, *206*
Embassy Suites New Orleans-Convention Center and Lofts Club Tower ⊞, *159–160*
Emeril's ✕, *136*
Emeril's Delmonico ✕, *139*
Encore Shop, *227*
Ernst Café, *190*
Erzulie's Authentic Voodou (shop), *212*
Esoterica Occult Goods (shop), *212*
Essence Music Festival, *35*
Eunice, *252–253*
Eunice Depot Museum, *252*
Evangeline Oak, *28*
Evans Creole Candy Factory, *209*

F

F&M Patio Bar, *193*
Fair Grinds Coffeehouse ✕, *109*
Fair Grounds Race Course and Slots, *116*

Faubourg Marigny, Bywater, and Tremé, *18*, *65–76*
hotels, *158*
nightlife and the arts, *177*, *186–188*
restaurants, *67*, *126*, *128*
safety, *66*
shopping, *214–215*
Faubourg Wines (shop), *214*
Faulkner House, *50–51*
Faulkner House Books, *51*, *207*
Ferry travel, *36*
Festival Acadiens et Creoles, *251*
Festival International de Louisiane, *251*
Festivals and seasonal events, *34–35*, *38*, *53–60*, *251*, *253*
Fifi Mahoney's (shop), *211*
Film, *197*
Finn McCool's Irish Pub ✕, *109*, *195*
Fleur D'Orleans (shop), *225*
Fleurty Girl (shop), *207*
Fly, The, *99*
Fodor, Eugene, *13*
Football, *24*
Forever New Orleans (shop), *212*
Four Points By Sheraton French Quarter 🖬, *151*, *154*
Frankie & Johnny's ✕, *38*, *140*, *142*
Fred's Lounge, *252*
Free events, *36*, *83*
French Antique Shop, *204*
French Market, *45*
French Quarter, *18*, *40–64*
hotels, *150–151*, *154–158*
nightlife and the arts, *172–177*
restaurants, *41*, *119–126*
safety, *40*
shopping, *41*, *64*, *202–214*
French Quarter Festival, *34*
French 75 (bar), *173*
French Truck Roastery and Espresso Bar ✕, *88*
Frenchmen Street, *68*
Friend (shop), *218*
Friends of Music, *196*
Fritzel's European Jazz Pub, *176*
Funky Monkey (shop), *221*

G

Gae-Tana's (shop), *227*
Galatoire's ✕, *122*
Gallery for Fine Photography, A, *205*
Gallier Hall, *82*

Gallier House, *51*
Garden District, *19*, *87–96*
hotels, *163*, *165*
nightlife and the arts, *191–192*
restaurants, *88*
safety, *89*
shopping, *218–223*
walking tour, *30–31*
Garden District Book Shop, *221*
Garden District Pub, *191*
Gardens and courtyards
Avery Island, *259*
Faubourg-Marigny, *72*
Mid-City and Bayou St. John, *111–112*, *115*, *116*
St. Francisville, *244*
Gauche House, *51*
Gautreau's ✕, *142*
Gay and lesbian
nightlife, *175*
travel, *268*
George Schmidt Gallery, *217*
Germaine Wells Mardi Gras Museum, *51*, *60*
Gogo Jewelry (shop), *222*
Golden Lantern, The (gay bar), *175*
Good Friends (gay bar), *175*
GOOD Shop, The, *228*
Goodrich-Stanley House, *91*
Goorin Brothers (shop), *211*
Grace Episcopal Church, *242*
Grand Coteau, *38*
Grand Isle ✕, *130*
Grand Victorian Bed & Breakfast 🖬, *163*
Grant House, *101*
Great Artist's Collective, *206*
Great River Road, *237–242*
Green Goddess ✕, *122*
Green Serene (shop), *221*
Grill Room, The ✕, *130*
GW Fins ✕, *122*

H

Harrah's New Orleans Casino, *80–82*, *189*
Harrah's New Orleans Hotel 🖬, *160*
Harris Antiques, *204*
Harouni Gallery, *206*
Hazelnut (shop), *225–226*
HBO's Treme, *75*
Health matters, *268*
Hebert's Specialty Meats ✕, *260*
Henry Howard Hotel 🖬, *163*
Herbsaint ✕, *136*
Hermann-Grima House, *46*
Hermes Bar ✕, *122–123*

Hilton New Orleans Riverside 🖬, *160*
Historic New Orleans Collection, *46*
Holocaust Memorial, *48*
Hot Tin (bar), *192*
Hotel Le Marais 🖬, *154*
Hotel Maison de Ville 🖬, *154*
Hotel Mazarin 🖬, *154*
Hotel Modern 🖬, *163*
Hotel Monteleone 🖬, *154*
Hotel Provincial 🖬, *154*
Hotel Royal 🖬, *154*
Hotel Villa Convento 🖬, *155*
Hotels, *13*, *147–166*
bed and breakfasts, *151*, *155*, *157*, *158*, *161*, *163*, *165*, *166*, *238–239*, *241*, *242*, *244*, *249–250*, *253*, *257*
Breaux Bridge, *253*
CBD and Warehouse District, *159–163*
children, *149*
Faubourg Marigny and Tremé, *158*
Fodor's choice, *154*, *156*, *160*, *162–163*, *165*
French Quarter, *150–151*, *154–158*
Garden District, *163*, *165*
haunted, *157*, *243*
Lafayette, *249–250*
Mid-City, *166*
neighborhoods, *150*
New Iberia, *258*
price categories, *149*, *234*
reservations, *149*
St. Francisville, *244*
St. Martinville, *257*
services, *149*
side trips from New Orleans, *233*, *241*
Uptown, *165*
Houmas House, *38*, *238*
Houmas House B&B 🖬, *241*
House of Blues, *176*
House of Broel's Victorian Mansion and Dollhouse Museum, *91–92*
House of Dance and Feathers, *69–70*
Hové Parfumeur, Ltd. (shop), *213–214*
Howlin' Wolf (club), *190*
Hurricane Katrina Memorial, *113*
Hyatt French Quarter 🖬, *155*

I

Idea Factory (shop), 212–213
InterContinental New Orleans
 ⚏, 160
International House ⚏, 160
Irene's Cuisine ✕, 123
Island of Salvation Botanica
 (shop), 215
Italian Barrel, The ✕, 123
Itineraries, 28–29

J

J&M Music Shop, 74
Jackson, Andrew, statue of, 47
Jackson Square, 46–47
Jacques-Imo's Cafe ✕, 144
James H. Cohen & Sons Inc.
 (shop), 204
Jax Brewery, 203
Jazz and Heritage Festival, 34,
 184, 185
Jazz funerals, 76, 183
Jazz National Historic Park,
 62, 76
Jazz Playhouse, The, 176
Jazz Quarters New Orleans
 ✕, 158
Jean Lafitte National Park
 Visitor Center, 51
Jean Therapy (shop), 224
Jelly Roll Morton House, 70
John Minor Wisdom United
 States Court of Appeals
 Building, 83
Johnny's Po-boys ✕, 123
Joint, The ✕, 128
Jonathan Ferrara Gallery, 217
Johnson's Boucanière ✕, 249
Jungle Gardens, 259

K

Keil's Antiques, 204
Kermit's Tremé Mother-in-Law
 Lounge, 188
Kerry Irish Pub, 173
Kevin Stone Antiques & Interi-
 ors (shop), 223
Killer Po Boys ✕, 123
King Cake, 124
Kingfish ✕, 123
Kingpin, The (bar), 193
K-Paul's Louisiana Kitchen ✕,
 123–124
Krewe du Optic (shop), 211
Kurt E. Schon, Ltd. (gallery),
 206

L

La Belle Galerie & the Black Art
 Collection, 206
La Belle Nouvelle Orleans
 (shop), 220
La Boca ✕, 136
La Crêpe Nanou ✕, 142
La Petite Grocery ✕, 142
LaBranche Houses, 47
Lafayette, 38, 247–251
Lafayette Cemetery No. 1,
 89, 92
Lafayette Courthouse, 248
Lafayette Natural History
 Museum and
Lafayette Science Museum, 248
Lafayette Square, 83
Lafitte Guest House ⚏, 155
Lafitte's Blacksmith Shop, 173
LA46 General Store & Vintage
 Market, 214
Lagniappe, 221
Lake Lawn Metairie Cemetery,
 22, 113
LaLaurie Mansion, 51, 61
Latil's Landing Restaurant ✕,
 241
Latrobe House, 61
Laura Plantation, 238
Laura's Candies (shop), 209
Le Bon Temps Roulé (club),
 193–194
Le Meridien ⚏, 160
Le Pavillon Hotel ⚏, 160–161
Le Richelieu in the French
 Quarter ⚏, 155
Lee Circle, 85–86
LeMieux Gallery, 217
Librairie Book Shop, 207
Lilette ✕, 142
Lionheart Prints (shop),
 222–223
Lions Inn ⚏, 158
Little Toy Shop, 214
Liuzza's by the Track ✕, 146
Loa (bar), 188–189
Loews New Orleans Hotel ⚏,
 161
Loft 523 ⚏, 161
Longfellow-Evangeline State
 Historic Site, 257
Lonsdale House, 92
Louis Armstrong Park, 74, 76
Louisiana Arts & Science
 Museum and Irene W.
Louisiana Children's Museum,
 27, 84
Louisiana Historical Center, 63
Louisiana Music Factory (shop),
 214

Louisiana Philharmonic
 Orchestra, 196
Louisiana's Civil War Museum
 at Confederate Memorial
 Hall, 86
Lower Ninth Ward, 71
Loyola University, 102
Loyola University School of
 Law, 102
Lucullus (shop), 204
Lucy's Retired Surfers
 Restaurant and Bar ✕, 79
Luling Mansion, 116

M

M. S. Rau (shop), 205
Madame John's Legacy, 61
Madewood B&B ⚏, 241
Magazine Antique Mall, 220
Magazine Street, 89, 218–227
Magazine Street Merchants
 Association, 219
Magic Box (shop), 226
Magnolia, The ✕, 244
Mag's 940 (bar), 177
Mahalia Jackson Center for the
 Performing Arts, 78
Mahony's Po-Boy Shop ✕, 142
Maison, The (bar), 177
Maison des Amis ⚏, 253
Maison Dupuy, The ⚏, 155
Maison Perrier Bed & Breakfast
 ⚏, 165
Mamou, 38
Mandina's ✕, 144
Maple Leaf (club), 194
Marcello's ✕, 136, 138
Mardi Gras, 53–60, 251
 cuisine, 124
 history, 55
 parades, 34, 57–58
 safety, 59
 shopping, 212
 visitor information, 60
 vocabulary, 60
Mask Gallery (shop), 211
Maurice, 260
Maurice Flea Market, 260
Maypop ✕, 138
McCarthy House, 101
McGee's Swamp Tours, 255
Melrose Mansion ⚏, 155
Mercedes-Benz Superdome,
 81–82
Meyer the Hatter (shop), 216
Michalopoulos Galleries,
 61–62, 206
Mid-City and Bayou St. John,
 19, 107–116
 hotels, 116, 166

nightlife and the arts, 195–196
restaurants, 109, 144–146
safety, 109
shopping, 227–228
Mignon Faget (shop), *225*
Milton H. Latter Memorial Library, *101*
Mimi's (bar), *186*
Mississippi River, *47*
Molly's at the Market (bar), *174*
Money matters, *13, 268*
Moon Walk, *48*
Mopho ✕ , *145*
Morning Call ✕ , *145*
Morris F.X. Jeff Municipal Auditorium, *76*
Moss Antiques, *204*
Mother's ✕ , *130*
Mouton Plantation ⌂ , *250*
Movies about New Orleans, *25*
Mr. B's Bistro ✕ , *124*
Mulate's (club), *190–191*
Murals, *247*
Muriel's Jackson Square ✕ , *124*
Museums, *27*
CBD and Warehouse District, 84–85, 86
Eunice, 252
Faubourg Marigny, Bywater, and Tremé, 70, 71, 72–73
free, 36
French Quarter, 45, 46, 47, 48, 50–51, 61–62
Garden District, 91–92, 93, 96
Great River Road, 240
Lafayette, 247, 248
Mardi Gras, 27, 60, 84
Mid-City and Bayou St. John, 111, 112–113, 115, 116
New Iberia, 258
St. Francisville, 242–244
Music, *176–177, 186–187, 188, 179–185, 190–191, 193–194, 195–196*
Cajun and Zydeco, 230
classical, 196–197
festivals, 34–35, 38, 53–60, 184, 251, 252, 253
Jazz and Heritage Festival, 34
shops, 224, 228
Music Box Village, *72*
Musson House, *93, 96*
Myrtles, The ⌂ , *243, 244*

N

Nadine Blake (shop), *213*
Napoleon House Bar and Café, *41, 174*
Napoleon's Itch (gay bar), *175*

National World War II Museum, *84–85*
New Iberia, *38, 258*
New Orleans Ballet Association, *197*
New Orleans Botanical Garden, *111–112*
New Orleans Center for Creative Arts (NOCCA), *70, 196–197*
New Orleans Christmas, *35*
New Orleans Film Festival, *197*
New Orleans Glassworks and Printmaking Studio, *86, 217*
New Orleans Healing Center, *69*
New Orleans Historic Voodoo Museum, *62*
New Orleans Jazz & Heritage Festival, *34*
New Orleans Jazz Collection, *63*
New Orleans Jazz National Historical Park, *62, 76*
New Orleans Marriott Hotel ⌂ , *156*
New Orleans Museum of Art (NOMA), *111, 112–113*
New Orleans Museum of Art gift shop, *228*
New Orleans Opera Association, *198*
New Orleans Original Cocktail Tour, *37*
New Orleans Pelicans, *24*
New Orleans Pharmacy Museum, *62*
New Orleans Saints, *24*
New Orleans School of Cooking and Louisiana General Store, *209*
New Orleans Wine and Food Experience, *34*
New Year's Eve, *34*
Nightlife and performing arts, *167–198*
bars and lounges, 172–174, 177, 186, 187, 188–189, 190, 191–193, 194, 195, 196, 250, 252
Breaux Bridge, 253
casinos, 80–81, 189
classical music, 196–197
cocktails, 37, 169
cover charges and drink minimums, 170–171
dance, 197
dress, 170
Eunice, 252–253

Faubourg Marigny, Bywater, and Tremé, 177, 186–188
Film, 197
French Quarter, 172–177
gay and lesbian, 175
hours, 170
Lafayette, 250–251
music clubs, 252, 253
opera, 198
safety, 171
theater, 198
tipping, 171
Nola ✕ , *124–125*
NOLA Boards, (shop), *209*
NOLA Brewing Tour, *37*
NOLA Couture (shop), *211*
NOPSI Hotel ⌂ , *161*
Nottoway, *38, 238–239*
Nottoway B&B ⌂ , *242*
N7 ✕ , *128*
Nuance/Louisana Artisans Gallery, *224*

O

Oak Alley, *38, 239–240*
Oak Alley B&B ⌂ , *242*
Oak Wine Bar and Bistro, *194*
Octavia Art Gallery, *217–218*
Octavia Books, *224*
Ogden Museum of Southern Art, *85*
Old Absinthe House (bar), *174*
Old Castillo Bed and Breakfast ⌂ , *257*
Old New Orleans Rum Distillery, *37*
Old No. 77 Hotel & Chandlery, The ⌂ , *161*
Old Ursuline Convent, *62–63*
Omni Royal Orleans Hotel ⌂ , *157*
One Eyed Jack's (club), *176*
1000 Figs ✕ , *146*
Opelousas, *38*
Opera, *198*
Orient Expressed Imports (shop), *226*
Orleans Ballroom, *63–64*
Outlet Collection at Riverwalk Marketplace, The, *216*
Oz (gay bar), *175*

P

Packing, *268*
Palace Café (French Quarter) ✕ , *50, 125*
Palm Court Jazz Café, *176, 190*
Palmer Park, *102*
Pal's (bar), *196*
Parade Disco, *175*

Parades, *34–35*
Jazz and Heritage Festival, 34
Mardi Gras, 34
Parasol's Restaurant & Bar, *192*
Park View Guest House ☶ , *165*
270
Parkway Bakery & Tavern ✕ ,
146
Parleaux Beer Lab, *187*
Pascal's Manale ✕ , *142*
Pat O'Brien's (bar), *174*
Patois ✕ , *143*
Patrick's Bar Vin, *174*
Paul and Lulu Hilliard Univer-
sity Art Museum, *38, 248*
Peaches Records (shop), *222*
Pearl Wine Co. (shop), *228*
Pêche Seafood Grill ✕ , *138*
Pelham Hotel ☶ , *161*
Pelican Club ✕ , *125*
perch (shop), *222*
Perlis (shop), *207, 224*
Perseverance Hall, *76*
Phoenix (bar), *186*
Pirate's Alley Faulkner Society,
51
Piscobar, *189*
Pitot House, *115*
Pizza Delicious ✕ , *128*
Plantation Country, *38,*
230–231, 236–244
Plantation tours, *230, 237, 266*
Poche's ✕ , *253*
Pontalba, Micaela, *49*
Pontalba Buildings, *50*
Pontchartrain Hotel ☶ , *163*
Port of Call ✕ , *125*
Porter Lyons (shop), *211*
Poupart's Bakery, *251*
Prairie Acadian Cultural Center,
252
Praline Connection ✕ , *126*
Prejean's ✕ , *249*
Presbytère, The, *47–48, 60*
Preservation Hall, *177, 190*
Price categories
hotels, 149, 234
restaurants, 119, 234
Pulp and Grind ✕ , *79*

Q

Q&C Hotelbar ☶ , *161–162*
Quarter Smith (shop), *211*
Quisby, The ☶ , *165*

R

R Bar, *186*
Ralph's on the Park ✕ , *145*
Randal's (club), *251*

Rayne Memorial Methodist
Church, *101*
Refuel Café ✕ , *98*
Remoulade ✕ , *125*
Renaissance Arts Hotel ☶ , *163*
Renaissance Pere Marquette
Hotel ☶ , *162*
Rendez-Vous des Cajuns, *252*
Rendezvous Inc. (shop), *213*
Republic (club), *191*
Restaurants, *13, 26, 117–146*
Abbeville, 259–260
American, 121, 125, 126, 130,
136, 138, 139, 140, 142, 234
Asian fusion, 138
Breaux Bridge, 253
cafés, 121–122, 130, 139, 144,
146
Cajun, 123–124, 129, 136, 145,
241, 249
Caribbean, 130, 136
CBD and Warehouse District,
79, 128–130, 136, 138
Creole, 120–121, 122–123,
124–125, 126, 138, 139, 140,
143–144, 145, 146
cuisine, 133–135, 233, 250
delis, 121, 123, 142
dress, 119
eclectic, 122, 125, 126, 128
Faubourg Marigny, Bywater,
and Tremé, 67, 126, 128
food glossary, 137
French, 142, 143, 146
French Quarter, 41, 119–126
fusion, 129
Garden District, 88, 138–139
Israeli, 143
Italian, 123, 129, 130, 136,
138, 139–140, 142
Lafayette, 249
Latin American, 136
Maurice, 260
Mediterranean, 146
Mid-City and Bayou St. John,
109, 144–146
Middle Eastern, 129
modern American, 120,
128–129, 139, 142, 145
New Iberia, 258
pizza, 128
price categories, 119, 234
reservations, 118–119
seafood, 120, 122, 129, 138,
140, 142
side trips from New Orleans,
233, 241
Southern, 120, 128, 130, 136,
140, 142, 143, 144, 241,
241, 249

St. Francisville, 244
steakhouses, 122
sushi, 144
Tapas, 128
Thai, 126
tipping, 119
Uptown and Carrollton-River-
bend, 98, 139–140, 142–144
Vietnamese, 145
R'evolution ✕ , *125*
RHINO Contemporary Crafts
Co. (gallery), *220*
Richard's Seafood Patio ✕ , *260*
Rink, The, *96*
Ritz-Carlton New Orleans ☶ ,
156
River Road African American
Museum, *240*
Riverboat cruises, *266*
Rock 'n' Bowl (club), *22, 195*
Rodrigue Studio, *64, 206–207*
Roosevelt Hotel New Orleans,
The ☶ , *162*
Root ✕ , *139*
Rosedown Plantation and
Gardens, *38, 244*
Rosenberg House, *101*
Royal Antiques, *205*
Royal Sonesta Hotel New Orle-
ans ☶ , *156*
Rubensteins (shop), *216*
Rue 127 ✕ , *145*
Rusty Nail (bar), *189*

S

Saenger Theatre, *198*
Safety, *21, 40, 59, 60, 79, 89,*
99, 109, 268–269
St. Augustine Catholic Church,
76
St. Charles Avenue Christian
Church, *101*
St. Charles Avenue Presbyte-
rian Church, *101*
St. Charles Avenue Streetcar,
79, 98
St. Claude Arts District, *70–71*
St. Francisville, *38, 242–244*
Saint Hotel, The ☶ , *156–157*
St. James Cheese Company
(shop), *224–225*
St. Joe's (bar), *193*
St. Louis Cathedral, *48*
St. Louis Cemetery No. 1, *73*
St. Louis Cemetery No. 3, *113,*
115
St. Martin de Tours, *257*
St. Martinville, *38, 256–257*
St. Mary Magdalen Catholic
Church, *259*

St. Patrick's Day, *34*
St. Patrick's Church, *86*
San Francisco Plantation, *240–241*
Sans Souci Fine Craft Gallery, *251*
Santa's Quarters (shop), *213*
Satchmo SummerFest, *35*
Satsuma Café ✕, *67*
Savoy Music Center and Accordion Factory, *252*
Sazerac Bar, The, *189*
Scriptura (shop), *226*
Second line and jazz funerals, *76*
Secondline Arts and Antiques, *205*
Shadows-on-the-Teche, *258*
Shaya ✕, *143*
Sheraton New Orleans Hotel ⌂, *162*
Shopping, *199–228*
antiques and collectibles, 203–205, 214, 215, 219–220, 223, 251
art and crafts galleries, 205–207, 216–218, 220, 223–224
books, 207, 221, 224, 226
CBD and Warehouse District, 215–218
centers and markets, 45, 85, 203, 216
clothing, 207–208, 216, 218, 221, 224, 226–227
coffee, 213
Fauborg Marigny and Bywater, 214–215
flea markets, 260
food, 208–209, 218, 222, 224–225, 228, 251
French Quarter, 202–214
Garden District, 218–223
hours, 201
housewares, 209, 222
jewelry and accessories, 209, 211, 216, 222, 225, 227
Lafayette, 251
lingerie, 225
Magazine Street, 218–223
Mardi Gras, 212
masks, 211–212
Maurice, 260
Mid-City, 227–228
music, 214, 222
novelties and gifts, 212–213, 215, 222–223, 225–226, 228
perfumes, 215
shoes, 226
spa and beauty, 213–214, 223, 226

tours, 206
toys, 214, 226
Uptown and Carrollton-Riverbend, 223–227
voodoo, 204, 212
wine and spirits, 214, 218, 224–225, 227
Shops at Canal Place, The, *64, 215*
Siberia Lounge, *186*
Side trips from New Orleans, *19, 38, 229–260*
Smith House, *101*
Snug Harbor (club), *187*
SoBou ✕, *125–126*
Soniat House ⌂, *157*
Soren Christensen (gallery), *218*
Southern Decadence (festival), *22, 35*
Southern Food and Beverage Museum, *92*
Southern Food and Beverage Museum gift shop, *224*
Southern Repertory Theater, *198*
Southwest Louisiana Zydeco Music Festival, *38, 252*
Sovereign Pub, *193*
Special-interest tours, *267*
Spotted Cat, The (club), *187*
Spruce Eco-Studio (shop), *222*
Spuddy's Cajun Foods ✕, *241*
Stanley ✕, *126*
Stein's Market and Deli ✕, *88*
Sterling Silvia (shop), *211*
Storyland, *112*
Streetcars, *20, 79, 88, 98, 100–102, 109, 263–264*
Studio Be, *72–73*
Sucré ✕, *139, 222*
Sukho Thai ✕, *126*
Superior Seafood ✕, *143*
Swamp tours, *230, 237, 255, 267*
Swap (shop), *227*
Swirl (shop), *228*
Sydney and Walda Besthoff Sculpture Garden, *111, 112–113*
Sylvain ✕, *126*
Symbols, *13*
Symmetry Jewelers (shop), *227*

T

Tabasco Country Store, *209*
Tabasco Factory, *259*
Tales of the Cocktail (festival), *35, 37*
Taxes, *269*
Taxis, *20, 263, 265*
Tchoup Industries (shop), *221*

T-Coon's Café ✕, *249*
Temple Sinai, *101–102*
Tennessee Williams/New Orleans Literary Festival, *34*
T'Frere's House ⌂, *250*
Theater, *198*
Theatres at Canal Place, *197*
Thomas Mann Gallery I/O, *220*
Three Muses ✕, *126 136*
Timing the visit, *21*
Tipitina's (club), *194*
Tipping, *119, 269*
Toby-Westfeldt House, *96*
Tommy's Cuisine ✕, *138*
Toups' Meatery ✕, *145*
Tours and guides, *27, 30–33, 37, 206, 230, 237, 266–267*
Tracey's (bar), *192*
Train travel, *20, 246, 265*
Transportation, *20, 262–265*
Trashy Diva Boutique, *207–208*
Tremé, *18, 73–76, 158, 188*
Treo (club), *195*
Trinity Artist Series, *197*
Troubadour Hotel, The ⌂, *162*
Tulane University, *102*
Turkey and the Wolf ✕, *139*
Twelve Mile Limit (bar), *195*

U

United Apparel Liquidators (shop), *208*
Upperline ✕, *143*
Uptown and Carrollton-Riverbend, *19, 97–106*
hotels, 165
nightlife and the arts, 192–194
restaurants, 98, 143–144
safety, 99
shopping, 223–226

V

Van Benthuysen-Elms Mansion, *92*
Venusian Gardens and Art Gallery, *70*
Vermilion Parish Tourist Commission, *259*
Vermilionville, *249*
Victoria's Shoes (shop), *226*
Victory (bar), *189*
Vintage 329 (shop), *205*
Violets (shop), *208*
Visitor information, *269–270*
Cajun Country, 247, 253, 259
Mardi Gras, 60
nightlife and the arts, 171
Plantation Country, 237
Voodoo Experience (festival), *35*

W

W Hotel New Orleans French
  Quarter ☷ , *157–158*
Waldhorn & Adler (shop), *205*
Walking tours, *30–33, 37, 267*
Warehouse District, *18, 32–33,
  83–86, 130, 136, 138, 163,
  189–191, 216–218*
Washington Artillery Park, *64*
Wayne Jacob's Smokehouse
  Restaurant ✕ , *241*
Weather, *21, 235*
Websites, *21, 269–270*
Wedding Cake House, *101*
Wehmeiers (shop), *218*
Westin New Orleans Canal
  Place, The ☷ , *158*
What's New (shop), *213*
Whisnant Galleries, *205*
Whitney Hotel, The ☷ , *162*
Whitney Plantation, *38*
Windsor Court Hotel ☷ ,
  162–163
Wine Institute of New Orleans
  (WINO), *218*
Woldenberg Riverfront Park,
  47, 48
Women's Guild of the New
  Orleans Opera Association
  House, *93*

Y

Ye Olde College Inn ✕ , *145*
Yvonne LaFleur (shop), *227*

Z

Zeitgeist Multidisciplinary Arts
  Center, *197*
Zemurray House, *102*
Zoos, *27, 99*
Zydeco music, *181, 184, 252,
  256*

PHOTO CREDITS

Front cover: Peter Unger/Getty Images [Description: Wrought iron lace in the French Quarter, New Orleans, Louisiana]. 1, dbimages / Alamy. 2, Dwight Nadig/iStockphoto. 4 and 5 (top), Paul Broussard/NOTMC. 5 (bottom), f11photo/Shutterstock. 6 (top left), Roy Guste/Allways Lounge. 6 (top right), Ljoy25 I Dreamstime.com. 6 (bottom right), Paul Broussard/NewOrleansOnline.com. 6 (bottom left), Commander's Palace. 7 (top), JAMES LANGE / Alamy. 7 (bottom), Walleyelj I Dreamstime.com. 8 (top left), Daniellenhassett I Dreamstime.com. 8 (top right), Courtesy of The Pharmacy Museum. 8 (bottom right), Dbvirago I Dreamstime.com. 8 (bottom left), Chuck Wagner/Shutterstock. 9 (top), NOTMC. 9 (bottom), Andriy Blokhin/Shutterstock. 11, dahon/Flickr, [CC BY-ND 2.0]. **Chapter 1: Experience New Orleans:** 14-15, Lars Plougmann/Flickr, [CC BY-SA 2.0]. **Chapter 2: The French Quarter:** 39, JTB Photo age fotostock. 41 and 42, Carl Purcell/New Orleans Convention and Visitors Bureau. 44, GTS Productions/Shutterstock. 46, Pgiam/iStockphoto. 52, Luis Castañeda / age fotostock. 53, dahon/Flickr, [CC BY-ND 2.0]. 54, Alvaro Leiva / age fotostock. 55, Public domain. 56 and 58 (top), Mark Gstohl/Flickr, [CC BY 2.0]. 58 (bottom left), Tulane Public Relations/Flickr, [CC BY NC 2.0]. 58 (bottom right), Infrogmation of New Orleans/Flickr, [CC BY-SA 2.0]. 59 (left), Infrogmation of New Orleans/Flickr, [CC BY 2.0]. 59 (top right), Paul Wood /Alamy. 59 (bottom right), Infrogmation of New Orleans/Flickr, [CC BY 2.0]. 60, Molly Moker. **Chapter 3: Faubourg Marigny, Bywater, and Tremé:** 65, Heeb Christian / age fotostock. 67, Andrea Ciambra/Flickr, [CC BY 2.0]. 68, Infrogmation of New Orleans/Flickr, [CC BY 2.0]. 69, Team at Carnaval.com Studios/Flickr, [CC BY 2.0]. 72, Molly Moker. 74, Jovannig I Dreamstime.com. **Chapter 4: CBD and Warehouse District:** 77, Mr. Littlehand/Flickr, [CC BY 2.0]. 79, Payton Chung/Flickr, [CC BY 2.0]. 80, Cheryl Gerber/ Ogden Museum of Southern Art. 81, vxla/Flickr, [CC BY 2.0]. 82, SuperStock/age fotostock. **Chapter 5: The Garden District:** 87, Heeb Christian / age fotostock. 89, Frank Kovalchek/Flickr, [CC BY 2.0]. 90, Kent Wang/Flickr, [CC BY-SA 2.0]. 94-95, Chris Waits/Flickr, [CC BY 2.0]. **Chapter 6: Uptown and Carrollton-Riverbend:** 97, RIRFStock I Dreamstime.com. 99, Richard Nowitz/New Orleans CVB. 100, Carl Purcell /New Orleans Convention and Visitors Bureau. 101 (top), Ken Lund/Flickr, [CC BY-SA 2.0]. 101 (bottom), Chris Waits/Flickr, [CC BY 2.0]. 103, Lindsay Glatz/Arts Council of New Orleans. 106, Audubon Nature Institute New Orleans. **Chapter 7: Mid-City and Bayou St. John:** 107, SnippyHolloW/Flickr, [CC BY-SA 2.0]. 109, Chuck Wagner/Shutterstock. 110 and 112, Infrogmation of New Orleans/Flickr, [CC BY 2.0]. **Chapter 8: Where to Eat:** 117, Michael Palumbo/Commander's Palace. 118, Cochon Restaurant New Orleans. 132, easyFotostock / age fotostock. 133, Kaige/Flickr, [CC BY-SA 2.0]. 134 (left), Reika/Shutterstock. 134 (right), Cathy Yeulet/Hemera/ Thinkstock. 135 (left), Jupiterimages/Comstock Images/Thinkstock. 135 (right), K Chelette/Shutterstock. **Chapter 9: Where to Stay:** 147, The Roosevelt, A Waldorf Astoria Hotel. 148, Royal Sonesta Hotel. **Chapter 10: Nightlife:** 167, Prisma by Dukas Presseagentur GmbH / Alamy. 168, Brian Huff. 169 (top), The Museum of the American Cocktail. 169 (bottom), Jennifer Mitchell. 170, Gary J. Wood/Flickr, [CC BY-SA 2.0]. 178, Franz Marc Frei / age fotostock. 179 (top), Jim West / age fotostock. 179 (center left), djnaquin67/Flickr, [CC BY-SA 2.0]. 179 (middle center), Ted Drake/Flickr, [CC BY 2.0]. 179 (center right), Tulane Public Relations/Flickr, [CC BY 2.0]. 179 (bottom), Public domain. 180 (left), Ishwar/Flickr, [CC BY 2.0]. 180 (top right), Public domain. 180 (bottom right), Herman Hiller/ Library of Congress Prints & Photographs Division. 181 (left) Stephen Kennedy/Flickr, [CC BY 2.0]. 181 (right), Janet Spinas/Flickr, [CC BY 2.0]. 182 (top left), Robbie Mendelson/Flickr, [CC BY-SA 2.0]. 182 (bottom left), rickh710/Flickr, [CC BY 2.0]. 182 (bottom right), Linda Marie/Flickr, [CC BY 2.0]. 182 (top right), Zjbrewer/Wikimedia Commons. 183 (top), Franz Marc Frei/ age Fotostock. 183 (bottom), Infrogmation/Flickr, [CC BY 2.0]. 184 (left), Infrogmation/Flickr, [CC BY 2.0]. 184 (top right), Ray Devlin/Flickr, [CC BY 2.0]. 184 (bottom right), djnaquin67/Flickr, [CC BY-SA 2.0]. 185, Infrogmation/Flickr, [CC BY 2.0]. **Chapter 11: Shopping:** 199, Christian Goupi / age fotostock. 200, Ray Laskowitz / age fotostock. 203, Giuseppe Masci / age fotostock. 210, Adalberto Ríos Lanz/ age fotostock. 219, Travel Division Images / Alamy. **Chapter 12: Side Trips from New Orleans:** 229, David Lyons / age fotostock. 232, Corey Harmon/Flickr, [CC BY-ND 2.0] 239, Ed Schipul/Flickr, [CC BY-SA 2.0]. 240, Walter Bibikow / age fotostock. 243, FRILET Patrick / age fotostock. 254, Kathryn8/iStockphoto. **Back cover from left to right:** Dwight Nadig/iStockphoto: f11photo / Shutterstock; Meinzahn I Dreamstime.com. **Spine:** Lori Monahan Borden/Shutterstock.

About our writers: All photos are courtesy of the writers except for the following: Cameron Quincy Todd, courtesy of Sara Todd.

NOTES

NOTES

NOTES

NOTES

NOTES

NOTES

NOTES

NOTES

ABOUT OUR WRITERS

 New Orleans resident Karen Taylor-Gist is the editor of *Wish Magazine,* an upscale shopping guide that is published monthly by *The Times-Picayune.* Gist updated the Experience, Side Trips, and Travel Smart sections of Fodor's New Orleans 2016.

 Cameron Quincy Todd has been in love with New Orleans since she first visited the city fifteen years ago. A graduate of the Creative Writing MFA Program at the University of New Orleans, Cameron lives in Algiers Point and writes about hotels and culture for ⊕ *Fodors.com.*